The Jamaica Reader

THE

JAMAICA

READER

HISTORY, CULTURE, POLITICS

Diana Paton and Matthew J. Smith, editors

DUKE UNIVERSITY PRESS   *Durham and London*   2021

© 2021 Duke University Press
All rights reserved
Printed and bound by CPI Group (UK) Ltd, Croydon, CR0 4YY
Typeset in Monotype Dante by BW&A Books, Inc.

Library of Congress Cataloging-in-Publication Data
Names: Paton, Diana, [date] editor. |
Smith, Matthew J. (Caribbean history scholar), editor.
Title: The Jamaica reader : history, culture, politics /
edited by Diana Paton and Matthew J. Smith.
Other titles: Latin America readers.
Description: Durham : Duke University Press, 2021. |
Series: The Latin America readers | Includes index.
Identifiers: LCCN 2020040507 (print)
LCCN 2020040508 (ebook)
ISBN 9781478010494 (hardcover)
ISBN 9781478011514 (paperback)
ISBN 9781478013099 (ebook)
Subjects: LCSH: Jamaica—History. | Jamaica—Civilization. |
Jamaica—Politics and government.
Classification: LCC F1881 .J36 2021 (print) | LCC F1881 (ebook) |
DDC 972.92—dc23
LC record available at https://lccn.loc.gov/2020040507
LC ebook record available at https://lccn.loc.gov/2020040508

Cover art: A sister and brother stand in front of an inspirational mural
by Jamaican artist Djet Layne. Layne's mural is part of the Paint Jamaica
street art project. Fleet Street, Kingston, 2019. Photograph: Kwame Miller.
Used with permission.

produced with a grant from
Figure Foundation
publication of the global nation

For Jamaicans
There, here, on the way.

Contents

Introduction

Jamaica is often imagined as two distinguishable and opposite parts. The more attractive part is immediately recognizable. It is the brightly lit Jamaica seen in Hollywood films. This Jamaica is the holiday capital of the Caribbean favored by royalty and global vacationers in search of tropical splendor. It is easy to appreciate the power of this imagined island. Jamaica—a small place, 144 miles long, with 2.8 million inhabitants and fourteen parishes—is blessed with white sand beaches that stretch for miles and are framed by deep green mountains and a warm crystal-blue sea. Its island culture appears removed from the rapid pace and anonymity of metropolitan life. Jamaican tourist posters command you to come to this Jamaica and "feel all right," borrowing a lyric from the 1977 song "One Love" by its most famous offspring, Rastafarian reggae singer Robert Nesta (Bob) Marley. This Jamaica is marketed heavily to the foreigner to encourage tourism, the island's leading industry. The ubiquity of all-inclusive hotels, "Jamaica, No Problem" T-shirts, fake dreadlock caps, uniformed bamboo carvings, and ancillary businesses of restaurants, nightclubs, sex tourism, water sports, makeshift spas, ganja (marijuana) sellers, and hair braiding along the North Coast all cater to tourist needs and indicate the importance of this Jamaica to the local economy.

The other Jamaica is also well-known, though far less promoted. It is urban and gritty. It contains gray narrow streets of oppressive poverty, communities pockmarked by generations of brutal violence. It is the Jamaica that for more than five decades has inspired reggae songs about deprivation, justice, and equal rights. It is the Jamaica of shirtless street children, traffic jams, zinc-roofed self-built houses, loud music, and squalor that sprawls around the capital city, Kingston. This is the Jamaica that investigative journalists search out and document in gripping reportage on the "other side of paradise." It is most commonly referenced by the island's leaders as the setting from which global superstar Bob Marley and his colleagues and descendants rose. Otherwise it draws no lasting attention from the island's elite. The visual distinction between these two parts of Jamaica is striking. Perhaps appropriately it was Bob Marley's son, Damian, a reggae legend in his own right, who most famously exemplified the contrast in his 2005 song "Welcome to Jamrock," which differentiated between "Jamaica" as an idyllic concept sold to foreigners by privileged sectors of the society and "Jamrock" as the horrific reality lived by the majority of urban Jamaicans.

Jamaicans habitually position themselves within this neat division of their country. One is either from "town" (generically used to refer to Kingston) or "country" (anywhere outside the capital). Politically one is either a supporter of the Jamaica Labour Party (JLP) or the People's National Party (PNP), the two political parties. Kingston's urban geography is split between "uptown"—the postwar central business district New Kingston and the wealthy residential areas scattered across the hills surrounding the city—and "downtown," the older capital and densely populated impoverished communities close by, the latter widely perceived by middle-class Kingstonians as dangerous spaces to be avoided at all costs. Social classes are broadly divided between a small, privileged, mostly "brown" (of mixed-race origins) middle class and a "black" popular class. Ethnic minority groups on the island—a small population of Indian, Chinese, Jewish, and Arab-descended Jamaicans, and whites born both on the island and elsewhere—are absorbed into these bifurcated social categories depending on language, wealth, and cultural preferences. Even one's choice of one of the two leading daily newspapers can reflect class affiliation.

It is tempting to explain all of Jamaica's outcomes, celebrated or shunned, as a product of the tension generated by these two poles. But that would be quite misleading. To view Jamaica as two distinct halves glosses over the complex processes by which the place and its people were formed. There are in fact many Jamaicas between these extremes.

The island's indigenous residents arrived more than a millennium ago. They left a resonant heritage. The island's most likely original name, Xamaye/Yamaye or Xamayca, popularly understood to mean "land of wood and water," comes from its inhabitants at the time of the Spanish conquest, the Taíno. Spanish marauders first came to Jamaica at the end of the fifteenth century and violently seized the land in the sixteenth, extinguishing the Taíno as a distinctive people in the process and beginning centuries of imperial rule. By the time the English wrested Jamaica from the Spaniards in 1655, it was already seen as strategically valuable in the group of islands that encircle the Caribbean Sea. The English developed their new colony into a place dominated by a plantation economy and worked by the forced labor of enslaved Africans. This past haunts the island. Jamaica became the British Crown's leading sugar- and coffee-producing colony, and by many accounts the most abusively managed.

The racial subordination of the majority of Jamaica's inhabitants, the black Africans and their creole descendants, was central to colonialism. A tiny proportion of resident white Britons ruled over a population that was 90 percent black, made up of people forcibly brought from Africa on a torturous transatlantic voyage. The end of slavery in 1838 modified this situation but left overarching structures of domination untouched. Jamaica's poor majority had precious few rights and remained marginalized from the political process. In slavery and freedom Jamaicans resisted this oppression. Major confrontations took place in 1760, 1831, 1865, and 1938. Resistance also took other forms. Marronage (the process of flight to the interior from the plantations), centuries of migration, and cultural resistance are all important elements of the Jamaican experience.

Independence in August 1962 required the idea of a unified nation. National symbols exaggerated sameness in much the same way the insistence on two Jamaicas exaggerates difference. The 1960s nationalist mission homogenized the varied experiences of Jamaicans into one story of an island's struggle for self-definition. Independent Jamaica's leaders emphasized this single story through the creation of a national motto, "out of many, one people"; national heroes, including rebel leaders Sam Sharpe and Paul Bogle; national holidays, including Labour Day and Independence Day; and the promotion of a national culture, including foodways, dance, and music. Their efforts could not conceal the incongruity in social life. The capital continued to expand. Urban poverty was exacerbated by economic pressures and insecurity. The inability of the independence governments of the 1960s and 1970s to come to terms with the reality of Jamaica's divisions is revealed in the tragic history of those years.

Today, more than a half century after independence, the scars of the past remain and the contests among the multiple parts of Jamaica have become more pronounced. While the national anthem's final stirring refrain, "Jamaica, Jamaica, Jamaica land we love," promises unified patriotic attachment, disenfranchised Jamaicans challenge a vision of "One Love" Jamaica. Reggae legend Burning Spear (Winston Rodney) exemplifies this in the question that closes the chorus of his song "Black Wadada" (1976): "Where is your love, Jamaica?"

This book does not aim to reconcile these alternate visions. Instead, we have tried to illustrate the range of life experiences, the historical and cultural influences, and the creativity of people in Jamaica. Selections enable readers to understand change and development over Jamaica's history, in people's work lives, political engagement, and cultural production, among other themes.

For most, it probably seems natural or intuitive to consider Jamaica as a single place for a reader like this one, but it is worth pausing to consider why this might be. As an island, Jamaica has been considered a single administrative unit since the appointment of the first Spanish governor in 1510, a year after the earliest Spanish permanent settlement began, although it did not become an independent nation until 1962. Its whole territory did not fully come under European power until the treaties with the Maroons who controlled much of the island's interior until 1739. The treaties allowed the Maroons to retain limited sovereignty but required them to accept a resident representative of the British Crown. Unlike for many continental territories, there has been no significant movement of Jamaica's external borders that might have led to challenges to a sense of essential coherence and self-identity.

The one attempt to form a larger state—the West Indies Federation project of the mid-twentieth century—unraveled on the eve of independence due to populist appeals to Jamaican nationalism and the fanning of fears of economic obligations to smaller and poorer islands. Nevertheless, Jamaica has always been firmly connected to places beyond the island itself. Some connections have been forged through proximity (as with Jamaica's larger neighbors, Cuba and Haiti), while others have been created through colonial history (Britain and the rest of the former British colonies in the Caribbean), cultural heritage and elective affinity (most prominently Africa), and migration (the Greater Caribbean region, plus the United States, Canada, and the United Kingdom).

This book is organized into eight parts. The first seven trace a chronological history of the island. Part I introduces precolonial Jamaica and explores its early colonial history as an outpost of the Spanish Empire. The Taíno heritage is treated in readings on their life and culture. This part also presents the English conquest of the island in 1655, which led to more than three hundred years as a British colony. In part II, we examine the emergence of a society absolutely dominated by race-based plantation slavery, which reached its full extent in the late eighteenth century. By that time a tiny minority of white Britons sought to control a much larger population of enslaved Africans. Part III takes the story through the contradictory late slavery period, ending with the achievement of "full freedom" in 1838. The effects on Jamaican society of the global transformations of the early nineteenth century are addressed through this part's selections.

In part IV we move to the period after emancipation, ending at World War I. From the point of view of the dominant plantation economy, this was a period of decline. Ordinary Jamaicans experienced considerable economic hardship in these years, but it was also an era of creativity, when the majority could for the first time develop patterns of culture and social organization outside the constraints of slavery. The Morant Bay Rebellion of 1865 was a turning point for freed Jamaicans' claims against race- and class-based domination. Among the rebellion's tragic results was a tightening of the colonial grip on the island. Part V examines the mid-twentieth-century decades during which a consistent nationalism developed, culminating in independence in 1962. The part begins with World War I, which initially confirmed Jamaicans' loyalty to the British Empire but by the end undermined it, as Jamaicans, like other colonial soldiers, encountered metropolitan and institutional racism. It moves on to consider the explosive riots of the 1930s, which led to transformations across the British Empire, and in Jamaica stimulated the formation of both of the two main political parties, the PNP and JLP, which continue to dominate Jamaica's politics today.

The period since independence is covered in parts VI and VII. Part VI focuses on the tumultuous years after independence during which Jamaica was strongly influenced by and also contributed to global movements. The *Reader* pays particular attention to Prime Minister Michael Manley's policy of "Democratic Socialism." Manley's vision responded to urgent demands for social change in postcolonial Jamaica. It fast fell victim to Cold War imperatives and contributed to the ruthless division in the island's politics. The watershed event of this period was the extreme violence during the 1980 election, won by Manley's successor, Edward Seaga of the JLP. More than eight hundred Jamaicans died violently during the election campaign.

Part VII attends to the period since 1980, when Jamaican governments have with greater or lesser willingness acquiesced in the "Washington consensus" of neoliberal reform and "free trade." This part also considers the creative responses of Jamaicans who came of age after the turbulent 1970s. Writers, athletes, and musicians became the dominant voices of the era, rising in international recognition above political leaders. This part highlights the global influence of Jamaican culture.

The final part of the *Reader* gives full attention to migration and its consequences, one of the most profound constants of the Jamaican experience. This part reveals the many forms of migration from Jamaica, over several centuries, including by those who have returned to the island. Jamaican achievement beyond the island's borders is remarkable. Jamaica's immense contributions to sport, literature, academia, and popular music have brought recognition to the country and its daughters and sons who settle elsewhere.

Taken together, these selections present the complex relationship Jamaicans have had with their homeland and the human impact of the events covered in the earlier parts.

The narrative threaded through the volume should enable readers to trace the main points of political and economic development in Jamaica's history: from early arrival of indigenous people and European conquest, through slavery and its abolition, then the partial reframing of the post-emancipation economy, and on to nationalism, independence, and postcolonial concerns. But we have also attended to matters outside the political and economic that are just as critical for an understanding of Jamaica, particularly the (strongly interconnected) development of religion and of music, both areas in which Jamaican-originated forms have had global reach.

As editors of the volume—one of us from Jamaica, one from Britain, both with long-standing interests in the island's history—we have pieced together a history of Jamaica through the voices of a wide range of the island's residents, both unknown and celebrated, along with many of the country's most important academic analysts. This anthology consciously blends familiar selections with lesser-known texts to more accurately reflect Jamaica's realities. A volume such as this cannot possibly be comprehensive. Nevertheless, we hope the *Reader* will serve as a guide for those new to Jamaica, whether as tourist, visitor, or student, and will also provide food for thought for those who already know the country well.

I

Becoming Jamaica

Human settlement on the island that we now call Jamaica is relatively recent. Although societies in the Caribbean were established by at least 5000 BCE (the dates of the earliest archaeological sites found in Trinidad), these early cultures seem to have bypassed Jamaica. The earliest Jamaican archaeological site that has been found, Little River in St. Ann, dates to around 650 CE. The people who settled Jamaica around that time are known to archaeologists as "Ostionoid," after their style of pottery, which is similar to that found at the Ostiones archaeological site in Puerto Rico. In Jamaica it is known as "Redware," because it is characteristically painted red. Ostionoid society, which was based on agriculture and fishing, developed within the Caribbean, probably from cultures that had been brought earlier by migrants from Central America.[1]

Over time, the Ostionoids developed into a characteristic society that scholars since the 1980s have referred to as the Taíno, a term that probably derives from the Arawakan words *tayno*, meaning "good," or *nitaíno*, referring to the elite group in their society.[2] The Taínoan peoples were for a long time referred to as Arawaks, because of their supposed similarity to the Arawak peoples of the Guianas. While the Taíno and Arawak languages are part of the same linguistic family, they diverged a long time ago and shared few terms with one another. Much early commentary in the past presented the Taíno or Arawak as peaceful, contrasting them to the supposedly warlike Caribs of the eastern Caribbean. More recent archaeological work avoids these essentialist characterizations. Some scholars now reject even the term *Taíno* as a name for the region's people on the grounds that it imposes an artificial unity on what were in practice diverse societies.[3] Nevertheless, all agree that people who drew on a shared set of cultural resources and assumptions, though probably not a unified identity, lived across the Greater Antilles. Archaeological sites with recognizably Taínoan material have been found in Jamaica, Puerto Rico, Cuba, and Hispaniola, and also extend into the Bahamas, although there is diversity within the material found at these sites. Taíno society developed around the tenth century and was changing rapidly at the time of the Spanish conquest.

Jamaicans have undertaken extensive research into indigenous societies. But mainstream archaeology mostly ignored the island, focusing more on Hispaniola and Puerto Rico. These larger islands attracted attention because of their greater importance to the Spanish empire and because intellectual agendas followed the lead of early US-based archaeologists such as Irving Rouse, whose research focused on those sites rather than locations in Jamaica. There are few written sources about indigenous society at the time of the conquest. Nevertheless, sufficient investigations have taken place to enable scholars to be confident that late precolonial Jamaican society and culture were in many ways similar to that of the other islands of the Greater Antilles. Jamaica shared the most with its nearest neighbor, Cuba. Mid-twentieth-century archaeologists included Jamaica in a group of "Western Taíno" societies, which may have had sparser populations, smaller political groupings, and perhaps a less hierarchical society than in the "Classic Taíno" area to their west, although as with the term *Taíno* itself, these categories are debated.[4] Most contemporary archaeologists think that the Taíno in Jamaica had few differences from those in the so-called Classic areas. Spanish written sources tell us that Taíno-speaking people resident in Jamaica and in Hispaniola called the island Yamaye or Xamayca, most likely variants of the same word.[5]

Jamaican society in the late pre-Columbian period was based on fishing and agriculture, especially the cultivation of manioc (cassava). Women did much of the everyday labor. The Taínoan peoples shared religious practices and beliefs including the use of *zemis*, which were physical objects made of stone or wood that represented and sometimes hosted the gods. Their society was matrilineal, with status reckoned through the female line, but political power was held by men. Taínoan society was organized into "complex chiefdoms," that is, confederated groups of communities under the rule of caciques (chiefs) who were supported by the surplus production of the commoners. Eight caciques have been identified in Jamaica at the time of Columbus's arrival, based on Spanish sources: Aguacadiba, Ameyao, Anaya, Guayguata, Huareo, Maynoa, Oristan, and Vaquabo. The extent of the caciques' authority is unclear, however; it may be that some had substantial power to direct behavior, while in other areas the caciques depended on persuading ordinary people to do their bidding. We do know that Jamaica was densely populated in the Taíno period. Recent scholarship suggests that there were at least one hundred villages at the time of the Spanish conquest.

Estimates of population are contested, ranging from around sixty thousand to half a million.[6]

The first Spanish journeys to the Americas had momentous consequences for the Caribbean. The Spanish Crown and the expeditions it sponsored hoped to find a more direct route to their trading partners in Asia. In particular they were driven by the search for precious metals, especially gold. On Christopher Columbus's first voyage (1492–1493), indigenous people in Hispaniola told him about an island to the south of Cuba: "He says that he found out that behind the island Juana [Cuba] to the south was another great island, in which there is a much greater quantity of gold than in this, and they gather pieces bigger than beans; and in the island of Hispaniola they gather pieces of gold as large as grains of wheat. They called that island, he said, *Yamaye*."[7]

On his second voyage (1492–1496) Columbus briefly visited Jamaica. He landed on the North Coast at the site now known as Discovery Bay in St. Ann parish. Indigenous Jamaicans strongly resisted the European incursion, and no settlers remained behind. Columbus visited Jamaica once again during his fourth voyage (1502–1504), when his fleet was hit by storms that forced him to sink his remaining ships in St. Ann's Bay on the North Coast. He and his followers were stranded there for a year, from June 1503 until they were rescued by a ship sent from Santo Domingo in June 1504, but again left no colony behind. However, Columbus did claim the island for the Spanish Crown, which awarded it to him as his personal property. After Columbus's death, the claim to Jamaica, along with the rest of Spain's New World colonies, passed to his heir, Diego. In 1509 Diego sent a party of settlers to the island under Juan de Esquivel. These settlers first established a colony at Nueva Sevilla (near today's Ocho Rios, St. Ann parish), and then in 1534 made their capital farther south, at St. Jago de la Vega, which eventually became known as Spanish Town.

During the Spanish period few settlers came to Jamaica. The island proved not to have large deposits of precious metals. It never generated the huge profits of the silver and gold mines of Peru and Mexico, so it remained a backwater within the Spanish Empire. The few settlers there lived primarily by raising livestock, and the island served mainly as a supply station for ships crossing the Atlantic en route to and from the mainland Americas.

Nevertheless, early colonization had dramatic effects. By the early seventeenth century fewer than one hundred indigenous people remained, a drastic reduction from the precolonial population.[8] The devastation was mainly due to imported diseases to which the inhabitants had no immunity

—particularly smallpox—but also to the Spanish practice of enslaving indigenous Jamaicans and taking them to Hispaniola to work in the gold mines.[9] The Spanish Crown first authorized the direct slave trade across the Atlantic in 1518, and the first enslaved Africans probably arrived in Jamaica in the 1530s.

After a century and a half of Spanish rule, during which the nonindigenous population probably never exceeded ten thousand, Jamaica became an English colony.[10] In 1655 Oliver Cromwell sent a fleet of ships to the Caribbean with the goal of taking Spain's Caribbean colonies for England. This "Western Design" took place at a time of increasing rivalry among European powers for dominance in the region. The English aimed to gain power in relation to Dutch and French as well as Spanish colonizers. Cromwell's expedition began with an unsuccessful attack on Hispaniola. In order to avoid complete failure, the leaders of the fleet, Admiral William Penn and General Robert Venables, headed for Jamaica, which had a much smaller population and was less defended than Hispaniola. They successfully seized the island, but were disappointed in what they found—in the words of an anonymous English letter writer, "Imaginary mountains of gold are turned into dross."

The Jamaican Maroons established themselves as distinct communities in the immediate aftermath of the English conquest. The first Maroons were Africans enslaved by the Spanish who took their freedom when the Spanish settlers evacuated after their defeat. Maroons in Jamaica shared much with fugitive communities of Africans in other slaveholding territories in the Americas. The term *Maroon* comes from the Spanish *cimarrón*, a word also used for escaped domestic animals. As is demonstrated both in this part and later in the *Reader*, the Jamaican Maroons were to play a particularly significant and controversial political role, first in providing a barrier to colonial expansion and later as an autonomous community that paradoxically facilitated European control.

This part of the *Reader* traces Jamaica's history up to the point when it became an English colony. Although often overlooked, the foundations of Jamaica's later development were laid in this early period of conquest and colonization.

Notes

1. Samuel M. Wilson, *The Archaeology of the Caribbean* (Cambridge: Cambridge University Press, 2007), 102–105.

2. L. Antonio Curet, "The Taíno: Phenomena, Concepts, and Terms," *Ethnohistory* 61, no. 3

(2014): 467–495; José R. Oliver, *Caciques and Cemí Idols: The Web Spun by Taíno Rulers between Hispaniola and Puerto Rico* (Tuscaloosa: University of Alabama Press, 2009), 6.

3. William F. Keegan and Corinne L. Hofman, *The Caribbean before Columbus* (Oxford: Oxford University Press, 2017).

4. The categories Western and Classic Taíno are especially associated with Irving Rouse. See his *The Tainos: The Rise and Decline of the People Who Greeted Columbus* (New Haven, CT: Yale University Press, 1992).

5. Christopher Columbus, "The Journal of the First Voyage," ed. and trans. Samuel Eliot Morison, in *Journals and Other Documents on the Life and Voyages of Christopher Columbus* (New York: Heritage Press, 1963), 146; Francisco Morales Padrón, *Spanish Jamaica*, trans. Patrick E. Bryan (Kingston: Ian Randle, 2003), 19, 23; B. W. Higman and B. J. Hudson, *Jamaican Place Names* (Mona, Jamaica: University of the West Indies Press, 2009), 24–25.

6. Kit W. Wesler, "Jamaica," in *The Oxford Handbook of Caribbean Archaeology*, ed. William F. Keegan, Corinne L. Hofman, and Reniel Rodríguez Ramos (Oxford: Oxford University Press, 2013).

7. Columbus, "The Journal of the First Voyage."

8. Frank Cundall and Joseph L. Pietersz, eds., *Jamaica under the Spaniards, Abstracted from the Archives of Seville* (Kingston: Institute of Jamaica, 1919), 34–55.

9. Wilson, *Archaeology of the Caribbean*, 162.

10. Lawrence R. Walker and Peter Bellingham, *Island Environments in a Changing World* (Cambridge: Cambridge University Press, 2011), 208.

Taíno Society

Kit W. Wesler

Archaeologist Kit W. Wesler summarizes the state of current knowledge of indigenous Jamaica on the eve of Columbus's arrival. Mid-twentieth-century scholars, most notably Irving Rouse, divided the Taíno people into a "Classic" group, living in Hispaniola, Puerto Rico, and eastern Cuba, and a "sub" or Western Taíno group, including those of Jamaica. More recent research suggests that the Taíno-speaking people living in Jamaica in the fifteenth century shared a great deal with their neighbors in Hispaniola. Wesler emphasizes Jamaica's dense population and relatively decentralized political system.

Jamaica first entered European history in 1494, when Columbus visited its coast for about a week during his second voyage. During his fourth voyage, Columbus and his crew spent a year (June 1503–June 1504) at St. Ann's Bay on the North Coast, living on beached ships and relying on the native people for supplies. Despite this close interaction, the Spanish chroniclers recorded little firsthand information about the Jamaican Taíno, leaving later scholars to generalize Taíno culture largely on the evidence of Hispaniola and Puerto Rico.

Even early commentators saw little difference between the Jamaican Taíno and their better-described neighbors. For example, the 1576 Tommaso Porcacchi map of Jamaica states that the Jamaicans "had the same language and customs as the people of Spagnuola [Hispaniola] . . . they keep the same rites and ceremonies as in Cuba, practice the same idolatry and are involved in the same nefarious rituals." The 1606 description of Jamaica on a map by Gerard Mercator asserted that the "people differ in no way from the people of Hispaniola and Cuba in laws, religion and customs."[1]

[Irving] Rouse, however, characterized the Jamaican Taíno with a less complex culture than the Classic Taíno of Hispaniola, Puerto Rico, and eastern Cuba, first using the term *sub-Taíno* then, with less subjective overtone, placing them among the Western Taíno, which included the people of

One of many Taíno pictographs on the wall of Mountain River cave, St. Catherine parish, showing two human figures wearing bird masks while holding spears or throwing sticks. Archaeologists think the cave served as a center for Taíno religious ceremonies. Photograph by Evelyn Thompson, from *Rock Art of the Caribbean*, edited by Michele Hayward, Leslie-Gail Atkinson, and Michael A. Cinquino (Tuscaloosa: University of Alabama Press, 2009), 51. Used by permission of the photographer.

Jamaica, Central Cuba, and the Bahamas. He did show some doubt about the Jamaicans:

> The density of Jamaica's population suggests that its inhabitants practiced the same advanced form of agriculture as the Classic Taíno . . . The chronicles indicate that the native Jamaicans had the greatest variety of ornaments among the Western Taíno, many showing rank. The class system of the Classic Taínos may therefore have extended into Jamaica . . . cemís were worshiped in homes . . . especially in Jamaica.[2]

Recent scholarship has emphasized the variability or cultural mosaic within the Taíno supergroup, and scholars must parse the scant historical sources and the archaeological record of the Jamaican Taíno before reintegrating them into a broader Taíno synthesis.

Jamaica was densely populated. Cundall's (1915) figure of 600,000 is derived by analogy to Martyr's estimate of 1,200,000 on Hispaniola and may be high. However, "Las Casas says that the islands abounded with inhabitants as an ant-hill with ants," and Columbian sources said that the island was "thickly inhabited." After Columbus's first visit, Michele de Cuneo's letter of October 28, 1495, reported "an excellent and well populated harbor . . . during that time some 60,000 people came from the mountains, merely to look at us."[3]

Wilson suggests that Jamaica contained "polities of more than 100 allied villages, with combined populations in the tens of thousands." According to Rouse, "It has been established that there were 8 or 10 chiefs on the whole island, but the names of only 2 along the northeastern coast have survived: Ameyao and Huareo." Swanton named eight "Indian tribes of Jamaica": Aguacadiba, Ameyao, Anaya, Guayguata, Huareo, Maynoa, Oristan, and Vaquabo (excluding some names he thought were place-names).[4]

The Columbian accounts of the year in Jamaica during the fourth voyage are surprisingly sparse in ethnographic observations, being focused largely on the internal affairs of the Spanish. They mentioned several villages: Maima, "about a quarter league from the ship"; Aguacadiba, an unnamed village "three leagues away"; and the *cacique* Huareo's seat "in a place now called Melilla" (Port Maria). The references to *caciques* suggest a variable and perhaps fluid system of authority. Columbus called "the principle Indians of that province" around St. Ann's Bay, rather than a single *cacique*. At Aguacadiba, Diego Mendez "agreed with the Indians and the *cacique*" for provisions, while at the unnamed village he "made the same agreement with the *cacique* and the Indians," and often the Spanish gave gifts to "the kings or chief men." In the East, Spanish renegades pillaged among "the *caciques* through whose territory they passed." Mendez's attempts to reach the eastern end of the island to find a canoe for Hispaniola were interrupted by his capture by "Indian pirates" and threats from Indians in spite of a local *cacique's* friendship.[5]

These references suggest both numerous chiefs and that authority was limited or shared in many groups. It is likely that no simple model of social organization fits all of the Jamaican polities, and structures may have included both simple and complex chiefdoms and conceivably even tribal groups. One tidbit worth noting is that Mendez escaped captors while they were playing a ball game, which establishes a game in Jamaica though not necessarily formal ball courts.

One recurrent issue, often tacit, is the relationship of the Jamaican Western Taíno to the Classic Taíno of Hispaniola, Puerto Rico and eastern Cuba. Rouse identified four artifact or feature types that distinguish the Classic group as ball courts/*bateyes*, wooden stools/*duhos*, stone zemis and petroglyphs. All but the ball courts have been documented in Jamaica, though as noted above, there is historic evidence of a ball game. In addition, the elite items which Righter et al. identify as markers of Classic Taíno culture (sculptured stone, shell ornaments and inlays, and stone beads) have been recovered in Jamaica. Hints of plazas at Stewart Castle and Retreat indicate village organization. Finally, [geologist James] Lee found a gold artifact associated with White Marl [St. Catherine parish] style pottery. Given the ethnohistoric accounts of chiefs of varying levels of authority and dense populations, all of these Jamaican traits argue for indigenous societies comparable to their Classic Taíno neighbours.

Notes

1. J. W. Lee, "The Tommaso Porcacchi, 1576, Map of Jamaica," *Archaeology Jamaica* 81, no. 4 (1981): 3; H. D. Cameron, "Description of Jamaica from a Map of 1606 by Gerard Mercator," *Archaeology Jamaica* 82, no. 4 (1982): 28.

2. I. Rouse, *The Tainos: Rise and Decline of the People Who Greeted Columbus* (New Haven, CT, 1992), 11.

3. F. Cundall, *Historic Jamaica* (Kingston, 1915), 1; S. E. Morison, *Journals and Other Documents on the Life and Voyages of Christopher Columbus* (New York, 1963), 356, 222.

4. S. M. Wilson, *The Archaeology of the Caribbean* (Cambridge, 2007), 110; I. Rouse, "The Arawak," in *Handbook of South American Indians*, ed. J. H. Steward (Washington, DC, 1948), 543; J. R. Swanton, "The Indian Tribes of North America," *Bureau of American Ethnology Bulletin* 145 (1952): 7–8.

5. Morison, *Journals*, 361, 364, 367, 392, 394.

Taíno Worship

Ramón Pané

Spanish priest Ramón Pané joined Columbus's second expedition. Although he traveled only to Hispaniola and wrote about what he observed there, his description of the Taíno people is relevant to Jamaica, which was inhabited by people with a similar culture. Pané considered Taíno religion a form of deception and devil worship. Nevertheless, his account is one of the most significant written sources through which archaeologists and historians have reconstructed pre-Columbian society in the Greater Antilles. This section recounts the production of zemis (or cemís), the spiritual objects made of wood or stone that were a materialization in the physical world of a vital spiritual force. The term zemi was used for both the vital force and the object that it inhabited. Although we cannot be certain that zemis in Jamaica were produced in the same way as in Hispaniola, we know that similar objects existed in both societies, and it is reasonable to infer that they were similarly understood. Pané also explains the role of the behique, *or shamanic spiritual leader, and describes* cohoba, *a hallucinogenic powder made from a tree, inhaled to induce spiritual visions.*

How they make and keep the zemis made of wood or of stone

The ones of wood are made in this way: when someone is walking along, and he says he sees a tree that is moving its roots, the man very fearfully stops and asks it who it is. And it answers him: "Summon me a *behique*, and he will tell you who I am." And when that man goes to aforesaid physician, he tells him what he has seen. And the sorcerer or wizard runs at once to see the tree of which the other man has told him; he sits next to it and prepares *cohoba* for it.

Once the *cohoba* is made, he stands up and tells it all his titles, as if they were those of a great lord, and he asks it: "Tell me who you are, and what you are doing here, and what you wish from me, and why you have had me summoned. Tell me if you want to be cut down, or if you want to come with me, and how you want to be carried, for I will build you a house with land."

Taíno carved wooden *cohoba* stand in the shape of a bird, perhaps a pelican. This object was found in a cave near Aboukir, St. Ann parish, in the 1940s and has been carbon-dated to the fourteenth century CE. *Cohoba* stands were used to hold the hallucinogenic powder used as part of Taíno religious rituals as described by Ramón Pané. Other examples have been found elsewhere in Jamaica and in other parts of the Caribbean. From the National Gallery of Jamaica, Kingston. Photograph by Franz Marzouca.

Then that tree or zemi, turned into an idol or devil, answers him, telling him the manner in which he wants it to be done. And he cuts it and fashions it in the manner he has been ordered; he constructs its house with land, and many times during the year he prepares *cohoba* for it. That *cohoba* is used to pray to it and to please it and to ask and find out from the aforesaid zemi good and bad things and also to ask it for riches. And when they want to find out if they will achieve victory over their enemies, they enter into a house in which none but the leading men enter. And their lord is the first one who begins to prepare *cohoba*, and he plays an instrument; and while he is making the *cohoba*, none of those who are in his company speaks until the lord

Anthropomorphic carved Taíno mahogany figure, 153 cm in height, thought to be a *zemi*. Some scholars have suggested that the figure represents one of two Taíno deities, Baibrama or Yúcahu, although others warn that we have insufficient knowledge of Jamaican Taíno religion to be able to make such clear identifications. Like the previous illustration, this object was found in a cave near Aboukir, St. Ann parish, in the 1940s; the two items were probably used together. Carbon dating shows that the figure was made in the fourteenth century CE. Artist unknown. From the National Gallery of Jamaica, Kingston.

has finished. After he has finished his prayer, he stays awhile with his head lowered and his arms on his knees; then he lifts his head, looking toward the heavens, and he speaks. Then they all answer him aloud in unison; and after that all have spoken, they give thanks, and he relates the vision he has had, inebriated from the *cohoba* he has inhaled through his nose and that has gone to his head. And he says he has spoken with the zemi and that they will achieve victory, or their enemies will flee, or there will be a great loss of life, or wars or hunger or another such thing, according to what he, who is drunk, may relate of what he remembers. You may judge in what state his brain may be, for they say they think they see the houses turn upside down, with their foundations in the air, and the men walk on foot toward the heavens. And they prepare this *cohoba* not only for the zemis of stone and of wood, but also for the bodies of the dead, as we have related above.

The stone zemis are of different constructions. There are some they say the physicians take out of their bodies, and the sick maintain that those are the best ones to make pregnant women give birth. There are others that speak; they have the shape of a thick turnip with their leaves spread out on the ground and long like those of the caper bush. Their leaves are in general similar to those of the elm tree; others have three points, and they believe they cause the *yuca* [cassava] to sprout. They have a root similar to the radish. The leaf of the *yuca* has at most six or seven points; I do not know to what it might be compared because I have not seen anything like it in Spain or any other country. The stalk of the *yuca* is as tall as a man.

Translated by Susan C. Griswold

The First European Account of Jamaica

Andrés Bernáldez

Christopher Columbus's first voyage to the Americas departed from Spain in August 1492, in search of a westward route to the East Indies. He visited Jamaica on his second voyage, which began in September 1493. His fleet of seventeen ships paid most attention to colonizing Hispaniola, but a smaller group of ships also briefly visited Jamaica, anchoring initially at what is today St. Ann's Bay on 5 May 1494. Here Andrés Bernáldez, a cleric and chronicler at the Spanish court in Madrid working from papers left by Columbus, describes the visit. His account includes a description of the indigenous population's canoes, weapons, and military tactics. Bernáldez emphasizes the island's beauty partly to encourage his Spanish audience to value the new colonies, but also reveals that Columbus's fleet met considerable resistance from the indigenous population. He presents the indigenous defense of the island as illegitimate, describing the Spanish use of dogs in warfare as "chastisement." Bernáldez's account suggests that the indigenous cacique submitted to the Spanish the day after the attack, but the island's inhabitants would have had a different interpretation. From their perspective, this was a short encounter with little lasting political meaning.

They navigated in search of the island of Jamaica, to the southward, and at the end of two days and two nights, with a fair wind, they reached it, striking a central point in it.

And the island is the most lovely that eyes have seen. It is not mountainous, and the country seems to rise towards the sky. It is very large, greater than Sicily, having a circumference of eight-hundred leagues—I mean, miles—and all full of valleys and fields and plains.[1] It is a very mighty land, and beyond measure populous, so that even on the sea-shore as well as inland, every part is filled with villages and those very large and very near one another, at four leagues' distance. They have more canoes than in any other part of those regions, and the largest that have yet been seen, all, as has been said, made each from a single tree trunk. In all those parts, every *cacique* has a great canoe, of which he is proud and which is for his service,

Engraving by Theodore de Bry showing a scene from Christopher Columbus's fourth voyage to the Americas. In the foreground are three Taíno men, two of them in a dugout canoe. Behind, Christopher Columbus and his allies fight against mutineers within their group, led by Francisco Poraz. From *Americae pars quarta. Sive, Insignis & admiranda historia de reperta primùm Occidentali India à Christophoro Columbo anno MCCCCXCII,* by Girolamo Benzoni (Frankfurt am Main: Johann Feyerabend, 1594), plate XIIII [14]. John Carter Brown Archive of Early American Images, record no. 09887-13, call no. J590 B915V GVL4.1 / 2-SIZE. Used courtesy of the John Carter Brown Library at Brown University. https://creativecommons.org/licenses/by/4.0/legalcode.

as here a *caballero* prides himself on possessing a great and beautiful ship.[2] So they have them decorated at the bow and stern with metal bands and with paintings, so that their beauty is wonderful. One of these large canoes which the admiral measured was ninety-six feet long and eight feet broad.

As soon as the admiral arrived off the coast of Jamaica, there immediately came out against him quite seventy canoes, all full of people with darts as weapons. They advanced a league out to sea, with warlike shouts and in battle array. And the admiral with his three caravels and his people paid no attention to them and continued to steer towards the shore, and when they saw this, they became alarmed and turned in flight. The admiral made use of his interpreter, so that one of those canoes was reassured and came to him with its crew. He gave them clothes and many other things which they held in great regard, and accorded them permission to depart. He then anchored at a place which he named *Santa Gloria*,[3] on account of the extreme beauty of its glorious country, in comparison with which the gardens of Valencia are nothing, nor is there anything to compare with it elsewhere, and so it is in all the island. And they slept there that night. Next day, at dawn, they went to seek for a sheltered harbour, where they might be able to careen and repair the ships. And having gone four leagues to the westward, they found a very remarkable harbour and the admiral sent the boat to examine its entrance.[4] And two canoes with many people came out to it and shot many darts at it, but they fled as soon as they found opposition and that not so quickly that they suffered no punishment. The admiral entered the harbour and anchored, and so many Indians came down to it that they covered the land, and all were painted a thousand colours, but the majority black, and all were naked as is their custom. They wore feathers of various kinds on the head and had the breast and stomach covered with palm leaves. They made the greatest howling in the world and shot darts, although they were out of range. And in the ships, there was need of water and wood, and it was further necessary to repair the vessels. The admiral saw that it was not reasonable to allow them to be so daring without chastisement, in order that on another occasion they might not be so bold. He assembled all three boats, since the caravels could not proceed and reach the place where they were owing to the shallows, and that they might become acquainted with the arms of Castile, they approached close to them in the boats and fired at them with crossbows and thus pricked them well, so that they became frightened. They landed, continuing to shoot at them, and as the Indians saw that the Castilians were speaking with them, they all took to flight, men and women, so that not one was to be found in all that neighbourhood. And a dog which they let loose from a ship chased them and bit them, and did them great damage, for a dog is equal of ten men against the Indians.

Next day, before sunrise, six men of those Indians came to the shore, calling and saying to the admiral that all those *caciques* asked him not to go away, because they desired to see him and to bring him bread and fish and fruits. And the admiral was much pleased with this embassy, and they protested their friendship and assured him of his safety, and the *caciques* and many Indians came to him, and they brought to them many provisions with which the people were much refreshed, and they were very content with the things which the admiral gave to them. And, having repaired the ships and rested the people, they departed thence.

Translated by Cecil Jane

Notes

1. In fact, the area of Jamaica is less than half that of Sicily. [Editors' note]
2. *Cacique* is the Taíno word for chief or leader. *Caballero* is Spanish for gentleman but has the specific meaning of a horseman, so Bernáldez is comparing the function of the canoe in Taíno society to that of the horse in Spain. [Editors' note]
3. St Ann's Bay. [Note by the original editor, Cecil Jane]
4. The mouth of the Rio Bueno. [Note by the original editor, Cecil Jane]

A Spanish Settler in Jamaica

Pedro de Maçuelo

Only in 1509 did substantial numbers of Spanish settlers arrive in Jamaica. They came under the command of Juan de Esquivel, acting on the orders of Christopher Columbus's son, Diego, who had just inherited his father's titles, including nominal control of Jamaica. For a century and a half the Columbus family would be the personal rulers of Jamaica. Writing to the king of Spain six years after the Spanish settlement of Jamaica and six months after his own arrival, Pedro de Maçuelo, the Spanish treasurer of Jamaica from 1514 and future governor, describes the current economic and political situation of Jamaica. It is largely a pessimistic view, noting the small size of the Spanish population and the difficulty of maintaining Spanish settlers on the island. The letter sheds light on the contest between the Spanish Crown and Columbus's allies for authority over the small number of Spanish settlers. Maçuelo also notes the ill treatment of the indigenous population by the settler population. The letter mentions the repartimiento, a forced labor system used throughout the early Spanish Empire, in which settlers claimed rights to the labor of indigenous people. The original letter is no longer extant; this is a translation of a secretary's summary.

To Your Highness
From Pedro de Maçuelo, 21st April, 1515

He says he arrived at that island on October 10 of the said year [of 1515] and that the land appears to be very good and healthful and temperate, and that there is no gold in it, because great diligence has gone into searching for it and more will be done; and that the land is well suited for [raising] livestock and for the cultivation of yucca and sweet potatoes and maize and birds, and that the island can support the sixty settlers (*vezinos*) who now live there in two towns, but that more settlers could not be maintained, because there are not as many Indians as was thought; that when [the Indians] are divided among the settlers and those whom Your Majesty has designated, they will have plenty to do.

He says that on the island he found two estates belonging to Your
Majesty, with some settlers, and from these estates seven ships have
been loaded thus far, five to the mainland (*tierra firme*) and two to Cuba,
with cassava bread, pigs, and maize. The two ships to Cuba were sent
on credit, because they said there was no gold (*oro fundido*); they wrote
to him that the smelting would be done after Easter. As for the other
five ships, since they have not returned from the mainland, he cannot
yet inform Your Majesty of the profit to be made.

He says the said ships were loaded in the months of November and
December, 1514, and in January and February of this year, and that the
said [royal] estates are in such good shape that it is as though nothing
were taken from them. He thinks it will be possible to make . . . *castellanos* per year from these estates, because they have in them 355 mounds
for growing yucca, sweet potato, and maize, and many pigs, and each
day they multiply. It requires no more than the eight Christians who are
there, and with 100 *castellanos'* worth of tools, or less, they will continue
to be productive each year. The shirts that Your Majesty orders be given
to the Indians do not need to be purchased, because they are made on
the estates, and there are even enough to sell. And these estates would
do well with [the labor allotment of] two thousand Indians, because at
present they do not have any; and they could provision the mainland
and Cuba at a lower cost. He thinks Your Majesty should not enter into
any business partnership (*compañía*) to run these estates, because half
the yearly profit to be made from them would be lost, and it would not
be good, given the low cost it takes to run these estates, to increase the
cost or give a half share to anyone. He makes the truth known to Your
Majesty to better enable him to order what he thinks best; to do otherwise would result in a significant loss of income for Your Majesty. If
there were two lead-hulled caravels, it would pay off significantly in the
provisioning of Cuba and the mainland, because without this, very few
[ships] return due to the [damage caused by] barnacles.

He says that to collect the rents owed to Your Majesty, he specifically
asked the Admiral's [i.e., Diego Columbus's] lieutenant for some houses
and a fortress belonging to Your Majesty, so that the rents could be held
securely, and that in order to collect the rents he had to request assistance from the magistrates (*alcaldes*) and council members (*regidores*);
and since these men were handpicked by the Admiral's lieutenant, they
do not serve Your Majesty with the appropriate diligence; and that for
each thing that needed to be collected, he had to go around giving orders and singling people out by name, and that everyone takes the side

DESCRITTIONE
DELL'ISOLA IAMAICA
HORA DETTA DI S. IACOPO.

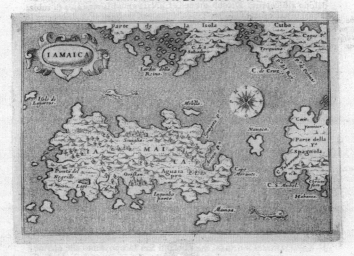

 AMAICA Iſola gia coſi chiamata, & hora di S. Iacopo, è nel grande Oceano Occidentale dirimpetto all'Iſole Spagnuola & Cuba uerſo Mezogiorno: dalla qual parte è poſta in gradi xvii. dalla linea Equinottiale: ma doue ell'è piu uerſo Tramontana, in gradi xviii. Da Leuante con fina con l'Iſola Spagnuola: percioche dal capo di Iamaica, ch'è la punta Oriental dell'Iſola, & è detta Capo Morante, al capo di S. Michele, da altri detto del Tiburone, che è la parte piu occidental della Spagnuola ſono xxv. leghe, benche altri có maggior differentia dica xl. Da Ponente è per xxxv. leghe lungi dall'Iſole dette de'Lagarti: ma perche queſte ſon dishabitate; le danno per confino da Ponente la terra ferma del Iucatan, & la foce, o porto dell'Aſcenſione. Verſo Tramontana ell'è xxv. leghe diſcoſto dall'Iſola Cuba, cioè dalla punta de'Giardini: & dalla parte di Mezogiorno ha l'Iſole di S. Bernardo, & la prouincia di Carta-

One of the earliest printed maps of Jamaica, which also shows part of Cuba and Hispaniola. Engraved by the Italian artist Giralomo Porro and published in 1572 in Tomasso Porcacchi Castilione's book *L'Isole più Famose del Mondo* [The most famous islands of the world] (Venice: Apresso Simon Galignani e Girolamo Porro, 1576), 203. John Carter Brown Map Collection, file name 1794-041, call no. H576 P8331 / I-SIZE (copy I). Used courtesy of the John Carter Brown Library at Brown University. https://creativecommons .org/licenses/by/4.0/legalcode.

of the Admiral and says that up until now they have known no other
king.

He says that those who have served as officials for one year nominate
those who will serve the following year, and they bring before the aforesaid lieutenant eight *regidores* and four *alcaldes*, and he picks the men
he wants for these offices. He says it would better serve Your Majesty
for council positions to be perpetual [i.e., lifetime rather than yearlong
offices] and the *alcaldes* to be elected by vote; Your Majesty should order
whatever he thinks best.

He says that he has asked the settlers of the island for the tithes,
rents, and payments they owe Your Majesty for the time they have been
there, and that they make excuses, saying that until now they have
been at war and have been pacifying the island, and that they should
enjoy the same exemption [from payments] as [the settlers of] Hispaniola, who now are beginning to thrive and make their fortunes; that
Your Majesty should decide what to do.

He says that he has been informed by persons who serve Your Majesty, especially one Diego Ramírez, that the wars and hardships have
not been as numerous as they say, because in five years no more than
four Christians have been killed; and when they arrived in the island,
they found plenty to eat. He says that Diego Ramírez has been, and is, a
good servant of Your Majesty; he begs that he be granted a council position (*regimiento*) in the town of Sevilla [recently founded in Jamaica].[1]

He says that the Indians have been very mistreated by the settlers of
that island, who beat them and burn them and otherwise abuse them, to
such an extent that if they continue unpunished, there will be no Indians two years from now; and that he found certain Christians had been
apprehended on account of such abuses, but the only punishment they
received was at most a fine of six *castellanos*, and seeing what a grave dis-
service that was to God and to Your Majesty, and because [Francisco de]
Garay had not yet arrived,[2] acting on orders for the good treatment of
the Indians, he restrained the Admiral's lieutenant and put two inspec-
tors (*visitadores*) in charge of making sure that from now on the Indians
are treated as Your Majesty commands and that anyone who acts to the
contrary will be punished.

[He says] that in the distribution (*repartimiento*), Indians will be given
to each in accordance with his status and service; and he makes known
to Your Majesty that there are some who have more Indians than Your
Majesty, and these men are the Admiral [Diego Columbus] and his lieutenant, who each have 1,600 [Indians].[3]

He says that there are some settlers who married in Spain but live in the island with their mistresses (*amancebados*); he asks that Your Majesty order them to return, and if they want to stay in the island, that they take their wives with them.

Translated by Kathryn Burns

Notes

1. Sevilla, on the North Coast, had been founded in 1509 as the Spanish capital, a status it retained until 1534, when it was largely abandoned in favor of Villa de la Vega (Spanish Town), in the south. [Editors' note]

2. Garay was to serve, among other things, as *repartidor* or "assigner" of Indians to particular Spanish settlers. See Irene Wright, "The Early History of Jamaica (1511–1536)," *English Historical Review* 36 (1921): 73–74. [Translator's note]

3. Wright's transcription continues, "mas no para que tenga tanta cantidad." This is hard to understand or translate and is perhaps a transcription error. [Translator's note]

The Spanish Capital

James Robertson

The Spanish settlers made their initial capital at New Seville, now in the parish of St. Ann, but in 1536 established a new capital farther south, naming it St. Jago de la Vega. After the English conquest this would become Spanish Town. Here James Robertson, a historian at the University of the West Indies, Mona, describes the founding of the new capital. Robertson emphasizes the town's position at a transit point for Taínoan communities and outlines early free and unfree migration to the island. The sixteenth-century population grew slowly, incorporating Christian settlers from Portugal, Iberian Jews and New Christians escaping the Inquisition, and captives from Africa who arrived in the early slave trade.

Over a century after Spanish Town's foundation a newcomer described its setting: "The Town stands on almost plaine ground, but a little inclining towards the East, for the better fall on the Raines downe into the River, w[hi]ch is very shallow, & Runs a pretty distance below the Towne & Emptys it selfe into the Arme of the Sea."[1] The site's location on a gradual slope towards the river appeared conspicuous, though it faced out towards the savanna to the west. The river provided the third key element, even if sailors who had just walked the seven miles up from the landing place at the river's mouth stressed the distance and that a shallow river was unnavigable. When the first Spanish settlers arrived to establish a town on the south side of the island, the ford across the Rio Cobre here not only dictated the choice of this site but then shaped the town plan they laid out.

The town straddles a road junction rather than simply providing a convenient stopping place. Later residents could characterise its location as "centrical with respect to the whole of the island," which made it "extremely convenient for holding the chief courts of justice."[2] In selecting a site on the south side of Jamaica for an administrative centre, the resulting settlement benefited from its hub position in the network of routes across the island's central mountains as well as its proximity to what is now called Kingston Harbour. One track continued south along the west bank of the Rio Cobre and another extended the line of the main cross-island road south across the savanna; both reached a sheltered landing place near where the river ran into the harbour.

The area around this ford across the Rio Cobre was a major transit point even before Europeans arrived in Jamaica. When the townspeople began to lay out their town, the gentle slope on the river's west side already held a few Taino burial mounds, though by 1534 these may already have been obscured by a crop of sugar or else would have simply appeared as so many hummocks in a cattle pasture. The largest pre-Columbian settlement identified on the island was at White Marl, which lay one mile to the east of the Spaniards' town. An archaeological section that cut through eight feet of deposits demonstrated prolonged residence there, perhaps dating back as early as 800 AD. Shells and fragments of Taino pottery found mixed into early Spanish layers in site in St Jago de la Vega suggest that when the Spaniards excavated and built, they dug through Taino middens and other features on the western side of the ford. There were some continuities. The Spanish settlers used a Taino name, "Cagway," for today's Rio Cobre. Their use of this name extended south to include the landing place at the river's mouth. Archaeological research may yet identify more substantial Taino features underlying today's town. Though the English conquerors who later took over the town were convinced that the Spaniards had employed Taino labour in its construction, current archaeological scholarship still suggests that the town the Spaniards established did not incorporate a preexisting Taino settlement into its plan.

St Jago de la Vega remained a small town throughout the sixteenth century. In the 1590s a clergyman's census of the number of Spanish colonists on the island gave a figure of 160 households. Other estimates at this juncture ran from "over one hundred" to 120 or else 130 Spanish households.[3] Deriving a total of individuals from such figures is difficult, as no estimates were offered for the amount of people an average household contained. What is clear is that the population had expanded from the 20 households who moved from New Seville in 1536 and the 30 Portuguese families whose immigration was licensed the same year, even if Jamaica was still not a particularly densely settled place. The town came to hold between 400 and 600 houses. The number of free settlers on the island rose slowly over the first half of the seventeenth century although a smallpox epidemic in 1650, which killed 100 slaves and 50 Spaniards, cut into a heavily concentrated population. Jamaica's inhabitants in 1655 totalled approximately 1,500 people, most of whom lived in St Jago. During the Columbus family's rule the island's population became a distinctive cultural blend. By the mid-seventeenth century, very few new settlers migrated from Spain to Jamaica. Meanwhile a trickle of slaves continued to arrive.

Different population groups expanded or contracted at different rates. The Spanish population gained numbers gradually, while the Taino appear to have disappeared or died out after this estimate. Other groups grew faster. Both the Portuguese and the African populations in Jamaica continued to increase during the early seventeenth century as slave ships from the Portuguese settlement in Angola stopped en route to Cartagena and Porto Bello and landed sick slaves in Jamaica on their first landfall after crossing the Atlantic. Many died; some lived. During the seventeenth century, protracted civil wars in Angola's neighbouring Christian kingdom of Kongo resulted in many of these newcomers being Roman Catholic refugees or prisoners from these wars. For what it was worth, Portuguese law required that all slaves be baptized before they were shipped out of Africa. Although the island always remained short of clergy and chaplains, the goal of sustaining some of these slaves' existing Christian beliefs was not impossible.

Jamaican immigration therefore diverged from that of the other Spanish islands as it retained a significant Portuguese component. When other Spanish governors followed royal orders by restricting immigration into the West Indies from Portugal during the early seventeenth century, Portuguese were still permitted to settle in Jamaica. The Columbus family had married into the Portuguese nobility, which may have influenced this policy, but the island also remained underpopulated, providing a welcome for any settlers. These immigrants included Christian families from Portugal who emigrated as labourers, together with other families of Portuguese stock who moved to the Caribbean from Portuguese settlements in West Africa. The incomers also included some "new-Christian" families whose Jewish ancestors had converted outwardly in the 1490s. While a very few of these converts did make free choices, many Spanish and Portuguese Jews were forced to adopt Christianity. Some of them managed to retain Jewish beliefs and customs. Individuals of Jewish ancestry were officially forbidden to sail to the New World. However, some did and, because Jamaica did not have an office of the Inquisition, it offered them a safer harbour. Although all residents shared a common official religion, race divided Jamaica's population, while the island's principled population growth came from forced immigration.

Notes

1. Caird Library, National Maritime Museum, WYN 10/2 W[illiam] B[urrows], "A journal of every dayes proceedings in the expedition of the Fleet sent into the West indies under the command of General William Penn," 20 December 1654–5 September 1655, unfoliated, 15 May 1655.

2. Edward Long, *The History of Jamaica*, vol. 2 (Montreal: McGill-Queen's University Press, 2002), 2, 39.

3. National Library of Jamaica Ms 291, 1597, testimony of Antonio Hernandes, inhabitant of Santo Domingo.

Slavery in Spanish Jamaica

Francisco Morales Padrón

The Spanish historian Francisco Morales Padrón published the first and still the only substantial study of the Spanish period in Jamaican history in 1952. Here Morales Padrón outlines the early history of African slavery in Jamaica. He focuses in particular on Jamaican colonists' difficulties in acquiring a steady supply of enslaved people to meet their labor needs.

It is possible that a few Blacks had entered the island with Juan de Esquivel. A small number of slaves who had been brought by individual colonists would probably have gone. But it was at the end of the third decade of the sixteenth century that the need to import African labour began to assume greater importance. The indigenous population had become greatly diminished, and the white population had begun to disperse due to the attractions of the Continent. In 1523, the Crown ordered a consignment of slaves, of which three hundred were destined for Jamaica. However, the solution was not definitive, either because the said slaves did not arrive or did not arrive in sufficient numbers. After a few years, it became necessary to establish an asiento with the King of Portugal, who agreed to supply the Indies with five thousand Africans. Of that number, seven hundred were for Jamaica. This agreement should have been a useful one since there was a labour shortage in agriculture. The Crown had a stake in the importation, and therefore would have endeavoured to offer the maximum facilities possible. In order to encourage the growth of a settled slave population, the contract specified that female slaves were to be included in the consignment to provide wives for the male slaves. An effort was made to ensure a balanced and a rising African population by increasing the number of males, by prohibiting the sale of slaves, and by insisting that those who died were to be replaced immediately. In his discussion of this question, [Antonio de] Herrera observed that though the gold collected in the island was very scanty, there were sugar mills and some farming. Grape culture, for example, had made possible the production of claret wine, and to ensure that the harvest would not be lost, an asiento with the King of Portugal became necessary.[1]

One of the first shipments of Blacks entered the island in 1534 when the Treasurer Pedro de Mazuelo was laying the foundations of a new settlement on the south coast of the island. In this area Mazuelo had a sugar mill, around which he wished to raise a town. There was, then, a personal interest, since he was short of the labour needed to increase the productivity of the mill. He sought and obtained through the King the importation of thirty slaves from either Portugal or Cape Verde.

The slaves performed a variety of tasks. The first slaves went to a decided area of production which would later become their major field of endeavour—the manufacture of sugar. Secondary tasks included the construction of fortifications, capturing wild cattle, working in households, clearing forests, tanning leather and so on.

At the beginning of the second half of the sixteenth century and indeed for the rest of the century, the need for the introduction of a sizeable number of African slaves was seen as an urgent priority. It was the only way to halt economic decline. The colonists petitioned the Duke of Veragua imploring him to seek from the King licenses to import slaves. Slaves were needed to man the *trapiches* (sugar mills) for it was impossible for white men to endure that kind of labour. Life in the trapiche was hard. The smaller number and higher economic value placed on the Jamaican slave ensured that he would be more leniently treated than black slaves in other Caribbean islands. At the end of the sixteenth century the colonists were complaining about the shortage of slave labour. This shortage was affecting work in the fields, trapiches and *ingenios* (sugar refineries). They were few in number. A few dozens more would improve the island and ensure that the fleets call to take on supplies. But so rarely did ships arrive from Paria or Guinea that years passed by without the arrival of even one coloured man. The French, by abandoning 150 African men on the island's shores [in 1588], eased the problem a little. Judges and officials immediately appropriated them and organised their sale. The state of the economy was such that there was no money to buy them. The slaves had to be sold on credit, and the Crown agreed to accept payment in the form of island produce, which would be remitted to the Peninsula via Cartagena de Indias.

Translated by Patrick E. Bryan

Note

1. Antonio de Herrera, *Historia general de las Indias Occidentales o de los hechos de los castellanos en las Islas y Terra Firme del Mar Océano* (Ediciones de Amberers por Juan Bautista Verdussen, 1728), Decade III, liv. V, cap. VIII.

A Description of Spanish Jamaica

Francisco Marques de Villalobos

Francisco Marques de Villalobos was the leader of the Catholic Church in Jamaica (the abbot) from 1581 to 1606. In this letter, written shortly after his arrival, he complains of the poor management of Jamaica by the Spanish governors and previous religious authorities. In attacking the governors he was criticizing the Columbus family, who were granted authority over the Spanish colonies in the Caribbean by the Spanish Crown. He also describes the island, arguing that it could be of great value to the Spanish Crown if properly managed.

As his most mighty Majesty the Emperor Charles the Fifth, of glorious memory who is with our Lord in heaven, gave this island to the Admirals of these parts and they are so exhausted by law suits and other troubles, they have not improved one inch of land in it. The Governors have not visited nor governed for the term that was right and proper, thus helping these poor people and the great poverty in which they live, but rather, have called upon them to attend to their needs and in every way ill-treated the inhabitants. If the latter wish to go and seek redress from the Royal Audiencia of Santo Domingo, they will not give them process or even certified papers, and if they send letters and other papers they seize them, so that no letter goes to Santo Domingo, nor do any come that they do not take, and the worst is that they interfere in ecclesiastical jurisdiction, abusing the priests and prelates because they reprove their effrontery. When the Governor has become rich the Admiral sends another creature as Governor to take the accounts (residencia) from him which he does entirely to the Governor's liking, and publicly shews himself very friendly to him. Knowing this, the poor inhabitants do not venture to demand their rights.

This island is in a position and latitude so convenient that if any of the enemies who molest your Majesty and are in rebellion against your Royal Service contrary to all right, should make a settlement and take possession there, as they have said and boasted of, it would mean total destruction for the neighbouring islands and be very dangerous to your Majesty's naval and mercantile fleets, for it has very good and commodious ports, deep and spacious enough to hold more than two hundred sail.

This island is fifty leagues long and twenty-five wide. It has only one town. It is called the town of la Vega. It contains one hundred inhabitants (*vecinos*). They live on the products of the land, that is by cultivating cassava and maize and Castillian vegetables which grow in abundance. This on the south side. As it is flatter than the north it is stocked with domestic cattle. On the north, as it is a broken and mountainous country: wild cattle are bred and there is a great quantity of pigs, so much so that very often the smaller ones are caught by hand.

The town lies north to south in level country. On the eastern side it has the river Caguaya of very excellent water.[1] It runs from north to south and discharges at the chief port of Caguaya which is not frequented as it used to be because enemies go there. Ships go three leagues lower to the port of Maymon.[2] The river can be forded at all parts. The houses are of wood and tiles. It is very poor. It has no property or income other than what the tithes yield it each year, which is one-third of the nine parts into which they are divided. The people of this island live in health from the good air and site of the town and the good waters that flow in it. There is a monastery of the order of Preachers where one or two monks reside. They live in poverty as they have nothing but the alms given to them. There are two hermitages, Saint Lucy and Saint Barbara without any caretaker. Their name-day is observed and other days of devotion. This place is two leagues from the chief port Caguaya by a level cart road by which produce and other things needed are carried to the ships. There is a fort or stockade close to the water in front of a tiled wooden house which serves as a guard against anything coming from outside. It is surrounded with lignum vitae, a hard wood, fascine and earth. Though it is not very strong yet it is a protection for those who take refuge in the house against the balls that enemies discharge. If these wanted to make a landing, there are many places where they can do it with great ease.

Translated by Joseph L. Pietersz

Notes

1. The Rio Cobre. [Editors' note]
2. Maymon may have been Old Harbour. [Note by the original editors, Frank Cundall and Joseph Pietersz]

The Economy of Spanish Jamaica

Alonzo de Miranda

This detailed description of the physical geography of Jamaica and of Spanish so-ciety and economy there includes an estimate of population, the complaint that the "people are so lazy and indolent," and the assertion that "all these Spaniards are from only three parentages . . . they are all related." It was written in 1611 by Alonzo de Miranda, who had been governor of Jamaica since 1607. Miranda's estimates of population add up to just over 1,500 people, of whom slightly more than one-third were enslaved. The letter also includes describes the leather industry, Spanish Ja-maica's most important economic activity.

This island of Jamaica in the Ocean Sea, that now belongs to the estate of the Admirals of the Indies, Dukes of Veragua, is in 17 and a half degrees north latitude. Its temperature is hot and humid as is general in all the In-dies falling within the two tropics. The longest day there is 13 hours and a half and the nights accordingly. Although it is a hot country there is less excess and more mildness than in any of the neighbouring islands and lands. It is abundant and suitable for growing all the seeds and grains that are culti-vated in Spain; but the people are so lazy and indolent and opposed to work that through this fault it generally suffers great misery. The Admiral of the Indies places a Governor here and a Lieutenant who holds the courts of first instance with the ordinary alcaldes. There are some clergy born in the is-land with a lot of chaplaincies but these are poor like the people in general. There are two monasteries, one of Saint Dominic and one of Saint Francis, and at present three monks in each and among them two preachers. In the whole island, from the note of the number of confession that I ordered to be made this year, 1611, with particular care, there were one thousand five hun-dred and ten persons of all classes and conditions, five hundred and twenty-three Spaniards, including men and women, one hundred and seventy-three children, one hundred and seven free negroes, seventy-four Indians, natives of the island, five hundred and fifty-eight slaves and seventy-five foreigners. All these Spaniards are from only three parentages and are so mixed with one another by marriage that they are all related. This causes many and grave incests to be committed by which this country is remarkably stained. The remedy is so difficult that it is almost impossible to find as is being experienced in this general visitation I am making in which I find this sin so widespread and deep rooted that it keeps me tied and checked not knowing what to do because except by depopulating the country and injuring many reputations so great a fire cannot be put out for censures and other ecclesiastical means serve more as hindrances than as a remedy. So much for the population.

The whole of the rest of the island which is about 50 leagues long and a little more than 15 wide is uncultivated and uninhabited although there are many hunting grounds of horned stock in which the colonists have their shares similar to the ranches they formerly had stocked with tame cattle from which have sprung those that are now wild in these grounds. Nearly the whole year is taken up in killing cows and bulls only to get the hides and the fat, leaving the meat wasted. There are also large herds of swine raised in the mountains, which are common to all who may wish to hunt them as is ordinarily done, obtaining therefrom a great quantity of lard and jerked pork. All the products of the country are cheap, so that while a silver *real* is worth thirteen quartos, they give for one quarto four pounds of beef at the butchery. The bread eaten here is made from a root called cassava and when made is preserved many months. Two *arrobas* of it which are called one load (*carga*) usually cost eight *reales* and seldom rise to twelve. The island is surrounded with ports with very secure harbours and rivers of fresh water that flow from the mountain ridges, of which there are many, covered with groves of cedars, brasil trees, mahogany and other woods, very suitable for ship building and so convenient for this that if Your Majesty should desire to command some ships or galleons to be built there, any such works would from the natural fitness of the country, the great abundance of woods and cheap provisions, as well as from many other advantages it has, prove much cheaper and more profitable than those that have been done and are going on in other parts, for it is known by experience that the cedar, brasil and other woods of this island are better than those of other places. Among other trees there is one called granadillo (red ebony). It is incorruptible and not quite as black as ebony. It answers just as well for mouldings and ornamentations and is much esteemed. There is another called thorn (*espino*), of variegated colour with the other properties and lustre of the granadillo and ebony. There are trees called cinnamon because the leaf in taste and smell has the same characteristic as cinnamon and as fruit bear pepper (*pimienta*) of the taste, smell and colour of that of India but the grains are larger. There is a great quantity of brasil wood spread all over the island and though up to now it has been used for building houses it has not been extirpated.

A venture has been made in it and cargoes sent to Spain, but up to this it is not known how it will turn out as this is the first year they have dealt with it. Here experiments have been made with it and it gives three different dyes, all very fine both for wool and for silk. If it gives satisfaction over there also it will be a great wealth for this island through the quantity there is in all parts of it.

With all these good possessions, the inhabitants, by their natural laziness are so poor that they hardly manage to feed themselves with cassava and beef which are the cheapest commodities there.

Translated by Joseph L. Pietersz

The Western Design

Juan Ramírez

In 1654 Oliver Cromwell sent a military force of around 2,500 men and thirty-eight ships to the Caribbean in his "Western Design," the goal of which was to capture Hispaniola from the Spanish for England. A further three or four thousand troops were raised from the population of England's eastern Caribbean colonies. In April 1655 the expedition landed west of Santo Domingo in Hispaniola but was quickly defeated. In retreat, the English forces decided to try to capture Jamaica. The island was largely undefended, and the English took it relatively easily. The Spanish surrendered officially on 27 May 1655. From Spain's point of view, the loss of Jamaica was significant more because it gave the English a strong base in the heart of the Caribbean, from which they could threaten the Spanish fleet and its colonies, than for the island's intrinsic economic value. Writing a few days after the surrender, the former Spanish governor, Don Juan Ramírez, explains to his king his failure to prevent the loss of Jamaica to the English. In his letter, Ramírez exaggerates the number of English troops and ships.

Sir,

I would not like to give your Majesty bad news, but as it is a matter of importance to your royal service and the duty I owe to my position, I must advise your Majesty that on the 20th of the present month of May, Robert Buenables [*sic*] Governor of Ireland and general of an English fleet composed of 53 ships of war, 11 small ones and more than 40 pinnaces, with 15,000 seamen and soldiers came in sight of the port of this island;[1] the same day he entered it, and, although I am crippled in hands and feet, in a bed I went to the port, which is very defenceless, to see if with the colonists of this island anything could be done, although to such strength there was no resistance, as I immediately experienced, for the colonists abandoned the port and town and went to the mountains with their families. Whereupon the enemy took possession of everything, and now capitulations are being drawn up for them to give us ships to leave the island. I do not know where this will end; I only know,

Sir, that it is a painful thing to have a port in the Indies that is not your Majesty's. That is felt in what has happened to this island with more than eight thousand souls scattered about the mountains, children, women and slaves without any hope of protection except from God, with the enemy's knife every hour at their throats. What I have managed to learn from the enemy up to the present is that he left England eight months ago, and that he comes to settle this island, and from here undertake greater enterprises such as going to Habana, Cartagena and Santo Domingo. What is most to be regretted is that there will be no security for your Majesty's galleons and fleets of merchant ships if the enemy fortifies himself in this island. Both fleets pass in sight of or very close to it. The trading ships of New Spain, Maracaybo and Caracas do the same, and there is no defence against such a powerful fleet except the arm and might of your Majesty. The island, Sir, is most fertile in every description of provisions and cattle and tobacco, which is what the enemy wants.

Translated by Joseph L. Pietersz

Note

1. The ships really numbered 38, and the soldiers 7,000, with a sea regiment of 1,000 [note by the original editors, Frank Cundall and Joseph Pietersz]. A pinnace is a small boat carried aboard a larger one [editors' note].

Mountains of Gold Turned into Dross

Anonymous

Two letters from an unknown English participant in the invasion of Jamaica demonstrate the initial confidence of the English settlers, followed by their rapid disillusionment. The first emphasizes the ease with which the island was taken from the Spanish and goes on to include a physical account of Jamaica, a description of the "commodities" that will grow there and the island's "innumerable" cattle and horses. The writer emphasizes the advantages of Jamaica in comparison to Hispaniola, which the English expedition had just failed to take. The second letter, written five months later, is much less optimistic. The anonymous correspondent emphasizes the difficulties of the new settlement, particularly the diseases that overtook many of the new settlers.

1 June 1655

On Wednesday morning, being the 9th of May, wee saw Jamaica Iland, very high land afarr off.

Thursday the 10th our souldiers in number 7000 (the sea regiment being none of them) landed at the 3 forts, or rather breast workes, about the point, [in] which there were 8 peece of ordnance yet had but 3 mounted, which played at us making about 20 shott; there were of the enemie about 300 men likewise to resist us with small shott, but all missed our men, who seeing them desperately bent to land, leaping up to the middle in water, they abandoned the forts; the Martin gally playing apace upon the Spaniard under whose gunns wee landed.

These 3 forts, or rather breast workes, were very strong and cannon proofe; from these forts our men marched through a sevanno to the high way in a wood leading to the towne, where about half a mile farther, there was another brest worke for cannon and musquetiers, which without resistance we passed, and within a little mile of the towne, which lay 5 miles from the sea side, there was another strong brest worke with 2 very great murderers to scoure the lane, where the enemie likewise appeared not; breif their strength was such that if the en-

43

emie had behaved himselfe manfully he mought have worsted us. It was
Fryday the 11th of May when the army marched into the towne, about 2
in the afternoon. In the afternoon of Saturday the 12th a Spaniard with a
white flagg comming to our outguards, desiring a treaty was conducted
unto the Generall. A treatie was agreed on, and 3 comissioned by their
Governour, who was carried out of towne in a hammock for the pox;
meane while the enemie sent us 300 head of leane cattle, on purpose to
make the least of the country.

As for the country it is much like that of Hispaniola, never a whit
inferior in any particular, it is fuller of plaine, and better water'd by
odds, most pleasant and healthful to the utmost, we have a land wind
and a sea wind as at Hispaniola. The commodities of this country are
sugar, Spanish tobacco, cotton, chocolate, hides, severall sorts of wood
as Lignum vitae, Brazill, or such sorts. Indigo will grow, so alsoe wine
and oile. The King of Spaine to advance those 2 commodities having
prohibited the growth thereof as the Spaniard tells us. Barley we have
found and pease, so that we hope to brew beere and ale in time. Tis not
soe hot as Italy by day, and cooler by night and mornings. The dayes
differ a little in length; at 7 of the night it growes dark, and it is light at
5 in the morninge. There are noe other cities nor townes, but this on
the Iland, and heere wee have above 1000 houses; the streets not regular
onely some, many of the houses of good brick and timber covered with
tile made heere, other houses of clay and reeds, which doe reasonably
well. Wee found onely 2 small shipps in the harbour, one was sunke, the
other had chocolate, with wood tables and bedsteds readie made, and
other goods. Wee have innumerable many wilde and tame cattle that
feed by thousands on the sevannos, hoggs, and horses alsoe. The horse
much better and larger than those of Hispaniola, soe that better horse
are [not] to be seen in England. Victuals here is therefore reasonable.
Wee have butchers heere that kill for the army, and we have sufficient
thereof, and bread of Cassavi with beskett. The 3 rainy winter months
are August, September, and October, after which the horse and cattle
are very fatt, and now at the worst some of them fatt enough. Wee have
now 2 of our amunition and provision shipps come to us, and the rest
are at Barbadoes expected hourely: when wee shall be soe well provided
of all things, that when wee shall be satisfied, as we shall be suddainly,
at the entringe in by the point and other places by sea, and at the landing, and at the towne, wee hope by God's gracious assistance to keep
our station, maugre the enemie who is round about us from the maine
and the Ilands. Whereof I trust he shall be made sencible suddenly, and

that wee are in respect of our good harbour and scituation better than if wee had taken Hispaniola, as now our councell and officers plainely see and acknowledge, soe that it is to be questioned whether any place in the world would have advantaged our nation more than this.

Jamaica the 5 of November 1655

The 11 ships lately arrived to this place with &c. poore men I pitty them at the heart, all their imaginary mountains of gold are turned into dross, and their reason and affections are ready to bid them saile home againe already. For my owne part greater disapoyntments I never met with, having had noe provision allowed me in 10 weeks last past, nor above 3 biskets this 14 weeks, soe that all I can rape and scrape in ready money goes to housekeeping, and the shifts I make are not to be written heer. Wee have lost halfe our armie from our first landing on Spaniola, when we were 8000, besides 1000 or more seamen in armes. Never did my eyes see such a sickly time, nor soe many funerals, and graves all the towne over that it is a very Golgotha. Wee have a sevanno or plaine neere us where some of the souldiery are buried soe shallow that the Spanish doggs, which lurke about the towne, scrape them up and eate them. As for the English doggs they are most eaten by our souldiery; not one walkes the streets that is not shott at, unlesse well befreinded or respected. Wee have not only eaten all the cattle within neare 12 miles of the place, but now alsoe almost all the horse, asses, mules flesh neere us, soe that I shall hold little Eastcheap in more esteeme than the whole Indies if this trade last, and I can give nor learne noe reason that it should not heer continue soe; besides this wee expect noe pay here, nor hardly at home now, but perhapps some ragged land at the best, and that but by the by spoken of, for us generall officers not a word mentioned. I could dwell long upon this subject, and could tell you that still halfe our armie lyes sick and helpelesse, nor had wee victuals for them before this fleet, nor expect ought now save some bread, and brandy, and oatmeal, and if that with phisick will not keepe them alive, wee have noe other remedie but death for them. For my owne part in 25 yeares have not I endured soe much sicknesse as here with the bloudy flux, rhume, ague, feavor, soe that I desire earnesly to goe for England in March next, if permitted, for I am fallen away 5 inches about.

Amongst the dead persons your brother J. M. is one, who died of the dropsie, consumption, and other complicated diseases, the 22 of August 1655 last &c.

The Establishment of Maroon Society

Robert Sedgwicke and William Goodson

In a letter to Oliver Cromwell, Robert Sedgwicke and William Goodson, two lead-ing officers in the English army in Jamaica, describe the appalling state of the mili-tary forces there in the months after the invasion. They recount the high death rates among the colonists, their lack of provisions, and the continuing presence of Span-iards in parts of the island. This extract is particularly important for its descrip-tion of the original Jamaican Maroons. In their haste to escape the island, Spanish settlers made no effort to retain their relatively small number of enslaved Africans. Those who thereby became free established themselves as communities in Jamai-ca's mountainous interior, where they, along with additional recruits, were able to prevent the English from gaining control over the whole of the island for nearly a century.

Jamaica, January 24, 1655/6

May it please your highness

Your commands, and our duty, make us bold to present these to your highness. We hope the letters sent by the Augustine, and other convey-ances, are arrived long before this. It is no small trouble to us our being so much streightened in opportunities, of more frequent giving account to your highness of the state and condition of your affairs here in these parts.

We humbly crave, that we offend not in our plainness and naked lay-ing open before you, how things stand with us at present, although we should have accounted it a mercy to have our letters and lines filled with more pleasing subjects; but God is wise and faithful in his crossing our earthly expectations.

The numbers of the army are much lessened since our last letters; the whole not extending to three thousand, many of them sick and weak, the best and soundest much abated of their strength and vigor, and God goes on every day to shorten our numbers. We die daily not less than fifty every week, which is much considering our small numbers.

As touching the state of the enemy upon this island, we can give no certain relation of them, but yet of late do know them to be more than formerly apprehended. We lately sent one of the smaller frigats and a brigantine to survey the island, to search the harbours on the north side, and to make what discoveries they could of the island and the enemy. The frigat and brigantine both are returned some ten or twelve days since, which in general report thus: They were in some harbours on the north side of the island, three especially good and large, in one of which they found many Spaniards quietly settled. Our frigat landed sixty men, the enemy only faced them, and then retreated. Our men burnt all their houses, and took some small store of old clothes and the like, and in some other places found some few Spaniards: and as they were returning on the south side, to windward of point Pedro, the frigat landing some men found two Spanish houses, in one of which he found seventeen fixed fire arms, which he brought away, and burnt the houses, but took only one Mulatto. The brigantine put to the shore to the leeward of the said cape, where faced him forty Spaniards mounted, who, as he came near the shore, marched up into the wood. The Mulatto upon his examination being demanded what the Spaniards intend to do, answered, they lay up and down expecting we would leave the island, that they might again possess what formerly was their own. Our soldiers do also in the out quarters sometimes see some few Spaniards mounted killing cattle, who sometimes wound, then kill one or two of our men.

As for the Negroes, we understand, and to satisfaction, that they, for the most part of them, are at distance with the Spaniards, and live by themselves in several parties, and near our quarters, and do very often, as our men go into the woods to seek provisions, destroy and kill them with their launces. We now and then find one or two of our men killed, stripped, and naked, and these rogues begin to be bold, our English rarely, or seldom, killing any of them. Never was there any either Spaniard, Mulatto, or Black, that since our generals went away did so much as make any tender of a desire of a composition. Both contrary; those few Blacks we had amongst us, that did formerly belong to the Spaniards, are run from us, even all but seven or eight, that are now kept with shackles to prevent them; amongst which Blacks that run from us there were two Irishmen went with them, who, as we apprehend, are with the Spaniard, and who cannot but know our condition, and we must, and cannot but acknowledge it as a great favour from God, that hath restrained them from cutting off our men, who are in as low and weak an estate as can be thought of.

As touching your highness's advice of raising some quantity of horse, we have put the army upon it, but we fear the condition of our men, and the difficulty of attaining horse are such, that they will effect little; yet what can shall be done. The truth is, they have with much difficulty kept so many horses as will draw up their provisions to their quarters; besides the horses in this country feeding upon nothing but light grass, in three days riding are unfit for service, when with much difficulty taken.

As for our provisions, both fleet and army subsist wholly on those provisions sent to us; only some few refreshments now and then gotten on shore, but not any thing that saveth a basket cake. Our provisions spend much, some decay by worms, and other ways, the climate being such, that our English provisions are much more subject to decay here than in Europe. We have provisions for the fleet and army for about five months, being the greatest part of them in New-England provisions, which we hope may prove good.

We are all satisfied as concerning your highness's great care in our seasonable supplies, and wish, if it were the good pleasure of God, we were in a capacity to come forth in some action, that might answer so great love and tenderness to us. We had long since attempted St. Jago de Cuba, could our army have afforded us but 500 men; but from that full intelligence we had of the strength of the place, we thought it not convenient to hazard our chief sea forces without a convenient number of men fit to land.

We daily expect the arrival of the other ships your highness is sending to us: in the mean time are fitting all those we have, which we hope will be all equipt and fit for sailing and fight in six days.

II

From English Conquest to Slave Society

In its early years as an English colony, Jamaica was valued by its new colonial masters primarily for its strategic location close to the wealthy Spanish colonies and to the sea routes traveled by the Spanish fleet bearing gold and silver from Mexico and Peru. Jamaica became a stronghold for pirates and especially for state-sponsored privateers. Its residents acquired substantial wealth from plundering Spanish ships and ports and from illicit trade with the Spanish colonies. Port Royal, on the peninsula across the bay from what today is Kingston, became a notorious town in this period before it was destroyed in an earthquake in 1692. Some of the profits from piracy and privateering were invested in land and in purchasing enslaved people, laying the foundations of the Jamaican sugar industry.

African slavery had been introduced to Jamaica under the Spanish but did not become dominant until the mid-eighteenth century. Jamaica's sugar boom followed those of Barbados and other parts of the eastern Caribbean, adopting the established system of plantation slavery. The government initially claimed the whole island as Crown territory, then distributed land to settlers who committed to import enslaved Africans. In Jamaica, this system was pushed to extremes: settlers received much larger allocations of land than did those elsewhere in the region. The plantation system, coupled with British dominance of the expanding Atlantic slave trade in this period, transformed Jamaican society. Hundreds of thousands of people arrived on slave ships from Africa, particularly from areas that today form parts of Nigeria, Ghana, and the Democratic Republic of Congo. Jamaica was the largest British importer of enslaved people in the Americas, and in some decades it accounted for nearly half of all Africans shipped by British ships to the hemisphere. It rapidly became a society in which more than nine people were enslaved for every one who was free. The entire economy and society were oriented toward the maintenance and reproduction of slavery. The system was designed to maximize the growth and export of sugar, a crop that shifted in the eighteenth century from being an exotic luxury to an everyday necessity in the European diet. In 1748, two-fifths of all British sugar imports were grown in Jamaica.[1] The wealth generated by slavery enabled many slave owners to return to Britain, where they became absentee landowners, managing their estates remotely and building lavish country estates.

Most records document the experiences of Europeans in Jamaica in this period. Very little evidence directly records the voices of enslaved people. Nevertheless, historians, archaeologists, and anthropologists have been able to partially reconstruct enslaved people's experience through close examination of extant archival sources; the survival of African and creole heritage; and excavations of former plantations. Part II examines the formation of an entrenched racially based slave society and economy in the island. It pays particular attention to the responses of enslaved people to their oppression, encompassing multiple forms, from music to armed revolt.

Note

1. Trevor Burnard and Kenneth Morgan, "The Dynamics of the Slave Market and Slave Purchasing Patterns in Jamaica, 1655–1788," *William and Mary Quarterly* 58, no. 1 (2001): 205–206.

Pirate Stronghold

Nuala Zahedieh

In the early years of English settlement, the town of Port Royal became a famous center of piracy and privateering. Pirates and privateers gained wealth by attacking the Spanish galleon fleets, which carried silver and gold extracted from Spanish American mines to Europe. Port Royal was also the center of the important contraband trade between English traders and the Spanish colonies. This illegal trade defied the mercantilist system, in which metropolitan powers attempted to regulate colonial commerce by prohibiting trade outside their own empire. Mercantilism aimed to ensure that the economic benefits of the colonies flowed directly to the metropolis. Here economic historian Nuala Zahedieh argues that despite mercantilism, capital acquired through legal and illegal trade with, and plunder of, the Spanish colonies generated significant wealth for the first English ruling class of Jamaica. As a result, Port Royal became an unusually wealthy colonial town.

The English founded a town at Port Royal with its large, sheltered harbour immediately after the seizure of Jamaica. The port quickly became a base for freebooting activities against the Spaniards, attracting disorderly elements from all over the Caribbean. In 1663 Jamaica had a fleet of fifteen privateers. By 1670, the island had over twenty such vessels with about two thousand men. Marauders continued to operate from Port Royal throughout the seventeenth century despite the Anglo-Spanish Treaty of Madrid, promising peace and friendship in 1670. Both opponents and advocates of so-called "forced trade" declared that the town's fortune had the dubious distinction of being founded entirely on the servicing of the privateers' needs and a highly lucrative trade in prize commodities. A report that the three hundred men who accompanied [Captain] Henry Morgan to Portobello in 1668 returned to the town with prize to spend of at least £60 each (two or three times the usual annual plantation wage) leaves little doubt that they were right.[1] Although Jamaica planting had scarcely begun, the port's trade increased fivefold in the 1660s. The Portobello raid alone produced plunder worth £75,000, more than seven times the annual value of the island's sugar exports, which at Port Royal prices did not exceed £10,000 at this time.

Port Royal was also ideally situated for contraband trade with the Spanish colonists. Foreigners had long obtained a substantial share of the official Spanish colonial trade which was conducted in two, supposedly annual, fleets from Seville or Cadiz. The goods were shipped to Portobello and Vera Cruz where they were exchanged for rich American commodities, mainly bullion. However, the traders' profits were eroded by innumerable difficulties and delays, particularly as the fleets became increasingly irregular and high defence costs pushed up charges. The advantages of direct trade via a base in the Caribbean were apparent to both sellers and customers. Suppliers reduced costs and delays considerably, which enabled them to increase turnover and profits. The Spanish colonists could buy goods more cheaply and dispose of their own products more regularly, which was particularly important if they were selling perishable agricultural commodities. The economic logic was too strong to be denied and, despite the Spanish authorities' persistent refusal to condone the trade, it grew and flourished, attracting merchants to Port Royal who participated on their own, and their correspondents' behalf. Part of this trade was conducted in the island's own sloop fleet, stimulating growth from 40 in 1670 to 80 in 1679 and about 100 in 1689. A further considerable part was carried on by English and colonial ships which called at Port Royal before making for the Spanish Indies, but did not return to Jamaica on their way home. Reginald Wilson, the Naval Officer, reported that forty of the eighty-seven ships which had sailed from Port Royal in 1679 had gone on to trade with the Spaniards in this way. A close examination of Wilson's returns in the 1680s suggests that it continued to be usual for about half the ships entering Port Royal to be destined for Spanish markets. Jamaican agents hired skilled supercargoes and strengthened the ships' crew, earning commission for their services.

The contraband trade was mainly carried on "underhand" in bays and creeks or the smaller towns. The larger, strongly fortified towns of Portobello, Cartagena and Havana were more difficult and risky to penetrate. The one commodity which could open their doors was slaves, for the Spaniards did not pretend to provide them for themselves, and so had to turn to a middleman who did. The contractors, or *asientistas*, obtained supplies where they could and Jamaica was ideally suited to serve them; transport costs being 20 per cent lower than they were from the rival Dutch base at Curaçao. There is no record of a formal agreement to supply the Spaniards in the early years but there are references to their coming to Jamaica. By the 1680s the trade was substantial. The African Company alone sold about

25 per cent of its annual supplies to the Spaniards (i.e., an average of about five hundred slaves) and there are also records of large sales by interlopers. However, it was a small group of merchants who benefited most. They bought slaves from the African Company, then sold them to the Spaniards, providing their customers with an armed convoy and accepting payment in the Spanish home port. The Spaniards paid 35 per cent extra for this convenience. It was a highly lucrative and relatively safe business which was, as the planter John Helyar remarked, "a much easier way of making money than making sugar."[2]

Unfortunately the lack of detailed statistical evidence makes it impossible to quantify the value of Port Royal's Spanish trades, either peaceful or forced, with any precision. However, their combined importance is clear. It was most obviously reflected in the unusual abundance of cash in Jamaica, which enabled the islanders to use coins as currency, rather than commodities as in other colonies. In 1683 a visitor remarked that "there was more plenty of running cash proportionately to the number of its inhabitants than is in London."[3]

The value of the Spanish commerce is also indicated by the fact that the growth and prosperity of Port Royal predated the development of the agricultural hinterland. Although the island's sugar trade was in its infancy, the port's white population increased from 630 in 1662 to almost 3,000 in 1680 and to 4,000 in 1689, making it the largest English town in the Caribbean. The importance of trading opportunities in attracting people to Port Royal is shown by the very large number of merchants in the town. There are 118 Port Royal inventories surviving from the period 1686–1694, a fair-sized sample of a town with about 1,000 households in 1689; 49 of these were merchants.

Visitors remarked on Port Royal's easy lifestyle. [John] Taylor, the diarist, described the merchants and gentry living "in the height of splendour," served by negro slaves in livery. The craftsmen also lived better than in England. There was plentiful employment and wages were three times as high as at home. There was abundant food. Three daily markets were well stocked with fruit, fish and meat. Luxuries were easily available too. There was also a wealth of entertainment: a bear-garden, cock-fighting, billiards, music houses, shooting at targets and also "all manner of debauchery" which the prudish blamed upon "the privateers and debauched wild blades which come hither." Many raised eyebrows at the large number of alehouses and the "crue of vile strumpets and common prostratures" which crowded the town, undeterred by frequent imprisonment in a cage near the harbour.[4] All this reflected the surplus cash in the place. The Port Royal inventories which survive from the period 1674–1694 also indicate that it was a prosperous town. In the whole period 44 out of a total of 212 left estates worth over £1,000. This suggests that the townspeople had succeeded in making themselves at least as rich as their famous New England counterparts. As Taylor remarked, "With the help of the Spaniards' purse" inhabitants on the island "have advanced their fortune" and were now rich.[5]

The wealth of Jamaica was created out of the profits of Jamaica; far from supporting the liberal theory that empire was a cost and burden on the mother country, the island provides a good example of imperialism as theft, albeit by one colonial power from another, rather than by a developed from a developing country. It was plunder and illegal trade which provided England's largest sugar producer with much of its initial capital.

Notes

1. In 1688 Henry Morgan, a Welsh privateer based in Jamaica, captured Portobello, Panama, a crucial city in the Spanish network through which Peruvian silver was exported to Europe. Morgan held the city for two months before ransoming it back to the Spanish, after extracting considerable wealth. [Editors' note]

2. Scottish Record Office Helyar MSS, WHh/1089, John Helyar to father, 16 September 1686.

3. F. Hanson, ed., *Laws of Jamaica* (1683), introduction.

4. Institute of Jamaica MS 105, Taylor, "Multum in Parvo," folios 491–507.

5. Institute of Jamaica MS 105, Taylor, "Multum in Parvo," folio 589.

Port Royal Destroyed

Anonymous

In 1692 a massive earthquake hit Jamaica. It was felt through much of the southeast-
ern part of the island, but the most serious destruction was to the hitherto thriving
town of Port Royal. The effect of the tremor was intensified by a tsunami. Damage
was also amplified because the largely sandy soil on which the town was built under-
went a process known to seismologists as "liquefaction," in which saturated sandy
soil under stress behaves like liquid. As a result, more than half of the fifty-acre site
of Port Royal was submerged beneath the sea. Around two thousand people were
killed immediately; another two thousand died later from injuries or disease. The
destruction of Port Royal led directly to the establishment of Kingston across the bay.
Many interpreted the earthquake as punishment for the lavish and loose lifestyles of
those who had lived in the town. This firsthand account of the earthquake presents it
as a moral tale. The extract also reveals the significance of slavery even in this early
period of English Jamaica.

Sir,

Waving all other Private and Particular Concerns at this time, give
me leave to present you with an Account of a late and dismal Calamity
and Judgement, which hath befallen us here in this Countrey by a Terrible Earthquake, which a just God hath sent upon us on *Tuesday* the 7th
of *June*, about a quarter of an Hour after Eleven of the Clock, and continued with great Violence and Terror, (as most say, about one Quarter of
an Hour) but in my Opinion not above six or seven minutes; in which
time it overthrew all the Brick and Stone buildings in the countrey,
whereof several in my own Parish, which now are either levelled with
the ground, or standing Monuments of the Wrath of God, are so shattered and torn that they are irreparable: While these were tumbling,
the Earth opened in my Parish in multitudes of places, and through
their dire Chasms spew'd out Water to a considerable heighth above
ground, in such quantities in some places that it made our Gullies run

on a suddain, tho before exceeding dry; insomuch that some were afraid of being overwhelmed at once by the River and Sea joining together to swallow up the Countrey.

Our noted town of *St Jago de la Vega*, or *Spanish Town*, is utterly down to the ground, with its Church devoured in the same Ruines. Our Magazeen and only Store house of *Port Royal* is three parts swallowed in the sea, ships and shallops now riding at Anchor where great numbers of fine Fabricks have been not long since;[1] the Relation of which single Places Sufferings to give you in particular, would not only weary your Eyes, but make your Heart ake to read it; many very eminent Merchants, before worth thousands, are now scarce worth more than the blew Linnen on their backs; several are dead, either overwhelmed with their Houses, or drowned in the Sea, which flowed in suddenly upon them, and while they fled from the gaping Chasms of the Earth, or the tottering Buildings, the Sea met them and swept them away. A whole street, which we call the *Wharf*, where most of the noted Merchants lived, and where much of the Planters Goods was landed for convenience of Sail and Shipping, (more especially sugar and cotton) sunk at once from one end to the other, with a general crack at the very beginning of the Earthquake, together with two Forts, Guns, &c, built thereupon; and which is more dreadful, all those poor Wretches perished that were either upon, or nigh it, without any Warning; and presently after this, while the People were in the greatest Horror and Consternation imaginable, neither having time to fly, or thoughts where to fly for safety, two or three more streets in their whole length tottered and fell, and were immediately sunk, Land and all together deep into the Sea, as far as the *Jews* Street: All the upper part of the Town, together with the Church and all above towards the Pallisadoes, is under Water, even their Pallisadoes it self where their Burying place was, is now no longer Earth, but Sea and (ghastly to behold) the very dead Corps that were submerged (I may say) instead of Inhumed, even at their Funerals floated thence to all parts of the Harbour.

The reputed number of the Dead, according to the general estimation (for perhaps there will never be any true Account) is commonly reckoned at fifteen hundred persons, besides Blacks, who 'tis probable may be six or seven hundred more, a multitude of whose Corps floated a great many days after from one side of the Harbor to the other, which caused such an intolerable stench, that the Dead were like to destroy the living.

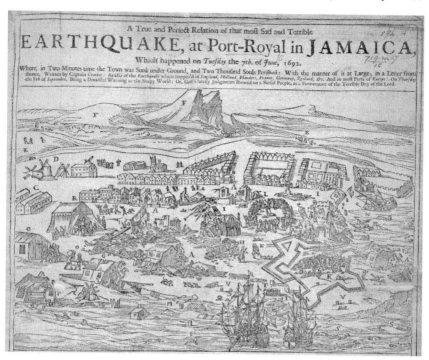

An anonymous account and visual representation of the Port Royal earthquake, published in London shortly after the event: *A True and Perfect Relation of that Most Sad and Terrible earthquake, at Port-Royal, Jamaica which happened on Tuesday 7th June 1692* (London: R. Baldwyn, 1692). British Library, General Reference Collection 74/719.m.17.(15.). © British Library Board. All Rights Reserved. Bridgeman Images no. BL58247. Used by permission of British Library, General Reference Collection / Bridgeman Images.

Immediately upon the Cessation of the extremity of the Earthquake, your Heart would abhorr to hear of the Depredations, Robberies, and Violences that were in an instant committed upon the Place by the vilest and basest of the People; no Man could call any thing his own, for they that were strongest, and most wicked seized what they pleased, and whose they pleased, and where they pleased, without any regard to Propriety. Gold and Silver, Jewels, Plate, or Goods was all their own that they could or would lay their hands on: nothing but breaking open of Houses, rushing into Shops, and taking what they pleased before the Owners faces, forcing Goods or Money from them in the open street, as they were carrying it elsewhere for better Security, succeeded the horrors of this dreadful time; while others in Canoo's, Wherries, Ship-boats, &c., were plundering Chests, Boxes, Screwtores, &c. of what they could find in them upon the Water, even the very Slaves thought it their time of Liberty, wherein they committed many barbarous Insolencies and Robberies, till they were supress'd by the Death of some, and punishment of others. Many days did these Depredations last, especially upon the Water, where the Dead were robbed of what they had about them, some stript, others searched, their Pockets pick'd, their Fingers cut off for their Rings, their Gold Buttons taken out of their Shirts, and then they were turned adrift again; from thence was taken all manner of Stores that would swim, every one taking that for his own which he could lay his hands on, as Pork, Beef, Mackril, Salt fish, Coaca, Candles, Soap, Wine, Beer, Brandy, and a vast deal of other things.

Port Royal being thus ruined, and utterly despaired of being a place of Safety for Habitation, it is intended utterly to be deserted, most people believing that in a few Months it will either be all under water by reason of its daily sinking, or at least but a very small remnant of that narrow Neck of Land will shew it self after a while: Wherefore the Council have very lately agreed upon another place, called *The Rack*, whereupon to build a Town for the Reception and Accommodation of Merchants, which is within the same Harbour as the other, but some Leagues farther up in the Countrey, at the farther end of the Haven, whereunto an approved of Channel leads, and which is not only more safe for Shipping both against Enemies and Storms, but is described also to be very nigh, and with very little Labour may be made altogether as convenient as the famous Harbour of *Port Royal*; it being Capable (now as nature framed it) to receive Ships of the greatest Burden very nigh to the shore, which may be much advantaged in a small time by the building of Wharfs &c. for the benefit of lading and unlading of Ships, as at *Port Royal* before. From thence it is but a short way to *Ligania*, the first and principal place for Planting, (whereunto my own Parish is immediately the next) which for the most part imitating, if not exceeding the stateliness of *Port Royal*, is now the more terribly brought to Desolation, together with its fine New Built and not yet finished Church, buried in the same Ruines with the Houses; above which place the lofty blew Mountains lift up their Heads, but are now so rent and torn that they are fearful to behold, and are like to stand for lasting Marks of the Wrath of God. And yet for all these great Disasters, great Numbers of People are not at all reformed of their Wickedness which brought this upon us, but there is the same

Whoring and Drinking, the same Cursing and Swearing, if not worse than formerly, so that we may fear the Judgment of *Sodom* will be the next punishment you will hear of.

Note

1. A shallop is a type of sailing boat. [Editors' note]

White Servants

Government of Jamaica

After settlement the English set about searching for a labor force to work in their Caribbean colonies. The pattern established in Barbados in the seventeenth century was repeated in Jamaica. Among the first colonial workers were white immigrants from England, Ireland, and Scotland, as well as from Barbados, who came to the island as indentured laborers under contracts that bound them to work for between three and seven years. Most were poor and had few options but to sign themselves over to plantation labor and the promise of a better life in the Caribbean. Others were forced into indentured labor in service of a debt, or hoodwinked by callous "spirits" who combed the country, especially the port towns, in search of able-bodied men and women. Still others were convicts whose punishment included transportation into indentured labor. White servitude was widely used across the English colonies. In Jamaica, it proved inadequate for the scale of sugar production. Enslaved Africans already outnumbered whites by the 1670s.[1] Nevertheless, a small population of indentured workers played a significant role in the Jamaican economy in the late seventeenth and early eighteenth centuries. The 1681 Act for Regulating Servants sets out the legal framework for the management of indentured laborers as well as hired servants, who received wages.

As well as compelling masters of servants to provide specified rations of food and clothing for servants, this act introduced the "deficiency clause," which attempted to ensure there would always be enough white men on the plantations to defend against enslaved insurrection. This clause specified a required ratio of "white Man-servant[s], Overseer[s], or hired m[e]n" to slaves. If the ratio was not met, slave owners had to pay a fine. In practice, as African slavery came to dominate Jamaica's economy completely, most slaveholders chose to pay the fine rather than maintain sufficient white servants.

The act also played an important role in consolidating the strong associations between blackness and slavery, whiteness and freedom, in the Caribbean and the broader British Empire. For the first time, it used the term white to distinguish servants from slaves.[2]

Be it enacted and ordained by the Governor, Council, and Assembly; and it is hereby Enacted and Ordained by the Authority of the same, That all and every Master or Mistresses of Slaves, for the first Five working Slaves, shall be obliged to keep One white Man-servant, Overseer or hired Man, for Three Months at least; and if the Number increase to Ten, Two; and for every Ten after the first, One, to be resident in the Plantation where the Negroes are employed: And if any shall be wanting, for the Space of Six Months, of the Proportion aforesaid, he, she, or they, for every Servant so wanting, shall forfeit Five Pounds to the Use of the Parish where such Default shall be made; to be recovered by the Church-wardens by Action of Debt in any Court of Record in this Island.

That all Servants shall serve according to their Contract and Indenture; and where there is no Contract or Indenture, Servants under Eighteen Years of Age, at their Arrival in this Island, shall serve seven Years; and above Eighteen Years of Age, shall serve Four Years: and all convicted Felons, for the Time of their Banishment, and at the Expiration of their Times aforesaid, shall receive from their late Master, Mistress, or Employer, Forty Shillings, and a Certificate of their Freedom upon Demand; and whosoever shall refuse, without just Cause, to give such Certificate to any Servant, Artificer, or Labourer, whose Time is expired, or Contract performed, shall forfeit Forty Shillings for every such Refusal.

And whosoever shall Employ any free Person without a Certificate from the last Employer, of the Performance of his or their last Bargain or Contract, shall forfeit Ten Pounds.

That no Person or Persons presume to trade with any Servant or Slave without the Master or Mistress's Consent, on Penalty of forfeiting to the Master or Mistress of such Servant or Slave treble the Value of the Things traded for, bought, or sold, and also Ten Pounds current Money of this Island; to be recovered by such Master or Mistress, by Action of Debt in any Court of Record: And all Contracts made with Servants or Slaves to be utterly void.

That if any Servant or hired Labourer shall lay violent Hand upon his or her Employer, Over-seer, or other Person put in Authority over him or her, such Servant or Labourer shall, for such Offence, serve his or her Employer without any Wages Twelve Months, by Order of any Justice of the Peace, on Conviction.

And be it further enacted by Authority aforesaid, That if any Freeman of this Island shall at any Time hereafter beget a Woman Servant with child he shall (upon due Proof thereof made, which Proof shall be by the Oath of the said Woman, as in other Cases of Bastardy) give good Security to save the Parish harmless; and as a further Punishment for his Offence, and for and towards Satisfaction of the Master or Mistress of such Servant, shall forfeit and pay unto the said Master or Mistress the full Sum of Twenty Pounds current Money of this Island; and shall likewise provide for the Maintenance of the said Servant and Child; and in case of Failure herein, shall serve the Master or Mistress of such Servant double the Time that she had to serve at the Time of the Offence committed, or shall procure one in his or their Stead that shall be obliged so to do; and in case one Servant shall beget another with Child, then the Man-servant shall, after the Expiration of his Term, serve the Master or Mistress of the Woman-servant double the Time she had to serve at the Time of the Offence committed.

That all Suits between Servants and their Masters or Mistresses, relating to their Freedom, shall be heard and determined by any two Justices of the Peace, without any Appeal; and if any Servants absent themselves from their Master's or Mistress's Service without Leave, or a Ticket from their Master, Mistress, or Overseer, shall, for every such Day's Absence, serve one Week, and so in proportion for a longer or shorter Time; the whole Punishment not to exceed Three Years.

That no Servant be whipped naked without Order of a Justice of Peace, upon Penalty of Five pounds, to be recovered by the Party injured, by Action of Debt in any Court of Record.

And whosoever shall not give to each White Servant weekly Four Pounds of good Flesh, or Four Pounds of good Fish, together with such convenient Plantation Provision as may be sufficient, shall forfeit to the Party injured Ten Shillings for each Offence.

And whosoever shall not yearly give to each Servant-man Three Shirts, Three Pairs of Drawers, Three Pair of Shoes, Three pair of Stockings, and One Hat or Cap, and to the Woman proportionably, shall forfeit to the Party injured Forty Shillings.

And also if a Servant, or hired Labourer, shall be guilty of hiding or entertaining any Person's Servant or Slave, he shall forfeit one Year's Service to the Master or Mistress of such Servant or Slave, or receive Thirty-nine Lashes on the naked Back, at the Election of the Party Injured; to be ordered by any Justice of the Peace to any Constable in the Precincts.

Notes

1. Richard S. Dunn, *Sugar and Slaves: The Rise of the Planter Class in the English West Indies, 1624–1713* (1972; repr., Chapel Hill: University of North Carolina Press, 2012), 155.

2. Edward B. Rugemer, "The Development of Mastery and Race in the Comprehensive Slave Codes of the Greater Caribbean during the Seventeenth Century," *William and Mary Quarterly* 70, no. 3 (2013): 446–448.

The Rise of Slave Society

Richard S. Dunn

Plantation society in Jamaica dates to the late seventeenth century. With more than double the land space of the other British possessions in the Caribbean combined, Jamaica was well suited to large-scale agricultural development. The English were keen to incorporate all the elements of a plantation system, especially large acres devoted to sugar cultivation and the importation of an enslaved labor force. The process took decades and involved ecological transformation as well as the establishment of new types of human relationships in the colony. Historian Richard Dunn emphasizes the large scale of early landholdings compared with those in the eastern Caribbean, but also stresses the gradual accumulation of property that lay behind the development of the large plantations of the eighteenth century.

Pioneer life in seventeenth-century Jamaica was a harsh winnowing process that separated out the great majority of the early English colonists. The domestication of this island turned out to be a greater challenge than the eastern islands, for Jamaica was wilder, more ruggedly mountainous, more thickly jungled, in every way harder to tame. Like the Spaniards before them, the English learned that it was no easy thing to cultivate this "garden of the Indies," and the first settlers only started the job. Yet, of course, the island had far greater agrarian potential than Barbados or the Leewards. The planters who stuck it out, through luck or skill or strength, founded the greatest sugar fortunes in the English Caribbean. They built a network of plantations that returned good profits in the late seventeenth century and spectacular profits by the mid-eighteenth century, when production reached full swing.

The most obvious difference between planting in Jamaica and the eastern islands was the grand scale on which land was distributed. Each new settler was encouraged to patent as much land as he could conceivably work. After paying a small fee to the land office, he held this acreage in free tenure forever, subject only to a nominal annual quitrent, which was rarely collected in the early days. By 1683, according to Governor Lynch, three thousand patents had been issues for 1,080,000 acres. This means that the average individual tract was 360 acres, the size of the largest plantations in Barbados or Nevis. During the course of the century eighty-eight Jamaicans patented two thousand or more acres apiece. Actually the truly land-hungry planters built up much larger allotments than the patent books show, because they bought, sold, and exchanged their lands among themselves at a dizzy rate. Lynch himself, for instance, took out ten patents for 6,040 acres, but in addition he bought 26,744 acres from other landholders and sold 11,346 acres, so that he ended with 21,438 acres, acquired in fifty-nine separate transactions between 1662 and 1684.

Very little of this acreage, so freely bandied about, was put under cultivation in the seventeenth century. The most fertile land in Jamaica was heavily forested, generally speaking, and it took the colonists many long years to clear and plant these woodlands. For example, a planter named Francis Price, the founder of one of Jamaica's premier sugar fortunes, patented 3,784 acres in three parishes between 1664 and 1676 and bought another thousand acres in addition. Price may have recognised that the richest land he selected was in Lluidas Vale, future seat of the great Worthy Park sugar plantation, but he did not attempt to grow cane at Worthy Park. Instead he kept a cattle pen in this remote and inaccessible tract and put all of his effort into building a sugar plantation closer to the coast on 450 acres in Guanaboa Vale.

Initially planters like Francis Price had few servants or slaves to help work their land. In 1662 the Jamaicans collectively owned only 552 slaves, which helps explain why, seven years after the conquest, they had a meagre 2,917 acres under cultivation. Most of the first comers had scant capital as well as scant labor, and they farmed accordingly. Some of them set up as ranchers; they rounded up the remnants of the Spanish livestock herds, built cattle pens and hog crawls in the coastal grasslands, sold the meat locally and exported the hides to England. Others planted provision crops such as peas, cassava, plantains, and yams amongst the stumps in their half-cleared fields and cash crops such as ginger, pimento, cotton, and tobacco for export. Indigo was another relatively easy, foolproof commodity that fetched a good price. Cocoa production offered alluring prospects to the first English planters, particularly since they could take over the existing Spanish cacao groves. But it required a considerable investment of labour, capital, and time to start a new cacao walk.

So sugarcane remained the most alluring crop of all—but of course sugar works required considerably more capital and labour than a cacao walk or an indigo works. One can trace through the island records the cases of numerous Jamaica planters who built themselves up to sugar by stages. They started out with provision crops, indigo or ginger, bought a slave or two and cleared an acre or two every year, and when they had assembled a work force of twenty or thirty blacks, converted their fields to cane. In the 1660s Jamaica sugar exports trailed well behind cocoa and indigo in value, but by the 1680s sugar had become the leading island export.

The chief planters of Jamaica were a mixed lot, even more so than in Barbados and the Leewards. Some had been soldiers in 1655, others were civilians; some came as Roundheads, others Cavaliers; some migrated directly from Britain, others from the eastern islands; some lived on their estates, some in Port Royal or Spanish Town, and others were absentees in England. Very few of the officers who commanded Cromwell's army when it landed in Jamaica in 1655 lived long enough or stayed long enough to become big planters. But a good many men who arrived with the army in 1655 or joined it during the next five years did end up among the island magnates.

Surprisingly few surnames from the Barbados plantocracy turn up in the early Jamaica records. Sir Thomas Modyford was by far the most conspicuous ex-Barbadian, unless one counts Sir Henry Morgan, who is supposed to have started his West Indian career as an indentured servant in Barbados. Richard Guy, Thomas Sutton, and William Drax were prominent Barbadians who became sugar magnates in Jamaica, and perhaps a dozen others could be added to the list. It is quite possible that fewer younger sons and brothers of established Barbados planters transferred their operations to Jamaica than to South Carolina in the 1670s and 1680s.

One point is clear. Most of the planters who succeeded in Jamaica arrived early, within the first decade of settlement. Three-quarters of the eighty-eight biggest patentees (those who acquired two thousand acres during the seventeenth century) took out their first grants by 1670. [Even so,] we must remember that the Jamaican plantocracy was still in embryo in the seventeenth century. The planters who controlled the best land and the top offices were more numerous and wealthy than the Leeward gentry, but most of them were fairly small entrepreneurs by Barbados standards, and such they remained until the Peace of Utrecht.[1] Eventually Francis Price's son and grandson would set up a grandiose sugar estate at Worthy Park in Lluidas, which dwarfed any of the initial Guanaboa plantations and equalled or surpassed the finest Barbados establishments. But this was in a new century and a new era, when the planters who had stuck it out through fifty years of trouble and disorder began to reap a rich reward.

Note

1. The Peace of Utrecht, a series of treaties signed in 1713, ended the War of the Spanish Succession. [Editors' note]

African Music in Jamaica

Hans Sloane

Hans Sloane is best known as the man whose vast collections provided the foundations of both the British Museum and the Natural History Museum in London. He went to Jamaica to serve as a physician to the newly appointed governor, the Duke of Albemarle, in 1687. He later married into a slave-owning family and gained significant income through his wife's slavery-derived wealth. Although he lived in Jamaica for only fifteen months, he kept detailed notes of his observations and later published a two-volume book about Jamaica and his voyage there. It focused mostly on the natural history of the island, but the introduction recognizes the significance of slavery. Sloane includes an encyclopedic description of Jamaican geography, flora, and fauna alongside accounts of the medical conditions he treated and matter-of-fact discussion of the brutal "punishments" imposed on enslaved people for their "crimes." Although he was not critical of slavery, Sloane was interested in the cultural lives of enslaved people. He left behind detailed descriptions of their everyday lives and cultural practices, including the fragments of music reproduced here. Sloane labels the three fragments Angola (that is, from West Central Africa); Papa (from Dahomey in what is now Benin); and Koromanti (from the Gold Coast, now Ghana). Recent research suggests that Mr. Baptiste, whom Sloane refers to as the man he asked to "take the Words they sung and set them to Musick," may have been a free man of color.[1]

The *Negros* are much given to Venery, and although hard wrought, will at nights, or on Feast days Dance and Sing; their Songs are all bawdy, and leading that way. They have several sorts of Instruments in imitation of Lutes, made of small Gourds fitted with Necks, strung with Horse hairs, or the peeled stalks of climbing Plants or Wichs. These instruments are sometimes made of hollow'd Timber covered with Parchment or other Skin wetted, having a Bow for its Neck, the Strings ty'd longer or shorter, as they would alter their sounds. The figures of some of these Instruments are hereafter graved. They have likewise in their Dances Rattles ty'd to their Legs and Wrists, and in their Hands, with which they make a noise, keep-

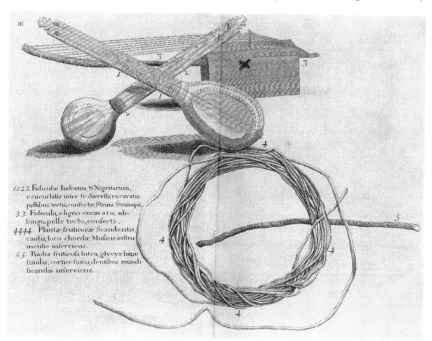

11.22. Fidiculæ Indorum & Nigritarum,
e cucurbitis inter se diversis excavatis,
pellibus tectis, confectæ, Strum Strumps.
3.3. Fidicula, e ligno excavato, ob-
longo, pelle tecto, confecta.
4444. Plantæ fruticosæ Scandentis,
caulis, loco chordæ Musicis instru-
mentis inserviens.
5.5. Radix fruticosa lutea, glycyrrhizæ
similis, cortice fusco, dentibus mundi-
ficandis inserviens.

An engraving showing musical instruments in use in seventeenth-century Jamaica. The long-necked stringed instruments, which Sloane described as "Strum Strumps," are the earliest available images of the banjo. The instrument at the back, a harp attached to a box resonator, may have been from Jamaica or from Africa. Engraver unknown, from Hans Sloane, *A voyage to the islands Madera, Barbados, Nieves, S. Christophers and Jamaica: with the natural history of the herbs and trees, four-footed beasts, fishes, birds, insects, reptiles, &c. of the last of those islands* (London: Printed by B. M. for the author, 1707), following p. cliv. John Carter Brown Map Collection, file name 08845-3, call no. D707 S634V / 2-SIZE. Used courtesy of the John Carter Brown Library at Brown University. https://creativecommons.org/licenses/by/4.0/legalcode.

ing time with one which makes a sound answering it on the mouth of an empty Gourd or Jar with his Hand. Their Dances consist in great activity and strength of Body, and keeping time, if it can be. They very often tie Cows Tails to their Rumps, and add such other odd things to their Bodies in several places, as gives them an extraordinary appearance.

Upon one of their Festivals when a great many of the Negro Musicians were gathered together, I desired Mr *Baptiste*, the best Musician there to take the Words they sung and set them to Musick, which follows.

You must clap Hands when the Base is plaid, and cry, *Alla, Alla*.

They formerly on their Festivals were allowed the use of Trumpets after

Musical notation by "Mr. Baptiste" of fragments of African music in late seventeenth-century Jamaica, from Hans Sloane, *A voyage to the islands Madera, Barbados, Nieves, S. Christophers and Jamaica: with the natural history of the herbs and trees, four-footed beasts, fishes, birds, insects, reptiles, &c. of the last of those islands* (London: Printed by B. M. for the author, 1707), l–li. John Carter Brown Archive of Early American Images, record no. 08845-2, call no. D707 S634V / 2-SIZE. Used courtesy of the John Carter Brown Library at Brown University. https://creativecommons.org/licenses/by/4.0/legalcode.

their Fashion, and Drums made of a piece of a hollow Tree, covered on one end with any green Skin, and stretched with Thouls or Pins. But making use of these in their Wars at home in *Africa*, it was thought too much inciting them to Rebellion, and so they were prohibited by the Customs of the Island.

Note

1. See the website Musical Passage (http://www.musicalpassage.org), which also includes modern performances of the musical fragments.

A Maroon Tradition

Collected by Kenneth M. Bilby

Women and men who escaped from slavery to settle in the interior at the time of the English conquest formed the initial core of the Jamaican Maroons. By the early eighteenth century these communities had become strongly established in the interior of central and eastern Jamaica, effectively limiting the expansion of colonial society. Maroons played an important role in many American slave societies but were particularly significant in Jamaica. They maintain a distinct identity in the country today. These four versions of a similar oral tradition were collected from Maroons in and around Moore Town in the Blue Mountains by anthropologist Ken Bilby in the 1970s. They detail the Maroon perspective on their own origins and the origins of non-Maroon African Jamaicans, referred to as "Bongos" in two of these narratives. The Maroons explain the difference in terms of a mythic split between two African sisters: one who fought against slavery, and another who accepted her enslaved fate. The parenthetical information after each narrative reveals the time and place where Bilby collected the account.

Hear me now. This is what I want to tell you. They all came here as slaves . . . They all were from Africa. But they were from different-different districts, different-different tribes that had come down here. There were two leaders of those tribes of people. And they were two sisters, what you would call the elder ones, and you would call them leaders. They were two sisters. One was Grandy Nanny, and the other was her sister. One was Fanti Rose and one was Shanti Rose. In other words, the Maroons called her "Grandy Nanny," because of a certain type of honour. Now, in the days when they came here, they all were slaves and they all worked here. Well, the two sisters met and they were arguing. One said, well, she was going to fight, and one said she wouldn't fight. And I will tell you as far as this: one said, "o biamba shanti, o biama shanti, o kotoku, o biamba so brinding" (Kromanti language).[1] And she stopped right there. And one said, "o biamba ashanti, o biamba ashanti, kotoku, o biamba so brinding, seh o shanti kotoku, seh konkondeba!" One said she wouldn't fight, for she didn't like the shedding of blood, so she wouldn't fight, it was better for her to become a slave. The other side said she would fight, right? And she was going to fight until the battle was rotten. Well, it was that side that became the Maroon side. For she did fight and became victorious. That's how the split came about. After we fight, and I become free and you become a slave, there are certain different types of rules existing in my state of freedom than exist in your state, though all of us are from the same place. That's how the bars were made between both of us (Moore Town, 4th June 1978).

One sister said she wouldn't fight, for she didn't like bloodshed. Well, the other one said she would fight. That's how the separation came about. You find now that you get the Maroons, who are different from the outsiders, whom we call "niega." But they are all Africans (Moore Town, 20th August 1978).

Bongos aren't as strong as Maroons. You know why the Bongos aren't as strong as the Maroons? The Maroon people scattered in the woods. They're named Kyatawud, you know: "scatter-wood." Because when Grandy Nanny was fighting—Grandy Nanny and Grandy Sekesu, two sisters, you know—Bakra (the white man) wanted the Maroons to become slaves. And Grandy Nanny said they her people . . . she could not let them become slaves. So she took her portion of the people, and scattered in the woods with them, to a place named Stony River. She scattered in the woods with her set of people. And the other sister who was named Sekesu took her set of people and clung to St Thomas. And then she went on to raise the Bongo children. So they call Maroon people now "Scatter-wood." That's why they're stronger than the Bongo, because they went into the woods and they ate leaves, ate all those leaves and everything . . . That's why Grandy Nanny is stronger—Maroon people are stronger—than the Bongos (Kent, near Moore Town, 1st June 1978).

The Bongos now, and the Maroons, are actually one people, actually, one people. The reason they split up . . . they're not really split up. They will greet one another, and they will move together still. But it is the language. Bongo language is different from the Maroons' language. So they're not really split. The Bongos came from Africa, but the Maroons came first. The Bongos took one part, they took St Thomas. And the Maroon men took Portland. There were two peoples. The Maroons were free. And the Bongos refrained from working. And the government overthrew them. That is the point. Well, they had refused to work. But the Maroons never worked. The Maroons never worked. The Maroons stood up to them, dead or alive. But before the Bongos would fight, they would go away and go hide. They wouldn't fight (Comfort Castle, near Moore Town, 25th May 1978).

Note

1. Kromanti language is a secret ritual language spoken by some Maroons and used for spiritual purposes. [Editors' note]

Treaty between the British and the Maroons

Anonymous

By the late 1730s, the British military had been fighting the Maroons for decades. Realizing that a full victory was impossible, the colonial government decided to attempt to make peace. In 1739 the Leeward Maroons in the Cockpit Country, led by Cudjoe (Kojo), signed a treaty with the British.[1] A similar treaty, though more restrictive of the Maroons, was signed later the same year between the British and the Windward Maroons in eastern Jamaica. The Windward Maroons were led by both Quao and Nanny—future national hero of Jamaica—but only Quao signed the treaty, leading to speculation that Nanny did not approve. However, Nanny's absence from the treaties may also be explained by British expectations that women did not engage in politics.

For the Maroons, the treaties guaranteed freedom and considerable economic autonomy but also made them politically subordinate to the British. In exchange for recognition of their freedom, the Maroons agreed to provide military assistance to the British, suppress rebellions, return escapees from slavery, and accept a resident British "superintendent" in their settlements. The treaties enabled the expansion of the plantation system into interior areas of Jamaica and ushered in a period of fast growth in both sugar production and the enslaved population.

Articles of Pacification with the Maroons of Trelawny Town, concluded March 1, 1738

In the name of God, amen. Whereas Captain Cudjoe, Captain Acompong, Captain Johnny, Captain Cuffee, Captain Quaco, and several other negroes, their dependents and adherents, have been in a state of war and hostility, for several years past, against our sovereign Lord the King, and the inhabitants of this island; and whereas peace and friendship among mankind, and the preventing the effusion of blood, is agreeable to God, consonant to reason, and desired by every good man; and whereas his majesty George the Second, King of Great Britain, France, and Ireland, and of Jamaica, Lord,

Defender of the Faith, &c. has, by his letters patent, dated February the twenty-fourth, one thousand seven hundred and thirty-eight, in the twelfth year of his reign, granted full power and authority to John Guthrie and Francis Sadler, esquires, to negotiate and finally conclude a treaty of peace and friendship with the aforesaid Captain Cudjoe, and the rest of his captains, adherents, and others his men; they mutually, sincerely, and amicably, have agreed to the following articles:

First, That all hostilities shall cease on both sides for ever.

Second, That the said Captain Cudjoe, the rest of his captains, adherents, and men, shall be for ever hereafter in a perfect state of freedom and liberty, excepting those who have been taken by them, within two years last past, if such are willing to return to their said master and owners, with full pardon and indemnity from their said masters or owners for what is past; provided always, that, if they are not willing to return, they shall remain in subjection to Captain Cudjoe and in friendship with us, according to the form and tenor of this treaty.

Third, That they shall enjoy and possess, for themselves and prosperity for ever, all the lands situate and lying between Trelawny Town and the Cockpits, to the amount of fifteen hundred acres, bearing north-west from the said Trelawny Town.

Fourth, That they shall have liberty to plant the said lands with coffee, cocoa, ginger, tobacco, and cotton, and to breed cattle, hogs, goats, or any other stock, and dispose of the produce or increase of the said commodities of the inhabitants of this island; provided always, that when they bring the said commodities to market, they shall apply first to the custos, or any other magistrate of the respective parishes where they expose their goods to sale, for a license to vend the same.

Fifth, That Captain Cudjoe, and all the Captain's adherents, and people now in subjection to him, shall all live together within the bounds of Trelawny town and that they have liberty to hunt where they shall think fit, except within three miles of any settlement, crawl, or pen; provided always, that in case the hunters of Captain Cudjoe, and those of other settlements meets, then the hogs to be equally divided between both parties.

Sixth, That the said Captain Cudjoe, and his successors, do use their best endeavours to take, kill and suppress, or destroy, either by themselves, or jointly with any other number of men, commanded on that service by his excellency the Governor, or commander in chief for the time being, all rebels wheresoever they be, throughout this island, unless they submit to the same terms of accommodation granted to Captain Cudjoe, and his successors.

Seventh, That in case this island be invaded by any foreign enemy, the said Captain Cudjoe, and his successors herein-after named or to be appointed, shall then, upon notice given, immediately repair to any place the Governor for the time being shall appoint, in order to repel the said invaders with his or their utmost force, and to submit to the orders of the commander in chief on that occasion.

Eighth, That if any white man shall do any manner of injury to Captain Cudjoe, his successors, or any of his or their people, they shall apply to any commanding officer or magistrate in the neighbourhood for justice; *and in case Captain Cudjoe, or any of his people, shall do any injury to any white person he shall submit himself, or deliver up such offender to justice.*

Ninth, That if any negroes shall here-after run away from their masters or owners, and fall into Captain Cudjoe's hands, they shall immediately be sent back to the chief magistrate of the next parish where they are taken; and those that bring them are to be satisfied for their trouble, as the legislature shall appoint.

Tenth, That all negroes taken, since the raising of this party by Captain Cudjoe's people, shall immediately be returned.

Eleventh, That Captain Cudjoe, and his successors, shall wait on his Excellency, or the commander in chief for the time being, every year, if thereunto required.

Twelfth, That Captain Cudjoe, during his life, and the Captains succeeding him, shall have full power to inflict any punishment they think proper for crimes committed by their men among themselves, death only excepted; in which case, if the Captain thinks they deserve death, he shall be obliged to bring them before any justice of the people, who shall order proceedings on their trial equal to those of other free negroes.

Thirteenth, That Captain Cudjoe with his people, shall cut, clear, and keep open, large and convenient roads from Trelawny town to Westmoreland and St. James's, and, if possible, to St. Elizabeth's.

Fourteenth, That two white men, to be nominated by his Excellency, or the commander in chief for the time being, shall constantly live and reside with Captain Cudjoe, and his successors, in order to maintain a friendly correspondence with the inhabitants of this island.

Fifteenth, That Captain Cudjoe shall, during his life, be chief commander in Trelawny town; after his decease the command to devolve on this brother Captain Accompong; and in case of his decease, on his next brother Captain Johnny; and, failing him, Captain Cuffee shall succeed; who is to be succeeded by Captain Quaco; and after all their demises, the

Governor, or Commander in Chief for the time being, shall appoint, from time to time, whom he thinks fit for that command.

Note

1. The treaty is dated 1738 because this was before the shift to "new style" dating. Until 1752, the year was taken to begin on 25 March in Britain and British colonies.

African Arrivals

Audra A. Diptee

Most of eighteenth-century Jamaica's population came as captives in the holds of slave ships. They came from a wide range of distinctive African societies and were enslaved via many different means, including war and judicial procedures. Historian Audra A. Diptee explains the main regions of Africa from which enslaved people in Jamaica originated: the Bight of Biafra, the Gold Coast, and West Central Africa. Each of these regions was large and complex and contained multiple states or political groups, which were often in competition with one another.

In the Bight of Biafra, the three main slave-trading ports were Bonny, Old Calabar, and Elem Kalabari (New Calabar)—with Bonny supplying the most captives by far. Between 1776 and 1808, Bonny exported just under 56 percent of all the captives transported from the region. During the same period, Old Calabar and Elem Kalabari accounted for 17 percent and 12 percent, respectively. Jamaica, the largest single destination for captives from this region, received 46 percent of the enslaved.

By the late eighteenth century, the Bight of Biafra had become a leading source of captives in the British slave trade. This region, which traditionally played a relatively minor role in supplying captives, received a new prominence after the 1730s. Its supply of captives peaked in the last quarter of the eighteenth century, but it continued to be an important supplier in the British slave trade until abolition in 1807.

The Igbo (contemporaneously known as "Eboes") predominated among the ethnic groups enslaved and transported from Bonny and Old Calabar, with the Ibibio (or "Mocos," as they were known in Jamaica) making up most of the rest. Close proximity to the Niger waterway meant that captives exported from Elem Kalabari were drawn in larger proportions from the northern and Middle Belt regions. Although it is tempting to suggest that Jamaican planter preference for "Eboes from Bonny" accounts for this port's predominance in Biafran slave trading, there were, in fact, a number of internal variables that facilitated the expansion of trade in this region. In part,

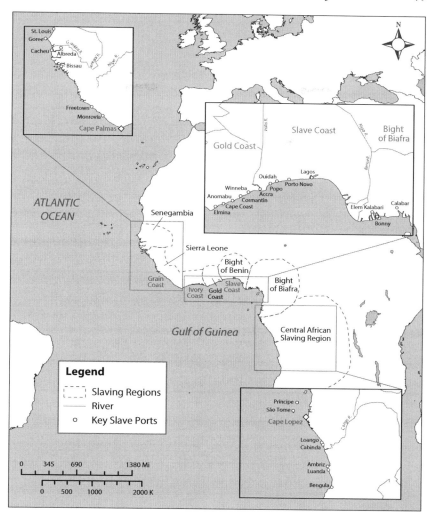

Map showing important regions in Africa from which enslaved people were sent to Jamaica. Based on the original drawing by Stephanie Shoobert for Audra A. Diptee's *From Africa to Jamaica: The Making of an Atlantic Slave Society, 1775–1807* (Gainesville: University Press of Florida, 2010), xvii. Used courtesy of the University Press of Florida.

it can be explained by the development and expansion of Aro networks, which generated increasing numbers of captives. Bonny's ascendancy as the chief port in the region is to be partly explained by its proximity to two central water routes. As the Aros established large diaspora settlements in central Igboland, they shifted the trade away from Old Calabar to Bonny, which was centrally located, could be more easily accessed, and could better facilitate the transport of captives.

Like the Biafran slave trade, there was also an expansion of slave-trading activities on the Gold Coast in the second half of the eighteenth century, peaking in the final twenty-five years. Between 1751 and 1808, approximately 57 percent of all captives put on British ships in this region were purchased at the ports Cape Coast Castle and Anomabu. Although in absolute numbers Gold Coast captives purchased for sale in Jamaica could not match those of the Biafran region, Jamaica was still the largest importer of men, women, and children from the region in the final decades of the slave trade. Approximately 53 percent of all the captives leaving the region on British ships were exported to the island, and it seems that few were re-exported from Jamaica to other islands.

Captives sold from this region were generally Akan. In the British Caribbean, however, they were often referred to as "Coromantee"—after the coastal settlement Cormantin. Ironically, Cormantin was *not* a major port for slave ships: only 1.1 percent of captives were known to have left from this area between 1700 and 1808. In reality, the notion of a "Coromantee nation" was an invention of the Americas that was "based on ethnolinguistic identity" and had no basis in indigenous African social organizations of the eighteenth century. In Africa, an individual's identity was tied into kinship, religious societies, and political organization. The tendency for captives to identify with other Africans on the basis of language, as in the case of the Coromantee, was a manifestation of African ideas about social interaction in the context of slavery in the Americas.

As can be expected, the eighteenth-century expansion and the related peaks and troughs in slave trading in the Gold Coast were closely linked to wars and political rivalries in the Gold Coast region. By the early eighteenth century, the Asante had emerged as the dominant power in the region. Its expansion continued well into the century, and although the original political rivalries in this region were for control of the gold trade rather than the slave trade, this was to change in later years. Asante's success during these Akan wars was aided by both the "gunpowder revolution" and the construction of a sophisticated road network system known as the Great Roads. The introduction of firearms, facilitated by the export of captives, was crucial to Asante's dominance in the region. The Great Roads also changed the dynamics of warfare in Asante's favor. These roads allowed for the rapid movement of Asante armies in the forested inlands and so gave them an important advantage during war. By the end of the eighteenth century, the Asante had only one significant rival—the Fanti.

The impact of internal African politics on the supply mechanisms of the slave trade is well reflected in the competing interests of the Asante and Fanti. Although the Asante controlled slave trading inland, the Fanti dominated the stretch of land along the Gold Coast. The Asante and Fanti had competing but complementary roles in supplying captives to the Atlantic market. Asante, the primary supplier of captives, was actively involved in the enslavement process. Captives taken by the Asante during the Akan wars accounted for many of the captives exported from the Gold Coast in the first half of the eighteenth century. As Asante consolidated its power, its slave-trading activities increased and reached their peak in the 1780s and 1790s. The Asante also supplied captives by demanding, from subordinated societies, that taxes be paid in human beings. These individuals were subsequently sold into the Atlantic slave trade.

The Fanti generally acted as the middlemen who brokered with the Europeans on the coast. In that role, they restricted Asante access to the coast and consequently to Europeans aiming to purchase captives. In general, few captives were enslaved by the Fanti in the coastal areas, as they relied heavily on the Asante to provide captives from the inland forest. There were, however, some exceptions to this. Coastal wars between political factions operating in Fanteland often resulted in war captives being sold into the Atlantic slave trade. The Atlantic slave trade also led to changes in Fanti social institutions, such as criminal justice and pawning, and so provided a source of captives that could be sold.

The primary means by which the Fanti, and presumably other coastal Africans, became victims of the Atlantic slave trade was through legal forms of punishment. Men were more likely than women and children to be sold for crimes. Children, of course, would rarely be convicted of a crime, unless they were unfortunate enough to be part of a family that was accused of witchcraft. They were, however, likely to be sold into the slave trade to pay off debts.[1]

In West Central Africa, British slave-trading activities were less dominant than in the Bight of Biafra and on the Gold Coast. Nonetheless, captives were transported to Jamaica in sizeable numbers and accounted for 34 percent of all captives put on British ships in this region. Unfortunately, between 1750 and 1808, records for the vast majority (63 percent) of captives purchased by the British do not specify at which ports they were purchased. Based on the data for the remaining 37 percent of the captives, it is clear that significant points of embarkation for British vessels were the Congo River, Malembo, Loango, Ambriz, and Cabinda.

Most of the men, women, and children sold in this region were taken from the same populations that supplied Luanda, the key trading port south of the Congo, which was under Portuguese dominance. The suppliers that provided the African traders with captives north of the Congo River were the African states Jinga and Kongo, both of which were located to the south. Another, far more easterly, state (Lunda) also supplied captives north of the Congo, though its trading activities were primarily at Cabinda.

Not surprisingly, political upheaval in the region served to feed the supply lines of the slave trade and so ensured that large numbers of captives were transported across the Atlantic. The introduction of European goods into the region fueled slaving activities and contributed to the increasing levels of social chaos and political instability in the region. South of the Congo River, the Kongo civil wars over succession to the throne also contributed to the supply of captives. These wars began in the second half of the seventeenth century and reached intense levels by 1780. Although periods of conflicts were sometimes followed by periods of relative peace, not until 1794 was there a period of some political calm in the region. During this period, it was largely prisoners of war who were taken during military campaigns and sold as captives. Although French slave traders benefited from tensions in Kongo the most, British slave-trading activities also reflected the vagaries of these internal conflicts.

As with other regions, the problems of determining the ethnicity of captives purchased in West Central Africa is problematic. In British slave-trade records, captives from this region were often given very general "ethnic" labels. One British slave trader reported, for example, that captives transported to Loango were from "three nations": the "Congues, Majumbas, and Madungoes." More often, however, they were categorized quite simply as "Angolan" or "Kongo." Interestingly, in late eighteenth-century Jamaica, evidence from one study suggests that captives from the region were often relabeled upon their arrival at the island. This analysis of runaway advertisements shows that they were more likely to be referred to as "Kongo," with only a small minority referenced as "Angolans."

Despite the use of such generalized ethnic labels, many of the enslaved came from villages or urban areas and tended to identify with the local communities in which they had resided. In many ways, the broad categories were used by traders for convenience; they were part of the "trading jargon." These labels made up a mutually comprehensible vocabulary that was common to both Africans and Europeans as they negotiated the terms under which captives were to be traded. Even slave traders of the time recognized that these labels were inaccurate and did not necessarily indicate the "ethnic origin" of captives. One French trader reported that the ethnic labels assigned to captives were often derived from either the ethnicity of the Africans who supplied them or the people whose territory the captives were transported through on their way to the coast. In other words, captives called "Kongo" purchased at Loango were not necessarily so labeled because they were of Kongo origin. They may, in fact, have been referred to as Kongo either because they were first purchased in Kongo or because they were transported through Kongo territory.

Nonetheless, although captives constructed their identities in relation to their local environment, there were strong social, cultural, and linguistic similarities throughout the region. Most of the enslaved men, women, and children leaving on British ships belonged to one of three "regional cultures": Kongo, Mbundu, and Ovimbundu. Captives were either from these areas or were from regions that were part of the same language family (West Bantu). In other words, it was possible for them to communicate with each other—even if only to a limited degree.

Note

1. Jerome Bernard Weuves, in Answers Returned by the Committee of the Company of Merchants Trading to Africa (1788), Board of Trade, BT 6/9 (no folio number), National Archives.

Spiritual Terror

Vincent Brown

Slave-ownership was based on a claim to complete control over people, extending to life and death. Yet the reality in Jamaica was that those who claimed ownership of people did not fully control their human captives. Enslaved people took actions to control their own bodies, including using their power to destroy themselves. In Jamaica suicide among the enslaved was high. Suicide was traumatic for enslaved communities but defied the planters' efforts to gain total conquest. Focusing on plantocratic mutilation of the bodies of suicides and "criminals," historian Vincent Brown argues that slave owners pursued a deliberate policy of "spiritual terror" aimed at securing the authority of the planters by connecting their power to that of the sacred.

Africans continued to kill themselves with distressing frequency in the Caribbean, and slaveholders kept resorting to grisly techniques of deterrence. In Jamaica, such practices were widespread throughout the eighteenth century. Just before midcentury, an anonymous Jamaican planter wrote that to prevent Africans from believing that they could escape the island in death their bodies were "often hanged up" by their masters to show the living that the dead remained in Jamaica.[1] Around midcentury, masters began to apply the punishments for outright rebellion—burning the body down to ash—to suicide as well. And to dramatize the impossibility of repatriation in death, masters threatened to deny suicidal slaves their final rite of passage. In 1751 the Anglican rector of Westmoreland Parish wrote to his bishop that "to deprive them of their funeral Rites by burning their dead Bodies, seems to Negroes a greater Punishment than Death itself. This is done to Self-Murderers."[2] As late as the final decade of slavery, John Stewart could remember a time when newly arriving Africans committed suicide to "return to their native country, and enjoy the society of kindred and friends, from whom they have been torn away in an evil hour."[3] He also remembered the "dismal and disgusting spectacle" of their heads adorning poles along public roads, and their bodies "sometimes consumed by fire."

Whether such mutilations in fact constituted an effective deterrent is open to question. Dismemberment certainly represented a compelling metaphysical threat to English Protestants, but there is little or no direct evidence that Africans believed that losing their head or a limb would prevent their return to ancestral lands. Indeed, in parts of West Africa, slaves were routinely beheaded after the death of nobles so that they could continue to serve their masters in the spiritual world. Whether or not European masters were aware of African precedents, in Jamaica they beheaded and dismembered their own slaves with a similar desire that the dead continue their service. Through dead bodies they attempted to seize and manipulate African visions of the afterlife in an effort to govern the worldly actions of the living.

Mutilating the bodies of Africans who committed suicide was only part of a broader agenda that used ritual execution to give governing authority a sacred, even supernatural, dimension. As with the punishments for suicide, the punishments for rebellion were meant to inspire in the enslaved terror of their ultimate fate by visiting extraordinary torments on their bodies before and after death. By at least the late seventeenth century, the bodies of slave rebels were burned alive. Sir Hans Sloane, who visited Jamaica just before the turn of the century, described the grisly tortures meted out to slaves and the meticulous method of executing rebels, "by nailing them down on the ground with crooked Sticks on every Limb, and then applying the Fire by degrees from the Feet and Hands, burning them gradually up to the Head, whereby their pains are extravagant."[4] Only two weeks after Thomas Thistlewood arrived in Savanna la Mar in 1750, he watched his host, William Dorrill, order the body of a dead runaway dug up and beheaded, with the head to be fixed on a pole and the body to be incinerated. Just months later, Thistlewood "saw a Negro fellow nam'd English belonging to Fuller Wood Tried, lost, and hang'd upon ye 1st Tree immediately (for drawing his knife upon a White Man), his head Cutt off, Body left unbury'd."[5]

Notes

1. Anonymous, *The Importance of JA to Great Britain Consider'd* (London, 1741), cited in Orlando Patterson, *Sociology of Slavery: An Analysis of the Origins, Development and Structure of Negro Slave Society in Jamaica* (Rutherford, NJ: Fairleigh Dickinson University Press, 1969), 196.
2. John Venn to Bishop Sherlock, 15 June 1751, Fulham Papers, Lambeth Palace Library, vol. 18, Jamaica, 1740 (undated), p. 47.
3. John Stewart, *A View of the Past and Present State of the Island of Jamaica, with Remarks on*

the *Moral and Physical Condition of the Slaves, and on the Abolition of Slavery in the Colonies* (Edinburgh, 1823), 281.

4. Hans Sloane, *A Voyage to the Islands Madera, Barbados, Nieves, S. Christophers and Jamaica,* 2 vols. (London, 1707–1725), 1:lvii.

5. Thistlewood diary, 2 October 1750, quoted in Michael Craton, *Testing the Chains: Resistance to Slavery in the British West Indies* (Ithaca, NY: Cornell University Press, 1982), 39.

Two Enslaved Lives

Trevor Burnard

Historians face a challenge in gaining a sense of enslaved people's everyday lives. Records produced by slave owners reveal a great deal about the demographic and economic development of slave societies, including Jamaica. But they rarely recorded anything personal about enslaved people, and direct historical evidence produced by those who were slaves is extremely rare. Historian Trevor Burnard uses the journal of slaveholder and attorney (plantation manager) Thomas Thistlewood to track the life histories of two women, Coobah and Abba, who lived on estates managed by Thistlewood in the second half of the eighteenth century. Burnard suggests that these two women exemplify two different ways in which women survived their experience of slavery: Coobah was a "rebel" who repeatedly ran away, while Abba was defined by her struggle to provide for her children. Thistlewood is notorious for the horrendous and often grotesque punishments he inflicted on enslaved people, and in particular for his rape of many of the women on his estates, including Coobah. His meticulous journals of his daily life and brutality, when tracked over a period of time, ironically allow for some insight into the lives of individuals.

The Slave Rebel

Thistlewood faced dissent and insubordination from one slave in particular —Coobah. Coobah was a rebel who refused to accept the strictures of slavery. She was what white Jamaicans in the eighteenth century called "an incorrigible runaway." Thistlewood bought her on 7 December 1761, at which time he described her as "4 ft 6 6/10 ins. Tall, about 15 yrs. Old, Country name Molia, an Ebo." He assigned her quarters with Egypt Princess and, the following week, sent her, with five other new slaves, to work in the fields. He initiated her in another way nine months later when he had sex with her, noting in his diary, "Stans! Backwd: gave her a bitt."[1] By August 1765, she had suffered her first bout of venereal disease. She had already had yaws in 1762 and had spent much of the first few months of 1764 ill in the hothouse. On 12 November 1766, at about twenty years of age, she had a

515   Trelawny, Nov. 4. 1784.
          R U N   A W A Y,

FROM Silver Grove, two Coromantee
    negro men, named DOBBIE and
ARCHER; Dobbie is a ft ut, young
fellow, and very black; Archer is a flender
young negro, inclining to a copper colour:
they have been in the country fince February laft, but neither of them has any
brand mark. Any perfon bringing them
home, or lodging them in gaol, giving information thereof to Jofeph Lake, Over-
feer on laid eftate, fhall receive FORTY
SHILLINGS reward for each.

───────────────────────────

517   Montego Bay, Nov 19, 1784.
          R U N   A W A Y,

FROM the fubfcriber on the 3th of Au-
    guft laft, a ftout new negro man named
WILL, of the Chamba country, the marks
of which are very plain on his face; is
about 6 feet high, had a fore on his right
foot nearly healed, and fpeaks very little
Englifh. Whoever apprehends faid negro,
and delivers him to the fubfcriber, fhall
be thankfully rewarded.
                    JAMES BARRATT.

Enslaved people frequently re-sisted slavery by escaping the site of their captivity. Plantation managers placed advertisements in newspapers to try to locate them, as in these examples from the *Jamaica Mercury and Kingston Weekly Advertiser* of 1779. Such advertisements are an important source for historians about enslaved people's lives and identities. Bridgeman Images no. MGS188100. Used by permission of Bridgeman Images / a private collection.

child with her husband, a free black man, but the child did not survive long, dying at fifteen months old on 16 March 1767. Whether the death of her child triggered something in Coobah is impossible to tell, but she increasingly became unmanageable. She first ran away in August 1765, a five-day absence that resulted in her being flogged and having a collar and chain put around her neck. She did not run away again until 20 March 1769, but from 1769 onward, she ran away at every opportunity when she was not sick. Coobah's persistent running away resulted in increasingly harsh punishments. By 1770, she was receiving severe floggings and was being kept in the stocks overnight. She was branded on the forehead and forced to wear a collar and chain for months at a time.

In addition to running away, Coobah indulged in what both Thistlewood and his slaves considered to be antisocial behaviour, such as stealing food from white neighbours of Thistlewood and fellow slaves. She also had arguments with other slaves when working in the fields about the amount of work she was expected to do.

By this time, she had become openly rebellious to Thistlewood, refusing to accept his authority in any manner. The nadir was reached on 4 October 1770, when Thistlewood reported: "[A] punch strainer hanging up against the buttery, Coobah sleeping in the cookroom, last night took the strainer and shit in it, wrapping it up and covering it with a piece of board, this breakfast time had it rubbed all over her face and mouth, but she minds not." Her rebelliousness made her a liability. Thistlewood had to divert slaves from the fields to go look for her on the frequent occasions she was away, and it often took these slaves three or four days to find her. He also could not employ Coobah as he wished. He was not able to send her, for example, to work on neighbouring estates because "she is so troublesome in running away, &c," thus depriving him of one of his most profitable sources of income.[2]

What provoked Coobah's intransigence is, of course, unknown, but it did result in Coobah being parted from her master. Thistlewood resolved to get rid of Coobah, which he eventually did on 18 May 1774, when he sold her for £40 and had her transported to Georgia. Coobah succeeded in ridding herself of her owner and managed to escape the harsh sugar regime of Jamaica for the relatively more benign one of Georgia, but at a considerable cost. She left for Georgia with the marks of her insubordination on her body, pocked by smallpox, debilitated by repeated bouts of venereal disease, lacerated by numerous floggings, and branded on her forehead as troublemaker. Thistlewood was not sorry to see her go. She had produced no money for him as a field hand, had borne no children who could augment his fortune, and had caused him grief.

The Slave Mother

Abba's story also has elements of tragedy about it, although in her case this has less to do with her reactions to slavery than with the difficulties she faced as the mother of a large family. Purchased in February 1758, Abba remained with Thistlewood until his death in 1786. In that time, she became pregnant thirteen times, had ten live births and one stillbirth, and had six children who survived the first year of life, four of whom were still living at Thistlewood's death (between the ages of five and twenty-five), and one grandchild. Such fecundity was highly unusual. Most slave women in Jamaica in the period of the Atlantic slave trade were either childless or had no more than one or two children.

Abba's high fertility affected her experience as a slave. She never entered into a permanent monogamous relationship with any man. She was the matriarch of a family of four children and a grandchild by 1785. Nevertheless, even though she cared for her family mostly by herself, she seldom had independent control over how her family was treated. In the first place, her precarious financial position and the many mouths she had to feed made her dependent on her master for support. She also relied on other slaves, especially slave men, for help in providing for her family. Abba had many partners, several of whom were not slaves under Thistlewood's care.

Abba's life was defined more by motherhood than by her serial relationships. What sort of mother was she? Abba cared for her children as much as she was able to, was solicitous about them when they were ill, and was distraught when they died. Abba lost four children soon after birth and two sons who were about six years old. When her son Johnnie fainted on 5 January and died on 8 January 1771 from "a spasm, or locking of the jaws" and her young boy Neptune died on 2 August 1773 of "a most violent cold, got I suppose by the water running thro' her house & making the floor wet," Abba was beside herself with grief. Thistlewood described her as "almost out of her senses" and "quite frantic & will hear no reason." Johnnie's death, in particular, affected her deeply. She buried him near her house with singing and dancing, as was the custom in West African funerals, and mourned his loss six months later in a post-interment ceremony by "Throw[ing] Water (as they call it)" and by "beating the Coombie loud, singing high &c. Many negroes there from all over the country."[3]

The apparent cause of Neptune's death, however, suggests that Abba found it difficult, despite her best intentions, to look after her children and ensure that they had enough food to survive and safe conditions in which to live. Thistlewood's brief description of her house—so open to the elements that water could flow easily through it—indicates that she lived in abject poverty. Her inability to provide for herself and her large family meant that she was more reliant on Thistlewood's largesse than most slaves. The inadequate house that she had was given to her by her master, as was the more substantial dwelling he finally provided in the last month of his life. Abba lived so close to the edge that she was forced to rely heavily on Thistlewood's assistance. She could not afford to rebel or offer resistance to her enslavement when she had so many mouths to feed. Significantly, Abba never ran away. To do so would have meant abandoning her family.

Notes

1. Diary of Thomas Thistlewood, 14 September 1763, Monson 31/1, Lincolnshire County Archives, Lincoln. All subsequent citations to Thomas Thistlewood's diaries are by date only. [Editors' note: The Thistlewood diaries are now held by the Beinecke Library at Yale University.]

2. 21 March 1772.

3. 7 July 1771.

Increase and Decrease

Managers of Haughton Tower Estate

Hundreds of thousands of names of those who suffered enslavement appear in documents produced in slave societies, almost all of which were created as part of managing the slavery-based economy. As such they tell us frustratingly little about the individuals named, although historians have used them to establish demographic patterns, while artists and activists have created memorials from them. This document, from a substantial sugar estate in the western parish of Hanover, is one of many similar annual accounts of "increase and decrease" sent from Jamaican plantation managers to absentee owners. It is typical in many ways, including its list of "stock" (mules and cattle) alongside a list of human beings, treating the latter as having the same status as the former. The document suggests a preoccupation with women's reproductive capacity. It names the mothers but not the fathers of the four babies born that year. It also shows that, as was typical on sugar estates, more people on Haughton Tower died than were born. Ned, "shot at Sam and stealing," may have been sold or perhaps executed through a judicial procedure. The document's failure to specify what happened to him is typical of this genre; what mattered to the estate was the accountancy, not the lives of the people named.

An Account of the Increase and Decrease of Negroes & Stock
on Haughton Tower Estate for the Year 1768

NEGROES DECEASED	INCREASE OF NEGROES
Fiba, with Old Age	Chloe's Quashey
Quashey with a Dropsy	Moll's Queen
Mathey, with Old Age	Mary's Hero
Hannah, with —ditto	Lucca's Charley
Franky, with —ditto	
Ned, Shot at Sam &: stealing	
King John, with Sickness	These were the only working slaves
Jasminta, with Eating Dirt	

DECREASE OF STOCK

Johnny, a mule, of old age
Stephen, ditto, of ditto
Maria, ditto, of ditto
Hamlet ditto, of ditto
Jasper ditto, of ditto
Nanny ditto of ditto
Kittah ditto of Belly Ache

DECREASE OF CATTLE

Fisher, a steer, killed in Graham's plantane walk
Rachel an Old Cow
Bacchus, with a purging
Pompey with ditto
Chucks staked
Passage Mort, with Age

INCREASE OF CATTLE

5 Calves

A Free Black Poet

Francis Williams

Francis Williams belonged to the small minority of free black people in eighteenth-century Jamaica. His parents, John and Dorothy Williams, were both free. They acquired property and successfully petitioned the Jamaican legislature to grant them and their three sons (though not their daughter) some of the "privileges" automatically enjoyed by white people—a sign that they were among the most well-off and "respectable" of free people of color. Francis was probably born in 1697, and by 1723, when his father died, was living in England, where he had been sent for education. After his father's death he returned to Jamaica, where he lived off the wealth inherited from his father and also kept a school in Spanish Town, teaching Latin, mathematics, and reading and writing. At his death in 1762 his estate included fifteen enslaved people.

Williams is the earliest published black writer in the English-speaking world. He wrote primarily in Latin, and this is the only work of his that has survived. As a result, he is less well-known than later writers such as Phillis Wheatley or Olaudah Equiano. Williams wrote this poem to honor the newly arrived governor of Jamaica, George Haldane, in 1756. In many ways it is a conventional poem, emphasizing the benefits of Haldane's governorship. It is notable for its complex discussion of race. In some ways Williams defers to his period's assumptions of black inferiority, for instance writing that his poem should be understood as "valuable" even "though poured forth from one very black." But he also contests racist understandings by claiming equal intellectual status with whites.

Williams was well-known in Jamaica and throughout the English-speaking world. In the 1770s white writers repeatedly enlisted him in debates about race, particularly about the alleged inferiority or otherwise of people of African descent. The proslavery intellectual Edward Long translated Williams's poem into English to include it in his History of Jamaica. Long was dismissive of Williams's poetic abilities, arguing that anyone who valued his poetry did so "merely because it came from a Negro." On the other side, abolitionist writers defended the quality of Williams's work and used it to argue for black potential. Long's is the best-known translation, but because it focused on maintaining the form of Williams's verse, he substantially

Portrait of Francis
Williams, c. 1745, oil
on canvas. From the
Stapleton Collection,
London. Bridgeman Im-
ages no. STC167415. Art-
ist unknown. Used by
permission of Bridge-
man Images / Stapleton
Collection.

changed the content. The prose translation included here was produced in the late
nineteenth century and in most respects is more faithful to the original in meaning.

A poem in honour of Sir George Haldane, KNT.,
A Most Virtuous and Brave Man,

Governor of the Island of Jamaica, on whom all the endowments of morals and of warlike virtues have been accumulated.

Since the fates wish that the year should come at last, all the joys which
are to be seen through a lengthened day are present. The people having
shaken off their anxieties, are prosperous under a bright image, and the land
flourishing under law. While thou art ruler, the useless things which had
been done by an ill-advising mind will not return at thy appearance. Therefore all the people, even the rabble, will see that thou hast removed the yoke
clinging to their necks, and the ills which the guiltless island has formerly
endured with dreadful tortures. The burden would have been excessively
painful did not thy victorious hand, previously renowned for valour, wish
of its own accord to aid our state going to ruin. The British king has no bet-

ter servant than thou art, while Scotland rejoices in thy talent. Thou art the best of heroes to prop up the fall of a nation; while the island survives, the memory of thee will also survive. Guadaloupe will recognise thee as her conqueror, and will deservedly despise the plundered camp of its governors. The golden Iris will weep for her boastful standards, and together with her inhabitants will groan for the conquered towns. Believe me, it is not in my power, O man, dear to Mars! Minerva denies to an Ethiopian to celebrate the wars of generals. Buchanan would sing thee in a poem, he would describe thee as equal to Achilles in council and in war. That famous poet, the honour of his country, is more worthy to relate thy exploits, and is scarcely inferior to the majestic Virgil. We live under an Apollo driving his own flame-bringing team. Every kind of eloquence is lacking to slaves. Receive this at any rate. Though poured forth from one very black, it is valuable, coming from a sonorous mouth; not from his skin, but from his heart. The bountiful Deity, with a hand powerful and firm, has given the same soul to men of all races, nothing standing in his way. Virtue itself, and prudence, are free from colour; there is no colour in an honourable mind, no colour in skill. Why dost thou fear or doubt that the blackest Muse may scale the lofty house of the western Caesar? Go and salute him, and let it not be to thee a cause of shame that thou wearest a white body in a black skin. Integrity of *morals* more adorns a *Moor*, and ardour of intellect and sweet elegance in a learned mouth. A wise heart and the love of his ancestral virtue the more remove him from his comrades and make him conspicuous. The island (of Jamaica) gave me birth the renowned Britons brought me up; the island which will not grieve while thou its father art well. This I pray: O may earth and heaven see thee without end, ruling a flourishing people.

Translated by E. J. Chinnock

Jamaica Talk

Frederic G. Cassidy

Patwa, the most widely used though not the official language of Jamaica, belongs to a family of languages that linguists call Atlantic Creoles. These languages fused African and European languages in a context of extreme power difference. The process began on the African coast and continued rapidly in Jamaica. By the nineteenth century the language was strongly established. Patwa has a vocabulary derived predominantly though not exclusively from English, but it follows many grammatical rules that draw on African languages. Some of the most obvious grammatical differences between patwa and English are found in the forming of plurals, which in patwa is done through the addition of the suffix -dem to the singular form (thus, man-dem rather than men), and in the use of pronouns. Where standard English distinguishes sharply between subject and object pronouns (e.g., I and me), patwa-speakers generally use the same word, me (sometimes spelled mi), for both.

For many years Jamaicans' everyday speech was widely understood as a form of "bad" or "broken" English, and facility with standard English is still necessary for professional advancement or middle-class status. Schools still teach in standard English. Public documents, newspapers, and reports are all delivered in standard English. Linguists today, though, recognize that patwa is a language with its own grammatical rules. The situation is complicated by the absence of clear boundaries between patwa and standard English. Throughout Jamaica's history, patwa-speakers have needed to interact with visitors and settlers who speak English but not patwa. As a result, most Jamaicans can move with relative ease among various locations on what linguists term the "Creole continuum," using more or fewer patwa terms and grammatical structures depending on the circumstances of the conversation. Such often-unconscious linguistic choices also act as markers of class and status in contemporary Jamaica.

Jamaican-born Frederic Cassidy was one of the mid-twentieth-century linguists who established the study of Creoles as a serious academic concern. He was one of the compilers of the groundbreaking Dictionary of Jamaican English, *which remains an essential work of reference for scholars of Jamaican history and society. This reading describes the "Creole continuum" and also discusses the varied origin of Jamaican vocabulary. Writing in the late 1950s, Cassidy uses the term "creolised English," where today's linguists would write "Creole."*

What language do Jamaicans talk? The question is asked not only by strangers to the Caribbean but also by English and American visitors who have heard Jamaicans speaking what they did not at first recognize as a type of their own tongue. It is a question raised as well by students of language, and they mean, How is Jamaica Talk to be classified—as a type of English, or as something quite different, though obviously related? A real question, this, which deserves a sound answer—one, however, that cannot be given until we have carefully examined the language as Jamaicans use it.

Another and equally interesting question is, How did Jamaicans come to talk as they do? The musical lilt and staccato rhythms, the mingling of strange words, the vowel sounds that go sliding off into diphthongs, the cheerful defiance of many niceties of traditional English grammar, the salty idioms, the wonderfully compressed proverbs, the pungent imagery of nicknames and epithets in the bestowals of which these islanders appear to be peculiarly adept—where do all these hail from, and how did they come to be?

It is now three hundred years since the English language, which has found its way to every corner of the earth, took root in Jamaica. There it has flourished and developed its own local forms and flavour, as transplanted languages do everywhere. For language—let us never forget—it is infinitely multiform, highly variable, ever on the change so long as it is alive. Only dead languages lie still. Even today, with all the effects of standardized schooling, Englishmen (to say nothing of Welshmen, Irishmen, and Scots) speak their language in countless variations. Considering the history of the British Isles, this is in no way surprising. Nor should one be disturbed to find yet other variations where people of many kinds in a new colony have pooled their home differences, seasoned them with the tropical spices of Arawak and Carib Indians, Africans, Spaniards, Frenchmen, and assorted others until a strong and tasty pepperpot of language is concocted. This, of course, is what has happened in Jamaica.

But even if we are able to name the ingredients of our mixture, and perhaps the proportion of each, this is not all. Jamaica Talk is not by any means of the same kind on all Jamaicans' lips. It exists in two main forms, which may be imagined as lying at opposite ends of a scale, with every sort of variation between, but each variant inclining in some degree toward the right or the left. At one end is the type of Jamaica Talk that aims toward the London "standard" or educated model. At the other end of the scale is the inherited talk of peasant and labourer, largely unaffected by education and its standards. This is what the linguist calls "creolised" English, that is, an English learned incompletely in slave days, with a strong infusion of African influences, and continued traditionally in much the same form down present.

These are at the ends of the scale. Moving toward the middle from the educated end, one finds an increasing inclusion of local elements—of Jamaican rhythm and intonation, of words that the Londoner would have no reason or need to know, of turns of phrase that have grown up in this island—what may be called "Jamaicanisms." Or, moving toward the middle from the uneducated end, one finds more and more adoption of the elements of standard English—the acquisition of grammatical features that were entirely lacking in the old creolised speech, a gradual tendency to pronounce in the standard way, at least when one is on guard or in formal situation. And, unfortunately, pride of education often brings with it scorn of the homely, or at least a tendency to hide the homely.

At the middle of the scale are the "bilinguals"—those who can use the speech of either end. Some live comfortably in this position, employing the folk talk in private or informal life, but switching to something closer to standard English in business or public life. Others—"old-time Jamaicans"—though brought up with standard English, can also handle the folk talk as they heard it from their *nanas* or nurses and the country folk in their childhood. The only painful group is that of the *parvenu* in education who, having crossed the middle of the scale, now feel that the folk speech is beneath them and scornfully reject it. This happens all over the world, of course, when people "go up" in the social scale, but the results are no less uncomfortable in Jamaica than in Birmingham or Chicago.

We may classify Jamaicanisms as belonging to five main types: preservations, borrowings, new formations, transferred meanings, and special preferences. Let us have some examples—first, of preservations. The *Oxford English Dictionary* (hereafter referred to as the OED) comments that *moonshine* is "now rare or poetic"—yet it is more current among the Jamaican folk than *moonlight*. The latest citation given for *tinnen* (made of tin) in the OED is from 1653—yet the word may be heard any day in Jamaica (and Barbados too). The latest citation for *roguing* is 1672; for *hold (one's) road* 1795; for *catch (to)* (arrive at), 1393; yet all of these are flourishing still in Jamaica, where they were undoubtedly brought by early English settlers and preserved among the common folk.

Next come borrowings—words of non-English origin which entered the English language via Jamaica, though many of them have ceased to be only Jamaican. An example is *cashew (Anacardium occidentale)*, which came into English from French *acajou* (from Portuguese *acaju*, from Tupi Indian *acaj Ú*) The OED first cites the word from 1703, but it was borrowed at least forty-five years before that time. In *The State of Jamaica* (dated post 1660), we find "Cashues" in a list of fruits along with "supotillia, advocatas, custard apples" and others, and in 1662 Stubbe denies to "the fruits of Jamaica call'd Cushu" the quality of an aphrodisiac.

The third kind of Jamaicanisms—new formations—has three subdivisions: alterations, compositions, and creations. A simple alteration of pronunciation may produce essentially a new word. For example, the vegetable known elsewhere as *scallion,* is *skellion* in Jamaica. In this word only one sound is changed. But far more complex changes have taken place in others, as when *Spanish elm* becomes, among the folk, *panchalam* or *panchalang.* Another sort of alteration is beheading, which may be illustrated in such standard words as *lone* from *alone,* or *fence* from *defence.* Another Jamaicanism of this sort is *jesta,* an iron cooking pot with a long handle, derived from *digester.*

By far the largest number of new formations are made by composition of existing elements, whether native or foreign or both. *Garden egg* is an example of the first. Though not recorded in any of the historical dictionaries, it has been in use in Jamaica since at least 1811, and is now the accepted term throughout the island and among all classes. In the Kingston area the presence of English and Americans in some numbers has introduced *egg-plant* to the market women, but its usage is recent and restricted. Reduplications might be put here too—such words as *tief-tief* (thieving), *fenky-fenky* (finisking), and *kas-kas* (using strong language, quarrelling).

Among creations a few are the result of back-formation—such a word as *reduck,* for example, a verb meaning to reduce, back-formed in all probability from *reduction.* Similarly formed is the interesting verb *devel* (with accent on second syllable) as in a fisherman's remark that the "breeze is develin' up," which would seem to come from the interpretation of *develop* as a verb-plus seem to come from the interpretation of *develop* as a verb-plus adverb phrase, *devel up.*

Onomatopoeia or echoism accounts for a number of Jamaicanisms, as the name for a large ant which makes a loud gnashing with its mandibles, and is therefore called *kap-kap.* Then there is the bird named *pechary* (pichíeri) in imitation of its cry; but this word may be ultimately Indian since it is paralleled in Cuba and Puerto Rico in the form *pitirre.* Every Jamaican child knows what a *fee-fee* is (a whistle); and another bird is well known as the *gimme-me-bit,* a name partly echoic, partly formed by folk-etymology.

The fourth type of Jamaicanism is that of the transferred meaning—a common type, of course, in all new lands, where it is easier to use a familiar word in a new way than to adopt or invent an unfamiliar one. The European dandelion is *Taraxacum officinale*; in Jamaica the name has been transferred to several different plants: *Cassia ligustrina* or *Cassia occidentalis* are "man dandelion"—having thicker stalks and coarser leaves, while *Cassia tora* is "woman dandelion"—with finer stalks and leaves.

The last type of Jamaicanism is that in which the word, though not exclusively Jamaican, is preferred term in the island—the one said more frequently than the word that is standard elsewhere. As good an example as any is *puss*, the usual word for *cat*. The native Jamaican would of course understand *cat*, yet it would not come first to his lips. Similarly, *vine* is understood, but the normal word is *wis* (from *withe*), which is vastly commoner and has entered into at least twenty combinations.

But it is not by peculiarities of vocabulary alone that Jamaica talk is characterised. The pronunciation differs in some striking ways from that of standard English, and in the grammar of the common folk we find the widest differences of all. The first time that an outsider hears spoken Jamaican he will be struck by unfamiliar sounds and rhythms; some words he will recognise fairly soon, others will be new; but the hardest to grasp will be the phrases in which—to him—some words are unexpectedly missing and others unexpectedly present. If he concludes that this is a chaotic babble he will be wrong. The rules are different but he may be assured that there *are* rules.

From the point of view of the standard language, these changes are usually thought of as "corruptions." The fact is that they do not pretend to standard, and therefore criteria of comparison are not the same. But a greater mistake comes when all sorts of unwarranted conclusions are drawn about the kind of people who could perpetrate such "corruptions," that they are at best simple children of nature at worst ignorant, lazy, wilful, or stupid. Such conclusions show a woefully unhistorical and uninformed view, unless one is to throw all people learning a foreign imposed speech into the same limbo. The English, in this case, were also, from the Norman conquerors' point of view, barbaric, ignorant, lazy and stupid in learning the upper-class language no better than they did. They corrupted French in horrible ways, and they clung wilfully to their corruptions. The point is, of course, that the African slave trying to learn English was in much the same position as the Anglo-Saxon commoner having to learn Norman—and the Jamaican has done no worse on the whole. The changes he has made have followed the same sorts of linguistic laws as those which governed the adoption of French words in eleventh-century England, and with no more outlandish results. An automatic belief in the superiority or purity of the English language may prove no more than that one has never truly observed it.

The War of 1760–1761

Edward Long

Enslaved people in Jamaica fought repeatedly against slavery. The biggest rising of the eighteenth century, often known as Tacky's Rebellion or Tacky's Revolt, began in the parish of St. Mary and spread across much of the island. A second, more sustained insurgency began in Westmoreland a few weeks later. The black combatants took advantage of the distraction of British forces by their involvement in the Seven Years' War, and built solidarity through their connection as "Coromantins" or "Coromantees" (those from the Gold Coast region of West Africa) and through the protection offered by spiritual leaders. Some drew on military experience in West Africa and in wars among European powers elsewhere in the Caribbean. Their rising terrified the Jamaican plantocracy. The British were forced to recognize their opponents as military enemies rather than simply "rebels"; they could not fully defeat the enslaved insurgents militarily, instead eventually accepting a negotiated surrender of some rebel leaders. The war did not end until late in 1761. Historians estimate that at least 1,500 enslaved people were involved in the fighting.

This account of the war is by Edward Long, a significant Jamaican planter and politician and one of the most important contributors to the intellectual defense of slavery and to the development of racism. He was also a historian and a careful observer of Jamaican society. His account of the war is one of the most detailed we have. Current research suggests that Long overestimated the level of coordination among insurgents in different parts of the island.[1]

In the year 1760, a conspiracy was projected, and conducted with such profound secrecy, that almost all the Coromantin slaves throughout the island were privy to it, without any suspicion from the Whites. The parish of St. Mary was fixed upon, as the most proper theatre for opening their tragedy. It abounded with their countrymen, was but thinly populated with Whites, contained extensive deep woods, and plenty of provisions: so that as the engaging any considerable number heartily in the scheme, would depend chiefly on the success of their first operations, they were likely to meet with a fainter resistance in this parish than in most others; and should the

issue of the conflict prove unfavourable to them, they might retreat with
security into the woods, and there continue well supplied with provisions,
until their party should be strengthened with sufficient reinforcements,
to enable their prosecution of the grand enterprize, whose object was no
other than the entire extirpation of the white inhabitants; the enslaving of
all such Negroes as might refuse to join them; and the partition of the island into small principalities in the African mode; to be distributed among
their leaders and head men. A principal inducement to the formation of this
scheme of conquest was, the happy circumstance of the *Marons*; who, they
observed, had acquired very comfortable settlements, and a life of freedom
and ease, by dint of their prowess. On the night preceeding Easter-Monday,
about fifty of them marched to Port Maria, where they murdered the store-
keeper for the fort (at that time unprovided with a garrison), broke open
the magazine, and seized four barrels of powder, a few musquet-balls, and
about forty fire-arms. Proceeding from thence to the bay, which lies under
the fort, they met with some fishing-nets, from which they cut off all the
leaden sinkers, made of bullets drilled.

The [insurgents] pursued their way to Heywood-Hall, where they set
fire to the works and cane-pieces, and proceeded to Esher, an estate of Mr
William Beckford, murthering on the road a poor white man, who was
traveling on foot. At Esher they were joined by fourteen or fifteen of their
country-men. The Whites on that estate had but just time to shut themselves up in the dwelling-house, which they barricadoed as well as they
could; unhappily they were destitute of ammunition, and therefore incapable of making any resistance.

The rebels, after this action, turned back to Heywood Hall and Ballard's
Valley, where they picked up some fresh recruits, so that their whole party,
including women, increased to about four hundred. The fatigues of the
opening their campaign had so exhausted their spirits by this time, that
they thought proper to refresh themselves a little before they renewed their
hostilities; having therefore a good magazine of hogs, poultry, rum, and
other plunder of the like kind, they chose out a convenient spot, surrounded
with trees, and a little retired from the road, where they spread their provision, and began to carouze. The white inhabitants, alarmed by Mr. Bayley,
had assembled in the meantime about 70 or 80 horse, and had now a fair
opportunity of routing the whole body; they advanced towards the place
where the rebels were enjoying themselves, and luckily discovered them
by their noise and riot, or they might have fallen into an ambuscade. The
Coromantins did not exhibit any specimen of generalship upon this occasion; on the appearance of the troop, they kept close in the wood, from

whence they poured an irregular fire, which did no execution. The drilled bullets, taken from the fishing nets, described an arch in their projection, and flew over the heads of the militia. After keeping their ranks for some time, it was proposed that they should dismount, and push into the wood; but on examining their ammunition, the militia found their whole stock, if equally divided, did not amount to more than one charge each man; they therefore held it more adviseable, for the major part to stand their ground on the reserve, while their servants, and some others well armed, advanced into the wood close to the rebels, several of whom they killed. The rebels, intimidated with this bold attack, retreated; but it was not judged proper at that time to pursue them.

In the mean while, the spirit of rebellion was shewing itself in various other parts of the island, there being scarcely a single parish, to which this conspiracy of the Coromantins did not extend. In St. Mary's parish a check was fortunately given at one estate, by surprizing a famous obeiah man or priest, much respected among his countrymen. He was an old Coromantin, who, with others of his profession, had been a chief in counselling and in-stigating the credulous herd, to whom these priests administered a powder, which, being rubbed on their bodies, was to make them invulnerable: they persuaded them into a belief, that Tacky, their generalissimo in the woods, could not possibly be hurt by the white men, for that he caught all the bul-lets fired at him in his hand, and hurled them back with destruction to his foes. This old imposter was caught whilst he was tricked up with all his feathers, teeth, and other implements of magic, and in this attire suffered military execution by hanging: many of his disciplines, when they found that he was so easily put to death, notwithstanding all the boasted feats of his powder and incantations, soon altered their opinion of him, and deter-mined not to join their countrymen, in a cause which hitherto had been unattended with success. But the fame of general Tacky, and the notion of his invulnerability, still prevailed over the minds of others, as that hero had escaped hitherto in every conflict without a wound. The true condition of his party was artfully misrepresented to the Coromantins, in the distant parishes; they were told that every thing went on prosperously, that victory attended them, and that nothing now remained but for all their country-men to be hearty in the cause, and the island must speedily be their own. Animated with these reports, the Coromantins on capt. Forrest's estate, in Westmoreland, broke into rebellion. They surrounded the mansion-house, in which Mr. Smith, attorney to Mr. Forrest, with some friends, was sitting at supper; they soon dispatched Mr. Smith and the overseer, and terribly wounded captain Hoare, commander of a merchant ship in the trade, who afterwards recovered. Three other Negroes belonging to this estate made their escape privately, and alarmed the neighbouring settlements, by which means the white persons upon them provided for their lives, and took measures which prevented the Negroes on three contiguous estates from rising. A gentleman, proprietor of one of these estates, remarkable for his humanity and kind treatment of his slaves, upon the first alarm, put arms into the hands of about twenty; of whose faithful attachment to him, he had the utmost confidence: these were all of them Coromantins, who no sooner had got possession of arms, than they convinced their master how little they merited the good opinion he had entertained of them; for having ranged themselves before his house, they assured him they would do him no harm, but that they must go and join their countrymen, and then saluting him with their hats, they every one marched off.

Among the rebels were several French Negroes, who had been taken prisoners at Guadeloupe, and, being sent to Jamaica for sale, were purchased by capt. Forrest. These men were the most dangerous, as they had been in arms at Guadeloupe, and seen something of military operations; in which they acquired so much skill, that, after the massacre on the estate, when they found their partisans of the adjacent plantations did not appear to join them, they killed several Negroes, set fire to buildings and cane-pieces, did a variety of other mischief, and then withdrew into the woods, where they formed a strong breast-work across a road, flanked by a rocky hill; within this work, they erected their huts, and sat down in a sort of encampment; a party of militia, who were sent to attack them, very narrowly escaped being all cut off. The whole party was thrown into the utmost confusion and routed, notwithstanding every endeavour of their officers; each strove to shift for himself, and whilst they ran different ways, scarcely knowing what they were about, several were butchered, others broke their limbs over precipices, and the rest with difficulty found their way back again. This unlucky defeat raised the spirits of the Coromantins in this part of the country, and encouraged so many to join the victorious band, that the whole number very soon amounted to upwards of a thousand, including their women, who were necessary for carrying their baggage, and dressing their victuals.

About the time of their breaking out, several other conspiracies were in agitation: in the Vale of Luidas, in St. John's, the Coromantins had agreed to rise, ravage the estates, and murther the white men there; they fixed a certain day for commencing hostilities, when they were to break open the house at Langher's plantation, *and seize the fire arms lodged there*; after which, they were to slay all the Whites they could meet with, fire the houses, and cane-pieces, and lay all the country waste. Three Negroes, who were privy to this machination, disclosed it to their overseer, in consequence of which, the ringleaders were taken up, and, upon conviction, executed; others, who turned evidence, were transported off the island: and thus the whole of this bloody scheme was providentially frustrated.

In the parish of St. Thomas in the East, a Negroe, named Caffee, who had been pressed by some Coromantins there to join with them in rebelling, and destroying the estates and white inhabitants, declined at first being concerned; but recollecting that some advantages might be gained to himself by a thorough knowledge of their intentions, he afterwards pretended to have thought better of their proposals, and, professing his zeal to embrace them, he associated at their private cabals from time to time, till he became master of the whole secret, which he took the first opportunity to discover, and most of the conspirators were apprehended.

Conspiracies of the like nature were likewise detected in Kingston, St. Dorothy, Clarendon, and St. James, and the partizans secured.

In Kingston, a wooden sword was found, of a peculiar structure, with a red feather stuck into the handle; this was used among the Coromantins as a signal for war; and, upon examining this, and other suspicious circumstances, to the bottom, it was discovered, that the Coromantins of that town had raised one Cubah, a female slave belonging to a Jewess, to the rank of royalty, and dubbed her *queen of Kingston*; at their meetings she had sat in state under a canopy, with a sort of robe on her shoulders, and a crown upon her head. Her majesty was seized, and ordered for transportation; but, prevailing on the captain of the transport to put her ashore again in the leeward part of the island, she continued there for some time undiscovered, but at length was taken up, and executed.

A fresh insurrection happened in St. James's, which threatened to become very formidable, had it not been for the activity of brigadier Witter of the militia, and lieut. colonel Spragge of the 49th, who dispersed the insurgents, and took several prisoners; but the rest escaped, and, uniting with the stragglers of the other defeated parties, formed a large gang, and infested Carpenter's Mountains for some time. Another party of twelve Coromantins in Clarendon, whom their master, from a too good opinion of their fidelity, had imprudently armed, at their own earnest intreaty, and sent in quest of a small detached band of rebels, of whose haunt he had gained intelligence, deserted to their countrymen, but were soon after surprized, and the greater part of them killed or taken. Damon, one of the Westmoreland chiefs, with a small gang, having posted himself at a place called Mile Gully in Clarendon, a voluntary party, under command of Mr. Scott and Mr. Greig, with three or four more, went in quest of them. They had a long way to march in the night, through the woods, and across a difficult country; but, having provided themselves with a trusty guide, they came up to the haunt about midnight, attacked the rebels without loss of time, killed the chief, and one of his men, wounded another, and took two prisoners; for which service, the assembly made them a genteel recompence, besides a good reward to the Negroes who assisted them in this enterprize.

The rebels in St. Mary's, under general Tacky, still maintained their ground. Admiral Holmes had dispatched a frigate to Port Maria, which proved of great use for the safe custody of prisoners, who were too numerous to be confined on shore, and required too large a party of militia to guard them; but after they were removed on board, where they were well secured, the militia were ready to be employed on more active service: no measure, therefore, could be more seasonable and judicious; and it was one good effect of the harmony then subsisting between the commander of the squadron and the lieutenant governor. The rebels now thought only of concealing themselves, and made choice of a little glade, or cockpit, so environed with rocky steeps, that it was difficult to come at them; but, in this situation, a party of militia and *Marons,* with some sailors, assaulted them with hand grenades, killed some, and took a few prisoners. Soon after this, they suffered a more decisive overthrow; the *Marons* of Scot's Hall, having got sight of their main body, forced them to an engagement; the rebels soon gave way, and Tacky, their leader, having separated from the rest, was closely pursued by lieut. Davy of the *Marons,* who fired at him whilst they were both running at full speed, and shot him dead. His head was brought to Spanish Town, and stuck on a pole in the highway; but not long after, stolen, as it was supposed, by some of his countrymen, who were unwilling to let it remain exposed in so ignominious a manner. The loss of this chief, and of Jamaica, another of their captains, who fell in the same battle, struck most of the survivors of their little army with despair; they betook themselves to a cave, at the distance of a mile or two from the scene of action, where it was thought they laid violent hands on another, to the number of twenty-five. A few miserable fugitives still sculked about the woods, in continual terror for their fate; but at length, they contrived to send an embassy to a gentleman of the parish (Mr. Gordon), in whose honour they reposed implicit confidence, and expressed their readiness to surrender upon the condition of being transported off the island, instead of being put to death. This gentleman had a congress with their leaders unarmed, and promised to exert his endeavours with the lieutenant governor; on their part, they seemed well pleased to wait his determination, and gave assurance of their peaceable demeanour in the mean while. The lieutenant governor's consent was obtained; but under an appearance of difficulty, to make it the more desireable; and upon intimation of it at the next private congress, they one and all submitted, and were shipped off, pursuant to the stipulation. The remains of the Westmoreland and St. James's rebels still kept in arms, and committed some ravages.

Captain Hynes, with his party, went in search of the rebels [in the West], and was four months on the scout; at last, after a tedious pursuit, he surprized them in their haunt, killed and took twelve, and the remainder were afterwards either slain or taken prisoners by other parties, or destroyed themselves. Thus terminated this rebellion; which, whether we consider the extent and secrecy of its plan, the multitude of the conspirators, and the difficulty of opposing its eruptions in such a variety of different places at once, will appear to have been more formidable than any hitherto known in the West Indies; though happily extinguished, in far less time than was expected, by the precaution and judgement of the lieutenant-governor in the disposition of the forces, the prompt assistance of the admiral, and the alacrity of the regulars, seamen, militia, and Marons, who all contributed their share towards the speedy suppression of it.

Note

1. Vincent Brown, *Tacky's Revolt: The Story of an Atlantic Slave War* (Cambridge, MA: Harvard University Press, 2020); Maria Alessandra Bollettino, "Slavery, War and Britain's Atlantic Empire: Black Soldiers, Sailors and Rebels in the Seven Years' War" (PhD diss., University of Texas at Austin, 2009).

Archibald Stevenson Forrest (1869–1963), a prolific British illustrator, produced this painting for his book *The West Indies*, published in 1905 with text by John Henderson. While Henderson's text was crudely negative in its depiction of Caribbean people, Forrest's watercolors present their subjects as people with dignity and some individuality. *Resting by the Way, Jamaica*, color lithograph based on a watercolor by Archibald Stevenson Forrest. Bridgeman Images no. STC364869. Used by permission of Bridgeman Images / The Stapleton Collection.

John Dunkley (1891–1947) was one of the most significant Jamaican intuitive (self-taught) painters. As a young man he worked in Panama, Costa Rica, and Cuba before returning to work as a barber in Kingston. Dunkley's work is distinguished by an originality in form and color. His paintings feature a darker, more surreal rendering of the Jamaican landscape, which contrasts markedly with the optimistic aesthetics of many of his peers. John Dunkley, *Banana Plantation*, c. 1945. From the National Gallery of Jamaica, Kingston. Used courtesy of Tina Dunkley.

One of Jamaica's most celebrated artists, Albert Huie (1920–2010), trained in London and Canada before returning to the island. He cofounded (with Edna Manley) and taught at the Jamaica School of Arts and Crafts, now the Edna Manley College of the Performing and Visual Arts. Through his encouragement of younger artists, Huie earned the popular title "Father of Jamaican Art." He honored Edna Manley with an acclaimed portrait of her, but was better known for his landscape works. *Crop Time* depicts workers on a sugar plantation, with the sugar factory in the background. The late David Boxer, who served for many years as chief curator of the National Gallery of Jamaica, regarded this painting as "the finest portrait yet of an activity which has been central to Jamaican life for centuries." Albert Huie, *Croptime*, 1955. From the National Gallery of Jamaica, Kingston. Used courtesy of Christine Huie-Roy.

British artist James Hakewill (1778–1843) published this print as part of a volume of drawings, mainly of rural landscapes, dedicated to the "noblemen and gentlemen, proprietors of estates in the West Indies." This image, one of a small number of urban scenes, is of the crossroad of Harbour Street and King Street, at that point the heart of Kingston, and still an important downtown intersection. As well as depicting vernacular architecture it shows soldiers, white residents, and black vendors. It emphasizes spaciousness and calm even while hinting, through the naked children and bare feet of some of the black figures, at the poverty and exploitation of enslaved Jamaicans. *Harbour Street, Kingston*, drawn by James Hakewill, engraved by Thomas Sutherland. Originally published in James Hakewill, *A Picturesque Tour of the Island of Jamaica, from Drawings Made in the Years 1820 and 1821* (London: Hurst and Robinson, 1825).

This satirical print, produced by British soldier Abraham Jones, depicts Jamaica as a land of indolence, heat, and death for whites. The image drew on and contributed to negative British interpretations of Jamaica and its white creole inhabitants. A. J., *The Torrid Zone, or Blessings of Jamaica*, colored aquatint (London: W. Holland, 1800). From the Harvey Cushing / John Hay Whitney Medical Library, Yale University, New Haven, CT.

Renée Cox (b. 1960) is a Jamaican artist who now works in the United States. This photograph is part of the series *Queen Nanny of the Maroons*, most of which depict the artist as the Maroon leader Nanny in a series of Jamaican locations. Here, she stands on a hill wearing a replica of a British military uniform and holding a machete, intensely looking into the camera. Renée Cox, *Red Coat*, 2006, photograph from the series *Queen Nanny of the Maroons*. Reprinted by permission of the artist.

Everald Brown (1917–2003) was an intuitive painter and sculptor, much of whose work derived from his spiritual experiences, in the Baptist Church in his early life and later as a convert to and leader of a Rastafari community. Among his esteemed works are his series of functional stringed instruments of various shapes, painted with colorful iconography. His unique constructions typically feature elements of instruments such as rhumba boxes, guitars, drums, and harps. Everald Brown, *Instrument for Four People—Starry Harp*, 1986, sculpture. From the National Gallery of Jamaica, Kingston. Photograph by Franz Marzouca. Used by permission of the Brown family.

Barrington Watson (1931–2016) trained in London, Paris, and the Netherlands, then taught in Jamaica and the United States. Many of Watson's paintings deal with profound moments in Jamaica's past. In *The Garden Party*, painted during Michael Manley's first term in office (1972–1976), he focused on the present. The mural was commissioned by the Bank of Jamaica and depicts idealized scenes of the 1970s, including rural pastimes, Rastafari cultural influence, foreign interest in Jamaican culture, labor, security, and community, all of which are infused in the sense of harmony in the image. Barrington Watson, *The Garden Party*, 1975, mural inside the Bank of Jamaica building, Kingston.

Laura Facey Cooper's sculpture was the winning entry for a competition to produce a sculpture for New Kingston's Emancipation Park, which opened in 2002. Alluding in its title to one of Bob Marley's most famous songs, the sculpture depicts male and female naked figures standing in water while looking to the sky, symbolizing their triumph over slavery. Although the nudity and pose reference Christopher Gonzalez's *Man Arisen* (1966), the sculpture has been controversial, with critics suggesting that the pose of the figures suggests passivity and their nakedness is excessively sexualized. Laura Facey Cooper, *Redemption Song*, 2003, bronze sculpture, Emancipation Park, Kingston. Photograph by the artist.

This photograph by Clinton Hutton (b. 1954) shows Priest Dermot Fagan of the School of Vision, one of a group of Rastafari elders reenacting the coronation of Ras Tafari at Scott's Pass, Clarendon parish, an iconic site of the Niabingi Order, on 2 November 2014, the eighty-fourth anniversary of the coronation of HIM Haile Selassie. Hutton is a scholar, photographer, painter, and activist and was a professor at the University of the West Indies, Mona. Used courtesy of the photographer.

Ebony G. Patterson (b. 1981) studied at the Edna Manley College of Visual and Performing Arts and in the United States. The title of this piece refers to a provocative 1985 large-scale mixed-media installation by Jamaican artist Dawn Scott. Scott's installation was encircled in zinc and objects of Jamaican poverty. Patterson instead presents viewers with a less claustrophobic depiction of urban Kingston. Doorless bejewelled cars framed by extraordinary portraitures and material objects emphasize the openness, individuality, and innovation of contemporary Jamaican dancehall culture. Ebony G. Patterson, *Cultural Soliloquy (Cultural Object Revisited)*, 2010, mixed-media assemblage. From the National Gallery of Jamaica, Kingston.

Blinded by the wretchedness of their situation, many of Jamaica's slaves, especially the black élite (those most exposed to the influence of their masters), failed, or refused, to make conscious use of their own rich folk culture (their one indisputable possession), and so failed to command the chance of becoming self-conscious and cohesive as a group and consequently, perhaps, winning their independence from bondage, as their cousins in Haiti had done. "Invisible," anxious to be "seen" by their masters, the élite blacks and the mass of free coloureds (apart from the significant exceptions already discussed within the body of this work, and those who, after Emancipation, were to establish, against almost impossible odds, the free villages and small peasantries of rural Jamaica), conceived of visibility through the lenses of their masters' already uncertain vision as a form of "greyness"—an imitation of an imitation. Whenever the opportunity made it possible, they and their descendants rejected or disowned their own culture, becoming, like their masters, "mimic-men."

The crucial test for the society came with the American Revolution. Had there not been the physical and psychological barriers between master and bondsman as had developed as a result of the nature of slavery in the New World, it might have been possible for the Jamaican politicians to present a more united and positive front to British mercantilism than was in fact possible or was felt to be necessary. Had the white creole élite not demeaned itself by debasing its labour force, it might have been possible for British European culture to have made a more radical contribution than it did to the process of creolization, and a Jamaican "identity" with deeper white Anglo-Saxon Protestant foundations might have been the result. As it was, the white contribution to Jamaica remained structural only, and resulted, because of its prestige position in relation to the mass, in the formation of a cultural dichotomy.

A second opportunity for social and cultural integration presented itself at Emancipation. But here again the physical and psychological barriers proved to be insurmountable. When, by 1865, the white élite admitted failure and, still refusing to cooperate with the black masses, accepted (and were made to accept) the knock of the British imperial hammer, colonial forms, in the descendent since 1728, rushed back in to fill the void created by the failure of the creole élite, and the society became even more estranged from itself and its several parts. The result was a further widening of the gap between colonial and metropolitan, colonial and creole, between élite and the mass of the population; and post-Emancipation industrial and political development in Europe and America have further retarded the possibility of creole autonomy.

Whether it can or will continue to survive in these terms is another matter. Jamaican society has in common with all other societies, one assumes, a natural built-in drive or gravitational tendency towards cultural autonomy. Cultural autonomy demands a norm and a residential correspondence between the "great" and "little" traditions within the society. Under slavery there were two "great" traditions, one in Europe, the other in Africa, and so neither was residential. Normative value-references were made outside the society. Creolization (despite its attendant imitations and conformities) provided the conditions for and possibly of local residence. It certainly mediated the development of authentically local institutions, and an Afro-creole "little" tradition among the slave "folk." But it did not, during the period of this study, provide a norm. For this to have been provided, the Euro-creole élite (the one group able, to some extent, to influence the pace and quality of creolization) would have had to have been much stronger, culturally, than it was. Unable or unwilling to absorb in any central sense the "little" tradition of the majority, its efforts and its continuing colonial dependence merely created the pervasive dichotomy which has been indicated in this study.

My own idea of creolization is based on the notion of an historically affected sociocultural continuum, within which (in the case of Jamaica), there are four interrelated and sometimes overlapping orientations. From their several cultural bases people in the West Indies tend towards certain directions, positions, assumptions, and ideals. But nothing is really fixed and monolithic. Although there is white/brown/black, there are infinite possibilities within these distinctions and many ways of asserting identity. A common colonial and creole experience is shared among the various divisions, even if that experience is variously interpreted. These four orientations may be designated as follows: European, Euro-creole, Afro-creole (or folk), and "West Indian."

With political power now in the hands of the black majority of the population, it remains to be seen whether the process of creolization will be resumed in such a way that the "little" tradition of the (ex-)slaves will be able to achieve the kind of articulation, centrality, prestige and influence— assuming, that is, that it is not by now too debased—that will provide a basis for creative reconstruction. Such a base, evolving its own residential "great" tradition, could well support the development of a new parochial wholeness, a difficult but possible creole authenticity.

Note

1. Orlando Patterson, *The Sociology of Slavery: An Analysis of the Origins, Development and Structure of Negro Slave Society in Jamaica* (London: Macgibbon and Kee, 1967).

Cane and Coffee

Robert Charles Dallas

Robert Dallas was a Jamaican-born slave owner and writer. In this selection from his book The History of the Maroons, *published in 1803, he describes the process of production of sugar, rum, and coffee, the most important commercial crops of the slavery era. Because of its prominence in the Jamaican economy, he devotes by far the most attention to sugar. But he also describes in some depth the other, secondary commercial crops of the island, demonstrating their significance too. With the exception of the production of sugar, Dallas says little about the work that goes into making the final products. Like many contemporary sources, particularly those by slaveholders, he hardly mentions the enslaved people who produced these commodities, but carefully reading phrases such as "the stem is topped, and the branches are pruned" (in relation to cotton) reveals their work.*

The [sugar]cane [is] one of the most valuable plants in creation. Its botanical name is *Arundo saccharifera*. In form it is a jointed reed terminating in leaves or blades, whose edges are finely serrated. Its stem is strong though brittle, and, when ripe, of a fine straw-colour. It contains a soft, pithy substance, that affords, in perfection, a copious supply of juice, and a sweetness the least cloying and the most agreeable in nature. The proper season for planting canes, is the interval between August and November. By thus insuring the influence of the autumnal rains, the foliage of the young canes becomes sufficiently luxuriant before the summer blazes, to keep their roots cool, and the contiguous earth moist. The usual mode of holing, that is, preparing to plant by manual labour, is as follows: The land being divided into plats of about twenty acres extent; each plat is then subdivided, by a line attached to wooden pegs, into squares of three or four feet. The field negroes are then placed in a row, in the first line, one to each square, which they excavate with hoes to the depth of five or six inches. It commonly requires forty negroes to hole an acre in the course of a day. For such labour, if hired, eight or ten pounds currency is commonly paid. The cuttings selected for planting, are usually the tops of the canes that have been expressed for making sugar. These placed horizontally on the bottom of the hole, are covered two inches deep with mold. In about twelve days the sprouts from the gems of the planted cane are seen: at the end of four or five months the banks of the holes are levelled. Till the young plants attain considerable maturity, the weeds that a rich soil highly manured rapidly nourish, are to be incessantly disturbed by the hoe. Plant canes are ripe for the mill early in the second year. From December till May is called crop-time in Jamaica. In Jamaica [sugar] is expressed by mills, worked by cattle, wind, or water. A sugar mill consists principally of three upright iron plated cylinders, from thirty to forty inches in length, and from twenty to twenty-five inches in diameter. The middle one, to which the moving power is applied, turns the other two by cogs. Between these rollers the canes are compressed twice, which squeezes them completely. The juice is received into a leaden vessel. The macerated rind of the cane, so pressed dry, serves (with dry cane leaves called trash) for fuel to boil the liquor.

The juice from the mill, running along a wooden gutter lined with lead, is carried to the boiling house, where it is received into a clarifying cauldron, of which there are commonly three. Each clarifier is provided with a syphon, or cock for drawing off the liquor. In establishments where two hundred hogsheads are annually manufactured, each clarifier has a flat bottom, is hung to a separate fire, with a separate chimney, to which belongs an iron slider, which being shut, the fire is suppressed. All cane juice is liable to rapid fermentation. As soon, therefore, as the clarifier is filled, the fire is lighted, and the temper (white lime of Bristol) is stirred into it. The alkali of the lime having neutralized its superabundant acid, a part of it becomes the basis of the sugar. An half pint of Bristol lime, dissolved in hot water, is commonly sufficient for an hundred gallons of liquor. The clarifier ought to be heated till the scum begins to rise into blisters, but not to actual ebullition. At this moment the damper is to be applied, and the fire extinguished. The warm liquor remaining a while undisturbed, the seculances attracting, entangle each other and rise in a scum. This scum sinks unbroken, and is left when the liquor is drawn off into the evaporating or grand copper. In this grand copper it is to boil, the additional scum being now taken off as it rises, till by skimming and evaporation, the quantity is considerably reduced, and becomes more viscid. It is then ladled into another copper, and undergoes further ebullition and skimming. After a certain time, when the liquor is reduced sufficiently, so as to be contained in the third smaller copper, it is ladled into that, and so on to the last, called the teache, so named probably from the practice, at this stage of the process, of trying the consistency of the boiled juice by the touch. In the teache the subject is finally boiled, till on trial of its fitness for granulation, it may be removed from the fire. This part of the business is called *stricking*; that is, ladling the thickened syrup like liquor into the cooler. As it cools, it runs into a coarse, irregular mass of imperfect chrystals, separating itself from the melasses. From the cooler in the boiling-house, the mass so granulated is conveyed to an hogshead in the curing-house. The melasses draining into the cistern the sugar in about three weeks becomes dry and fair. It is then said to be cured, and the process is finished. Of this precious commodity, when seasons are favourable, about one hundred and forty thousand hogsheads are annually shipped to Great Britain from Jamaica.

The bounty of the cane ends not here; the very dregs and feculencies of this invaluable plant, yield one of the purest, most fragrant, and salutary spirits in the world. The proportion of rum to the crop of sugar, is commonly estimated in Jamaica as three to four; but this is said to be too great an allowance on a general estimate, and that two hundred gallons of rum to three hogsheads of sugar, or two-thirds rum to the crop of sugar, is nearer the truth.

Another vegetable production, a native of the east, and an object of commerce, that flourishes in Jamaica, is coffee. Coffee-plants may be set out at all seasons of the year, even in the dryest. They will thrive in any situation, provided it will be screened from the north winds, which destroy its blossom. The best and highest flavoured fruit is the growth of a warm gravelly mold, or sandy loam, such as forms the slope of the dry red hills of Jamaica. The berry is sown, or the plants are set out about eight feet distant from each other on all sides. The holes in which they are placed must be of sufficient depth to receive the lower part of the stem about two inches under the surface of the ground. In the third year when the stem obtains the growth of five or six feet, the trees are topped. A single stem of this growth often affords forty-two bearing branches. The average of produce per acre, after the fourth year, is about 750 pounds weight of merchantable coffee.

In Jamaica, as soon as the berries acquire a black red colour, they are judged to be sufficiently ripe for picking. They are gathered into canvas bags from the trees at three different stages of ripeness. One hundred bushels in the pulp, give one thousand weight of dried coffee. There are two methods of drying it: 1st, to spread the fresh coffee in the sun, on a sloping platform of boards, about five inches deep, with the pulp on the berry, which ferments and discharges itself. The husks are afterwards separated by a mill, or by pestles in a wooden mortar. 2dly, To remove the pulp from the berry immediately as it comes from the tree, by passing it through a mill. The latter is the most expeditious mode, but the former gives the best flavoured coffee.

Women's and Men's Work under Slavery

Lucille Mathurin Mair

Although both sexes suffered under slavery, women's and men's experiences as enslaved people were significantly different. Lucille Mathurin Mair, an early historian of women and slavery, demonstrates the difference gender made in women's and men's working lives. Contrary to some stereotypes about slavery, which assume that enslaved women mainly did domestic labor, they were actually more likely than men to work in the fields.

The slaveholdings of the 1780s of William Beckford, the absentee planter and Lord Mayor of London, demonstrate the heavy participation of women in the "exaggerated labours of the field." This large complex of estates provides additional valuable evidence of a labour force consciously deployed in accordance with contemporary criteria of what was appropriate occupation for the sexes. It offers useful evidence, as well, of some of the effects of such labour policies on the condition of black women. Beckford's Jamaican properties included estates scattered over the three parishes of Clarendon, Westmoreland and St Ann.

Bodles Pen[, which was devoted to cattle raising,] had an expected high proportion of workers engaged in the care of livestock, which resulted in its purely agricultural activity left almost exclusively in the hands of women. [Beckford's] complex of twelve estates containing 2,204 slaves revealed that in 1780, 36 per cent, or 291 out of 802 men, and 57 per cent, or 444 out of 778 women, were field workers.

A varied range of skills, as William Beckford implied, was possible for the male slave. Nutt's River estate [owned by Sir Thomas Champnoys], for example, with twenty-five males, had fourteen artisans who included sawyers, carpenters, stone masons and boilers, as well as a blacksmith, a farrier and a cooper. The occupational openings for the men on the Beckford estates were even wider, for, in addition to the categories of work found at Nutt's River, they had on their 1780 establishment slaves classified as bricklayers, wheelwrights, distillers, fishermen, wharf-men, tailors and doctor's

This engraving, *Jamaica negroes cutting canes in their working dresses*, shows a gang made up of both men and women. Frontispiece to *Notes on the Present Condition of the Negroes in Jamaica* by H. T. De La Beche (London: Printed for T. Cadell, 1825). John Carter Brown Archive of Early American Images, record no. 82-116-1, call no. D825 D331N. Used courtesy of the John Carter Brown Library at Brown University. https://creativecommons.org/licenses/by/4.0/legalcode.

assistants; a high proportion were also engaged in the care of livestock. Male workers sometimes combined agricultural and nonagricultural work, so that on Esher estate, for instance, three men listed as field workers, Bob, Cudjoe and Caesar, were also respectively a boiler, a wainman and a distiller. On Bog Estate, Frank, Charles and Adam were simultaneously field men and sawyers. Drax Hall estate had six male field workers who also combined the skill each of either a boiler or a distiller.

In contrast, women were confined within a considerably more restricted area, and field women were exclusively field women. Indeed, often when women were listed in other categories of work apart from that of the field, a closer look reveals that they were in fact engaged in ancillary field tasks requiring little or no special skills. So that, for example, in addition to the 444 women on the Beckford estates in 1780 who were classified as "field negroes," there were nineteen who cut grass, worked in the estates' provisions garden and hoed fences. Other jobs allocated to women demanded little expertise: a further ten women did miscellaneous tasks; they carried water or watched gates or worked on the road. Seven women were drivers of field gangs. The care of poultry, pigs and sheep engaged thirty-three women, or 8 per cent of the adult female population.

Domestic work was the most significant work category next to agriculture, and accounted for fifty-nine women, or 13 per cent of the total sample. Within this group were to be found fifteen washerwomen, eighteen housewomen and twenty-six cooks. Eighteen of these cooks were assigned to the field gangs and prepared meals on the work site; half of the house slaves (nine in all) were mulattoes.

Women with "skills" numbered thirty-four, or 8 per cent. They included seven midwives, eight doctresses, five field nurses and fourteen seamstresses. This proportion of nonpraedial female workers overrates the black women's access to special expertise, for mulattoes dominated as seamstresses— eleven out of the group of fourteen—and the labels of "doctress," "midwife" and "nurse" were often euphemisms for superannuated field workers.

Estate inventories do not give much information about the training in skills, if any, which was made available to young female slaves. The only instances in all the samples which suggest a period of apprenticeship are: Dido, aged fourteen, at Bodles Pen, who was learning to be a washerwoman; Essey, a "fine healthy mulatto girl" at Nutt's River, who was learning to be a seamstress; and Sophia, a young girl at Mount Pleasant in 1787, who was "with the midwife."

With so few levels of expertise in the creole system to which she could aspire, the black slave woman was irretrievably the unskilled labourer in the field and, in the hierarchy of the "outer" plantation, no one ranked lower. Male slaves with advanced skills could become "important personages of great responsibility" on the estate. Distinction as "a good workman" earned authority and privilege. In contrast, the black woman, trapped in an occupational cul-de-sac, was the least able of all slaves, and of all women, "to attain positions of status and relative independence."[1]

Note

1. Thomas Roughley, *The Jamaica Planter's Guide; or, A System for Planting and Managing a Sugar Estate, or Other Plantations in That Island, and throughout the British West Indies in General* (London: Longman, Hurst, Rees, Orme and Brown, 1823), 79–87; Barry Higman, "Household Structure and Fertility on Jamaican Slave Plantations: A Nineteenth Century Example," *Population Studies* 3 (1973): 7.

Although a Slave Me Is Born and Bred

Recorded by J. B. Moreton

This song was recorded by J. B. Moreton, who worked as a bookkeeper in Jamaica in the 1780s. Moreton claimed to have heard it sung by a young enslaved woman. It wryly recounts the story of a woman who is violently whipped by both the white man and white woman who own her. Initially "kept" (that is, used as a sex slave) by her master, she nevertheless bears a black child, revealing a sexual relationship with another man. He whips her in response. Later, when the narrator bears a white child fathered by the estate overseer, the estate mistress believes that her husband is the second child's father. The song recounts how the mistress whips the narrator a second time. Although at times plaintive in tone, and speaking to a profoundly violent society, the song differs strikingly from abolitionist representations of enslaved sexuality, which often presented enslaved women as broken victims of immoral men. This song, with its final stanza that declares "me know no law, me know no sin," rejects a sense that the narrator's sexual encounters are shaming to her. Since the 1980s the song has attracted considerable critical attention, including analysis by the prominent Jamaican cultural critic Carolyn Cooper.[1] The song demonstrates the ongoing process of linguistic creolization while also commenting on the dynamics of race and sexuality in Jamaican slave society. It uses a number of Jamaican patwa words, including fum, "to flog"; busses, meaning "kisses"; Obisha, meaning "overseer"; pickinniny, meaning "child"; and rassa, meaning "ass/arse." Not all of these terms remain in use.

Altho' a slave me is born and bred,
My skin is black, not yellow:
I often sold my maidenhead
To many a handsome fellow.

My massa keep me once, for true,
And gave me clothes, wid busses:
Fine muslin coats, wid bitty, too,
To gain my sweet embraces.

When pickininny him come black,
My massa starve and fum me;
He tear the coat from off my back,
And naked him did strip me.

Him turn me out into the field,
Wid hoe, the ground to clear-o;
Me take pickinniny on my back,
And work him te-me weary.

Him, Obisha, him de come one night,
And give me gown and busses;
Him get one pickinniny, white!
Almost as white as missess.

Then misses fum me wid long switch,
And say him da for massa;
My massa curse her, "lying bitch!"
And tell her, "buss my rassa!"

Me fum'd when me no condescend;
Me fum'd too if me do it;
Me no have no one for 'tand my friend,
So me am forc'd to do it.

Me know no law, me know no sin,
Me is just what ebba them make me;
This is the way dem bring me in;
So God nor devil take me!

Note

1. Carolyn Cooper, *Noises in the Blood: Orality, Gender, and the "Vulgar" Body of Jamaican Popular Culture* (Durham, NC: Duke University Press, 1995).

Capture and Enslavement

Archibald John Monteath

*Archibald Monteath (sometimes spelled "Monteith" or "Monteeth") dictated his life
story to the Moravian missionary the Rev. Joseph Horsfield Kummer in 1853, after
the end of slavery. Monteath was a member of the Moravian church in New Carmel, Westmoreland, and worked across Jamaica as a "national assistant" to the
Moravian communities. The Moravians were the earliest Christian missionaries
to Jamaica. Born part of an "Eboe" (Igbo) community in what is today Nigeria, he
was kidnapped and taken to Jamaica on a slave ship in the early years of the nineteenth century, and in the 1820s he became a Christian. His narrative is particularly
interesting for providing an account of life in Igboland and of the Middle Passage.
Monteath—or Aneaso, as he was originally known—was one of an increasing proportion of children who experienced the Middle Passage in the later years of the Atlantic slave trade. The narrative uses a flat, unemotional tone to present Monteath's
experience of separation from his home and family. Monteath describes the trauma
of those around him but terms himself "happy" while on board the slave ship.*

I was born, as far as I can remember, taking into account the time when I
left my native land, in the year 1799.[1] I was born in Africa, and belong to the
nation or tribe called Eboe's. My father's name was ____.[2] My mother was
called Dirinejah; her father was a prince, and the daughter was named after
the father. My name was Aneaso. Although my native land is a heathen
land, and though my father was a heathen, and polygamy is generally preva-
lent, I can distinctly remember, that my father only lived with the above
mentioned Dirinejah, with whom he had 4 children, three daughters, and
myself was the only son. As an only Son I was the favourite of my father
with whom I generally labored in the field and provision ground, the yield
of which is very much the same as here in Jamaica; yams, potatoes, Indian
Corn, etc. etc. My sisters seldom went out of the house, but kept themselves
within, according to the custom of the land; and especially if any one of the
male sex came to see us; they would closely conceal themselves.

The God or Being in whose existence every heathen believes, because the works of creation declare this, was called Tschuku, or Tschuku-damma.[3] He makes the thunder and lightning etc., etc. We only prayed to him when we were sick, so that he should speedily make us well. Did we recover and get well again, then there was an end to the prayer. When death came, then every thing ceased to be, at least so we thought, and as is customary among the heathen, we did not trouble ourselves about futurity.

When I was about 10 years old, a young man came frequently to see us; he wished to have my sister for his wife. One day he asked me to go with him to the market place. Knowing nothing about the distance to the place, I, at once complied, without saying any thing to my father, who no doubt would not have given his consent. After we had walked for a whole day, we came to an acquaintance of the young man, and here we remained for several days. Then we all went together to the market which we soon reached. Here I saw a great many things I had never seen before, and which greatly astonished me; but most of all was I pleased with the great water, the ocean.

Then my companion and guide said, "Go nearer to the water, then you can see everything better." I did so, and leaning on a Kenepp tree, looked around, and was filled with astonishment to see the boats floating on the water, and most of all to see the great water itself. A man said to me, "Come into my boat, and try how you like the sailing about." I said, "No, that I will not do." Then he suddenly came upon me took me up, and carried me to his boat, and put me in.—Now I immediately knew that I would be made a slave, for I remembered that during the whole day I had frequently heard, when my guide was asked;—"What are you going to with boy; Sell him?" say in reply; "Oh no; he is a great man's son!" But still when the right man came along, and he sold me, and I could do nothing but to call to him, "tell my father where I am, and salute him." I was frightened and wept a little, but soon comforted myself, because I was fond of sailing in the boat. The other slaves screamed loud, and would neither eat nor drink. I however soon fell asleep. When I awoke I saw a large ship before me. I was not a little astonished to see such a beautiful house floating on the water; and when I was put on board nothing surprised me more, than to see the Captain with white face and hands, and with shining black feet without toes; (he wore boots). On the ship, there was scarcely any one else to be seen, as it was towards evening, and getting dark; hence I was not a little surprised the next morning, when various holes were opened to see 600 or 700 slaves brought upon deck, to whom yams were given for food, and rum for drink. Myself and 11 other boys were taken by the Captain into the cabin. We were happy; skipped about, eat and drank, and yet I felt very sorry when I saw the other slaves come up from the hold of the ship daily, into the air, and heard their heartrending cries of anguish; fathers & mothers longing for their homes and children, and often would neither eat nor drink, and were so strictly watched and held in such rigid confinement.

Notes

1. Maureen Warner-Lewis, in her study of Monteath, argues that the evidence of his narratives suggests that he was in fact born in 1792. *Archibald Monteath: Igbo, Jamaican, Moravian* (Mona, Jamaica: University of the West Indies Press, 2007), 41. [Editors' note]

2. The name *Durl* appears at this point in the German text. Missions-Blatt, 1864, p. 89. [Original editors' note]

3. A transliteration of the Igbo Chukwu, or supreme God or spirit. [Editors' note]

The Black Church

George Liele

George Liele, a black loyalist refugee from Georgia who came to Jamaica after the American Revolution, was one of the founders of what became the Native Baptist Church in Jamaica. "Native Baptist" was the term for the independent black-dominated Baptist church, distinguishing it from the congregations of the white Baptist Missionary Society, which were founded later. Many congregations that began as missionary churches subsequently became Native Baptist communities. Liele established the East Queen Street Baptist Church in downtown Kingston. This letter, dated Kingston, 18 December 1791, was reprinted in the British Baptist Annual Register as an appeal for funds. It begins with Liele's account of his early life, conversion, and preaching in Georgia. Here we pick up at the point where he turns to his time in Jamaica. Liele explains that the Baptists will only accept enslaved people as members with the permission of their owners. This policy recognized that without the tolerance of planters he could not have continued to preach. The Baptists would become one of the most important religious groups in Jamaica, nurturing the leaders of both the 1831 "Baptist War" and, in 1865, the Morant Bay Rebellion.

I began, about September 1784, to preach in Kingston, in a small private house, to a good smart congregation, and I formed the church with four brethren from America besides myself, and the preaching took very good effect with the poorer sort, especially the slaves. The people at first persecuted us both at meetings and baptisms, but, God be praised, they seldom interrupt us now. We have applied to the Honourable House of Assembly, with a petition of our distresses, being poor people, desiring to worship Almighty God according to the tenets of the Bible, and they have granted us liberty, and given us their sanction. Thanks be to God we have liberty to worship him as we please in the Kingdom. You ask about those who, "in a judgment of charity," have been converted to Christ. I think they are about four hundred and fifty. I have baptized four hundred in Jamaica. At Kingston I baptize in the sea, at Spanish Town in the river, and at convenient places in the country. We have nigh *three hundred and fifty* members; a few white people among them. Several members have been dismissed to other churches, and twelve have died. A few of Mr. Wesley's people, after immersion, join us and continue with us. We have, together with well wishers and followers, in different parts of the country, about fifteen hundred people. We receive none into the church without a few lines from their owners of their good behaviour towards them and religion. The creoles of the country, after they are converted and baptized, as God enables them, prove very faithful. I have deacons and elders, a few; and teachers of small congregations in the town and country, where convenience suits them to come together; and I am pastor. I preach twice on the Lord's Day, in the forenoon and afternoon, and twice in the week, and have not been absent six Sabbath Days since I formed the church in this country. I receive nothing for my services; I preach, baptize, administer the Lord's Supper, and travel from one place to another to publish the gospel, and to settle church affairs, all freely. I have one of the chosen men, whom I baptized, a deacon of the church, and a native of this country, who keeps the regulations of church matters; and I promoted a *free school* for the instruction of the children, both free and slaves, and he is the schoolmaster.

I cannot justly tell what is my age, as I have no account of the time of my birth, but I suppose I am about forty years old. I have a wife and four children. My wife was baptized by me in Savannah, at Brunton land, and I have every satisfaction in life from her. She is much the same age as myself. My eldest son is nineteen years, my next son seventeen, the third fourteen, and the last child, a girl of eleven years; they are all members of the church. My occupation is a farmer, but as the seasons in this part of the country, are uncertain, I also keep a team of horses, and waggons for the carrying goods from one place to another, which I attend to myself, with the assistance of my sons; and by this way of life have gained the good will of the public, who recommend me to business, and to some very principal work for government.

There is no Baptist church in this country but ours. We have purchased a piece of land, at the east end of Kingston, containing three acres for the sum of 155 l. currency, and on it have begun a meeting-house fifty-seven feet in length by thirty-seven in breadth. We have raised the brick wall eight feet high from the foundation, and intend to have a gallery. Several gentlemen, members of the house of assembly, and other gentlemen, have subscribed towards the building about 40 l. The chief part of our congregation are SLAVES, and their owners allow them, in common, but three or four bits per week[1] for allowance to feed themselves; and out of so small a sum we cannot expect any thing that can be of service from them; if we did it would soon bring a scandal upon religion; and the FREE PEOPLE in our society are but poor, but they are all willing, both free and slaves, to do what they can. As for my part, I am too much entangled with the affairs of the world to go on with my design, in supporting the cause: this has, I acknowledge, been a great hindrance to the Gospel in one way; but as I have endeavored to set a good example [of industry] before the inhabitants of the land, it has given general satisfaction another way. And, Rev. Sir, we think the Lord has put it in the power of the Baptist societies in England to help and assist us in completing this building, which we look upon will be the greatest undertaking ever was in this country for the bringing of souls from darkness into the light of the Gospel. And as the Lord has put it into your heart to enquire after us, we place all our confidence in you, to make our circumstances known to the several Baptist churches in England; and we look upon you as our father, friend, and brother.

Within the brick wall we have a shelter, in which we worship, until our building can be accomplished.

Your letter was read to the church two or three times, and did create a great deal of love and warmness throughout the whole congregation, who shouted for joy and comfort, to think that the Lord had been so gracious as to satisfy us in this country with the very same religion with our beloved brethren in the old country, according to the scriptures: and that such a worthy of London, should write in so loving a manner to such poor worms as we are. And I beg leave to say, That the whole congregation sang out that they would, through the assistance of God, remember you in their prayers. They altogether give their Christian love to you, and all the worthy professors of Jesus Christ in your church at London, and beg the prayers of your congregation, and the prayers of the churches in general, wherever it pleases you to make known in our circumstances. I remain with the utmost love Rev. Sir, your unworthy fellow-labourer, servant, and brother in Christ.

(Signed) GEORGE LIELE.

Note

1. A bit was seven pence halfpenny currency, or about five pence halfpenny sterling. [Original editor's note]

British Missionaries

Mary Turner

One of the most important changes to take place in the later period of slavery was the arrival of Protestant missionaries. German Moravians arrived first, in the mid-eighteenth century. Later, missionaries from the Wesleyan Methodist and Baptist Missionary Societies played important roles. The missionaries came to convert enslaved people to Christianity, rather than to oppose slavery. They often depended on planters to allow enslaved people to come to their meetings. Their home missionary societies usually instructed them to avoid public statements on slavery in order to maintain this access. Nevertheless, as historian Mary Turner explains, missionaries provided an alternative source of authority. Their presence led to conflicts between enslaved people and planters about religion and religious freedom that ultimately destabilized the system of slavery.

The missionary challenge caused the slave owners a many-faceted political problem. At a practical level the whites in Jamaica were a small minority, barely 10 percent of the total population, ruling a slave force augmented yearly by Africans who had to be absorbed into the routine of estate work. They faced a slave rebellion of some dimension about every five years. Any innovation in the system was regarded as a threat to security, and church attendance in itself meant a substantial innovation in the life of a people traditionally bound by the demands of estate labor. More disturbing was the fact that, even in England, the Wesleyan church was regarded by elements in the ruling class as yet another disruptive Dissenting sect. A church which raised up workingmen as preachers appeared to threaten the social order, and on this account English magistrates interfered with preaching and mobs were organized to drive preachers from the marketplace. The planters had reason to fear that the missionaries would teach the slaves not only the Christian virtues of industry and obedience but also that God made all men equal.

The most provocative element in the challenge was the relationship between missionary societies and the antislavery movement. In principle there was a vital division between the two. The antislavery movement, while it

Posthumous portrait
of William Knibb, one
of the most important
Baptist missionaries in
Jamaica, pointing to a
scroll stating "Slavery
Abolished, Jamaica
August 1838." Knibb
actively campaigned
for the end of slavery
in the 1830s, but earlier
missionaries focused
on conversion rather
than abolition. Artist
unknown. From the
George A. Smathers
Library, University of
Florida, Gainesville.

aimed only at abolishing the slave trade, condemned slavery. The missionary societies did not. They regarded slavery as a manifestation of the myste-
rious workings of God.

At a practical level, however, the missionary societies and the antislavery
movement shared a common conviction: that the most important single
benefit to bestow upon the slaves within the framework of the slave system was Christianity. It followed, therefore, that individual leaders of the
antislavery movement were closely associated with mission work. Wilberforce himself was a founding member of the Church Missionary Society
and an honored guest and patron of other societies. The situation was further complicated by the fact that some leading churchmen joined in the
principled condemnation of slavery, including Coke's mentor, John Wesley.
Wesley proclaimed, "Liberty is the right of every human creature as soon
as he breathes the vital air. And no human law can deprive him of that right
which derived from a law of nature."[1]

The missionary societies, however, did everything they could to preserve a political distinction between themselves and the antislavery move-

ment. Particular care was taken to instruct prospective missionaries to this effect. Baptist missionaries were warned, "Do not intermeddle with politics. . . . Remember that the object is not to teach the principles and laws of an earthly Kingdom, however important a right understanding of these may be, but the principles and laws of the Kingdom of Christ. Maintain toward all in authority a respectful demeanor. Treat them with the honour to which their office entitles them. Political and party discussions avoid as beneath your office."[2]

The planters' fears were not allayed by the missions' attempt to disassociate themselves from the political dimensions of the slavery question. They correctly perceived that the attack on the slave trade and the appearance of the missionaries were inextricably connected. They were always alive to the suspicion that the missionaries, by deed or by default, were subversives, agents of the antislavery party. Their suspicions were well founded. Missions to the slaves were an innovation; no precedents established what the effects would be. The questions of what the missionaries would teach and, even more important, what the slaves would learn were real ones that could only be answered by events.

The missions gained an initial foothold in Jamaica because outright opposition to them would have been impolitic. The planters could not, at one and the same time, advertise their benevolence and hound preachers to the slaves out of the island. Politic considerations, nevertheless, suggested that the planters' best move was simply to keep the missionaries, as they kept the black preachers, under vigilant supervision. The wars and slave rebellions engendered by the French Revolution, however, together with the success of the attack on the slave trade, made preachers to the slaves the focus of the full force of the planters' antagonism.

Notes

1. John Wesley, *Thoughts on Slavery* (London, 1774), 55–56.
2. Baptist Missionary Society, *Letter of Instructions* (London, n.d.), 13.

The Second Maroon War

Representatives of the Trelawny Town Maroons

This short statement of grievances relates to infringement of sovereignty and access to land, concerns which contributed to the Second Maroon War of 1795–1796. (The First Maroon War had ended in the peace treaties of 1739.) The war took place in the context of white anxiety about the ongoing revolution in nearby Saint-Domingue. On the Maroon side, the land allotted to them in the 1739 treaties was becoming inadequate to support their population. The immediate flash point was the judicial whipping in Montego Bay of two young men from Trelawny Town in the western part of the island, which violated Maroon sovereignty under the terms of the treaty. In response to the Maroon complaints recounted here the governor claimed he would negotiate, but instead arrested the Maroon envoys, declared martial law, and ordered the Maroons to submit to British troops. The Trelawny Town Maroons refused and formed guerrilla bands, successfully holding off the British for several months. It was not until March 1796 that the last fighting group surrendered. The Trelawny Town Maroons were deported to Nova Scotia, and from there to Sierra Leone.

State of grievances complained of by the Maroons of Trelawney Town, made this 19th of July, 1795.[1]

1. They complain of certain ill treatment suffered by two of their young men, by a whipping inflicted on them at Montego-Bay by the hands of a slave (ordered by magistrates); which they say is an infringement of the treaty.

2. That the lands granted them originally by the country for their subsistence, being worn out by long and repeated productions, are not sufficient to afford the provisions necessary for their support; they therefore claim from the island an additional quantity of land, and say, that the adjoining lands, the properties of Messrs. Vaughan and David Schaw, would suit them; and also, the lands commonly called and known by the name of Crews, now Robert Kenyon, would be convenient to them.

This scene, not drawn from life, shows a moment from the Second Maroon War. In the foreground, armed Maroons wait to ambush members of a British military unit who approach from the background along the wooded road. The aquatint, *The Maroons in Ambush on the Dromilly Estate in the parish of Trelawney, Jamaica*, was drawn by James Mérigot (London: Robert Cribb, 1801). Based on a painting by François Jules.

3. They complain against the conduct of Captain Thomas Craskell, the Superintendant appointed to regulate the Maroon Town; and say, that he is not qualified to discharge the necessary duties of the office; for when the young men quarrel and fight, instead of interfering with his authority to adjust their differences, he appears frightened, and runs to his house for safety; and as they have experienced the disposition and abilities of Captain John James (their late Superintendant), they are adverse to the appointment of any other person.

Note

1. Dallas uses "Trelawney town" here but "Trelawny town" in other parts of his text, including in his transcription of the treaty presented in part II. As the modern parish is spelled Trelawny, we follow this convention but do not correct Dallas's text. [Editors' note]

Jonkanoo

Michael Scott

Jonkanoo, more often in slavery-era sources spelled John Canoe, is an annual carnival-style festival that developed in the eighteenth century and is also found in other parts of the African diaspora, especially the Bahamas. It took place at Christmastime and involved music and dance. Slaveholders allowed and sometimes encouraged the Jonkanoo festivities. Jonkanoo was a period of permitted license, in which enslaved people were briefly in control of the streets. Some participants would dress up in masked costumes, including cow masks and characters with houses carried on the head, while others danced as "Set Girls." There has been considerable debate about the origins and meaning of Jonkanoo. Most scholars who have studied it believe it shows important African influence, and, while it was for a long time understood as a secular festival, more recent scholarship has emphasized its religious significance. Jonkanoo remains a live part of contemporary Jamaican culture.

Debates about the origins and significance of Jonkanoo form part of a broader set of considerations about how, and how far, Jamaica's African heritage has shaped its history and culture. Most scholars now agree that African cultural patterns and norms have strongly contributed to all aspects of Jamaican culture, both expressive (in areas such as music and dance) and everyday (foodways, family life, patterns of social interaction). This is despite institutional power's consistent favoring of European-derived cultural and social forms. Sophisticated historical research on Africa in the period of the slave trade has enabled scholars to connect specific Jamaican historical phenomena to particular events and processes in African history. This scholarship moves beyond an older debate between, on the one hand, the search for African "roots" and, on the other, an emphasis on the "routes" through which particular social and cultural practices were transformed in the Americas.

There are many descriptions of Jonkanoo from the period of slavery. This one is from Michael Scott's 1833 novel Tom Cringle's Log, *one of a series set largely at sea. Scott had spent time in Jamaica and was a close observer. His description is clearly proslavery and uses racist forms of description, such as referring to the Jonkanoo performer's hands as "paws." Nevertheless, Scott provides one of the most detailed*

*contemporary accounts of the costumes, music, dances, and behavior that made up
Jonkanoo.*

This day was the first of the Negro Carnival, or Christmas Holydays, and
at the distance of two miles from Kingston the sound of the negro drums
and horns, the barbarous music and yelling of the different African tribes,
and the more mellow singing of the Set Girls, came off upon the breeze loud
and strong.

When we got nearer, the wharfs and different streets, as we successively
opened them, were crowded with blackamoors, men, women, and children,
dancing and singing and shouting, and all rigged out in their best. When we
landed on the agents' wharf, we were immediately surrounded by a group
of these merry-makers, which happened to be the Butchers' John Canoe
party, and a curious exhibition it unquestionably was. The prominent character was, as usual, the John Canoe or Jack Pudding. He was a light, active,
clean-made young Creole negro, without shoes or stockings; he wore a pair
of light jean small-clothes, all too wide, but confined at the knees, below and
above, by bands of red tape. He wore a splendid blue velvet waistcoat, with
old-fashioned flaps coming down over his hips, and covered with tarnished
embroidery. His shirt was absent on leave, I suppose, but at the wrists of
his coat he had tin or white iron frills, with loose pieces attached, which
tinkled as he moved, and set off the dingy paws that were stuck through
these strange manacles, like black wax tapers in silver candlesticks. His coat
was an old blue artillery uniform one, with a small bell hung to the extreme points of the swallow-tailed skirts, and three tarnished epaulets; one
on each shoulder, and, O ye immortal gods! O Mars armipotent! the biggest
of the three stuck at his rump, the *point d'appui* for a sheep's tail. He had an
enormous cocked hat on, to which was appended in front a white false-face
or mask, of a most methodistical expression, while, Janus-like, there was
another face behind, of the most quizzical description, a sort of living An-
tithesis, both being garnished and overtopped with one coarse wig, made of
the hair of bullocks' tails, on which the *chapeau* was strapped down with a
broad band of gold lace.

He skipped up to us with a white wand in one hand and a dirty handkerchief in the other, and with sundry moppings and mowings, first wiping my
shoes with his *mouchoir*, then my face, (murder, what a flavour of salt fish
and onions it had!) he made a smart enough pirouette, and then sprung on
the back of a nondescript animal, that now advanced capering and jumping about after the most grotesque fashion that can be imagined. This was

This is one of seven images of urban Jonkanoo published by Isaac
Mendes Belisario, a Jamaican Jewish artist. It shows the masked and
headdressed "actor boy" figure lavishly dressed in "muslin, silk, satin
and ribbons," the Jonkanoo band of fife and drums, and a crowd of
onlookers. The participants and watching crowd include people of a
range of skin colors (although none are definitively white) and apparent
social backgrounds. The light-skinned woman and child on the left are
dressed in fashionable European styles, while some others wear cheaper
clothing, and other women wear African Jamaican–style head ties.
Belisario thus accentuates the cross-class interest in Jonkanoo. The actor
boy remains one of the most iconic images in Jamaica today. *Koo, Koo, or
Actor-Boy*, lithograph by Isaac Mendes Belisario, plate 5 from the series
*Sketches of Character in Illustration of the Habits, Occupation and Costume of
the Negro Population in the Island of Jamaica* (Kingston: Adolphe Duperly,
1838). Reprinted in *Belisaro: Sketches of a Character. A Historical Biography of
a Jamaican Artist,* by Jackie Ranston (Kingston: Mill Press, 2008), 251.

the signal for the music to begin. The performers were two gigantic men, dressed in calf-skins entire, head, four legs, and tail. The skin of the head was made to fit like a hood, the two fore-feet hung dangling down in front, one over each shoulder, while the other two legs, or hind-feet, and the tail, trailed behind on the ground; deuce another article had they on in the shape of clothing except a handkerchief, of some flaming pattern, tied round the waist. There were also two flute-players in sheep-skins, looking still more outlandish from the horns on the animals' heads being preserved: and three stout fellows, who were dressed in the common white frock and trowsers, who kept sounding on bullocks' horns. These formed the band as it were, and might be considered John's immediate tail or following; but he was also accompanied by about fifty of the butcher negroes, all neatly dressed—blue jackets, white shirts, and Osnaburgh trowsers, with their steels and knife-cases by their sides, as bright as Turkish yataghans, and they all wore clean blue and white striped aprons. I could see and tell what *they* were; but the *Thing* John Canoe had perched himself upon I could make nothing of. At length I began to comprehend the device.

The *Magnus Apollo* of the party, the poet and chief musician, the non-descript already mentioned, was no less than the boatswain of the butcher gang, answering to the driver in an agricultural one. He was clothed in an entire bullock's hide, horns, tail, and the other particulars, the whole of the skull being retained, and the effect of the voice growling through the jaws of the beast was most startling. His legs were enveloped in the skin of the hind-legs, while the arms were cased in that of the fore, the hands protruding a little above the hoofs, and, as he walked reared up on his hind-legs, he used, in order to support the load of the John Canoe, who had perched on his shoulders, like a monkey on a dancing bear, a strong stick, or sprit, with a crutch top to it, which he leant his breast on every now and then.

After the creature, which I will call the *Device* for shortness, had capered with its extra load, as if it had been a feather, for a minute or two, it came to a stand-still, and, sticking the end of the sprit into the ground, and tuck-ing the crutch of it under its chin, it motioned to one of the attendants, who thereupon handed, of all things in the world, a fiddle to the ox. He then shook off the John Canoe, who began to caper about as before, while the Device set up a deuced good pipe, and sung and played, barbarously enough, I will admit, to the tune of Guinea Corn, the following ditty:—

"Massa Buccra lob for see
Bullock caper like monkee—
Dance, and shump, and poke him toe,
Like one humane person—just so."

And hereupon the tail of the beast, some fifty strong, music men, John Canoe and all, began to rampauge about, as if they had been possessed by a devil whose name was Legion:—

"But Massa Buccra have white love,
Soft and silken like one dove.
To brown girl—him barely shivel—
To black girl—oh, Lord, de Devil!"

Here the morrice-dancers began to circle round old Tailtackle, keeping him on the move, spinning round like a weathercock in a whirlwind, while they shouted, "Oh, massa, one *macaroni*[1] if you please." To get quit of their importunity, Captain Transom gave them one. "Ah, good massa, tank you, sweet massa!" And away danced John Canoe and his tail, careering up the street.

In the same way, all the other crafts and trades had their Gumbi-men, Horn-blowers, John Canoes, and Nondescript. The Gardeners came nearest of any thing I had seen before to the Mayday boys in London, with this advantage, that their Jack-in-the-Green was incomparably more beautiful, from the superior bloom of the larger flowers used in composing it.

The very children, urchins of five and six years old, had their Lilliputian John Canoes and *Devices*. But the beautiful part of the exhibition was the Set Girls. They danced along the streets, in bands of from fifteen to thirty. There were brown sets, and black sets, and sets of all the intermediate gradations of colour. Each set was dressed pin for pin alike, and carried umbrellas or parasols of the same colour and size, held over their nice showy, well put on *toques,* or Madras handkerchiefs, all of the same pattern, tied round their heads, fresh out of the fold. They sang, as they swam along the streets in the most luxurious attitudes. I had never seen more beautiful creatures than there were amongst the brown sets—clear olive complexions, and fine faces, elegant carriages, splendid figures,—full, plump, and magnificent.

But, as if the whole city had been tom-fooling, a loud burst of military music was now heard, and the north end of the street we were ascending, which leads out of the *Place d' Armes* or parade, that occupies the centre of the town, was filled with a cloud of dust, that rose as high as the house tops, through which the head of a column of troops sparkled; swords, and bayonets, and gay uniforms glancing in the sun. This was the Kingston regiment marching down to the Court-house in the lower part of the town, to mount the Christmas guards, which is always carefully attended to, in case any of the John Canoes should take a small fancy to burn or pillage the town, or to rise and cut the throats of their masters, or any little innocent recreation of the kind, out of compliment to Dr Lushington, or Messrs Macauley [*sic*] and Babington.[2]

Notes

1. A quarter dollar. [Note in original]
2. Scott is referring to British abolitionists Stephen Lushington, Thomas Babington, and Zachary Macaulay; he is suggesting that abolitionism risks rebellion. [Editors' note]

Provision Grounds

Sidney Mintz

As well as working to produce the commercial crops of the plantations, most en-
slaved people in Jamaica also had to grow their own food. They did so on the poorer,
usually steeply sloping land that made up the backlands of many estates. This sys-
tem contrasted with that in use in some other slave societies, such as Barbados or
most of the US South, where slaveholders either purchased or organized the produc-
tion of the food consumed by slaves. The provision ground system had important
consequences. It forced enslaved people to do additional work, which they often had
to do at night. But it also created an area of work that was not directly under the
control of the slaveholders, and it gave enslaved people the chance to sell surplus
provisions they raised.

Sidney Mintz, a legendary anthropologist of the Caribbean, conducted fieldwork
in Jamaica in the early 1950s. His interest in the historical background of Caribbean
peasantries led to his research on enslaved people's work to raise subsistence crops.
In this piece, he describes the Jamaican provision ground system and the marketing
networks that it supported. Mintz argues that the growth of internal markets dur-
ing slavery was a crucial element that led to the construction of a peasant society
after emancipation.

Where an estate had land not wanted for cane, the slaves were usually allowed to cultivate food crops on it in their spare time. When war threatened
or when for other reasons food imports were insufficient to meet the demand for them, laws were usually passed requiring estate owners to undertake the cultivation of a stipulated quantity of land in foodstuffs as an estate
operation. At the same time, the unsupervised cultivation of food stocks by
the slaves themselves grew steadily more important whenever the estate
contained land to support this activity.

The slaves used such land to produce a variety of foods, such as tree
crops, vegetables, and edible herbs and roots, as well as craft materials.
These foods and materials were raised primarily for their own use. But
eventually—and the details of the process are regrettably dim—surpluses

Pencil and watercolor sketch, *Afro-Jamaicans Carrying Goods on Their Heads, Jamaica, 1808–1815,* by English artist William Berryman, who lived in Jamaica in the early nineteenth century. From the Library of Congress Prints and Photographs Division, Washington, DC, reproduction no. LC-DIG-ppmsca-13415, call no. DRWG 1—Berryman, no. 130 (AA size) [P&P].

came to be taken to local markets and exchanged for other commodities or sold for cash. The proceeds of these transactions accrued entirely to the slaves, apparently from the very first day. Market day, customarily held on Sunday so as not to interfere with estate cultivation, became an important social and economic institution.

Information on the agricultural implements used by the slaves is discouragingly scanty. The most important were the bush knife, or cutlass, and the short-handled hoe. With regard to the crops generally preferred for cultivation and cuisine, our information is again less than satisfactory. Several early authors suggest that the slaves preferred to cultivate plantains (and bananas?), corn, and vegetables rather than root crops, attributing this preference to either imprudence or laziness. The planters themselves preferred to see root crops planted since these would better survive hurricanes. Renny (1807: 87) believed it was the slaves' preference for plantains and corn that led them to neglect the root crops.[1] And yet yams, sweet potatoes, dasheen, tanniers, cassava, and the like could hardly have become established as preferred peasant foods only after the start of the nineteenth century. It seems fair to suppose, therefore, that any favouritism the slave cultivators may have shown for plantain, corn, and vegetables over root crops could have arisen as much from the market situation as from anything else, and it is possible that these items were supplied in significant quantities to naval and merchant vessels. That the planters never actively interfered with the slave cultivators' crop choices is in any case of great interest, and seems to underline the mutual respect for customary arrangements which held between the estate owners or managers and the slaves.

As settlement and the sugar industry and trade increased, activity in the capital town and in the ports of the island would also have grown. New demands for food supplies would have been met by slaves who sold in officially designated and other marketplaces the produce they raised in their spare time on estate lands.

Since it was the individual slaves or slave households who produced provisions on the estate backlands, then clearly they would be the sellers of surplus produce. Either individual slaves would go marketing, or else they would make voluntary agreements among themselves for marketing one another's produce.

By the time the nineteenth-century observers had begun to write of the markets and the slaves' role in them, the pattern had well over a century of traditional practice behind it. No really important new crops entered into the slaves' cultivation, diet, or marketing after 1800; and the slave code which guaranteed rights to market had long been in force. After Emancipation, many new markets would appear, and the scope of economic activity open to the freedmen would be much increased. But Emancipation, insofar as marketing and cultivation practices were concerned, only widened opportunities and increased alternatives; apparently it did not change their nature substantially.

Note

1. Robert Renny, *A History of Jamaica* (London: J. Cawthorn, 1807). [Editors' note]

The Liberation War of 1831

Henry Bleby

In December 1831 enslaved people in Jamaica took up arms for their freedom in the biggest rebellion ever to take place in a British colony dominated by slavery. Beginning on Kensington estate in the parish of St. James, the insurrection rapidly spread to encompass most of the western half of the island. The initial plan was to refuse to work after the Christmas holiday until slaveholders agreed to emancipation, but this strike quickly became a military struggle. For just over a week, rebels controlled parts of the island; the war for freedom was eventually suppressed using the forces of the Royal Navy as well as the local, largely white, Jamaican militia force. At the heart of the rebellion was a group of men who had carefully planned it over weeks, perhaps months. Their leader was Samuel Sharpe, commonly referred to as Daddy Sharpe, who lived in Montego Bay and was a member of a Baptist congregation. Hence the rebellion is sometimes called "Sam Sharpe's rebellion," the "Christmas rebellion," or the "Baptist War."

Henry Bleby, a missionary with the Wesleyan Methodist Missionary Society, was living in Jamaica at the time of the rebellion. Along with other Nonconformist missionaries, he was accused of fomenting the rebellion, and a mob of white men attacked him. After the suppression of the rebellion, Bleby frequently visited the jail where Sharpe and other prisoners were held. His detailed reports of his discussions with Sharpe give some insight into the planning and organization of their struggle.

Mr Murray and myself very frequently visited the gaol, and spent a great deal of time in conversation with [the prisoners]. Samuel Sharpe fully confirmed all that [Edward] Hylton had told us, adding many particulars which Hylton had failed to remember, and admitted himself to be the originator of the insurrection. The plan was devised entirely by himself; and it was he that led all the others to believe, that they had actually been made free, and persuaded them to assert their claim to freedom. The plan proposed to be acted upon by Sharpe was that of *passive resistance*, and to fight only in case the "buckras" used force to compel them to turn out and work as slaves.[1] He thought that if they all "sat down," and refused to go to work again in the capacity of slaves after Christmas, carefully abstaining from offering violence to any person, it would be a very difficult thing for the masters to force such an immense body of people to work against their will. It was probable that a few would have to be punished, and perhaps put to death; and he for one was prepared to die rather than continue in slavery: but if the people showed themselves firm in their refusal to work, they must in the end succeed in obtaining their freedom. The burning of the plantations, and the violence offered to the whites, were no part of his design; and he said that when he saw the first incendiary fire break out, and then another, and another, in rapid succession, he knew that his whole plan was rendered abortive; for now the "buckras" would shoot and murder the people without mercy, and have an apology for doing so; and he gave up all hope of their obtaining freedom at that time.

Gardner and Dove, well known as "Colonel Gardner and Captain Dove," stated that they were present one morning at a second breakfast, at the house of George Guthrie at Cunningham Hill; and there were several others present. Guthrie, who was one of Mr Grignon's slaves, said, "Well, friends, I hope the time will soon come when we shall have privilege, and we shall drink our wine in free. I hope we shall soon have Little Breeches under our feet." Gardner said, "What this 'Little Breeches' mean?" Guthrie answered, "He is my master, Mr Grignon; and I hear him say, *the king going to give us black people free; but he hope that all his friends will be of his mind, and spill our blood first.*" Gardner and Dove both said they believed that the free paper had really come, because Samuel Sharpe told them that he had read it in the papers, and they put very great confidence in Sharpe: and Sharpe sent a man, named Edward Ramsay, round to all the properties, to tell the people that the free paper had come. Gardner also said, that, at a meeting at which he and Dove and others were present, Sam Sharpe spoke to them for a long time on the subject of slavery, and told them what he had read in the papers concerning it: and he addressed them in such a manner that he, Gardner, was wrought up almost to a state of madness. He had not been very hearty in the cause before, but after that he entered into it with all his soul.

The insurrection, therefore, it is manifest, was planned by one person, and that individual himself a slave. Samuel Sharpe was the man whose active brain devised the project; and he had sufficient authority with those around him to carry it into effect, having acquired an extraordinary degree of influence amongst his fellow-slaves. I had much conversation with him whilst he was in confinement; and found him certainly the most intelligent and remarkable slave I ever met. I had an opportunity of observing that he possessed intellectual and oratorical powers above the common or-

This is an early work by Duperly, who went on to become a significant photographer of Jamaican scenes. Many estates, including Roehampton in St. James, were burned during the rebellion of 1831–1832. *The Destruction of the Roehampton Estate*, lithograph by Adolphe Duperly (Kingston: Duperly Lithographic, 1832).

der; and this was the secret of the extensive influence which he exercised. I heard him two or three times deliver a brief extemporaneous address to his fellow-prisoners on religious topics, many of them being confined together in the same cell; and I was amazed both at the power and freedom with which he spoke, and at the effect which was produced upon his auditory. He appeared to have the feelings and passions of his hearers completely at his command; and when I had listened to him once, I ceased to be surprised at what Gardner had told me, "that when Sharpe spoke to him and others on the subject of slavery," he, Gardner, was "wrought up almost to a state of madness."

Sharpe acknowledged to me that he had, as an individual, no reason to find fault with the treatment he had received as a slave. His master, Samuel Sharpe, Esq., and the family, were always very kind to him, and he had never been flogged beyond the occasional and slight correction which he had received when a boy. But he thought, and he learnt from the Bible, that the whites had no more right to hold black people in slavery, than the black people had to make the white people slaves; and, for his own part, he would rather die than live in slavery. "Minister," he said, while his frame expanded, and his eagle-eye seemed to shoot forth rays of light, "I would rather die upon yonder gallows than live in slavery!" He expressed deep regret that such an extensive destruction of property and life had resulted from the conspiracy which he had promoted, but declared that this formed no part of his plan. He did not wish to destroy the estates, nor did he desire that any person should be injured: his only object was to obtain freedom. But to his great disappointment he found that the spirit of revolt, once evoked, was not susceptible of control. He had not sufficiently taken into account the excitable character of the negroes whom he sought to benefit, and their probable want of self-government when they should be suddenly emancipated from the yoke to which they were subject; and he too hastily concluded that he should find them the same patient and submissive beings as he had ever known them, when, crouching under the lash, they yielded an implicit obedience to the despotic authority of their owners, which, until he suggested the idea, they never thought of shaking off or resisting.

Note

1. *Buckras* was a Jamaican term for white people. [Editors' note]

Apprenticeship and Its Conflicts

Diana Paton

An 1833 British act of Parliament abolishing slavery came into effect on 1 August 1834. Enslaved people did not immediately become free. Instead, slavery was replaced by a system known as apprenticeship, in which those who had been enslaved were required to work for their former owners for 40.5 hours a week without pay. The most significant change was that estate managers were not allowed to use physical violence against apprentices, but had to call on a newly created set of officials known as stipendiary magistrates to determine punishments. The system produced many conflicts, as apprentices tried to defend their new rights, while former slaveholders tried to maintain maximum control. Many conflicts began as disputes about the organization of time. Historian Diana Paton describes one such conflict, which took place in autumn 1834.

At the beginning of crop time, Thomas Learny, the overseer, tried to rearrange his apprentices' work schedule so as to increase the hours in which the sugar works ran. He claimed that he wanted to divide the gang into two spells, one working from 4 a.m. to noon, the other from noon to 8 p.m.; the apprentices reported that he tried to divide them into three spells, one from 3 a.m. to noon, one from noon to 10 p.m., and the remaining one working from 6 a.m. to 6 p.m. in the fields. The apprentices refused to work outside of daylight hours, grounding their refusal in the changed legal circumstances of apprenticeship. According to Learny, they declared themselves "as well aware of the law as I was myself."[1] Other apprentices reported that one of their number, Leanthe Allweather, said that "negro had no right to be worked at night—that Buckra was imposing on them, and that the law was not so."[2]

When, the next day, the apprentices did not divide themselves into early and late spells, but instead all arrived in the field and sugar works at 6 a.m., Thomas Learny called in [magistrate] Frederick White. The apprentices said that White "could do nothing for them" and in spite of his instructions that they must obey the overseer in the matter of work hours, continued to oppose the new arrangements.

White interpreted Leanthe Allweather's claim that "the law was not so" as a direct challenge to his authority and ordered her into the stocks to await a sentence in the house of correction. He also tried to force her to relinquish care of her infant child. When Allweather refused to go to the stocks without her baby, White, according to Gibraltar apprentices, tried to remove the infant by force. Another apprentice, Francis French, intervened to help her, calling out, "Eh can't you give the woman liberty to loose the child off her back instead of pulling and hauling it this way, are you going to kill the child."[3] The conflict had now come to be about White's interactions with the apprentices, and in particular his disregard for a woman's relationship with her child, as much as it was about the organization of labor time. White ordered that French be flogged. When none of the apprentice constables flogged French to White's satisfaction, he ordered multiple further punishments.

At this point, most of the apprentices left the estate. Their rejection of White's authority did not, however, entail complete rejection of the law. A group of nine walked through some of the most mountainous terrain in Jamaica, reaching stipendiary magistrates Archibald Palmer and Patrick Dunne in the parish of Port Royal three days later. Their complaints focused more on White's unfairness, refusal to listen, and arbitrary punishments than on the original conflict with Learny. Palmer and Dunne took down a detailed affidavit and sent it on to Sligo, where it became part of a dossier of cases that resulted in White's eventual removal from the magistracy. Palmer and Dunne then told the apprentices to go back to Gibraltar, assuring them "that redress would be afforded if their rights had been infringed on."[4]

We could surmise, though, that the apprentices' confidence in the law was diminished in the next week. There is no evidence that they received any of Palmer and Dunne's promised "redress." Instead, when they returned to Gibraltar, Learny once again called in White, who sent a group of four women to the Kingston house of correction for running away. By late November Learny reported that the estate's apprentices were "working well" according to the two eight-hour-spell system. But he also had to consider the fact that two fires had mysteriously appeared in the trash house the night of the "disturbances," and no one on the estate was willing to help put them out—an indication perhaps, that, while they hoped to be able to gain the support of lawful authorities, the Gibraltar apprentices did not put all their confidence in the state.[5]

White, the representative of the state, was called in by Learny with the intention of suppressing the resistance of the gang workers. Learny needed White because the law made it illegal for him to directly punish his workers, and because he knew that the apprentices were fully aware of that law, and would act against him if he tried to break it. The struggle began as one between a planter and his apprentices, but quickly drew in several stipendiary magistrates, pitting apprentices against one of them. It also expanded from its beginnings in a conflict over work hours to become a conflict around maternal rights as well, when White attempted to remove Leanthe Allweather's child from her. Finally, the apprentices made use of a wide variety of tactics which drew on slaves' traditional methods of struggle and which operated simultaneously within and beyond the law.

Notes

1. Statement of Thomas Learny 18 November 1834, enc. in Sligo to Spring Rice No 28, 29 December 1834, PP 1835 (177) L (hereafter "Learny statement").
2. Affidavit of John McLeod, Lavinia Duncan, Catherine Willis, and Betsy Shelly, 19 October 1834, enc. in Sligo to Aberdeen, 7 February 1835, CO 137/197 (hereafter "McLeod affidavit").
3. McLeod affidavit.
4. A. L. Palmer and Patrick Dunne to Sligo, Private, 19 October 1834, Rhodes House MSS Brit Emp S 22 G 60.
5. Learny statement.

An Apprentice's Story

James Williams

The conflicts produced by the new system of apprenticeship attracted attention from abolitionists in Britain. In 1836 two of the most prominent, Joseph Sturge and David Harvey, visited the West Indies to investigate the system. They aimed to gather information on the abuses taking place under apprenticeship in order to publicize them and thus strengthen the campaign for a full abolition of slavery. In Jamaica, Sturge and Harvey met James Williams, a young apprentice who had suffered repeated punishments. He had been repeatedly imprisoned by stipendiary magistrates as a result of complaints against him by his master and mistress. Sturge paid to purchase Williams's freedom and brought him to England, where he worked with another abolitionist, Archibald Palmer, to produce an account of his experiences. The resulting pamphlet recorded not only Williams's time as an apprentice but also the suffering of many other apprentices. The pamphlet was widely sold in Britain and helped to turn public opinion there against apprenticeship. The system was finally abolished in 1838, two years earlier than had been planned.

When them try me, massa said, that one Friday I was going all round the house with big stone in my hand, looking for him and his sister, to knock them down. I was mending stone wall round the house by massa's order; I was only a half-grown boy that time. I told magistrate, I never do such thing, and offer to bring evidence about it; he refuse to hear me or my witness; would not let me speak; he sentence me to get 39 lashes; eight policemen was present, but magistrate make constable flog at first; them flog the old driver first, and me next; my back all cut up and cover with blood,— could not put on my shirt—but massa say, constable not flogging half hard enough, that my back not cut at all;—then the magistrate make one of the police take the cat to flog the other three men, and him flog most unmerciful. It was Henry James, Thomas Brown, and Adam Brown that the police flog. Henry James was an old African; he had been put to watch large corn-piece—no fence round it—so the cattle got in and eat some of the corn—he couldn't help it, but the magistrate flog him for it. After the flogging, he got quite sick, and began coughing blood; he went to the hot-house,[1] but got no attention, them say him not sick. He go to Capt. Dillon to complain about it; magistrate give him paper to carry to massa, to warn him to court on Thursday; that day them go to Brown's Town, Capt. Dillon and a new magistrate, Mr. Rawlinson, was there. Capt. Dillon say that him don't think Henry James was sick; he told him to go back, and come next Thursday, and he would have doctor to examine him; the old man said he did not know whether he should live till Thursday. He walk away, but before he get out of the town, he drop down dead—all the place cover with blood that he puke up. He was quite well before the flogging, and always said it was the flogging bring on the sickness.

Same day Henry James dead, Massa carry me and Adam Brown before magistrate; he said I did not turn out sheep till nine o'clock on Wednesday morning; I told magistrate the sheep was kept in to be dressed, and I was eating my breakfast before dressing them; but Capt. Dillon sentence me and Adam Brown to lock up in the dungeon at Knapdale for ten days and nights; place was cold and damp, and quite dark—a little bit of a cell, hardly big enough for me to lie full length; them give me a pint of water and two little cocoa or plantain a day;—hardly able to stand up when we come out, we was so weak; massa and misses said we no punish half enough; massa order we straight to our work, and refuse to let we go get something to eat.

The week after we let out of dungeon, Mr. Rawlinson come to Penshurst, and tell some of the people he not done with me yet about the sheep; we only put in dungeon for warning, and he would come back next Thursday, and try we again for it; he did come Thursday about four o'clock, and send call us; when we come, him and massa and misses was at dinner—we sent in say we come—them said, Never mind till morning. We know this magistrate come to punish we for nothing, so we go over to Capt. Dillon at Southampton to complain; he write paper next morning to police-station, and policeman take us home. Mr. Rawlinson gone already, and Misses said he left order that we to lock up every night, and keep at work in day-time, till he come back—but police say no, Capt. Dillon order that we not to punish till he try we himself on Thursday, at Brown's Town;—Them took us there, but Capt. Dillon did not come, but send paper for the other magistrate to try it, and said them couldn't try us for the same thing again. Mr. Rawlinson said it was not the same thing; Mr. Senior said, No, we had been insolent to him; we call constable to give evidence, and he said we not insolent; Then magistrate say to Mr. Senior, "you mean insolence by manner." Massa answer, "Yes, that is what I mean, insolence by manner." It was magistrate self that put massa up to say this;—Then the magistrate sentence us to get twenty lashes apiece, which was given in front of court-house by police; the punishment was very severe—both of us fainted after it—we lie down on the ground for an hour after it, not able to move; A free man in the place sent some rum and camphor to bring we round. We went home that night, and went into hospital—them would hardly receive us, we stop there that night and Friday, lock up all day and night, and no feeding; Saturday morning massa turned both of us out—we back all sore, quite raw, and we not able to stoop.

Note

1. Hospital. [Note in original]

Because of 1833

Andrew Salkey

Andrew Salkey's epic poem Jamaica *retells history for a newly independent nation. Born in Panama in 1928 to Jamaican parents, Salkey was raised in the island and became one of the country's most prolific writers, though he lived most of his adult life in the UK and the United States. "Because of 1833" comes from a section of the work named "Slavery to Liberation," which defines and reflects on a chronology for the island's history, with poems entitled "Because of 1692" (the Port Royal earthquake), "Because of 1796" (the Second Maroon War), "Because of 1865" (the Morant Bay Rebellion), "Because of 1907" (the Kingston earthquake), and, here, "Because of 1833"— the abolition of slavery. Throughout, the poem emphasizes the importance of land as the foundation of the people's freedom: a place for the cultivation of one's own crops but also for the establishment of history and culture. First published in 1973, shortly before the start of Jamaica's period of Democratic Socialism, lines like "I always countin' somebody else benefits, / stackin' somebody else foreign balance" speak to contemporary concerns as well as to the historical experience of emancipation.*

And there are the dreams,
the waving corn,
free red hairs,
loose in the Undertaker Wind
that haunted Quashie's adobe huts;
there are the sessions
to which Clarkson and Wilberforce
were denied admission: slaves only

Other things slip
into these dreams:
a stifled laugh,
a small gesture towards a grand veranda;
and the dreamers shift
on torn skin;

Lithograph depicting the abolition of slavery in Jamaica, by Thomas Picken, published by R. Cartwright, London, 1838. Picken shows the central square in Spanish Town filled with newly free people, which the caption describes as members of the congregation of the Baptist missionary James Mursell Phillippo. Thomas Picken / © Michael Graham-Stewart / Bridgeman Images no. MGS120624. Used by permission of Bridgeman Images / a private collection.

vines, bitter cords,
strap sweet hopes,
while blindfolds drop
near our feet:
the bleary-eyed stumbling
in the half-light,
and latifundia profits
crash down
like quarry stones:

for we know one backyard,
one set o' lash; one life we know;
'cause is that all a-weekday time we did know . . .

nursing bucking urges
like blistered feet;
wanting to run
the length of the land:

'cause is that all a-weekday time we did know . . .

yet,
there are the other tears,
pride, propriety,
and the jangling chains
replaced by different noises:
bitterness,
acute suspects
(hanging around
the boiler house),
acute suspicions,
complexes
(the jangling never
really stopped);
natural right of independent thought,
economics aside,
freedom to choose a burial spot,
freedom to live, freedom to die:

we free! we free!
Lawd, today, we free!

A wash of light,
a swift kitchen knife!
Stupefaction, slice, slice,
disengaging thunderclap,
hammer on anvil (a different symbol,
now), a new position,
a groundin';

a voice asks for a path,
a path for those on their way,
a path with milestones
they'll make
as they go:

we free! we free!
Lawd, today, we free!

Caribbea,
even now,
know we ask;
prepare a path.

Caribbea,
prepare a path.

Consider
the case o' Country
the lonlies' man
in town.

Country jook the mornin'
wit' him finger,
an' ask the 'cestors them:
you did ever talk to the lan'?
You did ever talk real serious to it?
You been diggin' into it, from Africa,
an' you sleep right 'pon top o' it,
since you come,
an' you been slap nex' to dutty
all you' slavin' life. That no lie!
But, you did ever talk real serious to it?
You ever hear what it say 'bout freedom
an' the ways it got,
open up sometimes, sometimes p'rhaps not,
foot into door, ankle get chop off,
sun hot, cold night?

Freedom is as freedom does,
and it didn't accomplish much.

Take that up to the quarry,
and put it to the test.

"Free is shit,"
the man with the shovel said,
bending over and scooping up
the diced quarry pebbles
which were burying
his dusty scaled ankles,
and making a mechanical man of him.

"Free is when them gone,
an' you' lan' come back home
to you in one piece;
free is when them gone f'true,

when them lif' up an' fly 'way like wasp,
when shadow x itself out,
an' you' lan' wrap it two han' roun' you
wit' love," he said, putting a pebble
between his teeth and promising himself
to start discovering the new alternative
he'd had in his thoughts
from first light that morning.

"Free is when you' yard
only grow f'you own rich mineral,
f'you own sugar cane an' banana,
an' f'you own dandelion tea,
an' when the groun' spread out
an' is f'you own,
in life an' deat',
top an' bottom;
everyt'ing else,
any which way or ever,
is one self-foolin'
kind o' mirror."

He stepped out
of the quarry pebbles,
spat,
clasped his hands
into a bunched fist,
raised it to his lips,
blew a tune over it,
smiled (like his Port Antonio cousin
would certainly have
with his face turned away
from the loaded ship),
and said, "I always countin' somebody else benefits,
stackin' somebody else foreign balance,
livin' in somebody else hopes,
walkin' in somebody else clothes.
Is that them think this is, any at all?
Life don't go so."

He walked
slowly

out to the open road,
beat the quarry dust,
out of his shirt,
stamped his boots
hard on the baked marl,
and said, "Fight me an' lose,
an' give me back me lan'
an' give me back me sea
an' give me back me free,
right now."

Caribbea,
prepare that path.

IV

Colonial Freedom

The more than 300,000 apprentices who became free in 1838 greeted their new status with enormous hope, and with outpourings of loyalty to the British Empire and in particular to Queen Victoria. This part's title, "Colonial Freedom," draws attention to the paradox of this emancipation process: slavery's end entrenched colonial rule. In the years to come, many freedpeople's hopes were frustrated, but some were realized. Freedpeople built on their experience during slavery of working on provision grounds to establish "free villages," places where people owned the land they lived on and therefore were not subject to the will of planter landlords. Others settled without legal title on land that was not being used by estates, establishing autonomy at the cost of vulnerability to legal challenge.

Jamaica's sugar-oriented plantation economy nose-dived after 1838. Annual sugar exports fell by more than half between 1832 and 1880 and continued to decline until the beginning of World War I.[1] The change was partly due to freedpeople's reluctance to work on sugar estates at the wages and under the conditions offered by planters. It was compounded by the British Sugar Duties Act of 1846, a result of British campaigns for "free trade" that ended subsidies to agricultural producers. The act set the island's production in competition with sugar produced outside the British Empire, including in neighboring Cuba, which relied on enslaved workers until 1886. Because many of them had acquired land, Jamaican workers were not completely dependent on wage labor and therefore could hold out for wages that sugar planters did not want to pay. Many large landowners were absentees and responded by divesting themselves of Jamaican property, investing in economic activities elsewhere, including in Britain and other parts of the British Empire.

The decline of the white plantocracy opened space for a black and brown middle class, based in merchant activity and the professions, to consolidate itself after emancipation. This group grew out of the population of free people of color that had consolidated itself during the late slavery period.

Free men of color had by 1831 acquired the right to vote and sit in the House of Assembly, subject to property requirements that also applied to whites. After emancipation this group became increasingly separate, culturally and socially, from the majority of the population, even while often claiming to stand for their interests. Early defenses or "vindications" of the island and its people often came from middle-class brown and black Jamaicans, a section of society that would later produce some early nationalist leaders.

Throughout this period the country's black majority faced routine racism in their encounters with white people, who even in decline continued to control key political and economic institutions. Black Jamaicans were not legally excluded from citizenship as they were in, for example, the post–Civil War US South, but all aspects of state activity and official institutional practice assumed their inferiority. In particular, elite and middle-class Jamaicans of whatever color stigmatized cultural and religious practices that they considered African. Black Jamaicans increasingly engaged politically through religion. Missionary churches became African Jamaican–led and African-oriented in style of worship and theology.

In 1865 conflicts that had been developing for years erupted in an uprising in the town of Morant Bay, in St. Thomas in the East parish, led by a Native Baptist preacher, Paul Bogle. The rebellion was brutally suppressed on the orders of the governor, Edward Eyre, and the incident sparked massive debate in Britain and the Caribbean about race and the outcome of emancipation. Many white observers concluded that emancipation had failed. After Morant Bay the centuries-old Jamaica Assembly was abolished. The island lost its long-standing powers of self-government to become a Crown Colony, directly ruled from London. Advocates described the process as "benevolent despotism"; recent historians have seen it as "de-democratization."[2]

Jamaica was not entirely black and white, or even black, white, and a mix of the two, in this period. Significant numbers of people moved from India to work as indentured laborers on Jamaican sugar estates, while smaller numbers also came from China. Some indentured workers, the survivors of the illegal slave trade who had been taken from slave-trading ships by the Royal Navy, were imported from Sierra Leone. These migrations were not on the scale of the movement of indentured workers to Trinidad or Guyana in the same period, but they still significantly affected Jamaica's cultural, social, and political life. By the late nineteenth century the island welcomed migrants from the Levant and hundreds of itinerants from neighboring islands, particularly Cuba and Haiti. These migrations added to complex changes in Jamaica in the decades after slavery's end.

Toward the end of the nineteenth century a new crop, the banana, became a significant part of the island's production, surpassing sugar in export value by 1890.[3] Banana production renewed the local economy. The success of the crop attracted foreign businesses such as the United Fruit Company. The banana economy further stimulated the introduction of tourism as a subsidiary industry early in the twentieth century as the large companies encouraged visitors to travel to the island on the new "banana boats." New hotels and a campaign to promote Jamaica as a health resort for cruise ship travelers helped transform the island's reputation. Development in these areas was dramatically hampered by the Great Earthquake of January 1907. As the world entered the global crisis of World War I, Jamaican society had become more fluid and diverse but was still hierarchical, tested by natural disaster and internal social and political conflict.

Notes

1. Gisela Eisner, *Jamaica, 1830–1930: A Study in Economic Growth* (Manchester: Manchester University Press, 1961), 241–243.
2. Mimi Sheller, *Democracy after Slavery: Black Publics and Peasant Radicalism in Haiti and Jamaica* (Gainesville: University Press of Florida, 2001).
3. Eisner, *Jamaica, 1830–1930*, 239.

Free Villages

Jean Besson

Immediately after the end of slavery, land became the site of intense conflict between those who had been enslaved and those who had once owned enslaved people. Land-owners tried to force freedpeople to work for wages on their estates by charging high rents for estate-based houses to anyone who was not an employee. Many freedpeople responded by doing whatever they could to acquire land of their own, either by purchase or through informal occupation ("squatting"), so that they would not be vulnerable to planter manipulation. Much of the land in these villages became "family land," which could not be sold but was for the use of all the descendants of those who originally acquired it. Although family land has never been recognized in Jamaican law, it is an important element of everyday political economy and social life. Many "free villages" established during the early postemancipation period still have residents descended from those who originally established them, while Jamaicans across the world still make claims on family land.

Martha Brae, near Falmouth in the parish of Trelawny, was originally established by white settlers during slavery. It was transformed in the aftermath of emancipation through informal settlement by the newly free. Since the late 1960s, Jamaican anthropologist Jean Besson has been conducting research about the village and its history. Her work has involved oral histories which have enabled her to trace the establishment of the free village. She describes work with two of the "Old Families" of the village and quotes extensively from interviews she recorded with some of their members about the establishment of Martha Brae as an African Caribbean peasant village.

The Minto Old Family

The Minto Old Family, which was mainly Baptist with a Revival-Zion world-view, traced its ancestry to the parents (names unknown) of three brothers: George Finlayson Minto, John Jarvis Minto, and William Shakespeare Minto. These three brothers and their parents are said to have been emancipated slaves from Irving Tower Plantation bordering Martha Brae who all settled in the planter town. The parents and two of their sons, John Jarvis and William Shakespeare, reportedly purchased five plots in the colonial town, four of which (those bought by the parents and William) subsequently became the Minto family lands (the fifth plot, purchased by John Jarvis, had been forfeited to the Parochial Board). During my earlier fieldwork, the trustee for the Minto family lands was one of William Minto's daughters, Rhoda, who was born around 1897 and died in 1980 at the age of eighty-three. After Rhoda's death the trusteeship for the Minto family lands devolved to Morgan McIntosh, one of her sons from her first set of children, who lived on his own small plot of purchased land at the western edge of Martha Brae across the road from Holland Plantation. He died in July 2001 and was buried in the Martha Brae cemetery. The following is an extract from his narrative, recorded shortly before his mother's death and his assumption of the trusteeship:

> As far as what I know, we had two villages where the slaves used to live. One was Irving Tower. The other one was down "John Ewen" section [a part of Holland Plantation], which now they call it "Carib Road" where the factory is now and the School. The only thing that is down there now [from slavery] is the old breeze-mill [windmill], which is at the William Knibb Memorial High School yard. That's the old, old, breeze-mill; everything pull down save that.
>
> Well now, after slavery, the people began to move from one place to the other. Well, Martha Brae was the first [parochial] capital. You have the soldiers, the police, the government buildings. All those was situated here. Well, in those [slavery] days the [Martha Brae] river was used as the shipping port. Small craft take the produce from down the wharf there, down to the ship in the harbor out there. By process of time Falmouth start to develop. So by process of time, people began to move from the [slave] villages into the township [of Martha Brae].
>
> How did I learn all that? Well, look, I get to know them from the older people. Not even [just] me Mammy. Older than me Mammy. 'Cause there were a lot of old people that I know, you see. Because when I was a small boy, we have a lot of old people living here, which is even older than my [maternal] grandmother. And I know a lot of them, and they tell us what used to happen.
>
> If they were people who'd moved in from the slave villages? Yes, yes; *plenty* of them. Because they was alive in slavery days. My mother's father come from Irving Tower; he was born there . . . his forefathers was slaves; his parents. So you see, he was born there and he leave. That's where he leave from and come here and buy this place.

Sligoville was one of the first free villages established in Jamaica. *Sligoville, with Mission Premises*, engraver unknown, from *Jamaica: Its Past and Present State*, by James M. Phillippo (London: John Snow, 1843), following p. 222.

The Thompson Old Family

Amy Bruce was the oldest living member of the Thompson family line, and of all Martha Brae's Old Families, in the earlier years of my research. Born in Martha Brae in 1892, she died there in 1982, at the age of ninety, and was buried in the village cemetery. By the time of my fieldwork she was widowed and lived alone on a quarter-acre plot that was part of a family-land estate created by her paternal grandfather, an ex-slave from Irving Tower Plantation. This emancipated slave is said to have purchased two pieces of land in Martha Brae, near the lands bought by the Minto ex-slaves and close to the border of Irving Tower Estate: the quarter-acre piece nearer to the center of the village and a one-acre plot (bought for £20) across the street but closer to the river bridge. His family-land estate, which remained in the Thompson Old Family, comprised both of these plots.

Throughout many of my years of fieldwork, Amy's brother William Tapper lived on the second (one-acre) piece of family land. One of the great oral historians of Martha Brae, he died in 1985 at the age of eighty-two. Both he and his wife, who was still alive in 2001, were members of the William Knibb Memorial Baptist Church in Falmouth, for, as he explained, "most of the people here are Baptists in Granville and Martha Brae." William recounted in detail the evolution of Martha Brae as a free village and the history of the Thompson Old Family and its family lands:

All the districts [villages] generally in Jamaica, they are excerpts from slavery; handing down from slavery. The slaves were here working on the farms [plantations], and when they get freedom, you see, you have little districts here, districts there: Granville, Martha Brae, Bounty Hall, Rock, Perth Town, Daniel Town [Trelawny villages]. So you have all the little districts around [and] those older slaves go there and they produce children. . . .

How did they get the land? The churches. The Baptist Church was foremost. William Knibb was a foremost preacher here, and Charles Mann and all those men. I think William Knibb even lose his life [*sic*] fighting to get freedom and lands for the slaves. And the first educational system in Jamaica was through the churches principally. Then the Government began to form, then the people leave the churches and go on their own. But most of it through the churches.

After emancipation, the Baptists got the Martha Brae lands, in the 1840s. Most of the history of the black people don't come in big log-book. They keep it themselves, and grandparents told their children and grand-children. And my grandparents [ex-slaves] told me that the Martha Brae lands were acquired by the church. The church got the land and then despatched it to their members. And this also happened in Martha Brae. The Baptist church—see the Prayer House there [across the road from his yard]. And it was a school and Prayer House. Many of the children went to school there, and Sunday school also.

Well, you see, [in the case of] Martha Brae, the slaves was occupying over Irving Tower. That's the property over there [the plantation bordering the village]; Irving Tower. Well, when they get their freedom now, they launch from there out here to Martha Brae. They were stationed over that side of the property. Because you had a little [sugar] mill over there; Irving Tower mill. There were several estates [in the area]. You have Green Park Estate, Gayles Valley Estate, Tilston Estate—all those estates right up. So the sugar estates occupy the slaves. Well, when they get their freedom, some remain in the barracks there, but some launch out in the little districts. That's why you see you have the districts. Holland is another one too. Holland Estate concern [borders] Irving Tower, [which also] go away down touching Southfield [Estate] and join on with the place they call Potosi [Plantation], and join on to Maxfield [Estate]. Irving Tower was the part where the sugar mill was. The old works was there.

William then recounted the creation and evolution of the Thompson family line and family lands in the context of the free village system and the transformation of Martha Brae. His account underlined the significance of protopeasant capital for land purchase after emancipation. His paternal grandfather, one of eleven sons scattered throughout Jamaica, had been a slave on Irving Tower Plantation. After emancipation, he settled in Martha Brae and bought out two small plots. The grandfather stipulated that these lands should not be sold but should be retained as family land for his descendants in perpetuity:

> He [the grandfather] was in the slave days. Him was an *old* man before him die, but him touch a little of the slavery. Because he said he was over Irving Tower there, that him used to live there when him get the place [lands] to buy out here [in Martha Brae]. He bought it, you see, after the abolition of slavery—apprenticeship. There was an apprenticeship for the slaves. So they get allotted lands for them. That's why you find these little districts [free villages] all over Jamaica. The churches acquired land for the ex-slaves, so those who had a little accommodation [savings] bought land. That is how my grandfather come to get this piece. They had a little money, so they bought the land.
>
> Well, my grandfather, he bought the piece of land that I am living on now, and the part where my sister is living. He make the house over the part where my sister is. Well, my grandfather said the land should not be sold. It is for his heritage going down. It must go from children to grandchildren, right down the line. Well, the grandfather, when his time is expired, he hand it [lands] over to my father [the grandfather's only child]. Father said, "My time is ended"—he hand it to the children. Well, it was quite a few brethrens of us, but all died now, left only myself and me sister over there on the smaller plot, now. So she has that part—the same "lot" [two and a half square chains, i.e., a quarter acre].

Cholera

Samuel Jones

In 1850 the first of two cholera epidemics hit Jamaica, part of the second global cholera pandemic, which also affected India, Europe, and many other parts of the Americas. The disease killed about forty thousand people, or one in every ten. This letter from Baptist missionary Samuel Jones gives us some insight into the epidemic. Reporting back to the Baptist Missionary Society in England, Jones observes the extreme hardship caused by the disease and interprets it as divine punishment for sin. He also sees it as an opportunity for conversions.

Annotto Bay April 8th 1851

My Dear Brother

I write to you now in order to thank you and the Committee and the contributors to the "West India Cholera Fund" generally for your kindness towards us in the time our deep affliction and distress. On behalf of myself and the people under my care I can say that we feel truly grateful for such timely assistance given us in our deep trials. I have felt very great pleasure in being the Almoner of your liberality to the destitute and distressed and to see the big tear starting from the eyes of some of our aged females when I told them that I had a little assistance from their friends in England to give to them, they would exclaim, "Thank God Massa and thank them too." "The Lord mercy is great massa." If the donors had to witness what I have witnessed in this respect they would feel more than paid for contributions. They have the blessings of a great many upon them. In my distribution of that part of it entrusted to my care I have been very careful to give it almost entirely to those who are truly destitute and unable to do for themselves, feeling strongly that those who are able to work ought to work and ought not to be helped to indulge them in their idleness. We have a great number of aged and destitute belonging to our Church here. More in proportion to our number than any Church that I know of, and to them the aid afforded has been exceedingly valuable indeed. By the Missionary Heralds for Feby and March I have been much gratified to see that the Churches contribute so generally and so liberally towards the Cholera Fund. As to myself I never doubted the sympathy with the Jamaica Churches of either the Committee of our Society or of the Churches and when we are in actual distress that sympathy shows itself in a practical manner, much to the credit of all concerned. Several of our aged friends have had the Cholera severely, nevertheless they have survived it, but being aged their recovery is extremely slow, for several months they look haggard and worn having a strange appearance in their countenance which is deathlike. They are unable to do any thing for themselves and it is a question with me whether some of them will ever again be able to do any thing for themselves. I consider these objects of deep pity, and real objects of charity. On their behalf you will allow me to say that whatever help you may be able to afford will be very very serviceable to them. I do not ask for any thing for myself but leave that to be entirely at your own discretion, for though we were severely tried during the prevalence of the Pestilence yet our God was then a "present help to us in time of trouble" and we will trust him still. He has said "I will never leave thee nor forsake thee."[1] We have a God to trust in who is faithful to all his promises: what a strong consolation does that afford!

In the two churches Annotto Bay and Buff Bay we have lost some 120 members by Cholera, and many inquirers besides. I am happy to be able to say that it has now left this part of the Island for some time past in fact we have had but little of it in this Parish since February, but it pays a second visit to some places and takes a good many off the second time but generally the second visit is not of long continuance, but it soon disappears again. Whether we may be subject to a second visit of it or not is known only to Him who knows all things, and who disposes all things according to his unerring counsel. Our sins doubtless call loudly for another visitation upon us. Doubtless you are desirous to know what effects the visitation has left upon our people generally, and so far as we can see it is our duty to let you know this. We see now very plainly that it has left different effects upon different persons. It is evident that some instead of being softened down to deep repentance and sorrow for their sins by which they have been seen and felt, have been actually hardened and instead of being better, they are worse, more desperate and presumptuous in wickedness than they were before. Others are considerably frightened by it, so as to attend the means of grace much more than they did before, and many of them wish to be inquirers, but whether their fear of the Cholera will be blessed of the spirit of God so that it may issue in a change from sin to righteousness in their future conduct will be proved by time. We are willing to hope for the best, although looking what man is we hope as it were with trembling. In fact we now see some signs to give us alarm for as the Cholera seems to be at a distance carelessness and indifference to religious duties begin to creep on, some if not many break the vows which they made when it was as it were staring them in their faces. However we trust that it will prove to be a blessing to many and that there will be a permanent awakening both among professors and non-professors through out the length and breath of the [*sic*]. My heart yearns for such an awakening "O Lord revive thy work in the midst of the years, in the midst of the years O Lord in Judgment remember mercy."[2] We surely have had the Judgment heavily; O that following it we may have the revival.

My Dear Brother
Yours Affectionately
Samuel Jones

Notes

1. Jones here quotes from Hebrews 13:5. [Editors' note]
2. Jones here quotes from the Bible, Habakkuk 3:2. [Editors' note]

Black Voters

Swithin Wilmot

During slavery, only a tiny minority of Jamaicans were able to participate in elec-
toral politics. After 1838 there were no racial restrictions on the franchise, but only
those who owned or rented property of a certain value were permitted to vote, and
the vote was restricted to men. In these circumstances the electorate remained small.
Nevertheless, relatively successful black freedmen could vote. In the 1840s and 1850s
several black candidates ran for seats in the House of Assembly. Some of them, as
historian Swithin Wilmost explains, effectively appealed to this new electorate on
the basis of both racial and class solidarity.

Charles Price, a black builder and master carpenter in Kingston, successfully contested a seat for the parish of St John in the 1849 general elections.
Price served his political apprenticeship in the Kingston Common council,
and along with Edward Vickars, who in 1847 became the first black member
of the Assembly, strongly insisted on the blacks' entitlement to representation in Jamaica's public institutions. St John was ideal for Price to fulfil
his political ambitions. Before emancipation, large-scale coffee and sugar
cultivation had declined in the steep, fertile and well-watered lands of the
Juan de Bolas Mountains, and free black and free coloured small farmers,
who combined a variety of crops such as coffee, pimento, provisions, fruit
trees and hardwoods, had developed instead. This process accelerated after 1838 when freedpeople settled on abandoned coffee plantations and on
the margins of pens, as well as along the old sugar road from Lluidas Vale
to the shipping ports on the south coast, via the steep climb to Point Hill
and down to Guanaboa Vale. This altered pattern of land settlement found
its political expression in the immediate postslavery period. George Price,
planter at Worthy Park and Custos of St John, noted that St John's politics
was dominated "almost entirely [by] black men, mountain settlers."[1]

In 1849, Charles Price jointly canvassed with Samuel Queensborough
Bell, a coloured carpenter and a former bookkeeper, whose family roots
were grounded among St John's settlers who had already elected him to

One of the earliest photographic images of Jamaica. *Marketplace in Falmouth, Jamaica, 1844,* lithograph of a daguerreotype by Adolph Duperly, from his book *Daguerian Excursions in Jamaica* (Kingston, 1850). Courtesy of National Library of Jamaica.

the parish vestry. The settlers warmed to Bell and Price since they were members of the "middle class" and were "men from among themselves" who could be trusted "to watch over and guard their interests."[2] Their opponents were John Aris, a coloured sugar planter, who had represented the parish since 1841, and Francis Lynch, a white solicitor in Spanish Town, whose father-in-law, Dr William Turner, was the Custos of St Catherine and a member of the Legislative Council. Lynch, in particular, enjoyed the prestigious backing of the governor, Sir Charles Grey, who, with "a select party of ardent adherents" to the Queens House Party, visited St John and canvassed support for him.[3]

On election day, August 29, 1849, the four candidates and their supporters, accompanied by music bands, gathered at Point Hill for the poll, as did several "visitors" from the five adjoining parishes who witnessed what proved to be a historic election. The two men who nominated the respective teams of candidates reinforced their different class origins. Adam Thoburn, a white doctor who trained at Edinburgh and who owned two properties, Lookout and Top Hill, that spanned the mountainous borders of Clarendon and St John, which together totalled 985 acres, nominated Aris, the coloured sugar planter, and Lynch, the white solicitor. In contrast, John Thomas Bell, a coloured artisan with 32 acres at Retirement in St John, and whose father had been manumitted as a child in 1790, nominated Bell, the coloured carpenter and former bookkeeper, and Price, the black master carpenter. St John's black and coloured "mountain settlers" handed victory to Price and Bell, who received 51 and 50 votes respectively, while Aris with 43 votes and Lynch with 36 votes were defeated. It was an eloquent statement on how St John's political landscape had changed in the decade after emancipation that 40 (i.e., 85 per cent) of the 47 voters whose racial identities have been identified were either black or coloured, and two-thirds of them, including at least 11 free men, voted for Bell and Price. It is significant that 85 per cent of the 13 black or coloured men who voted for Aris and Lynch were either artisans or shopkeepers in Spanish Town or planters and penkeepers in St John. The first group reflected the influence of the members of the Queens House Party in the island's capital, while the second group of Aris and Lynch's coloured supporters voted with seven white planters who also exclusively endorsed the two "gentlemen" over the two craftsmen from the "middle class."

Clearly, black and coloured small freeholders, several of whom were freedmen who had established themselves after 1838, decided the election. Accordingly, the planters were alarmed that a black "uneducated Kingston operative tradesman" of "slender means" had defeated two men of fine "intellectual achievements," and some called for the abolition of the Assembly before "every man of a white skin" was excluded.

Notes

1. George Price, *Jamaica and the Colonial Office: Who Caused the Crisis?* (London: Sampson, Low, Son and Marston, 1866), 2.
2. *Morning Journal*, 13 January, 3 and 6 September 1847.
3. *Falmouth Post*, 13 July and 24 August 1849; *Morning Journal*, 3 September 1849.

Religion after Slavery

Hope Waddell

The end of slavery created new opportunities for freedpeople to take control of their religious lives. The result was a rapid turn to forms of religious expression independent of missionary churches. These new denominations combined Christianity with forms of worship prominent in Africa, including styles of singing and dance as well as possession by spirits. In some parts of Jamaica in the early 1840s there was an upsurge of Myal, a religious cleansing movement that aimed to destroy evil. Those involved in the movement referred to the evil they opposed as "Obea" or "Obeah," a term that was often used much more broadly to describe any religious movement that drew on African practice or theology. The development of autonomous black religion shocked the missionaries. Here Hope Waddell, a Presbyterian missionary who arrived in Jamaica in 1829, describes his encounter with a group of Myal worshippers. His description emphasizes their refusal of deference to the white missionary.

The wild outbreak of Myalism, in 1842, was one of the most startling events in the history of Jamaica missions, and showed how deeply rooted the old heathenism of their race still was among the negroes. As the corrective of Obea, it wore a benign aspect, and was favoured by the negroes; while both, as corresponding parts of one system, formed an extraordinary superstition. Anything might serve as the means or instrument of the malign Obea influence, and placed in a person's garden or house would find its way into his body, and afflict him with incurable disease, or blast his property and labours, producing all kinds of misfortune. A person under that curse felt condemned; his health and interest were ruined; everything went wrong with him; he pined away and died. The hidden "poison" could be discovered and counteracted only by its proper Myal antidote, which the initiated alone knew. The power, which could detect and eradicate the subtle and malignant evil, was regarded as a real saviour by the befooled people.

Long suppressed but never eradicated, these African superstitions began to revive after emancipation, when the old laws against them were no longer in force. The introduction of several thousand new Guinea people, taken from captured slavers, favoured their resuscitation; for as the Creoles attributed peculiar skill in the black art to the old Guinea negroes, so did these latter to its more recently imported professors.

After the occurrences formerly mentioned, instances took place here and there, from time to time, previous to 1842. The most considerable of these was at the Spring Estate, about the Christmas holidays of the previous year. A kind of frenzy seized on some people there, but none of my people, who went about crying that the estate was poisoned by Obea, and that people had been killed by it, the cause of their death being discovered near their graves. Then everything bad on the property was attributed thereto; and the disciples of that belief set themselves to discover and purge out the poison, wherever it existed. Men and women thus affected ran about the negro houses, as if deranged, and even to the field, stopping the people from their work, and calling them to prayers, breaking into houses to dig out the Obea, which the devil had set in them, and fighting in the name of God all who were supposed to be guilty of practicing the infernal art.

In July 1842 the delusion broke out again in one of its principal seats, *Flower Hill*; and a company of its agents invaded *Blue Hole* to cleanse that estate from its sins and miseries. They were sent by God, they said to purge and purify the world, they had the spirit, and were Christians of a higher order than common. Most or all of them, I am sorry to say, were members of one of the principal missionary churches. It was the strangest combination of Christianity and heathenism ever seen. After these fanatics had spent several days extracting the supposed pernicious substances from the houses and gardens of their own class, with singing, and dancing, and various peculiar rites, and had declared their purpose to enter and search every house in the village, my people were alarmed, and reported the matter to me, desiring advice how they were to act. Of course, I told them by no means to open their doors to them, nor to follow them elsewhere; and if violence were offered to force an entrance, they should go to the overseer and the attorney for protection.

It seemed needful I should visit the place, and have a special meeting with the people; and the following Sabbath evening I went, accompanied by a few trusty elders and members of our church. We used to meet in the old "great house," but on this occasion were attracted to the village by the noise of the Myal proceedings. There we found them in full force and employment, forming a ring, around which were a multitude of onlookers. Inside the circle some females performed a mystic dance, sailing round and round, and wheeling in the centre with outspread arms, and wild looks and ges-

Conflict between missionary Christianity and Jamaican African-Christian religions developed in the years following slavery. This depiction of African Jamaican funerary rites, captioned "Heathen Practices at Funerals," appeared in the Baptist missionary James M. Phillippo's book *Jamaica: Its Past and Present State* (London: John Snow, 1843), following p. 244.

tures. Others hummed, or whistled a low monotonous tune, to which the performers kept time, as did the people around also by hands and feet and the swaying of their bodies. A man, who seemed to direct the performance, stood at one side, with folded arms, quietly watching their evolutions.

Entering the circle, I attempted to address the assembly, but was unheeded. The dancing women engrossed all the attention. Addressing him who seemed the president, I requested him to quiet the people, and let me speak to them. He did so in a moment, and most gently. They were silent, and I mentioned my object, and proposed they should come with me to the former place of meeting in the old Great House. They objected to move from the spot, and desired me to stand and preach there. Some proposed I should first sing a hymn, and I commenced one; but observing how much it affected them, ceased, and began to pray. That calmed them for a while, but soon they grew impatient, and resumed their own song, and the dancing women their performances. Turning to the manager, I said, "If you don't keep these mad women quiet, we cannot go on with the worship of God." Thereupon a strange hubbub arose. "They are not mad." "They have the spirit." "You must be mad yourself, and had best go away." "Let the women go on; we don't want you." "Who brought you here?" "What do you want with us?"

Indentured Workers

Verene Shepherd

Some Jamaican sugar planters responded to the crisis in the sugar industry by importing workers from both India and Africa to do the work previously done by enslaved people. These workers were indentured, which meant that they were required to work for a set rate of pay for whoever bought their term of indenture for a fixed period, usually three to five years. As historian Verene Shepherd explains, around thirty-seven thousand indentured migrants from India came to Jamaica after emancipation. This was a small proportion of a much larger global process of labor migration in the nineteenth century, during which about 1.5 million Indians left India under indenture and many more moved without indenture. Although Indians did not come to Jamaica in sufficient numbers to completely transform the demography, culture, and economy of the society, they played a significant role in Jamaican history in the second half of the nineteenth century and continued to be a recognizable community for much of the twentieth.

Between 1845 and 1916, an estimated 37,000 Indian immigrants entered the island and served their period of indentureship on properties located primarily in the parishes of St. Andrew, St. Mary, Portland, Clarendon, Westmoreland, St. Catherine and St. Thomas-in-the-East (simply St. Thomas after 1867). After their arrival in the island (first at Port Royal and then on to various disembarkation depots) immigrants were dispatched in carts, schooners or by rail to the properties on which they were to serve out their indentures. These were the ones who after examination by the Medical Board on arrival were found to be "fit for service" and who were then issued with certificates of indenture. Despite the length and rigours of the journey from India—particularly before the use of steam ships in 1906—those rejected as "unfit" were remarkably few.

In the early years of immigration, Indians seem to have been allocated to estates in batches of about twenty, but between 1891 and 1916 some estates received as few as four and others as many as sixty-three from single shipments. In comparison to Trinidad and Guyana where much larger numbers

A group of Indian indentured workers in Jamaica, gelatin silver print by a member of the Duperly photography firm. The original photographer titled the image *West Indian Coolies, Jamaica*. Late nineteenth century. Used by permission of Archive Farms, Inc.

of Indians were densely concentrated, in Jamaica a much smaller number was widely dispersed, though there were concentrations in areas of high sugar and banana production. Thus, in Jamaica, the land areas into which Indians were absorbed—particularly after their employment on banana estates—was larger than in Trinidad and Guyana, where estates were concentrated in comparatively smaller ecological zones. Even when there was the possibility of movement off the estates into villages and the increase of the Indian population by natural means or the addition to their numbers through further importations, there were other factors militating against any significant growth in the Indian population in the island. These included repatriation, the lack of continuous importations and socioeconomic factors frustrating the evolution of "Indian Villages."

On the estates, Jamaican proprietors employed a variety of measures in an effort to render Indian immigrants a more controllable labour force than Afro-Jamaican labourers. The main strategy was, of course, to secure Indian labourers under indentured contracts. The rationale for such contracts was that when labour was not sufficiently cheap and servile, the free play of market forces had to be interrupted and an element of extra-economic compulsion introduced. Planters constantly agitated for longer contracts, though at first the British Government only allowed one-year contracts. By 1850 the Government had relented sufficiently to allow three-year contracts; this was because Indians from the 1845–1847 batches had generally refused to reindenture after the first year. A parish-by-parish survey conducted by the press in [1848] revealed that a large number had become vagrants and mendicants and that poverty was widespread among them. These factors combined with reactions to the Sugar Duties Act of 1846 led to the suspension of immigration in 1848. Importations restarted in 1860 and by 1862, five-year contracts were general throughout the region.

Before the beginning of the period of contract, each labourer was issued with agricultural implements, cooking utensils and a suit of clothing. Trousers were made out of oznaburgh and shirts out of striped Holland or flannelette. Women's clothes were made from brown calico and striped Holland. This represented a further break in tradition and the demise of the dhoti and sari for many. New immigrants were supplied with rations for the first few months but thereafter provided food out of their wages.

On sugar estates, indentured labourers worked in gangs supervised by either an Indian or Afro-Jamaican headman or "driver." Indian "drivers" were selected solely on the basis of their ability to implement plantation routine—not according to caste or religion. Thus low castes could be placed over high caste, Muslims over Hindus, and so on—factors which forced interethnic interaction.

The classification of gangs followed closely that of slavery, with strength and physical condition, age and gender being important criteria for the worker's allocation. Thus the weeding gang was invariably composed of the less physically able, and some women. At times there was also an invalid gang comprising children and convalescents. In Jamaica the criterion of "race" was also applied. Planter preference for Afro-Jamaican labourers for heavier tasks, combined with the stereotype of the physically weak Indian, caused certain gangs to consist heavily of blacks; correspondingly, certain tasks referred to as "women's work" tended to be assigned specifically to Indians—male or female. However, the list of tasks performed by Indian labourers, including digging stumps, preparing the land, planting and reaping indicates that ethnic factors in allocating work were not absolute. For instance, contrary to popular belief, Indian labourers were employed in sugar factory work.

Work on banana plantations and livestock pens was less regimented, but even on those units the gang system often prevailed. On banana plantations, a similar stereotype regarding the physical capacity of the Indian directed "delicate work" such as pruning bananas, to Indian labour gangs. Other tasks on banana estates ranged from hoeing grass, billing, forking and trenching to heading and carting.

The Indian's life—whether employed on pen, sugar estate or banana plantation—was arranged according to the schedule devised by the plantation. Neither routine nor tasks bore any relationship to caste or religion. About the only restriction which respected caste and religious sensibilities was the direction that Hindus should not be given jobs which involved the handling of meat. Governor Manning claimed that none were so employed in Jamaica, but as Indians worked on livestock farms it is unclear whether this denial was accurate.

The Morant Bay Rebellion

Gad Heuman

After abolition, conflicts developed over land, labor, taxation, family life, religious expression, and the judicial system, to name but a few. In the 1860s these divisions intensified due to drought and the adverse economic impact of the US Civil War. All these factors contributed to the armed resistance movement that took place at Morant Bay, in the parish of St. Thomas in the East, to the east of Kingston, in October 1865. Although not on the scale of the slavery-era insurrections of 1760 and 1831–1832, the rising had long-term consequences. The Morant Bay Rebellion and its brutal suppression by Governor Edward Eyre shocked people across the British Empire and contributed to a developing debate about "race." In Jamaica, the political consequences were also severe. The House of Assembly was abolished and a new form of government—Crown Colony rule, which gave much more power to the governor—was instituted. In the twentieth century, the rebellion became a touchstone for Jamaican nationalism. Two of the men who would become national heroes of independent Jamaica, Paul Bogle and George William Gordon, were executed for their parts in the rebellion: Bogle as its primary organizer, Gordon as a brown leader who was groundlessly accused of stirring up rebellion.

In this narrative from his book on the 1865 events at Morant Bay and their aftermath, historian Gad Heuman describes the course of the uprising and its repression. He draws mainly on the evidence given to the Jamaica Royal Commission, which later investigated the events. Heuman's account emphasizes the organized, quasimilitary aspects of Bogle's actions and those of his followers, and stresses that they were a determined response to long-standing grievances and to entrenched race and class domination.

The Morant Bay rebellion broke out in Jamaica on 11 October 1865. On that day, several hundred black people marched into the town of Morant Bay, the capital of the predominantly sugar-growing parish of St Thomas in the East. They pillaged the police station of its weapons and then confronted the volunteer militia which had been called up to protect the meeting of the vestry, the political body which administered the parish. Fighting erupted between the militia and the crowd, and by the end of the day, the crowd had killed eighteen people and wounded thirty-one others. Seven members of the crowd died. In the days which followed, bands of people in different parts of the parish killed two planters and threatened the lives of many others. The disturbances spread across the parish of St Thomas in the East, from its western border with St David to its northern boundary with Portland.

The crowd that day was unlike any other which had ever made its way to Morant Bay. Vestrymen were familiar with crowds which "used to come down there sometimes on vestry days and kick up a row—make a noise." But this gathering was different: the people were armed and "came in with some intention."[1] Only a small number had guns, but most of the others had either sharpened sticks or cutlasses. The crowd was also highly organized; the men marched four abreast, with the women on their flanks. As one observer noted, they "came in rows . . . they were well packed together close behind each other, but not at all straggling; they advanced slowly and deliberately."[2] Though dressed in ordinary labourers' clothes, they looked more like troops than like an irregular mob.

The immediate cause of the troubles was a court case held four days previously, 7 October. According to Custos Ketehodt, over 150 men had come into Morant Bay that Saturday "armed with sticks and preceded by a band of music" and with the intention of rescuing a man who was to be tried in court, were he found guilty. During the proceedings a boy was convicted of assault and ordered to pay a fine of 4s. and costs of 12s.6d. However, another man, James Geoghegan, interrupted the court, arguing that the boy should not pay any costs. Geoghegan was ordered out of the court, but he continued to make a noise while he was leaving. When a justice on the bench ordered him to be arrested, the crowd prevented it. The police apparently grabbed Geoghegan in the square, but the mob pulled him away. According to the clerk of the parish, some "40 or 50 people with sticks [were] licking at the police. The rioters were drawing away a man through the market, and the police trying to prevent them taking him away." Fearing that the policeman would be injured by such a menacing crowd, the magistrates called the police back into the court house. In the process one of the policemen suffered a broken finger and at least one other member of the police was beaten. Paul Bogle was among the people involved in the scuffle.[3]

The following Monday the justices issued warrants against twenty-eight people for the assault on the police at the court house. On Tuesday the police proceeded to Stony Gut, Bogle's village, to execute the warrants. They found Bogle in his yard, read him the warrant, and sought to arrest him. But Bogle refused to go and instead shouted for help. As one of the policemen

A sculptural tribute to the leader of the Morant Bay Rebellion. *Paul Bogle*, by Mallica "Kapo" Reynolds, lignum vitae wood sculpture, 1952. From the Larry Wirth Collection at the National Gallery of Jamaica, Kingston. Photograph by Franz Marzouca. Used by permission of Naomi Reynolds and the National Gallery of Jamaica.

reported it, as soon as Bogle appealed for help, "the shell blew, and drums rolled at the same time," and the police were surrounded. Immediately, upwards of 300 men armed with cutlasses and sticks appeared out of the nearby canefields and out of the chapel in the village. Although the police tried to escape, several were caught.[4] They were handcuffed, threatened with death, and eventually forced to swear an oath of loyalty. "So help me God after this day I must cleave from the whites and cleave to the blacks."[5] While at Stony Gut the policemen also witnessed other men taking the oath.

[On 11 October, after attacking the courthouse and killing a number of vestrymen,] the crowd marched to the district prison. Again, they proceeded in a military fashion, headed by Paul Bogle. There were three companies of ten men each, led by Bowie, Craddock and Simmonds as well as nearly three hundred other people at the prison. One of the officers in charge of the prison reported that as the mob entered the gaol, Bogle ordered a sentry to be put at the gate. The crowd liberated the fifty-one prisoners in the gaol, but Bogle insisted that the prisoners "must get their own clothes, for he would not like to rebel against the Queen, and he would not strike as a rebel against the Queen, and so they wanted their own clothing." The prison officer had to break open the chest where the personal clothes of the prisoners were kept and hand them out. Bogle also had the prison officers swear on a Bible that they would no longer serve as public officers. Bogle then formed the prisoners into a line and marched them out of the prison.[6]

The organized nature of the crowd may explain the lack of pillaging in the town. Apart from the burned-out buildings there was little other destruction in Morant Bay. The crowd demanded gunpowder from Mrs Lundie's shop, they took bread from the baker, and a range of items, including tobacco, fish, candles and soap, from Marshalleck's store. But even there, they left the rum and other spirits. The crowd had come to attack the vestry; they were not intent on destroying or looting the town. For them, the vestry was the symbol of oppression; its leading members were involved in disputes with the people over land, justice and wages. Moreover, Bogle and his allies were angry about the expulsion of their spiritual and political leader, George William Gordon, from the vestry. Their fury was reflected in the massacre at Morant Bay.

The response of the Jamaica authorities was swift and brutal. Making use of the army, Jamaican forces, and the Maroons, the government vigorously put down the rebellion. In the process, nearly five hundred people were killed and hundreds of others seriously wounded.

The outbreak was a rebellion, characterized by advance planning and by a degree of organization. The leader of the rebellion was Paul Bogle, who, with other associates, organized secret meetings in advance of the outbreak. At these meetings oaths were taken and volunteers enlisted in expectation of a violent confrontation at Morant Bay. The meetings were often held in Native Baptist chapels or meeting houses; this was important since the Native Baptists provided a religious and political counterweight to the prevailing white norms of the colonial society.

The common people were bitter about the continued political, social and economic domination of the whites. Among other things, this meant a lopsided and partial judicial structure; for many blacks the only solution was an alternative legal system which they themselves controlled. Another problem centred around land: the people believed that their provision grounds belonged to them and that they should not have to pay rent for those lands.

Access to land was symbol of freedom, a freedom which some believed might even be denied to them. In addition, there were repeated complaints about the low levels of wages paid on the plantations.

These grievances were not new. Protests over these issues were a recurring feature of the postemancipation period. Even during the Morant Bay rebellion itself, there was much that was similar to earlier protests in Jamaica as well as to other social movements elsewhere.

Notes

1. Jamaica Royal Commission (JRC), Evidence of Brookes Cooke, pp. 52–53.

2. JRC, Evidence of Edward House, p. 202; Evidence of Edward William Major, p. 28.

3. JRC, Evidence of Edward Eyre, Custos of St Thomas in the East to the Governor's Secretary, 10 October 1865, p. 83; Papers, In the Court held under Special Commission, January 1866: The Queen v. Bogle and others, Copy evidence for Mr Attorney-General, Statement of Stephen Cooke, p. 389.

4. JRC, Evidence of William Fuller, p. 80.

5. CO 137/140, Storks to Cardwell, 19 February 1866, no. 28, Enclosure: Statement of William Fuller, Policeman, 5 January 1866.

6. Papers, In the Special Commission, 7 March 1866: The Queen v. Bogle, Henry Theophilus and others by Felonious Riot, Evidence of Sligo Campbel, p. 359; JRC: Evidence of Sligo Campbell, p. 140; Evidence of W. Cuthbert, p. 139.

Dear Lucy

George William Gordon

George William Gordon was the leading critic of the government in the House of Assembly in the early 1860s. A man of mixed African and European descent, he insisted on justice for Jamaica's poor. This drew the ire of the plantocracy. When the Morant Bay rising took place, Governor Eyre and several other politicians used the crisis to target Gordon. Eyre had him illegally transferred to St. Thomas in the East, which was under martial law. He was tried in a court-martial for conspiracy, sentenced to death, and rapidly executed. Gordon's illegal execution was one of the aspects of the suppression of the Morant Bay uprising that drew the most criticism in Britain. In this letter to his wife, Lucy, written shortly before he was hanged, Gordon maintains his innocence, drawing on religious piety to prepare himself and his wife for his inevitable fate. The Royal Commission that investigated the events later concluded that Gordon had no direct involvement in the planning and actions of the protestors at the courthouse.

Dear Lucy

General Nelson has just been kind enough to inform me that the court-martial on Saturday last has ordered me to be hung, and that the sentence is to be executed in an hour hence; so that I shall be gone from this world of sin and sorrow. I regret that my worldly affairs are so deranged, but now it cannot be helped. I do not deserve this sentence, for I never advised or took part in any insurrection. All I ever did was to recommend the people who complained to seek redress in a legitimate way; and if in this I erred or have been misrepresented, I do not think I deserve the extreme sentence. It is, however, the will of the Heavenly Father that I should thus suffer in obeying His command to relieve the poor and needy, and to protect, as far as I was able, the oppressed. And glory be to His name! And I thank him that I suffer in such a cause. Glory be to God, the Father of our Lord Jesus Christ, and I can say it is a great honour thus to suffer, for the servant cannot be greater than his

The Cotton Tree at the Cross Roads near Morant Bay, where the rebels assembled immediately before the attack on the Court House.

Cotton trees have sacred significance in Jamaica. This photograph bears the handwritten caption "The Cotton Tree at the Cross Roads near Morant Bay, where the rebels assembled immediately before the attack on the Court House." Photograph by Alexander Dudgeon. From a photography album documenting the Morant Bay Rebellion in Jamaica (1865), with views of Malta, Ireland, Guernsey, Spain, and elsewhere. Graphic Arts Collection, Department of Rare Books and Special Collections, Princeton University Library, Princeton, NJ. Used courtesy of Princeton University Library.

Lord. I can now say with Paul, the aged, "The hour of my departure is at hand, and I am ready to be offered up. I have fought a good fight, I have kept the faith, and henceforth there is laid up for me a crown of righteousness, which the lord, the righteous Judge, shall give me." Say to all friends an affectionate farewell, and that they must not grieve for me, for I die innocently. Assure Mr. Airey and all the others of the truth of this. Comfort your heart, I certainly little expected this. You must do the best you can, and the Lord will help you, and do not be ashamed of the death your poor husband will have suffered. The Judges seemed against me; and from the rigid manner of the Court I could not get in all the explanation I intended. The man Anderson made an unfounded statement and so did Gordon; but his testimony was different from the deposition. The Judges took the former and erased the latter. It seemed that I was to be sacrificed. I know nothing of the man Bogle. I never advised him to the act or acts which have brought me to this end. I did not expect that not being a rebel, I should have been tried and disposed of in this way. I thought his Excellency the Governor would have allowed me a fair trial if any charge of sedition or inflammatory language were partly attributable to me; but I have no power of control: may the Lord be merciful to him! Now, my dearest one, the most beloved and faithful in the Lord bless, help, preserve, and keep you. A kiss for dear mamma, who will be kind to you and Janet. Kiss also Annie and Jane. Say good-by to dear Mr. Davison, and all others. I have only been allowed one hour. I wish more time had been allowed. Farewell also to Mr. Espeut, who sent up my private letter to him. And now may the grace of our Lord Jesus Christ be with us all.

> *Your truly devoted and*
> *now nearly dying husband,*
>
> G. W. *Gordon.*

Vindicating the Race

Rev. R. Gordon

On the fiftieth anniversary of the full abolition of slavery, 1888, a group of black Ja-
maicans, mostly clergymen, published a volume of essays titled Jamaica's Jubilee;
or, What We Are and What We Hope to Be. *The book was an important step in*
the development of Jamaican nationalism. It argued that Jamaicans had made enor-
mous progress since emancipation and challenged the claims of influential racist
British writers like Thomas Carlyle, James Anthony Froude, and Charles Kingsley
that emancipation had failed. The introductory essay by the Rev. R. Gordon takes
issue with the prejudiced view of British contemporaries that black Jamaicans were
incapable of achievement. Instead, it argues that despite their history of enslave-
ment, they have a bright future. Gordon's emphasis on the Jamaican as "a British
subject in a British colony" attests to the attachment of Jamaicans to the empire
during the Victorian era.

It has repeatedly been asserted that the black population of Jamaica have
had no history; and to prove this, arguments like the following have been
urged. They have been taunted with the statement that Jamaica is not their
country, inasmuch as they are not descendants of the Aborigines; nor have
they any relationship to Great Britain beyond that of British subjects. In
turning to Africa and claiming it as their home, they have been asked, how
is it they do not speak the language and abide by the customs peculiar to
that country? The Englishman, the German, the Frenchman, the Hindoo,
the Chinaman, speaks each the language of his country, and carries with
him wherever he goes certain badges distinctive of his nationality. But the
black man of Jamaica has no such marks of distinction. Not an Englishman, he speaks, notwithstanding, the English tongue, and moves in society
according to the laws and requirements of English etiquette. And thus, in
view of the colour of his skin, he is not an Englishman; with regard to his
speech and manners, he is not an African; and since he is not descended
from the Aboriginal Indians, he is not a Jamaican. Hence the taunt, "He has
no history!"

It is not our purpose to attempt a refutation of the censorious assertion; not from the difficulty, but from the non-necessity, of so doing. It is sufficient that he, as the lineal descendant of those who were kidnapped in, and stolen from, their African homes, and, to satisfy the rapacity of a dominant race, brought to this country and here kept for generations in iron bondage,—it is sufficient, we say, that he, as their offspring, stands to-day in the position of a British subject, thereby claiming, and that justly, the interest, sympathy, and protection of those who were instrumental in effecting the expatriation of his ancestors. As a British subject in a British colony, the black man of Jamaica *has* a history. His existence in the island for over two centuries cannot be altogether uneventful. And whether the facts and events recorded are such as to reflect on him creditably or otherwise, depends, in a great measure, on the circumstances into which he has been thrown.

Characters, we hold, cannot rightly be judged apart from their environments; and to conclude, as some have done—in (what they choose to call) the absence of that social, moral, and intellectual progress, that invariably indicates the existence of national life and activity, and which gives promise of future greatness, that the Jamaica negro is wholly devoid of those mental and moral qualities so indispensably necessary to his rise in the scale of true civilization, is as unreasonable as it is untrue. The questions to be settled are these: Has he been happily positioned since his introduction into this island? Have his advantages been of the best and most favourable kind? Has sufficient encouragement been held out to him? The only answer to these questions that can have any show of fairness and justice, must be in the *negative*.

For *two hundred years* under the galling yoke of slavery, what could be expected but a crushing out of his manhood—a gradual but certain destruction of every vestige of the principles and lingering virtues that distinguish him even as uncivilized man? Slavery exerts an admittedly demoralizing influence. Its tendency is to degrade, and not to elevate; to pollute, and not to purify; to imbrute, and not to humanize; to destroy, and not to save. And, writhing under its grinding tortures, unpitied and helpless, it is not to be wondered that the enslaved and, in consequence, demoralized and dehumanized negro almost ceased to be a man! Indeed, so far down in the scale of humanity had he been sunk, that his master no longer regarded him as equal, much more superior, to his horse. With nothing in his position to comfort and cheer; with nothing in the near or distant future to inspire or animate; with the very lifeblood of his manhood completely crushed out; it is certainly not surprising to find him where he was when, fifty years ago, emancipation dawned upon him.

And now it might well be asked, Can a people so disadvantageously positioned, so despised, so ridiculed, so crushed, be reasonably expected to take any prominent place amongst the nations of the world, or accomplish much, if anything, by way of distinguishing themselves? The past of their history presents a dark page, it must be admitted; but is the record always to be written in blood and tears, revealing nothing but wretchedness and woe? We think not. There are not only *probabilities*, but *possibilities*, in the negro character, which, we trust, time and favourable circumstances will develop and place beyond the region of uncertainty or doubt.

August Town Craze

Frederick S. Sanguinetti

Alexander Bedward was the most prominent of a number of significant millenar-ian preachers and religious leaders in late nineteenth- and early twentieth-century Jamaica. He was part of the tradition of Jamaican Revivalism, a religion that devel-oped in the 1860s and connected Jamaican Christianity to African religion. Bedward was so successful that his followers became known as Bedwardites. Bedwardism is often interpreted as a precursor to the Garveyite and Rastafari movements.

In 1891 Bedward established a religious center at the Hope River in August Town, St. Andrew, which he preached was a "healing stream." Here Frederick Sangui-netti, a clerk in the Jamaican colonial secretary's office, summarizes many docu-ments about Bedward from 1895. In that year, Bedward was arrested, tried for sedi-tion, and then briefly committed to the Jamaica Lunatic Asylum. After his release Bedward once more gathered followers in large numbers. During the late 1910s and early 1920s people traveled from all over Jamaica to hear him preach and be close to him. In 1921, after he and eight hundred followers were arrested when they began a pilgrimage from August Town to Kingston, he was once again committed to the Lunatic Asylum, this time for good. He died incarcerated in 1931.

Sometime in the latter part of 1893 the attention of the Police was attracted to the large crowds which assembled once a week at a spring in the August Town district of St. Andrew, a branch of the Hope River, to drink the water and to bathe in the stream in evident faith of its efficacy to cure disease.

A black man by the name of Alexander Bedward who lived in the neigh-bourhood claimed to have had the secret of the stream revealed to him in a dream and that he had received divine common to invite his fellow crea-tures to freely take of these healing waters. Wednesday in each week was the day chosen and the people assembled sometimes in thousands at a build-ing in the vicinity which is called the "Mission House"; Bedward presided and praying and singing took place. After about two hours of this exercise a procession was formed and was led to the river by Bedward. He then read passages from the bible, exhorted the people to drink of the "water of life"

Alexander Bedward. Photographer unknown, c. 1920. Previously published in Martha Warren Beckwith, *Black Roadways: A Study of Jamaican Folk Life* (Chapel Hill: University of North Carolina Press, 1929).

and those who wished to do so to bathe in the healing stream and with a show of solemnity he blessed the water.

A return was presently made to the Mission House where another religious service was carried on and ultimately the people dispersed to their several homes carrying with them vessels filled with the "sacred" water.

Bedward's life history as known to the Police began in 1883 when he exhibited signs of an unsound mind but proceedings were not taken to confine him in the Lunatic Asylum.

It was considered that there was great risk in these assemblies and the bathing together of such a number of people suffering from various diseases and the Attorney General was asked whether the Central Board of Health had power to act in the matter. He advised that he thought that it had not, but suggested that under certain circumstances the bathers might be indicted for indecent exposure.

The Governor did not consider it desirable to take any action in the matter at that time, but the movement was watched and reports were sent in weekly by the Inspector of Police for the parish, generally uniform in character as regards the proceedings at these meetings which have already been described. The craze seemed to die out somewhat in the early months of 1894 but in January 1895 the Police reported that the crowds attracted to August Town had recently very much increased and that Bedward's conduct tended to excite the ignorant people who flocked to hear him.

On an occasion mentioned he baptised a number of people—a new feature in his vagaries—and afterwards addressed them in seditious language. He told them that after baptism they had undertaken to throw off the oppression cast upon them by the white people and the Government. He spoke in a most insulting way of the Governor, the Government and the Clergy, designating the latter as vagabonds, thieves, robbers and liars, saying that they had filled our hospitals, alms-houses and prisons, that they were blasphemers and scoundrels who were worshipping Anti Christ, that he and Shakespeare (his assistant at the river) were the only servants of the true Christ and that they had been sent to stop all the tricks of the parsons and the Government, that he knew the Police and detectives were watching him but they could go and tell those who sent them that he defied them to touch him as he was right, that the Government had refused to interfere with him.

He called upon the people to drive out the white population who were oppressing them, holding out to them the fires of hell as their doom if they neglected to do it and reminding them of the Morant Bay rebellion. He referred to the black population as the "black wall" and the white as the "white wall" saying that the white wall had long enough oppressed the black wall and the time had now arrived when the black wall must knock down and oppress the white.

The papers were sent to the Attorney General who advised that proceedings should be taken against Bedward for seditious language and instructions were issued for Bedward's arrest.

The usual proceedings followed and the man was committed for trial at the Circuit Court on 22nd April on a charge of sedition.

In the Circuit Court in April last Bedward was put on his trial and the Jury returned a verdict of "Not Guilty by reason of Insanity" and the Chief Justice ordered that he should be kept in custody until the pleasure of the

Governor should be known. Thereupon the Governor's warrant was issued for his removal to the Lunatic Asylum.

On the 21st May after argument against the legality of his detention, in Court and in Chambers, Bedward's Counsel succeeded in obtaining an immediate Order for his release.

Anansi and the Tiger

Walter Jekyll

*Since slavery Anansi (also spelled Annancy and Anancy) stories have been an im-
portant part of Jamaican culture. Drawing on an oral tradition from the Akan peoples of today's Ghana, they feature a trickster man-spider who uses his cunning
and ability to dissemble to get the better of more powerful figures, and sometimes
of others who are less powerful than him. Anansi has often been interpreted as a
metaphor, both positive and negative, for Jamaican culture more generally. In keeping with their oral origins, "Br'er" (Brother) Anansi stories are often told to groups
of children in Jamaica today. Books and recordings of local storytellers are designed
for schoolchildren who are also encouraged to learn and recite them. Either hero or
villain depending on the circumstances of the story, Anansi is an enduring figure in
Jamaican culture.*

*In the early twentieth century, there was widespread interest in many countries
in collecting and preserving cultural forms that had until then been orally transmit-
ted. In Jamaica, Walter Jekyll was among the most prominent of those who collected
Anansi stories and other elements of what was becoming known as "folklore." Jekyll
was from England but lived for many years in Jamaica. He recorded stories from people working for him and in other contexts, trying to capture the sounds and rhythms
of Jamaican creole speech (patwa). The tale of Anansi and Tiger is one of the most
commonly retold Jamaican Anansi stories. In this version, Anansi outsmarts Tiger,
only to find himself beaten by the monkeys that he has attempted to use to his own
advantage.*

One day Annancy an' Bro'er Tiger go a river fe wash 'kin. Annancy said to
Bro'er Tiger:—"Bro'er Tiger, as you are such a big man, if you go in a de
blue hole with your fat you a go drownded, so you fe take out your fat so
lef' it here."

Tiger said to Bro'er Annancy:—"You must take out fe you too."

Annancy say:—"You take out first, an' me me take out after."

Tiger first take out.

Annancy say:—"Go in a hole, Bro'er Tiger, an' make me see how you swim light."

Bro'er Annancy never go in.

As Tiger was paying attention to the swimming, Annancy take up his fat an' eat it.

Then Annancy was so frightened for Tiger, he leaves the river side an' go to Big Monkey town.

Him say:—"Bro'er Monkey, I hear them shing a shing a river side say:—[1]

Yeshterday this time me a nyam Tiger fat.
Yeshterday this time me a nyam Tiger fat.
Yeshterday this time me a nyam Tiger fat.
Yeshterday this time me a nyam Tiger fat.

The Big Monkey drive him away, say they don't want to hear no song.

So him leave and go to Little Monkey town, an' when him go him said:— "Bro'er Monkey, I hear one shweet song a river side say:—

"Yeshterday this time me a nyam Tiger fat.
Yeshterday this time me a nyam Tiger fat."

Then Monkey say:—"You must sing the song, make we hear."

Then Annancy commence to sing.

Monkey love the song so much that they made a ball a night an' have the same song playing.

So when Annancy hear the song was playing, he was glad to go back to Bro'er Tiger.

When he go to the river, he saw Tiger was looking for his fat.

Tiger said:—"Bro'er Annancy, I can't find me fat at all."

Annancy say:—"Ha, ha! Biddybye I hear thing shing a Little Monkey town say:—

Yeshterday this time me a nyam Tiger fat.
Yeshterday this time me a nyam Tiger fat.

Bro'er Tiger, if you think I lie, come make we go a Little Monkey town."

So he and Tiger wented.

When them get to the place, Annancy tell Tiger they must hide in a bush.

Then the Monkey was dancing an' playing the same tune.

Tiger hear.

Then Annancy say:—"Bro'er Tiger wha' me tell you? You no yerry me tell you say them a call you name up ya?"

An' the Monkey never cease with the tune;—

Yeshterday this time me a nyam Tiger fat.
Yeshterday this time me a nyam Tiger fat.

Then Tiger go in the ball an' ask Monkey them for his fat.

The Monkey say they don't know nothing name so, 'tis Mr Annancy l'arn them the song.

So Tiger could manage the Little Monkey them, an' he want fe fight them.

So the Little Monkey send away a bearer to Big Monkey town, an' bring down a lots of soldiers, an' flog Bro'er Tiger an' Annancy.

So Bro'er Tiger have fe take bush an' Annancy run up a house-top.

From that, Tiger live in the wood until now, an' Annancy in the house-top.

Jack Mantora me no choose any.[2]

Notes

1. Anansi's speech is conventionally indicated with a lisp. [Editors' note]
2. This phrase, more often rendered "Jack Mandora mi no choose none," traditionally marks the end of an Anansi story. It means, "I retell the story as I received it." [Editors' note]

The 1907 Earthquake

Dick Chislett

On 14 January 1907 an earthquake devastated Kingston and its surroundings, reducing much of the city to rubble and killing at least eight hundred people. The earthquake was the worst natural disaster to hit the island in over a century, reminiscent of the 1692 Port Royal temblor.

Eastern Jamaica, including Kingston, sits on an earthquake fault line known as the Enriquillo–Plantain Garden fault zone, which stretches to neighboring Hispaniola. It was this fault that caused destruction in Port-au-Prince and Léogâne in Haiti in January 2010. A century before that, the Kingston earthquake drew considerable international interest. Survivors were taken to open fields such as the Race Course at the northern end of the city (now National Heroes' Circle), where they camped for months. Aftershocks and an immense fire that spread immediately after the quake added to the scale of destruction and human loss. As a result of the quake, several businesses, schools, and homes were relocated to other areas, thereby redrawing the metropolitan borders of Kingston. Some middle-class families, having lost their businesses and homes, left the city or the island altogether. Most Kingstonians were forced to fend for themselves, although the colonial government and leaders such as Bishop Enos Nuttall organized some relief and an impressive new plan for urban renewal. These efforts would eventually lead to the joining of Kingston and St. Andrew parishes in 1923.

Many extant sources reveal the immensity of the earthquake's wrath. The most moving of these are the personal testimonies of survivors. In this letter written only two days after the quake, Dick Chislett, a middle-class Jamaican, describes his experience in the earthquake to his brother, Jack. Dick had been shopping in Kingston's business area when disaster struck. As well as describing the earthquake's impact, the letter also gives a sense of the everyday transactions of middle-class Jamaicans in the early twentieth century.

Chestervale, Wednesday am, January 16th [1907]

My dear Jack

Mary and I are safe and well. We have just been through the most terrible experience. Monday at 3.30 pm Jamaica had an awful earthquake. Mary was here at Chestervale and I was in the worst place in Kingston. That I escaped was only due to God's kindness and my own quickness, but I will tell you my own movements and Mary will write hers.

Monday at 8.00 am Mr Comstock and myself left here on pony back to go to Bath We reached Kingston at about 1.00 o'clock, went to Mrs Cook's boarding house, had lunch, left our suit cases in our room, took a carriage and drove to the steamer office and bought our tickets to sail on the United Fruit Co's Steamer, "Sampson," next day, Tuesday, at noon. Then we went to the Bank of Nova Scotia, then to Nathan Sherlock's large General Store. I could not get the collars I wanted, so Comstock said he would go to the Post Office and to some Steamboat office (I do not know where it was) and I was to go down Harbor St to Ramsey's General Store and then down a square farther to Gardiner's Book Store and wait for him there. I went into Ramsey's (a good sized General Store). There were a good many people in there and a lot of clerks and a number of lady tourists. It is my belief that I was the only one to escape alive. I was near the door and the clerk had just put a box of collars on the show case when I heard a deep rumbling noise. The building shook all over, then in a second came an awful, deep, rumbling roar, the building rose in the air and came down a mass of ruins. In about 15 seconds every brick building in Kingston was a mass of ruins.

I rushed out of the door. The front walls of every building were falling out in the street, the wall of the building across the street on my right and just struck the ground, and glancing up I saw Ramsey's front wall at an angle of nearly 45 degrees right over my head. I rushed at a right angle right on top of the mass that had fallen almost before it fully struck the ground and Ramsey's wall fell right behind me, and the opposite wall on top of that. Then the air was full of suffocating white dust, something hit my back, and I was thrown down on the bricks. I could only see about three feet, but right beside me was a heavy iron beam and a small space beside it. I lay there, hoping that there would be some protection. I fully expected every minute—every second—to be killed, and could only say, "O God! Save me!," and thought I should never see any of my loved ones again. Oh! It was awful.

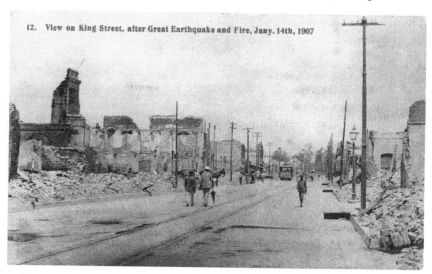

12. View on King Street, after Great Earthquake and Fire, Jany. 14th, 1907

A destroyed tramcar on King Street, the morning after the 1907 earthquake. *View on King Street, after Great Earthquake and Fire, January 14th, 1907*, photographer unknown. From the National Library of Jamaica Digital Collection, identifier D0005161. Courtesy of the National Library of Jamaica.

I suppose I lay there about 5 minutes and as nothing fell on me, and as I could see a little distance to the corner, I got up, made my way to the corner, where, as all the buildings were down, nothing could fall on me. A few walls were standing and the streets full of tangled wires and filled with bricks, mortar, and debris of all kinds. I cannot tell you what an awful sight it was as the dust gradually thinned. The narrow streets had been filled with horses and carriages and rigs and people. Hundreds were killed outright; hundreds were terribly injured; and hundreds imprisoned in the ruins. Heart Rending cries came from every direction. Right around me people were crying for help. "Oh! My back is broken!," "My legs are broken," "Help me, I am dying!" Near me a bloody hand stuck out of the bricks and the person unable to cry out was moving the hand up and down to attract attention. I saw at once that it would take a dozen men a long time to move away the debris and lift the heavy iron roofing on top. I was powerless to do anything. Many people around me were covered with blood. It was awful and I can't tell you any more.

My first thought was if I could do anything for poor Comstock, (I haven't heard anything from him since) but as he might have been anywhere within four or five squares, I could not tell where to look for him. Then every moment I expected another shock. Then as where I was, was only a few feet above the sea, I fully expected a tidal wave to sweep over the City, and then looking back I saw two columns of smoke rising up and saw that in a very short time the whole business portion of the town would be in flames with no way of fighting fire, as they have only the old-fashioned fire engines, and nothing could get along any of the streets.

Traveling from Kingston to Montego Bay

Herbert de Lisser

Herbert George de Lisser (1878–1944) was an influential early twentieth-century Jamaican voice. Journalist, novelist, short story writer, editor, and political commentator, de Lisser was extraordinarily prolific. Born in Falmouth, the capital of Trelawny parish, he relocated with his family to Kingston. At twenty-five he followed in his father's footsteps and became editor of the Daily Gleaner, *a position he held for forty years. His political views were generally conservative, and he was an energetic defender of empire. De Lisser was best-known for his literary works, including* Jane's Career (1914) *and* The White Witch of Rose Hall (1929). *He was also a perceptive travel writer who wrote extensively about the state of the Caribbean at the dawn of a new century. In this selection from his second book,* Twentieth Century Jamaica (1913), *de Lisser offers a rich description of a trip from Kingston to Montego Bay that reveals much about the landscape and attitudes of Jamaicans in the early twentieth century.*

Jamaicans are sometimes apologetic in speaking of their capital and of the towns of their island; but they hardly say anything about the country proper. They perceive that Kingston is sadly lacking in many of the attributes of a capital city; they know its defects, and are daily aware that its appearance is not calculated to dazzle or impress the stranger. But they will remind you that Kingston is not the island, just as the Canadian in Toronto or Montreal will solemnly protest that if you have seen only the eastern cities of Canada you have not seen Canada.

For two or three miles [from Kingston] our route leads northward. Past the market, which is already crowded with buyers and sellers, past houses dilapidated and old, but still crowded with people, past the northern boundary of the city, and into the contiguous parish of St. Andrew. The character and appearance of the buildings have changed. This part of St. Andrew's parish is in reality but an extension of the residential area of Kingston; every man who lives here works in Kingston; but land is cheaper here and the rates are low; it is cooler too, and hardly a house but has its own grounds, with fruit trees and shade trees, and grass and flower beds. Some handsome houses we pass, built of wood and brick, or of brick alone, in the West Indian fashion; the homes these of officials and prosperous merchants. We turn south-westward now, having reached the village of Half-way Tree. South-westward we run for a while, and now we are surrounded by wastes of green, enveloped in silence and overarched by a mighty dome of blue. How still it is! No sound is heard, save that made by our car; no human beings to be seen except ourselves. Even animals are rare; it looks as though this part of the countryside were deserted. Yet we know that behind the trees some curious youths may be peeping at us from behind that hedge or lolling within the shadow of that thicket.

Soon we come to a shallow river running across the road; we dash through it and speed onwards. We are in the parish of St. Catherine—saints seem to have been popular with the Jamaicans of the past—and on either hand of the hard white road, for miles and miles, are plantations of the banana.

The road here is dusty, so dusty that you cannot see far in front of you. It is one of the great highways of the island, and by night and day huge wagons filled with fruit, laden with sugar, or piled high with merchandise pass, continually over it. There they come, some of them slowly drawn by oxen, which nothing in the world will induce to a reasonably active pace, or by sturdy mules, which stand first amongst the local beasts of burden.

Thus through dust and carts and shouting men we come to Spanish Town. Here is the oldest town in the island, a place which was the headquarters of the Spaniards when an English buccaneer attacked Jamaica more than three hundred years ago. It is on record that when Cromwell's commanders captured Spanish Town (or St. Jago de la Vega, as it was and still is sometimes called) he found half of it deserted. Half of it is still deserted. This town, indeed, seems always to have lived up to its reputation of desertion; it has always had more houses than people to occupy them; it has always been a silent funereal sort of place.

Its population is over seven thousand, but you would never suspect it. You would drive through one of its long streets and not meet more than a dozen human beings, a sad-looking goat, and a score or so of dogs who look as if they too were historical chiefly. The problem has always been to find out what the people of Spanish Town do for a living, for there is very little commerce in the place, and but one industry. It is the centre of a banana and sugar parish, however, and it is to be presumed that many of those who are employed on the plantations and estates live or keep their families in Spanish Town. It has a handful of people of the professional, planter, and official class, and these form the upper crust of the society of the town.

From Spanish Town we go north by west and through the heart of the country. For some distance we have the Rio Cobre on our left, and great mountains of limestone on our right; the road is hard and level, and a cool wind makes the journey delightful.

Our way is now towards Moneague, a town where, in the very midst of summer, it is always cool. The temperature changes perceptibly as our car speeds upwards, a glorious breeze blows incessantly, and traveling is a delight.

Before reaching Moneague, we crossed one of the highest roads in the island and saw some of the most wonderful scenery. We crossed Mount Diablo, the devil's mount, called so, doubtless, because of the peril of it in days gone by. Time was when even the strongest pair of horses would strain and pant as they pulled a light buggy up the hill; and a slip was dangerous for on one hand was a towering wall of cliffs, and on the other a succession of yawning precipices. To-day a motor-car makes nothing of the steep incline, and parapets have been built to prevent an accident. But the view remains as of yore, a view which few writers can adequately describe; which, indeed, is indescribable. You look down upon sleeping villages aglow with sunlight, upon range upon range of greenest hills rolling away to the far-off horizon. But Mount Diablo has been passed and Moneague is reached, and now our journey lies directly northward and downward. We are going towards the sea.

Down, down, steadily downwards, and with every mile the temperature grows slightly warmer. And here you observe one of the commonest features of life in Jamaica; in a day you can pass from the warm lowlands to the coolest heights, to elevations which remind you of northern countries in the verdant spring months to a temperature that may be likened to that of an Indian summer. And as you travel you will be tempted at times to ask if Jamaica is very sparsely populated, so few, comparatively, are the people you see. Yet let your motor-car break down, and you will be surprised at the number of curious folk that will appear, whence, you can scarcely guess! Still it is true that the country could support a much larger number of inhabitants, and will, as time goes on.

The lowlands at last! We turn due west now, and in a little while, unexpectedly, the sea of the northern coast bursts upon our view. We have come to Ocho Rios, the place of the eight rivers; we are in the parish that has been called "the Garden of Jamaica"; we are in that portion of the country which

Columbus first saw and where he first landed, and where he lived a whole year in sickness and distress. In this parish was built the never-completed Spanish city of Seville.

Nowhere is the sea more beautiful than here. All the colours of the rainbow are reflected from its surface, and in the distance the waves dash themselves to foam against the line of breakers that here and there run parallel to the shore. This is cultivated country. Our journey is by the seashore; but sometimes the sea is hidden from our sight by trees and peasants' gardens, and for long distances we travel through a lane of green steeped in the shadow thrown by overarching trees. Hut after hut we pass, and large cattle pens, and peasants trudging their way along stolidly, and giving you politely "the time of day." They know you at once for a stranger, and gaze curiously, but never rudely, at you, and you know that you will be the source of a few minutes' speculation to them, and may even constitute the staple of that evening's conversation.

The roar of falling water has smitten our ears, and a glimpse of a great volume of something white has been caught by our eyes as we hurried along; we halt, and, alighting, walk back to look upon one of the waterfalls for which the island of Jamaica is famous. The noise is thunderous, as through a narrow gorge a huge body of cream-coloured water leaps into a chasm below. This is a branch of the Roaring River, and a little later on we shall see the real Roaring River Falls, the immense cascade that tumbles over a mass of rocks with an infinity of foam and flashes of pale green— shall see it through a tangled medium of tossing trees, and shall carry away an unforgettable memory of it: a joy for ever.

Starting in the early morning from St. Ann's Bay, we hug the sea-coast once more, and the farther we go the more sugar estates we begin to see. Sugar was once the chief product of Jamaica, and is still one of the principal exports. Farther on, alas! We come upon other sugar estates, but these are as quiet as the grave, as deserted as a churchyard. They are abandoned properties. This is one of the tragedies of old Jamaica industry. Once fortunes were made out of sugar, then a bare living, then came the time when the competition of European bounty-fed sugar told the Jamaican planter of his approaching ruin. But Jamaica will always make sugar, for modern machinery and modern science have come to the aid of the planter, and some of Jamaica's sugar soils are among the best in the world.

But it is when one has passed through the parish of St. Ann and entered that of Trelawny that the full extent and meaning of the decadence of the sugar industry become apparent. For a large part of Trelawny is deserted today; estate after estate is passed, all in a condition of ruin; it needs no further

Cutting the Sugar Cane, Jamaica, West Indies, postcard (Brown's Town, Jamaica: J. Johnston, c. 1906). From Look and Learn's Elgar Collection. Bridgeman Images no. LLE814372. Photographer unknown. Used by permission of Bridgeman Images / Look and Learn / Elgar Collection.

knowledge to convince one that this parish at any rate has never recovered from the blow which it received during the nineteenth century. The effect of so many ruins, of expensive sugar-works given over to absolute neglect, of fine mansions dismantled and falling slowly to pieces, is saddening in the extreme. We observe, too, that the people we meet in this part of the country seem poorer than those we have seen elsewhere, and that is indeed their condition. Still, they appear cheerful and happy. They scream out a request to us as we go by—"Beg you a tup!" a tup being equivalent to three half-pence. It is only about here that you will hear this word; it is, like some other terms, quite peculiar to the district. In other parishes the peasant will beg you a shilling. But in Trelawny, where probably few tourists go, the simple peasant is content with asking for a tup, and is apparently equally content if no attention is paid to his request.

It is while on our way to Falmouth, the chief town of Trelawny, that we see some of the finest scenery that the island has to show. Up a high hill we climb, then, as we reach its summit, a steep precipice breaks away upon our left. We look down, and below us lies a valley through which a wide dark-gleaming river flows—the River Nuevo on its way to the sea.

As we approach Falmouth, we once again have the sea in view. Falmouth is the classic example of a deserted city in Jamaica. Spanish Town is populous and a hive of activity compared with it. Once it rivaled Kingston; it was the chief sugar port of the island, the produce of two rich parishes was shipped from its wharves. To-day nearly all its wharves have rotted, and but a few planks remain in certain spots, or a few stumps of piers, to remind one that there once were wharves and warehouses along the sea-front of the town. We remark that most of the houses are large. We notice that most of the houses are closed, and that there is not one amongst them that looks less than a hundred years old. Two-thirds of the shops are closed—more than two-thirds. We count three persons in the principal street, one dray is standing outside an empty warehouse; we spy a man looking out of the window of the Government building which dominates the town. The dust is inches thick upon the street, grass grows everywhere; this surely is a town that has been dead for sixty years; some would say dead beyond the hope of resurrection. Yet it is not necessarily so.

Our journey will end at Montego Bay, twenty-one miles off. Our road is no longer level, but rolls up and down; the gradients are still easy, and it is pleasant to see that in this parish of St. James, which we have now entered, there are sugar estates at work and but few signs of desertion and poverty. When we come to Montego Bay, we find a town of wooden houses mainly, but a town that looks prosperous enough in its quiet, contented, tropical way. Six thousand six hundred people live in it, it supports a weekly newspaper, it has several large, well-built churches and good hotels; and it calls itself the capital of the Northern parishes. It is a busy town, as commercial and industrial activity goes in the British West Indies; its wealthier classes live "on the hill," the poorer people live on the levels, and every one seems to accord very well with every one else, in a placid provincial sort of way.

Our journey is at an end. It has been hurried; we have only caught a brief glimpse of things from the interior of a motor-car. Our impressions have been concerned with externals only, and we have only partially seen a part of those. And, when night finds us on "the hill" of Montego Bay, and we watch the town twinkling with lights below, with the dark sea rolling out to the far horizon in front of it, we know that we have passed through some of the most magnificent country in the world, but feel that by no effort of ours can we convey to any other mind a vivid and true impression of the things we have seen.

V

Jamaica Arise

Between World War I and independence in 1962, Jamaica's formal attachment to the British Empire tightened, strained, and then frayed. The lone British territory in the northern Caribbean, a space increasingly shaped by the dictates of the United States, Jamaica entered the period with both old and new challenges. Natural disasters continued in these decades, most dramatically with the calamitous Hurricane Charlie in 1951.

World War I presented evidence of Jamaican loyalty to empire. Overwhelming support for the Crown was manifest in the thousands of Jamaican volunteers who left the island to fight on the European frontlines. Larger numbers of Jamaicans traveled to the United States, to England, and across the circum-Caribbean, primarily in order to find work. Wherever they went, Jamaican migrants faced social and racial prejudice. The experience of overseas racism had profound influence. A few Jamaican emigrants such as Marcus Garvey and Leonard Howell built powerful black consciousness movements out of these experiences: Garveyism and Rastafari, which were influential both within and well beyond Jamaica. These interrelated pan-African movements drew on long-established undercurrents in Jamaican popular thinking to challenge white supremacy.

Travel to Jamaica also increased by midcentury. By the 1950s European and North American visitors increasingly perceived Jamaica as a desired holiday destination. New passenger airline companies facilitated tourism by introducing routes to the Caribbean. Tourism began to alter Jamaica's landscape through the development of private hotels along the island's coasts as part of a new industry enthusiastically promoted by the government.

The increase in tourism in the 1950s assisted the popularity of Jamaican mento, the first internationally successful music from the island. With roots in nineteenth-century rural Jamaica, mento required a small band of performers playing acoustic instruments and often singing of local concerns. Mento performers also promoted the island as an ideal location for foreign visitors, as in songs such as Lord Messam's "Take Her to Jamaica Where the Rum Come From" (1952). Mento's appeal facilitated the rise of international performers such as Lord Flea, who found success in the United States. The popularity of mento in the 1950s represented an important shift toward a more commercial Jamaican music that would become the foundation of other musical forms of later decades.

The era's greatest changes were political. The labor rebellions that engulfed much of the British Caribbean in the late 1930s were particularly important in Jamaica. Faced with low wages, poor living conditions, and a high cost of living, Jamaican workers protested vigorously for improvements. A vibrant labor movement developed, and increasingly turned to nationalism. The subsequent Royal Commission of Inquiry into the labor protests (the Moyne Commission) exposed the gravity of social inequality in the island and recommended important changes. The nationalist platform for independence, however, was not straightforward. Many Jamaicans retained a paradoxical attachment to Great Britain, or at least a wish to remain under the imperial umbrella. Even so, a significant minority, influenced by Garveyism and later the Black Power movement, rejected colonial ties completely.

Out of this context came the island's two political parties: the People's National Party (PNP), led by the articulate lawyer Norman Washington Manley, and the Jamaica Labour Party (JLP), led by his cousin, the charismatic Alexander Bustamante. Both leaders joined Jamaican nationalists within and outside the island who pressed the British to grant self-government: local control over all domestic political decisions within the British Empire. Universal adult suffrage in 1944 was a major step in the slow undoing of Crown Colony rule. The elections held that year brought about a change in the political administration of the island. Jamaicans voted directly for members of Parliament in the House of Representatives, and the JLP won the majority of the thirty-two seats. By 1959 Jamaica had achieved full internal self-government.

Party politics transformed the Jamaican political and social landscape. Allegiances to parties and leaders were strongly defended and differences were pronounced. A major source of political difference was the question of West Indian Federation. Under Norman Manley's leadership, in 1958 Jamaica joined nine other British territories in this political union. The JLP called for Jamaica's withdrawal from the federation, claiming that it slowed the progress of independence and that Jamaica, the largest of the islands, would have to support other members. The contention between the JLP and the PNP over federation led to the island's first national referendum in 1961. The result was Jamaica's withdrawal from the federation, which collapsed not long after. Jamaica then pushed forward to gain full independence from Great Britain the following year.

Life in Rural Jamaica

Lorna Goodison

There is a discernible contrast between lifestyles in rural and urban Jamaica. Although most Jamaicans live outside the island's two cities, Kingston and Montego Bay, it is those two locations that have come to define the island to outsiders. But each of Jamaica's fourteen parishes has its own distinguishable features, some of which have survived the passage of time. Transitions in rural life, especially before the midcentury migration to Kingston, are best evoked in generational stories such as this extract from the book From Harvey River *by acclaimed poet and writer Lorna Goodison.*

This award-winning work is a memoir about the author's mother, Doris. Goodison describes life in the early twentieth century in her family's home parish of Hanover in western Jamaica. Harvey River, Goodison explains, was named after her great-grandfather William Harvey. Doris was the seventh of eight children for William's son David and his wife Margaret. This large family was well-known in the area, which was located a good distance from the coast. Goodison draws deeply on the memories of relatives and close study of island history to provide a personal portrait of the experiences of her mother and sisters. One of the book's strengths is Goodison's engrossing depiction of the rhythms of country life in Hanover, which she reconstructed from the stories told her by her mother and other relatives many years before.

The narrative follows the Harvey sisters on a Saturday visit to the parish capital, Lucea, with generous insights on the setting, sights, and society. This weekly tradition is presented in fascinating detail, complete with comments on the personalities the sisters would meet in the stores and on the streets. Goodison's clear depictions of characters such as Mr. Reid and Mr. Shagoury lend a level of intimacy to the narrative, allowing the reader to see Lucea through the eyes of young country girls. As Goodison describes, life in the town was quite different from the interior of the parish. The excitement of the visit was heightened by the girls' dress. The practice of dressing up for weekend visits to the central town and to church remains an important feature of Jamaican life in the countryside. By including these colorful details Goodison succeeds in giving us the world that Doris and her sisters shared with generations of young girls from the country.

Lucea, the capital of Hanover, is situated on the western side of a horseshoe-shaped harbor that is approximately one mile wide. With the exception of the parish of Kingston and St. Andrew, Hanover is the smallest of the fourteen parishes in Jamaica. Hanover was almost named St. Sophia, in honour of the mother of King George I, but this name was voted down by the Legislative council in favour of Hanover, originally spelled Hannover. The name was chosen with reference to the German domain of the reigning family of England.

When the Harvey girls descended from their home in the hilly interior of Harvey River and rode into the town of Lucea, they never failed to look up in wonder at the Lucea Clock Tower, which held a red clock that looked like the high-domed helmet worn by German royal guards. Everyone in the town knew that the clock in the tower was brought to Lucea by mistake, that it had been destined for the island of St. Lucia, and that the captain of the ship which was transporting it had mistaken the Port of Lucea for the island of St. Lucia, and delivered it there in 1817. As it so happened, Lucea's town fathers had already ordered a new clock built, but it was of a more modern design, and not anything as grand as this German helmet. They decided forthwith that they could not and would not let the red helmet clock go and so they laid claim to it. It has remained there ever since.

After noting the time by the clock tower, the girls would dismount and leave the horses in the care of one of their relatives in Lucea, after which they would sometimes go to visit the Lucea Parish Church and pay their respects to some of their relatives who were buried in the churchyard. They would go by the Lucea Hospital at Fort Charlotte (named after George III's queen) and Rusea's High School, built towards the end of the eighteenth century with money left by a Frenchman, Martin Rusea, in thankfulness for the safe harbor and hospitality that he had found in Lucea. These were the town's main landmarks, situated fairly close together on the promontory overlooking the harbour. With the imposing Dolphin Head Mountains rising as high as two thousand feet, and an abundance of cabbage palms and tall coconut trees forming a lush backdrop to the azure harbour, the town of Lucea was a small but steady source of light.

The eligible young men of Lucea gathered to feast their eyes on the Harvey girls whenever they came to town. These included the young men who worked as clerks at the courthouse and as civil servants in the few colonial government offices in existence at that time, such as the Collector of Taxes. Some of them were apprenticed as surveyors in the Lands Department, and a few were members of Her Majesty's Jamaica Constabulary Force, but the Harvey girls would not consider giving the time of day to a policeman. For some reason (probably to do with their Irish grandfather, George O'Brian Wilson) their mother, Margaret, had a fierce prejudice against policemen and soldiers. Another of her edicts, in addition to "No child of mine will ever rule me," was "No policeman or soldier will ever sit in one of my chairs."

Dressed to the nines to come shopping for yet more fabric, the girls would go directly to Mr. Jim Reid's store on the Lucea main street. Mr. Reid, a slender, well-dressed and soft-spoken man, was known for his exquisite taste. He stocked the finest cloths, lace, buttons, buckles, belting and trimmings, accessories, lingerie and millinery, as he referred to his hats. Mr. Reid was unmarried. Such a pity, for any woman would have been glad to have him dress her every day. He adored the beautiful Rose. "Look Miss Rose, I ordered this blush pink crepe de chine with you in mind, and these carioca kid shoes are perfect, just perfect." Mr. Reid smelled nicely of Florida water. On Sundays he wore a crisp white drill suit and an expertly blocked Panama hat. He had a friend, Mr. Dixon, who owned a bicycle built for two. On Sunday afternoons, Mr. Reid and Mr. Dixon would go bicycling along the coast road, their well-seamed trouser legs secured by matching bicycle clips.

Shagoury's was the other store frequented by the Harvey girls. The goods there were not of the same quality as those stocked by Mr. Reid. Doris used the first one-pound pay-cheque from her job as a pupil-teacher to buy a pair of pumps from Shagoury's. Mr. Shagoury, who was not too long from Lebanon, recommended the shoes highly, saying, "These shoes strong, you wear them till they bark." Maybe that was a popular saying in his native country. But the shoes fell apart after a few weeks. The uppers and the sole separated, creating a flapping, gaping space in the front of the shoes when she walked. Her brother Howard said that was what Mr. Shagoury meant when he referred to the shoes "barking," for they now looked as if they had open mouths.

They would also shop at Emmanuel's Haberdashery, sometimes for special linens and lingerie, for each Harvey girl expected to be married, and they each had a bottom drawer. After shopping, they would visit their Aunt Fanny's bakery on what was called Back Lane, to buy fresh breads and pastries to take back to Harvey River. The girls had a particular fondness for the small, flat buttery loaves called *gratto*, a word which was probably a corruption of the French *gâteau* in the same way that other French words crept into the language and had been reshaped by the tongues of Jamaicans. For example, Château Vert, a village in Hanover, was now called *Shotover*, and the bunch of assorted vegetables—the legumes—that could now be bought in the local market for the Saturday soup were called *leggins*.

On their way past the blacksmith's forge, the Harvey girls would often have to push their way through gangs of schoolchildren who loved to stand outside the door and chant rude words in time to the ring of the blacksmith's hammer on the anvil.

After spending a Saturday morning shopping, the Harvey girls would pass by Animal Hill to have lunch with one of their relatives. Maybe their cousin Lily Musson, who was the daughter of one of their father David's half-brothers. On their way to her house they would go by a house called Glenmore, at the corner of Cressley Lane. This spot was once the site of the Jewish burial ground, and in the yard there could still be seen some scattered tombstones, one of which bore an inscription to Mr. Moses Levy, who died in Lucea but was born in New York.

At the end of a day's shopping in Lucea, the Harvey girls were always met outside of the town by a family helper who would have been sent to assist them with carrying their parcels back to Harvey River. The girls would ride home full of the latest news from Lucea and laden with purchases—from lengths of fabric, stockings, hats, and lingerie to bottles of Lydia E. Pinkham's Vegetable Compound for "female" complaint. They always brought back some small gift for David and Margaret, usually a bag of cakes and pastries from Aunt Fanny's bakery that were more "refined" than the substantial cornmeal and potato puddings that were baked every weekend in the Harvey household.

Many years later, my mother and her sisters would continue to fall into their fabulous-Harvey-girls-get-dressed-to-go-to-town routine whenever they were together. Even when they were old women, they were still the fabulous Harvey girls.

An Amazing Island

W. E. B. Du Bois

The influential African American intellectual and civil rights activist W. E. B. Du Bois visited Jamaica in May 1915, where he first learned of Marcus Garvey, who was launching his then fledgling Universal Negro Improvement Association (UNIA) in Kingston. Garvey and Du Bois would later become legendary rivals. They disagreed profoundly over strategies for the black struggle in the United States and internationally. While Du Bois argued for a strategy designed to end discrimination within mainstream institutions, Garvey sought to encourage black independence including black businesses and cultural institutions. At times their clashes drew on the differences between the black experience in the United States and in Jamaica. Such comparisons are particularly telling in Du Bois's comment on his trip to Jamaica, published a month after his return to the United States. While Du Bois notes the poverty of many Jamaicans, he also praises what he regards as the more favorable situation of black people on the island, going so far as stating that "in Jamaica for the first time in my life I lived beyond the color line," a reference to his celebrated sentence in The Souls of Black Folk *(1903): "The problem of the twentieth century is the problem of the color line."*

Jamaica is a most amazing island. I have seen something of the earth, more especially Europe and America which leave, to be sure, much unseen; but of the lands that I have looked upon hitherto Jamaica is the most startling. The ride from Spanishtown [*sic*] to the northwestern sea is one of the great rides of the world to be likened to the Horse Shoe Bend or St. Gotthard. The Wag Water is a beautiful stream and Montego Bay is the bay of Naples. The whole island is a mass of gray, green mountains thrown on the face of the sea with gash and shadow and veil. The rain of Jamaica is the maddest, wildest and wettest of rains and the sunshine is God's. There in Jamaica the world is met. Africa and Asia and Europe all meet which may mean little and yet may be the most fateful meeting the world ever saw. In Jamaica for the first time in my life I lived beyond the color line—not on one side of it but beyond its end. There in strange places I could sense its curious paths stopping and wavering and fading into uncertain threads. Of course, I was ever looking for it. That is my inborn nature. I saw that the moving picture films, for instance, were "approved" by "His Worship, the Mayor," and when I sat beside His Worship, the Mayor at dinner, behold, His Worship was colored. I almost hesitated at the barber shop but the barbers did not hesitate. It was a strange sort of luxury to ride on railways where engineers, firemen, conductor and brakemen were black. The smart, dark Constables in their gleaming white hats and coats gave me a double sense of security. In the stores there was usually a curl or a tint in the clerk that proclaimed the most ancient of blood and it was the same in the post office, the telephone exchange and the government buildings. In fact, though somewhat of an expert in knowing mine own, I confess that in Jamaica it was quite impossible for me to pick out the alleged 15,000 white people out of the 900,000 of population.

The peasants—a great mass of hard working black laborers—were to me perhaps more alluring. I can see now those black, straight and strong and fullbosomed forms, supple of hip and thigh and lithe of limb, sinewy yet fine and calm, treading their silent miles like fate. Soft of word and slow but sweet of smile and uncomplaining, of the blood and tears of such as these was built Jamaica. Threaded through all this curious beauty, with palm and mahogany, the scent of orange blossoms and the gleam of bananas, threaded through all this is the tragedy of a poverty almost incomprehensible. Think of a woman carrying sand all day, twelve endless hours in a Jamaica sun, for eighteen cents! Think of able-bodied men working for twenty-five cents and less a day. Think of walking fifty miles and carrying a hundred pound burden for forty cents. Think of raising and selling oranges at two cents a hundred!

Here is an island rich beyond dream; out of it for three centuries and more the white world has reaped its millions. Yet today the island lies poverty-stricken but facing the world proudly with one great gift of racial peace, the utter overturning of the barbaric war of color, with a chance for men to lift themselves regardless of the complexion of their grandfathers. It is the most marvelous paradox of this paradoxical western world.

Marcus Garvey Comes to the United States

Marcus Garvey

Marcus Mosiah Garvey (1887–1940) was one of the early twentieth century's most important black leaders. A native of St. Ann parish, he left the island as a young man, arriving in the United States in March 1916, along with thousands of other Jamaican migrants who moved to the United States in the early years of the twentieth century. Garvey hoped to find American financial backing for the Universal Negro Improvement Association (UNIA), which he had recently launched in Jamaica. He also wanted to learn about race relations in the United States, which in this letter, written shortly after he arrived in the US, he compared favorably to the situation in Jamaica. Garvey was inspired by the work of African American leaders Frederick Douglass and Booker T. Washington. He spent the first months after his arrival traveling the Northeast giving talks and closely observing urban black life. He eventually settled in New York, from where, in the 1920s, he transformed the UNIA into the largest black organization in the world, with chapters spanning the African diaspora. The success of the UNIA made Garvey enormously influential. His powerful ideas on black consciousness would inspire movements across the globe long after his death. For his monumental achievements, in 1969 the Jamaican government made Garvey the first person to be accorded with the Order of National Hero.

I have been in America eight months. My mission to this country is to lecture and raise funds to help my organization—the Universal Negro Improvement Association of Jamaica—to establish an industrial and educational institute, to assist in educating the Negro youth of that island. I am also engaged in the study of Negro life in this country. I must say, at the outset, that the American Negro ought to compliment himself, as well as the early prejudice of the South, for the racial progress made in fifty years, and for the discriminating attitude that had led the race up to the high mark of consciousness preserving it from extinction.

I feel that the Negro who has come in touch with western civilization is characteristically the same, and but for the environment, there would have been no marked difference between those of the scattered race in the west-

Portrait of Marcus Garvey, 1924. From Prismatic Pictures. Bridgeman Images no. DGC1065636. Photographer unknown. Used by permission of Bridgeman Images / Prismatic Pictures.

ern hemisphere. The honest prejudice of the South was sufficiently evident to give the Negro of America the real start—the start with a race consciousness, which I am convinced is responsible for the state of development already reached by the race.

A Fred Douglass or a Booker Washington never would have been heard of in American national life if it were not for the consciousness of the race in having its own leaders. In contrast, the West Indies has produced no Fred Douglass, or Booker Washington, after seventy-eight years of emancipation, simply because the Negro people of that section started out without a race consciousness.

I have traveled a good deal through many countries, and from my observations and study, I unhesitatingly and unreservedly say that the American Negro is the peer of all Negroes, the most progressive and the foremost unit in the expansive chain of scattered Ethiopia. Industrially, financially, educationally and socially, the Negroes of both hemispheres have to defer to the American brother, the fellow who has revolutionized history in race development inasmuch as to be able within fifty years to produce men and women out of the immediate bond of slavery, the latchets of whose shoes many a "favored son and daughter" has been unable to loose.

As I travel through the various cities I have been observing with pleasure the active part played by Negro men and women in the commercial and industrial life of the nation. In the cities I have already visited, which include New York, Boston, Philadelphia, Pittsburgh, Baltimore, Washington and Chicago, I have seen commercial enterprises owned and managed by Negro people. I have seen Negro banks in Washington and Chicago, stores, cafes, restaurants, theaters and real estate agencies that fill my heart with joy to realize, in positive truth, and not by sentiment, that at one center of Negrodom, at least, the people of the race have sufficient pride to do things for themselves.

The acme of American Negro enterprise is not yet reached. You have still a far way to go. You want more stores, more banks, and bigger enterprises. I hope that your powerful Negro press and the conscientious element among your leaders will continue to inspire you to achieve; I have detected, during my short stay, that even among you there are leaders who are false, who are mere self-seekers, but on the other hand, I am pleased to find good men and, too, those whose fight for the uplift of the race is one of life and death. I have met some personalities who are not prominently in the limelight for whom I have a strong regard as towards their sincerity in the cause of race uplift, and I think more of their people as real disciples working for the good of our race than many of the men whose names have become nationally and internationally known. In New York, I met John E. Bruce, a man for whom I have the strongest regard inasmuch as I have seen in him a true Negro, a man who does not talk simply because he is in a position for which he must say or do something, but who feels honored to be a member. I can also place in this category Dr. R. R. Wright, Jr., Dr. Parks, vice-president of the Baptist Union, and Dr. Triley of the M. E. church of Philadelphia, the Rev. J. C. Anderson of Quinn Chapel [AME Church] and Mrs. Ida Wells-Barnett of Chicago. With men and women of this type, who are conscientious workers, and not mere life service dignitaries, I can quite understand that the time is at hand when the stranger, such as I am, will discover the American Negro firmly and strongly set on the pinnacle of fame.

The West Indian Negro who has had seventy-eight years of emancipation has nothing to compare with your progress. Educationally, he has, in the exception, made a step forward, but generally he is stagnant. I have discovered a lot of "vain bluff" as propagated by the irresponsible type of West Indian Negro who has become resident of this country—bluff to the effect that conditions are better in the West Indies than they are in America. Now let me assure you, honestly and truthfully, that they are nothing of the kind. The West Indies in reality could have been the ideal home of the Negro, but the sleeping West Indian has ignored his chance ever since his emancipation, and today he is at the tail end of all that is worth while in the West Indies. The educated men are immigrating to the United States, Canada and Europe; the laboring element are to be found by the thousands in Central and South America. These people are leaving their homes simply because they haven't pride and courage enough to stay at home and combat the forces that make them exiles. If we had the spirit of self-consciousness and reliance, such as you have in America, we would have been ahead of you, and today the standard of Negro development in the West would have been higher. We haven't the pluck in the West Indies to agitate for or demand a square deal and the blame can be attributed to no other source than indolence and lack of pride among themselves.

The Negroes of the West Indies have been sleeping for seventy-eight years and are still under the spell of Rip Van Winkle. These people want a terrific sensation to awaken them to their racial consciousness. We are throwing away good business opportunities in the beautiful islands of the West. We have no banks of our own, no big stores and commercial undertakings, we depend on others as dealers, while we remain consumers. The file is there open and ready for anyone who has the training and ability to become a pioneer. If enterprising Negro Americans would get hold of some of the wealthy Negroes of the West Indies and teach them how to trade and to do things in the interest of their people, a great good would be accomplished for the advancement of the race.

Jamaica and the Great War
Daily Gleaner

The shock of World War I resounded across the British Empire, not least in the Ca-
ribbean. Jamaicans strongly supported the war effort beginning in 1914. Loyalty to
the Crown often superseded misgivings about colonial rule. A year later, when King
George V consented to the raising of a British West Indies Regiment (BWIR), hun-
dreds of Jamaican men from across the island responded to the call-up. In all more
than ten thousand Jamaicans would serve in the BWIR, two-thirds of the total from
the Caribbean territories. These two editorials from the Daily Gleaner *appeared*
during the fever of Jamaican recruitment in October 1915 and reflect the intensely
patriotic mood of the time. The first, "Jamaica's War," emphasizes the duty of all
Jamaicans, as British subjects, to the war effort and reasserts fealty to empire. It also
points out the importance of British over US imperialism for Jamaica. The second
editorial, "To the Women of Jamaica," is a specific appeal to Jamaican women,
claiming they had an important role in the struggle: they were duty-bound as British
subjects to support and encourage their men to join the BWIR.

Jamaica's War

When England is at war Jamaica is at war, and we Jamaicans have always
followed with the greatest interest and anxiety the fortunes of the Mother
Country's arms. But it seems to us that we shall feel even a more intimate
concern in the fighting going forward when we know that comparatively
considerable numbers of our sons are either in the thick of it or are busily
training to do their share. The concrete fact will impinge upon our minds,
making a vivid and indelible impression. Our sons and brothers, husbands,
cousins, fathers and friends—all are there. That is what we shall think in the
near future, and every battle we read of, every attack or defence, will appeal
to us as of intimate personal concern. We shall begin to think of this war,
not only as England's war or as the Empire's war, but as Jamaica's war, for
most of us think in images and we make a symbol of things most familiar to
us. We have always had interests at stake in this war. But now the supreme

interest are the lives of our heroes. And, strange though it may sound, for every Jamaican who loses his life in the most glorious way in which a man can die, there will always be another at home to leap forward gladly to take his place. For this war has got to be fought to the end, and in our mouths the end has but one meaning. The British Empire cannot be defeated. There is no part of it but has imbibed from the Mother Country something of that spirit of stern endurance which the world knows so well and which the world has yet again to see shining forth as a beacon and inspiration to those who are weak of heart. Having once begun, there is no looking back until victory is ours. And isn't it a proud thought that Jamaica shall have some part, however small, in that glorious end?

Yes, the war will now mean more to us than it ever did before, for we shall think of the men we have known, who will be fighting and enduring even while we think of them. And this sending of our sons to fight for the great and righteous cause for which this Empire is contending—what better way could there be of binding us more closely to England? An American paper was advocating the other day the purchase of Jamaica by the American Government. How would such an offer sound in the ears of a people whose children had fought for the Empire, fought because they loved and valued the Imperial connection, fought because they would willingly give their lives for Old England? When we are willing to shed our blood, who shall dare speak to us about material considerations, who will venture to think that we place peace before honour or would be mad enough to welcome a change from a place in the British Empire to a place in any other empire whatsoever? When we think of it calmly, what Empire is there like ours? What nation in the world can compare with the British nation taking it from every point of view? This is not arrogance, it is sober fact: England to-day stands for the world's freedom, must bleed for the world's freedom, will maintain that freedom in the face of the most powerful foe. And we, who are a part of the larger England, feel proud to be able to do our share in this work. Jamaica's war, we call it, even though our part in it may be infinitesimal. Yet what we do shall give us a new place in the Empire, shall have great future influence on our spirit as a British colony, shall teach us self-respect, shall lead us to take a keener interest in every question that concerns the Empire.

To the Women of Jamaica

Women of Jamaica, to-day you are called upon to play your part in the struggle which is taking place on the battlefields of Europe. To-day you are asked to make up your minds whether or not you will use your mighty influence on behalf of your King and of the British Empire; whether you will say to the young men of this country, "Go forth and do your duty," or will weakly hold them back, or at least remain inactive. You may have watched the progress of this world war with interested eyes—as British subjects you can have done no less. But you may also have thought that, being women, you had no part or lot in it, had and could have nothing to do with the sending of men who might accomplish much to uphold the ideals for which this Empire is fighting and to keep the honour of Jamaica untarnished in the eyes of men. It is not so. You are great factors in the present situation; England expects every woman to do her duty, and your duty is clear. There are men around you: sons, brothers, lovers. Mothers of Jamaica, it is not easy to part with a son. But the time has come for you to choose between your wish to have him near to you and your nobler desire that he shall prove himself a man, prove himself a worthy member of this great Empire, prove that Jamaica does not breed cowards and that the son of your body is not inferior in courage to any man of them all. Many mothers have already sent their sons. With tears in their hearts, but with brave faces, they have bidden them go forth to the field of glory, to fight side by side with other heroes, to play their part in driving the enemy out of down-trodden Belgium, where thousands of women have been forced to drink to the dregs the cup of humiliation and woe. Will you be less than these, can you be less than these? We do not believe it! And now we pray you to become conscious of your influence and power, to realize what you may accomplish with a word.

Returning from War

Glenford Howe

The enthusiasm with which Jamaicans signed up to serve in World War I turned for many to disillusionment in the war zones. Like all soldiers, troops from the British West Indies Regiment dealt with disease and squalid living conditions. In addition, Caribbean troops were subjected to racial discrimination. Their frustration at this was compounded when immediately after the Armistice in November 1918 white troops received a pay raise, but black troops did not. Anger culminated in a four-day mutiny among BWIR troops stationed in Taranto, Italy, and the subsequent formation of the Caribbean League, which sought higher wages and self-government for the West Indian colonies. This militance led colonial authorities in Jamaica to treat returning troops with anxiety and suspicion. In the immediate postwar period, protests and riots took place in Jamaica, as in many other parts of the world. The historian Glenford Howe here describes events in Jamaica in 1919.

The authorities in Jamaica were very concerned about ex-servicemen and seamen joining together to seek revenge for their treatment overseas. As a result, the first main shipload of returning soldiers was met by a warship and a military guard on the wharf. Because many people believed, perhaps correctly, that these measures were intended to intimidate the ex-servicemen, the authorities were forced to publish a statement claiming that this was not the case. If these security measures disturbed the soldiers, the warm reception they received on landing may have, as in British Honduras, made them temporarily forget their grievances. The town was gaily decorated, the streets were packed with cheering crowds and several prominent persons made speeches.

Importantly, however, the authorities did not wish the ex-servicemen to remain in Kingston too long, as it was feared that this could lead to disturbances. Thus, those from other parishes were usually despatched within twenty-four hours to their hometowns, where they were paid off. The strategy seems to have worked, especially with the first groups to arrive. In June 1919, the governor concurred with an article from the *Gleaner*, which noted that the behaviour of the ex-servicemen had been favourably commented on by all classes. Although the news that the ex-servicemen were planning to form an association to improve their condition did raise some doubts, the local authorities were fairly convinced that their intentions were honest. A Colonial Office official was less impressed, however, and minuted: "This appears to correspond very much with the 'Caribbean League' we have heard so much about," but another cautiously observed that the proposed society had on the face of it very laudable aims.[1]

Nevertheless, the Colonial Office did not wish the Jamaican officials to be lured into a sense of false security and warned them that the Caribbean League had discussed the possibility of a black uprising which was to involve the elimination of the whites in Jamaica and the other colonies. The inspector-general of the police reported, however, that there was no evidence of the league in Jamaica and no sign of unrest. Nevertheless, in the light of local fears of unrest, the arrival on July 5, 1919, of the Trinidadian F. E. M. Hercules, the general secretary of the London-based Society of Peoples of African Origin, was viewed with much concern by the authorities, especially when he addressed a group of strikers.

The confidence of the Jamaican authorities was shaken two days later when a riot erupted in Kingston. On the night of July 18, a crowd, which included ex-servicemen and seamen shouting "kill the whites," launched a "determined attack" on some white sailors from the *Constance*; a few local white civilians were also assaulted.[2] An armed party from the *Constance* was landed hurriedly to restore order and patrol the streets the rest of the night. The next morning the sailors were reinforced with guards from the West Indies Regiment, who were stationed at different locations in Kingston and its suburbs. These measures were partly prompted by rumours that there was going to be another outbreak of violence during the peace celebrations to be held on the nineteenth. Although the strategy seem to have prevented any major disturbance during the celebrations in Kingston, a rowdy element, according to the *Gleaner*, committed some acts of lawlessness with impunity. The festivities held at Morant Bay and Sav-la-Mar were also disrupted by unruly ex-servicemen. Although the officials desired to expel Hercules from the island, they could not find sufficient cause in his speeches or telegrams to justify his expulsion.

Later, a group of seamen, and apparently some ex-servicemen, sent a lengthy petition to the governor explaining their grievances and concerns and seeking redress. Their arguments focused on the violation of what they termed their "inalienable rights" as British subjects as a result of class and race oppression in England. They made it known that they felt "much aggrieved" and "deeply dissatisfied and disappointed at the insidious attack and illegal outrage" perpetrated on their constitutional rights and privileges, although they had served as soldiers, sailors and merchant-marines and had been subjected to all sorts of dangers, while some whites bluntly refused to do likewise. For these reasons, they stated, the treatment they received in England was unjustifiable, un-British and "against all the principles that sanctify humanity," and had shocked them "terribly all around in every way."[3] Clearly, their experiences overseas had forced them to question seriously their relationship with England and the empire. Yet their willingness to use constitutional means to seek redress was perhaps some indication that beneath their expressions of anger was an enduring loyalty to England and the empire, and that they still regarded England as their "Motherland." Indeed, the state aim of the petition was to ensure that they received justice, so that the honour and prestige of the empire might be upheld constitutionally, freed from class legislation, racial hatred and prejudice, and that harmony and peace would exist among the various races of the empire.

The authorities were willing to make some concessions, but this apparently did not satisfy the men. The situation was made worse with the subsequent arrival in Jamaica of the seamen from the *Orca*, as this soon led to further disturbances in Kingston. On the afternoon of October 9, 1919, a large crowd led by seamen who, according the police report, were in an "ugly mood" began demonstrating outside the immigration office. Attempts by the police to calm the protesters proved fruitless, and when the police began clearing the crowd from the streets, a riot ensued. The hostility of the crowd was directed against white people in general, but white sailors were especially targeted and severely beaten. During the disturbance there were thousands of people on the streets and the town was "in a state of high excitement."[4] The police believed, perhaps mistakenly, that in general, the sympathy of the crowd lay with the authorities, but there was a section which supported the seamen. Eventually the seamen were trapped and overwhelmed in the Queen's Hotel by a party of armed police.

On October 10, fifteen of the rioters were tried in court and eleven convicted, two discharged and two remanded. Four were sentenced to twelve months hard labour each, five to six months and two received sixty days. More arrests were made subsequently. The deputy inspector-general, B. Toole, who had been responsible for organising the police attacks on the rioters, was highly commended by the governor. The confidence of the officials was justified, as there were no more major disturbances associated with the resettlement of the ex-servicemen and seamen. A land settlement scheme was established to assist the ex-servicemen, but because the allocated land was in a remote area many could not take advantage of the scheme. The fact that approximately 4,036 of the ex-servicemen migrated to Cuba was probably a relief to the authorities and elites. Although the planters were always fretful about any loss of labour from the colony, it is not likely that they would have raised any or much objections to the departure of the potentially dangerous ex-servicemen to Cuba.

Notes

1. CO 318/355/45808 Probyn to Milner, 26 August 1920, Minute of THP, 7 June 1919.
2. CO 137/733/50990 Johnstone to Milner, 14 August 1919.
3. CO 318/349/60449 Petition of Seamen to Acting Governor H. Bryan, enclosed in Bryan to Milner, 21 October 1919.
4. CO 318/349/67533 Minute of Deputy Inspector-General, enclosed in Bryan to Milner, 7 November 1919.

Self-Government for Jamaica

W. Adolphe Roberts

The Jamaica Progressive League (JPL) was founded in September 1936 by Jamaican migrants living in New York City. This staunchly nationalist organization argued for full self-government in Jamaica, that is, for control of all domestic policy by an elected Jamaican government. At the time, most other Jamaican political leaders favored political reform but did not consider self-government or independence a viable possibility. A pamphlet by one of the JPL's founders—writer, journalist, and intellectual W. Adolphe Roberts—makes the case for self-government. Roberts's arguments anticipate the widespread push for self-government in the island that would emerge with the outbreak of the 1938 labor riots.

Jamaica is now being governed by a means of a remarkable device, under which the opinions of elected persons are heard, but need not be heeded.

The Governor usually is a career man promoted from a lesser charge. On occasions, he has been a retired Army General. He is chosen without consulting the wishes of the people of Jamaica. He comes instructed to carry forward the Mother Country's doubtless beneficent plans for her territorial possession. Thereafter, he is answerable to no one, save the Colonial Office which appointed him.

The Governor's task surely is executive. The very term "Governor" implies that. It is not surprising, seeing that he is an autocrat, that he also performs the functions which in democratic Britain, or in any of the Dominions, would be entrusted to a Prime Minister.[1]

The Governor presides over the Legislative Council, as the sole Chamber is called. He is in effect its Speaker. He has both an original and a casting vote. The ten chief Department heads of the Administration sit there as ex-officio members. Five residents of the Colony, nominated by the Governor, also have seats, which they hold under the formal proviso that they must vote "Aye!" on all administration measures, or resign. This gives His Excellency a total of 15 votes, not counting the decisive ballot which he may cast from the chair in the event of a tie.

The other side of the House is composed of only 14 elected members, one for each parish. The franchise is limited on a property basis, both for voters and candidates. Roughly, a Jamaican may not vote unless he occupies a dwelling on which he pays taxes of at least ten shillings, or holds a financially equivalent salaried job, or has a moderate private income.

I believe in universal suffrage. If the Government of Jamaica imposed an educational test for voters, one might respect its motives. But a property qualification is intolerable. The same applies, and with still greater import, to candidates for office. A member of the Legislative Council receives no salary, so a poor man cannot afford the time to sit in the Council. Legislators obviously should be paid, since they serve the country—as well as for the definite reason that a salary opens the way to any person of ability to make a career of statesmanship.

The unsalaried legislator is an anachronism handed down to the Crown Colonies from the ancient regime in Great Britain, under which only gentlemen were supposed to be elected to Parliament. England changed the system in the early years of the present century, when salaries were granted to members of the House of Commons. It should be changed in Jamaica, also.

The conditions which I have outlined did not always prevail in Jamaica. The form of government first set up in Jamaica was not Crown Colony government. In this respect, the island had an advantage over Trinidad, British Honduras and many British colonies in other parts of the world. Even after Jamaica had been made a Crown Colony, there were times when the Legislative Council had larger powers than it has now, and when the elected members showed greater independence and consciousness of the fact that they were the people's representatives.

Crown Colony? What does the term mean? It means a territorial possession governed arbitrarily by its owner. Such a relationship is one of master and dependent. Jamaica's condition is not—under the British Government—a cruel form of servitude. But then, some masters have always been noted for their kindness to dependents—have even coddled them—without being able to overcome their natural desire for greater freedom of action.

The British Government has never held the Crown Colony system to be ideal, or declared that it must be permanently maintained. British statesmen have said, over and over again, that self-government would be granted to the separate units, "when they are fit for it." This pledge has been redeemed in certain instances, apart from the setting up of Dominions.

I say that the moment has come for Jamaicans to realize that if they are to develop politically, they must set about the shaping of their own future. It is idle for them to expect that self-government will be initiated from Westminster as a bounty. They must show an aptitude for the responsibilities of liberty, or it will never be granted. They must begin to act as a people within the framework of the Empire and to cease speaking—or even thinking—as apathetic subjects under a Crown Colony system which has long outstayed its time.

The inhabitants of Jamaica are, in fact, a people; for national entity is a gift of God to every society that has seen its generations come and go on the same soil for centuries. The awakening of a consciousness of nationality is what is needed today.

The 70 years that have passed since the Morant Bay Rebellion are more than enough, I think, as a period of discipline for the Jamaican people. The time has arrived to ask the Mother Country to restore their ancient rights. When this is accorded, it will not be an experiment in the dark. It will be an act of justice to an old and loyal colony, allowing her to begin again politically where she left off in 1865.

Specifically, I advocate:

First: The immediate founding of a political party in Jamaica, pledged to work for self-government.

Second: The waging by Jamaicans, in Jamaica, of a campaign of cultural development in the broadest sense of the term. Knowledge of the Island's history, art and legitimate aspirations must be brought to the masses. It is of still greater importance to foster a proud, fine growth for tomorrow.

I set the ideal of nationalism before all Jamaicans. There is a definite sustaining and guiding strength in national sentiment, in a national consciousness, and this can be created only along the parallel lines of political action and artistic fruitfulness. Neither political action nor artistic fruitfulness has as yet come to flower in Jamaica, but I am confident that the moment in history has been reached when they are due to appear.

Note

1. The Dominions—Australia, New Zealand, Canada, the Irish Free State, Newfoundland, and South Africa—were self-governing territories within the British Empire. Under a law of 1931 the metropolitan British government could no longer legislate for them. The greater powers of self-government available to these white or white-controlled territories accentuated the lack of democratic power in Jamaica. [Editors' note]

The 1938 Rebellion

Richard Hart

Between 1934 and 1939 social unrest swept across the Caribbean, affecting almost every British colony, as well as Cuba and Puerto Rico. Strikes, hunger marches, demonstrations, and riots were common. In Jamaica, the disturbances were so intense that the government almost lost control of the island. They began with a successful strike over wage rates at the Frome sugar factory in Westmoreland in May 1938, which escalated into violence. A few weeks later, Kingston dockworkers struck, while those without work staged ever-larger demonstrations demanding employment. By the end of May, strikes and demonstrations were taking place across Jamaica, and they continued for several weeks. They eventually came to an end through a combination of suppression by state troops and, more importantly, the intervention of nationalist leaders Alexander Bustamante and Norman Manley, who convinced the people that trade unionism and political campaigning would lead to genuine change.

Richard Hart (1917–2013) had in 1938 recently returned to Jamaica, having been educated in England. He became quickly involved in Jamaican politics, supporting the strikers. He was one of the founders of the People's National Party (PNP) and was involved in the establishment of the first Jamaican trade union, the Bustamante Industrial Trade Union, led by Alexander Bustamante, who would later become the first prime minister of an independent Jamaica. In 1952 Hart was one of four men who became known as the "four H's": men who were expelled from the PNP for alleged Soviet sympathies. In later life he became a prolific historian. Here he explains the mounting political and social tensions in 1930s Jamaica.

In the first quarter of 1937 the growing unrest among peasants, many of whom both farmed their own or rented plots of land and also worked part time on larger properties, and landless agricultural workers, found organisational expression in upper Clarendon in central Jamaica. A movement to refuse to pay any more rent to landlords began to spread and, in some areas, land-hungry people seized estate lands. This was fuelled by the revival of a widely held belief that Queen Victoria had promised that, one hundred years after their emancipation, the slaves who had got nothing at the time of the abolition of slavery would inherit the land. Tenants and others who seized lands began to erect fences and offered to pay taxes on the lands the ownership of which they claimed to have acquired.

At the end of December 1937 workers on Serge Island Estate in St Thomas, at the eastern end of the island, refused to start reaping the crop at the rates of pay offered. Police were rushed to the area and, on 4 January 1938, they reported that some four hundred to five hundred strikers had forced others to cease work. Sixty-three of the strikers were arrested and, over a period of three days from 13 January, were tried before the Resident Magistrate. Three "ring-leaders" were sentenced to one month's imprisonment with hard labour, seven were fined £2 and eleven were fined 21/– each with the alternative in default of payment of thirty and twenty-one days' imprisonment respectively. Forty-five others were admonished and discharged. These were relatively lenient sentences.

On 29 March, warned that dissatisfaction among the lowest-paid manual workers was assuming island-wide proportions, the Government announced the appointment of a Commission to enquire into rates of wages and conditions of employment of labourers in receipt of not more than thirty shillings per week, its first session to be held on 11 April.

During the first quarter of 1938, large numbers of workers had been converging on Westmoreland at the western end of the island, attracted by the possibility of employment. On 2 May the *Daily Gleaner* published this report:

> One thousand labourers, a large proportion of them engaged on the erection of a giant Central Sugar Factory at Frome Estate . . . went on strike Friday. They are still out and state that they will only return to work when their demand—one dollar [4/–] per day—is met by the West Indies Sugar Company.

Next day the newspaper's reporter on the spot reported:

> The old factory on the estate, which up to Friday had been grinding canes, is entirely in the hands of the strikers. . . . I hear rifle firing, followed by shrieks and cries. . . . I can see men on the ground. Some are motionless, others are staggering to and fro or crawling away on their hands and knees. The strike has culminated in stark tragedy. A few minutes later I hear that three are dead, eleven wounded and that the police are making many arrests.

Four people were killed that day, three by police gunshot and one by a police bayonet.

The events at Frome had an electrifying effect. There were demonstrations of unemployed workers in Kingston, the capital. Waterfront workers in Kingston put forward demands for wage increases and, at the end of the second week of May, came out on strike. On 23 May many other workers in the city struck work and work in the city came to a halt; all the major stores were forced to put up their shutters by marching workers.

On 24 May, the Governor ordered the arrest of William Alexander Bustamante, a popular figure who during recent months had been addressing public protest meetings and writing letters to British Members of Parliament revealing the distressing economic conditions prevailing in the island. The arrest of Bustamante and his principal assistant St William Grant, and the initial refusal to grant them bail, was a provocation which, despite the appointment of an officially sponsored Conciliation Board on 26 May, unleashed a wave of further strikes and riots.

A week later realising that the only way to ease the situation was to release Bustamante and Grant, the Government agreed to bail being granted. By that time however the spirit of revolt had spread throughout the island and strikes and demonstrations were occurring in every parish. This situation continued for many weeks, despite the use of the battalion of British troops stationed on the island to supplement the police. Workers were killed and injured and many arrests took place.

By the end of June calm had been restored. A number of factors had contributed to this. Perhaps the most important had been the launching by Bustamante of a trade union and assurances from him and the much respected barrister N. W. Manley that the workers would receive proper representation. The announcement on 14 June that a Royal Commission would be arriving shortly to investigate conditions had undoubtedly created expectations that improvements would be forthcoming. On 28 June Acting Governor Woolley had announced in the Legislative Council that two loans would be raised to finance land settlements and other infrastructural developments.

Remembering the Rebellion

Lucius Watson

The 1938 rebellion partly responded to chronic unemployment and underemploy-
ment, exacerbated by the international depression of the 1930s. Kingston in particu-
lar was home to thousands who had been forced to return to Jamaica by nativist
responses to the depression in Cuba and other common destinations for migrant
workers. Garveyism and Jamaica's long history of radical religious engagement, in-
cluding Revivalism and the emerging Rastafari movement, also aroused popular
consciousness. Meanwhile, the Great Powers' minimal response to Italy's invasion
of Ethiopia in 1935 stimulated anger and increasing politicization.

Lucius Watson was interviewed in 1987 for an oral history project of the history
department at the University of the West Indies (UWI). Watson, an activist in the
dockworkers' strike, recounts the events of May 1938 in Kingston, emphasizing the
influence that Garveyism had on him. He stresses the involvement of St. William
Grant (1894–1977) and Alexander Bustamante (1884–1977). In the aftermath of 1938,
"Busta" became, along with his cousin Norman Manley, one of the most significant
political and labour leaders in Jamaica. Bustamante's style of leadership was in-
tensely personalistic. The trade unions he founded all bore his name; eventually they
merged into the Bustamante Industrial Trade Union, and Bustamante served as
president for life. Watson highlights Bustamante's rise and the way his personality
came to overshadow other popular leaders, such as St. William Grant.

Garvey had a strong influence on one person, dat was me. A strong influence, for at nights I use to go to Eloise [Edelweiss] Park. Every night you
have a service up there, and Legion march from the western part of the
balcony, and go right round and Garvey in front, and the lady in charge a de
choir wid de book and sing "Shine on Eternal Light" and march right round,
and sing and clap and keep service there every Sunday night. On Monday
night now, yuh have entertainment. Fally [The Follies] dance or anything
like that. Fally girl teach me a lot of things there. Garvey and whole a de
Garvey people dem, had an impact, great impact on de people. Garvey laid
the foundation in educating the workers—the masses of this country. But

the support was not there because we had a barrier, a class barrier. A brown or white man he will never get any support in supporting the poor man below. The class barrier was a hell of a thing! In 1938 there was no politics. You see, everywhere you turn nobody to represent you. The workers never had any say.

[In those days] even seven and eight year old boys had to be working for themselves and tilling for themselves at one shilling a day.

As for conditions in the rest of the country, oh Lawd, master, the conditions was very bad, the condition it was miserable. For you had men who was working shoving handcart fe Chiney getting eighteen shilling a week. And all those kinds of things. Unemployment was bad, bad, bad. It was terrible! Then the war came along and made things rather worse. While there was no work, everything had actually stand still. For nothing could come or go. Sometime a man would earn for the whole week, three shillings. Sometimes a man would work 5/– or 10/–. Well when you see a man work 30/– is plenty work dat him was to do, for fi de whole day you work from seven in the morning on the ship 'til six in the evening and you get 9/– for that. I don't know how to put it to you but the workers was suffering bad. The Depression was on. Everything was tight and when one ship come you would have three, four hundred waiting on the ship when it could only take on four gang of men for the ship and four gang for the dock. But the condition of work was very bad. It was one bone to a dozen lion. That was the kind of condition. Men was just grabbing and scraping to get a little work. And the men them was forced to the condition, for nobody ever thinking about the workers.

I have been working at the port of Kingston during the 1938 disturbances. The disturbances start in Westmoreland at Frome, then come to Kingston. Islington [St. Mary] break out too. People died at Islington, you know. De port shut down.

There really wasn't any rioting, in the true sense of the word, for it was people demonstrating against conditions that existed at the port, and it were fight peacefully until the thing start to spread all over Kingston. But there was no incident of violence or murder. People was just closing down everywhere, join the port workers who had struck down on the waterfront.

Let me give you the real breakdown of what happened in 1938. They had a boat company, I should say companies, come here with boat. They use to take some people from Aruba as stevedores to work on ship, and load cargo. It happen that the Kingston workers could get any work with that boat. It was foreign men who come with that boat. Well the morning, the Tuesday morning, when the boat come the dock men them take a stand. They are not unloading the ship unless they take on man from Kingston port that's working there. Port workers could only get jobs when a ship come in and man take dem at random, and you know there was more men than jobs. There was no organized system at that time. So this fellow him was there and him take a stand say well then call the other workers and say man we are not working unless they [employ us] on the ship. Well the boat went back with the cargo.

But what spark up it was on the Thursday now that United [Fruit] Company had a boat at Princess Street wharf named "Harboe Jenson." It came from Canada with flour. Well the port workers were called in to work. The port worker said they want one shilling an hour. They were getting eight pence for the dock and nine pence for the ship. Understand! Who work on the dock was getting eight pence, and who work on the ship was getting nine pence an hour. The company refused. They called the assistant-manager down, Mr Hyslop, and he asked them what they want. The workers were bargaining for themselves. There was nobody. Workers take it in their own action. What happened there at Princess Street, United Fruit Company wouldn't yield to one shilling an hour. Well the boat never work. So the ship went away with the Cargo to Portland. It was the Portland stevedores work the boat there.

Well, Sunday now, which was May 23rd was the big show down. The United Company had two boats came, at No. 2 pier—one from Panama, and the other from New York. One was the *Metopan*, and I believe the other was *Sixholder*. That time between them the two boats employed about 600 workers. Well the men [who were] asked to work the boat on Sunday morning said they will not work unless they get a shilling an hour. Well the United Company said they were not paying the shilling an hour. Well the men were there and nobody to negotiate. The men stick out say they are not working unless they get a shilling a hour. [The men] gathered themselves say them not working, and men start to block the gate, say nobody not to work unless them get a shilling a hour. Now when they start off and wouldn't work, the United Fruit Company ask the crew on board the ship, you know the steward them and so forth, offer them a shilling a hour to unload the mail.

Listen to me good, son! The workers had no leader. They were just doing on their own. Well about six of us, a fellow named Franke Isaacs, Jennings, Christie, one named Morgan, and myself—I don't remember the other fellow's name—we said, "well we don't have no leader, let us go call St. William Grant." Grant was living at 36 Rose Lane, so I went and call Grant.

Everybody know Grant. Grant use to have a meeting every Sunday evening at the park telling you about the history of different country, which

St. William Grant
(*left*) and Alexander
Bustamante (*right*) leaving the Central Police
Station, Kingston,
after being arrested
in 1938. Photographer
unknown. From the
National Library
of Jamaica Digital
Collection, identifier
D0002670. Courtesy of
the National Library of
Jamaica.

was very foreign to some of us. Also in those days you know, say about 40 percent of suffering people was illiterate. And he always draw a crowd. Grant wasn't a union man in New York. He was a UNIA man. He came down as a delegate from New York, with the UNIA convention. But he never return back to America. The park was the meeting spot and Grant used it at nights. Built up a little stand there, and start to lecture there each night, Sunday nights. Grant was the key man in the whole thing. For Grant use to keep this meeting and Busta always go out to Grant meeting. And Grant always project him as a rich man, come from Spain and dis and dat, blah, blah, you know. But there was nutten like that. He was just a brag on us.

So when I send and call Grant it was to address the port workers to see if they could get the shippers to come to agreement, for they ask for a shilling a hour. They wouldn't work. So it had no leader. Then, anyway, we go and call Grant at 36 Rose Lane, knock on the gate and push the gate. Saw Grant leaning on a broom, in the yard, and without any shirt on, and merino on. So we knock on the gate and we push the gate. We sey "Mr Grant is you we come to. Come to you." "So weh you want me so late?" We say there is a strike down the waterfront and we want somebody to come and talk to us. So Grant sey, "Alright, oonu wait on me. Wait deh, a coming." Im went to put on his shirt and put on his shoes and sey come and turn up Rose Lane, then turn Beeston Street and sey im just going to call somebody. Then all of us walk on Beeston Street straight on. We open a little iron gate, and the home is about six to seven feet, not even quite seven feet from the gate. And he knocks on the door and the voice inside sey, "Who dat?" Im sey, "Me, Mr Bustamante, me chief." Im sey, "What do you want, Grant?" Im sey, "Me have something here, Sir." And Busta just push im head out and sey "What is it Grant?" And he said, "these men strike on the waterfront and they come and call me to come and talk for them down there." Busta sey, "Alright, Alright, I'll come!"

So Busta take over same time. Then dem sey to Busta and Grant, they want a shilling a hour. And Busta sey if you are entitled to shilling a hour, and you want a shilling a hour, they are robbing you. And Busta same time go across the street. There was a barrier, you know, that when the train coming, it block the train, and Busta climb on the barrier and climb on the train and start to address the men them on strike. And im talk there and tell them not to work until them get the shilling an hour. The delegate from the United company—the one from New York—come and address the meeting, too. And when im [Busta] finish, im come down of the train. Im say "Well, I'll be back here tomorrow morning." Well the men them pick up $39.00 and give it to Busta say to buy some food. Everybody then started to picket the wharf right out. Men start to do their own picketing, but there was no leader to tell you to do this or do dat.

Well the following morning about after 8.00 Busta drive the same little old car and come round, im and Grant, and park and jump up on the bank and address the men dem again, and he walk with we go out to Hanover Street to Jamaica Producer office. And he stop here and hold a meeting and address a man upstairs there name Williams. [He said] "You men up there, you hold good men up there, and won't pay workers. Unoo gwine see!" Afterward he left with the gathering and everybody walk with him on Harbour Street, up King Street. And workers marched behind him and walked up to the Park.

[And so] on the 24th [May] Busta march with the men dem and come up to the Park and stay there and address [a gathering], and this time the crowd develop to a mass thing. When im [Bustamante] go to Parade im climb pon de Queen statue and start to talk dere, mi love. Dat time de crowd big you know, for mouth radio is a very hell of a radio. And when Busta climb on the statue, and start address the man dem, Orrett same time come on, Inspector Orrett, and [tell] Busta, "break it up now." And Busta came down, Yes man! Orrett draw him gun! Busta say "Orrett? You can't shoot the people, is me to shoot for is me addressing them." Orrett left him, and Busta walk and go up to the Brigade for him hear the Brigade was going stop work. That time everywhere shut down now, you know. There was no violence [until then]. Now Ah tell you when the violence began. Is when after they arrest Busta. (They arrested him from that [time] till about the other week.) When we went Sutton Street, Orrett and a police squad came out and stop Busta and tell Busta, well you under arrest. By the time im come out and tell Busta im under arrest. Orrett walk beside Busta wid im gun in im hand. Dem lick de police! 'Bout five police tumble down pon Grant wid de big stick, wid de big long staff and lawd, dem start to beat Grant! And dem give Grant one beating! Them never touch Busta. The black man them beat you, you know. Dem beat him you see? Bloodup! Dem nearly kill him. [The crowd did not intervene] you see, for that time everybody been 'fraid a police, for the police was in full strength and force. Grant nuh du nutten, you know. Dem neva touch Busta far im was de cousin of Norman Manley. Im was a brown man. The only arrest Busta.

When they arrest Busta then now the whole city of Kingston, the Monday, Tuesday, everything start to close down, and that time it turn out it getting out of hand. Everybody said now they want more pay. Everybody say they want to follow Busta. The workers never go back to work on the port. No work go on from dem lock dem up. The men dem sey them not working until Busta release. That happen on Monday. The shippers offer now to give them two-pence [increase]. They are not working until when Busta release. For is through them why Busta arrest. The men them say still hold on with the strike and they were there days after days. Now what happen about the Wednesday, everybody was there and we went out to Princess Street. They said they are not working now. De two a dem [Busta and Grant] dey a jail, and Busta, bway, everybody, de men now insist, sey to mek tings work, se no work till Busta and Grant release. Dat is de Monday. De Tuesday, Wednesday, and now de Thursday, everybody out ah No. 2 pier, and a man ride a bike and sey, Bustamante cousin, Mr Manley, call you round a Malabre Wharf. Everybody fe come round deh. When we go round deh, upstairs we see Mr Manley, de Malabre brothers and all de official dem, an de shippers come sey dey will compromise wid you and give you eleven pence a hour if you return to work. Workers sey not even pound a hour, we not working till Grant and Busta release.

1938 open the eyes of Jamaica. The events of 1938 helped the country. 1938 was the springboard of all what we have here come out of 1938. For that time you know, Son, you couldn't be talking as a little black man. It started in Westmoreland but it had died out in Westmoreland. After 1950 the worker came into his own.

Now We Know

Roger Mais

As nationalism gained pace after 1938, some intellectuals steadfastly opposed British control of Jamaica. The most celebrated critic was Kingston-based writer, poet, photographer, painter, and playwright Roger Mais (1905–1955), a prolific literary figure who won several awards and influenced generations of Jamaican writers. Raised in a middle-class family, Mais developed a sensitivity to the realities of Jamaica's urban and rural poor that infused his literary work. His political consciousness emerged during the 1938 labor riots. He objected strongly to the unfair treatment of the workers by the island's British rulers and was also critical of Jamaica's class structure. His fiction includes the celebrated novel Brother Man *(1954), a remarkable achievement for its focus on the poverty of Kingston and attention to the cultural nationalist power of urban movements such as Rastafari. In this work and his other writings, Mais expressed an urgent demand for social change.*

Mais's anticolonial protest is clearest in his political writings, including this extraordinary essay, published in 1944 in the People's National Party paper Public Opinion. *It provides a thoroughgoing critique of Great Britain's proposals for a new Jamaican constitution, which would come to fruition later that year. Mais draws attention to what he terms the "hypocrisy and deception" of Prime Minister Winston Churchill—"that man of brave speeches"—and the British Empire, then embroiled in World War II while reinforcing "aggression and inequality and human degradation" in its colonies. After he published this essay Mais was arrested for sedition and imprisoned for six months, an experience that inspired his later work.* Now We Know *remains a classic comment on the imbalances of British imperial rule.*

Now we know why the draft of the New Constitution has not been published before. The authors of that particular piece of hypocrisy and deception are the little men who are hopping about like mad all over the British Empire implementing the real official policy, implicit in statements made by the Prime Minister from time to time.

That man of brave speeches has told the world again and again that he does not intend the old order to change; that he does not mean to yield an inch in concessions to anyone, least of all to people in the colonies. Time and again he has avowed in open parliament that, in so many words, what we are fighting for is that England might retain her exclusive prerogative to the conquest and enslavement of other nations, and that she will not brook competition in that particular field from anyone.

For it is not the non-dissolution of the Empire that is aimed at—there are free Dominions within the Empire—but it is the non-dissolution of a colonial system which permits the shameless exploitation of those colonies across the seas of an Empire upon which the sun never sets.

That the sun may never set upon aggression and inequality and human degradation; that the sun may never set upon privilege and repression and exploitation. . . .

That the sun may never set upon the putting of one man's greed before the blood and the sweat of a million.

That the sun may never set upon urchins in rags and old men and old women in rags, prostrate with hunger and sores upon the sidewalks of cities and upon straw pallets among vermin in poorhouses and prisons and homes;

That the sun may never set upon the groaning of people of alien races who have been brought the blessings of Empire; of famine and plague and the sword. . . .

That the sun may never set upon the insolence and arrogance of one race toward all others; and especially to those whose manhood they hold in eternal bondage through their own straw-bosses and quislings and cheap jim-cracks and all the scabs and blacklegs and yes-men and betrayers of their own whom they can buy for a piece of ribbon to wear on their coats or a medal to wear on their coats some letters to come after their names or for the privilege of calling some big-wig by his first name, "Hello, Bill!" "Hello, Charlie, how's the boy!" or with a sinecure of office with access to travelling expenses or with some other such scraps which fall unnoticed from their full table where the unholy feast is devoured by their lords and masters.

For such things as these Colonials from all parts of the Empire are fighting. . . .

For such things as these our young men have added their names to the roll of honoured dead with their mothers and wives and sisters and sweethearts present at the unveiling and proud to honour their dead. . . .

For such things . . .

That the sun may never set upon the great British tradition of Democracy which chains men and women and little children with more than physical chains; chains of ignorance and the apathy of the underfed and the submissiveness which is a spiritual sickness in the thews and sinews of a man; chains them in dungeons of gold mines and silver mines and diamond mines and upon sugar plantations and upon rubber plantations and tea plantations.

For the great idea of Democracy which relegates all "niggers" of whichever race to their proper place in the scheme of political economy:

That we Colonials may ever sing in our schoolrooms those rousing songs like "There'll Always Be an England" and "Rule Britannia" and the rest. . . .

That we might take an equal pride with all Englishmen in the glory of the Greatest Empire upon Earth; that we may rejoice we are privileged to serve it seeing it couldn't exist without us.

That we may take pride if we are no more than the great hunks of red meat upon which the noble Lion feeds that he might have the great sinews and the fierce blood and the mighty roar to afright his enemies. . . .

That we may rise dutifully to our feet and sing with the rest "God Save the King" before we take our seats in the cinema or after the show. . . .

That we might rejoice in our bonds and join in sneering at the great socialist republics which comprise the greatest State upon earth. . . .

That we might rejoice in our poverty and degradation and sickness and ignorance and sores; for it is accounted more blessed to be poor. . . .

For such things as these we are fighting side by side with others in the good cause;

Now we know.

Cookshop Culture

Planters' Punch

Changes in eating customs indicate broader changes in society. From the vantage point of the 1940s, the elite magazine Planters' Punch *here compares the dining habits and preferred foods of urban Jamaicans in the nineteenth century with those of the post–World War I period. The fashion for eating out grew in popularity in the twentieth century. Eating out provided opportunity for social interaction as well as the enjoyment of favored local dishes. Some of the changes in eating habits described here have endured as Jamaican street food, including common foods such as patties and salted codfish. Cookshops remain staples for daily meals among a wide cross section of urban dwellers.*

"SALTFISH, rice and yam!"

  "Stewbeef, rice and yam!"

  "Steak and rice!"

  "Boil' freshfish and yam."

  "Soup and bread!"

The stout woman yelled these instructions to the maids in the neighbouring kitchen as she sat by an open door communicating from the dark, long, gloomy eating-room with the yard where the cooking took place from early morning until night. From her point of vantage she could see every customer that entered, could take his order and transmit it in stentorian tones to the busy servants beyond. Hers was an eating house of the cheaper sort, where the price was sixpence per meal; her customers were men of the old cab-driver type, and artisans; this place of meals and refreshment was one of those that flourished in the lower part of Kingston up to forty years ago; and wages were lower then, and prices lower also, and the meals served in these eating houses were sufficient in quantity and were well patronized.

Occasionally, because she suffered from indigestion, she emitted a loud belch which, in other surroundings, might have been considered more than enough to put her clients off their food. But of this they seemed to take no notice, each man continuing to eat his meal with gusto, some using the forks with which they were supplied, others finding a knife more appropriate to their needs. They talked to one another with their mouths filled with viands, they told of their day's experiences and laughed loudly at the jokes that were passed about. At three or four long tables they sat, each table covered with a dingy and greasy tablecloth spotted here and there with dried vestiges of gravy or of soup; the knives and forks were of steel with horn or wooden handles, the spoons of iron, the tumblers thick and heavy, the cups of coarse and ponderous earthenware. Coffee, tea or chocolate was extra, at three halfpence a cup, but the cups were large. Chocolate appeared the favourite beverage. Bread was served with the sixpenny meal, a small roll to each plate, and the seats were benches whose backlessness forced the diners to lean forward towards the table. From the raftered, unceilinged roof hung large kerosene lamps which were lit at dusk and which sometimes smoked profusely. The smoke had blackened the roof, the few windows that fronted the street admitted little air, the smell of cooking from the yard was strong and all-pervasive, but the customers took no notice of all this and seemed to enjoy the time they spent in this sultry apartment eating breakfast or dinner and engaging in conversation of a familiar and humorous kind.

Rival establishments of a similar description had each their clientele of customers; and farther up, in the centre of the city, were other dining places still. But these were of a lower social order. These were chiefly to be found in the lanes about the central market of Kingston, and in the one small room in which people were served there were usually but a couple of small tables, innocent of covering, and the charge for a plate of food was three-pence. Here labourers congregated, jacketless, not exactly odorous, and here too the knife was much more in evidence as a conveyer of morsels to the mouth than was the fork. But no one ate with his fingers, for that would have stamped him as a creature of the lowest stratum of human life. These men, indeed, never ate with their fingers anywhere. That sort of thing must have happened in Kingston in 1850. But those were the days of darkness before table-manners had come, as it were, to bring form and inconvenience into the city's working-class life.

You may picture the scene for yourself: the large, dark room, the crowd of men seated at the tables with their dingy coverings, the maids moving quickly to and fro, the staccato cries of "stewbeef, rice and yam," the entire place redolent of smells of cooking food and full of the sound of laughing, talking voices. But a change was coming. The horse vehicle gave way to motor cars and taxis, the artisans became better paid, earned more money. Prices increased, salaries rose, a new order in the way of providing refreshment for the better-off multitude emerged. The transition may not have been noticed until it had completely happened; yet where now are the dining rooms of an older day? One or two of them may linger still, but even they are not what their predecessors were. They are smaller, they ask from sixpence to a shilling a meal, they are chiefly luncheon rooms. The poorer classes now take their food from vendors who sell in the markets or in the open air, cheap food made all the cheaper because there are no rooms or tables. One sits upon a bench or a box in a market, or by a gate, or even stands, with his plate or his basin in hand with fork and spoon with the sky for roof, and devours his meal in huge content. It is luncheon that he eats thus: he dines at home. As for the descendants of those who fifty years ago would regularly patronize the sixpenny places where stout ladies shouted to their waitresses for saltfish, rice and yam, you will find them in quite a different sort of refreshment parlour now. They have risen in life, many of them have merged into the middle orders of society. What is more, while in the old days no woman went into one of the cheap popular restaurants of Kingston to lunch or dine, today young women freely visit the newer sort of luncheon room or rendezvous, most of which stand open for all the passing world to see.

The meals at these places are different quite from those that used to be served in former times. Drop in at one of them. Its doors are not closed and are many. Its windows are probably large and of plate glass. Inside, the room is furnished with neat little tables with a metal surface; there are individual chairs with backs. On each table is a printed card on which the various foods and drinks for sale are named, with their prices; the fare is the same day after day, but one may have one's choice of sausage or beef-patty, there are milk, cake, bread-and-butter, malted milk too—which has become a favourite in Jamaica—and ice-cream and half-a-dozen other things. The fare, you will observe, is light; but heavy meals do not seem to be as much consumed in public places in these days as they used to be. I fancy that people, even young men, now spend more on their backs than on their stomachs. But, remember, the patties sold in these places are large; the price of one is threepence, and two of them might be sufficient for an ordinary midday meal. Coffee is threepence also, a huge cup of it, and the milk to flavor it is served separately, as is the sugar to sweeten it—and this is the best sugar that Jamaica makes. And if one prefers cake to patty or sausage, the slice placed before one is generous: you wonder that so much can be given for threepence. And your order is taken by a girl in a clean, neat dress, who is as a rule good-looking, who is neat and quiet in manner, who is as different as anything can be from the waitress who in the days of yore planked down before you a plate of saltfish, rice and yam in a steam eating-house.

So in some forty years the outdoor life of the city has considerably changed; and the change is symbolized by the popular refreshment rooms, with their cleanliness, their blaze of light after dusk, their catering for classes of people who constitute new social orders. The mentality of the people who patronize these popular eating houses is also entirely different from the mentality of their forbears; a new and very much larger middle-class, graded here as it is elsewhere, has sprung into being. In feeling it is somewhat pagan, materialistic, believing in physical enjoyment, living mainly for the hour. It was born either during or shortly after the first great war: the old belief in stability, almost stagnation, it does not share. It feels that the world is changing and that it is part of this new, changing world of uncertain future; it believes far more in equality. In the country districts life may proceed along the ancient lines, but Kingston has gone modern. Or at least, its younger generation is determined to be so. What it will make of the future—what the future will make of it—remains to be seen.

My Mother Who Fathered Me

Edith Clarke

Published in 1957, Edith Clarke's My Mother Who Fathered Me *was one of the foundational works of Caribbean social science and social policy. Clarke, from a well-off Jamaican family, studied anthropology at the London School of Economics in the 1920s. Her research was commissioned by the Colonial Social Science Research Council as part of the Colonial Development and Welfare Programme instituted on the recommendation of the Moyne Commission. Clarke conducted research in three contrasting communities to which she gave the pseudonyms Orange Grove, a settlement of relatively well-off small farmers; Sugartown, a community in which most residents were employed as wage workers on the local sugar plantation; and Mocca, a poor village whose residents scraped by on the produce of family land. The book's title invokes the Barbadian novelist George Lamming's 1953 autobiographical novel,* In the Castle of My Skin, *in which the narrator describes how "my father who had only fathered the idea of me had left me the sole liability of my mother who really fathered me." Clarke's was one of several influential social scientific studies that depicted the importance of the mother and grandmother to Caribbean family life as pathological. But her work was also sensitive to the complexities of Caribbean families, and in particular to women's work, as the following portraits of different kinds of kin and class relationships demonstrate.*

An example of a married family of the extended type among the relatively well-off farmers of Orange Grove were the Wrights, who lived in a large two-story house with their six children, the eldest a girl of twenty-four with her baby. The two youngest were still going to school. The three eldest boys helped their father on the farm, where each had his allotted duties. The family rose early. Mr Wright and the sons went out to look after the animals and while the girls polished the floors and tidied the house, Mrs Wright cooked the breakfast. All the family sat at the table for this, though sometimes the menfolk were late in coming. Breakfast was generally at 7:30 and consisted of coffee for the grown-ups and bush tea for the children, eggs, bread and butter or biscuits and corn pone. On another day it might be saltfish and ackee, breadfruit and avocado pear. After breakfast the family dispersed: the younger children went off to school, other older boys went with their father to work on the farm, and the eldest daughter looked after her baby and helped her mother with the washing or other household duties. The Wrights, although well-to-do, kept no servant. Lunch was at noon and all the family assembled for it. There was considerable variety in the menus, but there was always a meat course—beef, mutton or chicken, yams, cocos, breadfruit or rice and vegetables. The children cleared the table and helped with the washing up. After this the men went back to the fields and the women took things easy and tidied up for the evening. Supper was between 6:00 and 6:30 whenever the men got home. It consisted of homemade cake or biscuits, bread and butter and hot mint tea. On these citrus farms adults and children alike picked and ate oranges at any time during the day when they felt thirsty. In contradistinction to Sugartown, or for that matter Mocca, the family is thus gathered together within the home in a series of joint activities and intimate personal relationships. The father as well as the mother plays with the children, teaches them patterns of behaviour, rebukes or praises. Moreover, the children observe their parents' interdependence and cooperation in all the details of daily life. When differences between husband and wife arise, as inevitably they do, there is not the violence or the tacit acceptance that it may mean a final breach.

Among the small farmers in Orange Grove it was quite proper for the wife to do more of the actual field work [compared to the wives of the better-off farmers]. One of these told us that her husband was a stonemason and did not concern himself with the cultivation. The farm of four acres was hers, she had inherited it from her grandmother and had the title and had paid the taxes. She and her two sons worked the land. She had an acre and a half of corn which is the staple crop; two hundred hills of yam and two acres in pasture. She had one cow, a pig and kept a few fowls. In the old days the land was better, but by stirring and stirring the soil without having a cow to manure it, the yields fell off. She planted peas through the corn and has already reaped that crop. She expected to get four bushels of corn and proposed then to grow potatoes in that bit of land. She grew small tomatoes which she thought the most paying thing in the island. She could sell them on the spot for sixpence for a small basin-full or in Kingston for one shilling and sixpence per pound. By September she would be reaping about 20 lbs a week for six weeks from the two squares she had planted.

Her account of their daily routine was as follows: The two sons rose before 6:00 a.m. and looked after the cows and weeded the land. She prepared the tea, which they had together at 8:00 a.m. unless her husband had to go

out early, in which case he had his separately, but it was his wish that she
sat with the children at meals. Breakfast consisted of yams, potatoes, coffee or bush tea, bread, cabbage and they each had an egg every day. After
breakfast the children want to school taking the lunch money with them.
Three pence was for bread and sugar but she knew they bought sweets with
it. The young man went back to the fields. She cleaned and tidied the house
and then by 9.30 a.m. was ready to go to the field herself. She did weeding
mostly, and the planting of potatoes, cassava and peas. She worked until
about 11:30 and then went back to the house to rest. By this she meant a
rest from field work, but she actually prepared the midday meal. At noon
everybody, except the children who were at school, returned for lunch. This
consisted of yam, flour made into dumplings, breadfruit and a meat dish.
The meat dish varied according to the butcher's schedule; on Monday they
had saltfish; on Tuesday and Thursday cabbage with fat or coconut oil, the
oil either from nuts from their own land or bought. On Wednesday and
Friday they had herrings. Sunday was rice and peas. After lunch the men
returned to the field and, after she had put away the dishes, she went back to
weeding by 1:30. At 3:30 she returned to cook the dinner. The children came
back from school at 4:20 and her sons and husband at 5:00. They all had dinner together. They had soup almost always for dinner followed by the same
vegetables as at lunch and occasionally they had pork. After dinner there
was nowhere to go. The children sometimes played about the yard and she
tidied them for bed by 8:00 p.m. She sometimes went to the prayer meeting
on Sunday night and to the Salvation Army meeting on Monday evenings.
Every second Monday she attended the credit union meeting. Her husband
did not bother with prayer meetings. He loved his sport but he slept in his
bed at nights. On Sunday, he walked and visited. The boys did not sleep in
their beds at nights. They went about and "sported." Sometimes when they
came in she was fast asleep and did not know. Praedial thieves gave them
a lot of trouble. They often had to sit up at night and watch their yams and
could not be sure of reaping their crops because of thieves. The poor fellows
who worked for wages could not afford to buy food, she said, and had no
cultivations so they stole other people's. There was a young man who used
to work in her fields. He was the prettiest young man in the whole district.
He came out one night and dug sixty hills of her yams and went out early
to sell them in the market. When her son missed the yams he went down
and matched the yams in the market with theirs. The thief had no cultivations of his own and, confronted with the proof, he confessed. He got two
months' imprisonment for it.

In Sugartown home life, in the sense in which we have just described it, centring in the home, and continually renewing itself in in a daily routine of cooperative tasks, did not exist. The father, if he was employed, left the home early in the morning and spent much of his leisure in the shops or taverns, returning home late in the evening. It is rare to see a man playing with his children or paying much attention to them. On a Sunday morning we occasionally saw a father carrying the baby, both dressed in their best clothes, along the village street. But it was unusual for him to devote sufficient time to the children to build up any intimate relationship. The house, consisting only too often of one small room or two at best, was little more than a dormitory. The kitchen, where meals were cooked and eaten, was a small wattle hut in the yard containing no furniture. A chair or stool might be brought from the house and put in the doorways for the woman to sit on, but more often than not, she and her children sat on the ground or on a stone with the dish on their knees and ate. The midday meal, which might be eaten any time between noon and 5:00, consisted of cocos, yams, potatoes or breadfruit cooked in a pot together with a small piece of salt fish or salt pork. Often there was only one plate and the woman would give the children pieces of food from hers which they ate with their fingers. The man of the household left after an early "tea" (which in contrast to the Orange Grove family breakfast usually consisted of bread, bush tea and sometimes cornmeal dumplings) and did not return until the evening. If he was a sugar worker he bought his midday meal from one of the food vendors. Supper consisted of bread, bush tea or coco. Among the poorest of the population meat was rarely eaten more than twice per week. During the day, life was lived in the yard, where the children had played, looked after one another or ran errands. Washing of clothes was done at the spring or river. It is done unhurriedly because it is an opportunity for meeting friends and exchanging views, but few adults or children have more than two sets of clothes, one for "drudging" and one for best, so that there were several washing days in a week. While the women were away the children were left in the yard to play, usually in charge of an elder sister who often was kept from school for the purpose. There was much freer movement from "yard" to "yard" in Sugartown than in Orange Grove for example, where class distinctions were operative, and children tended to collect in groups and play together where they were free from adult interference.

In Mocca, also, the men were absent from the homes for the greater part of the day but their activities rarely took them far afield and they normally returned for the midday meal. Although the houses did not allow for these to be taken round a table, it was noted that in several homes the man was served at a small table in the "hall" or second room of the house, while

252
Edith Clarke

the woman and children ate in or near the kitchen. In the afternoons the men generally remained at home until it was time to drive up the cattle, which were pastured some distances away. They did odd jobs in which their womenfolk were occupied or sat about gossiping together while the children played around. Coconut oil boiling was primarily a woman's industry but the men helped in the heavy work of husking the coconuts while the children fetched and carried. There were, in other words, considerably greater opportunities for companionship and shared activities between members of the family at Mocca than in Sugartown. While there was never the degree of familiarity and intimacy in the paternal as in the mother-child relationship, in Mocca, unlike Sugartown, it was not uncommon to see a father playing with his children, teaching the boys to perform some task, even nursing a baby. Whereas in Orange Grove, however, the child could rely upon his father at adolescence to give him a start in life, there was no way in Mocca where the father could help his grown-up children. As in Sugartown the hope was that he might be taken in by some member of the family who had gone away and made good in Kingston or one of the larger towns.

The Origins of Dreadlocks

Barry Chevannes

The Rastafari belief system, distinguished by its worship of Emperor Haile Selassie as the messiah and its rejection of life in Jamaica as exile in Babylon, developed in the milieu of Kingston in the 1920s and 1930s. Its early leaders—Leonard Howell, Archibald Dunkley, and Joseph Hibbert—had all spent time overseas and were influenced by Marcus Garvey. The first Rastas did not wear dreadlocks, and the origin of this way of styling the hair has been controversial among scholars of Rastafari. An influential Jamaican anthropologist, Barry Chevannes, here argues that the "matted hair complex" was advanced by a group of radical young Rastas known as Youth Black Faith during the early 1950s. Rejecting arguments made by other scholars that dreadlocks were modeled on the matted hair of the Hindu holy man the sadhu, and moderating claims that they emulated the style of Mau Mau warriors in Kenya, Chevannes argues that dreadlocks symbolized the outcast, the lunatic, and the derelict in Jamaican society. In adopting this style, Rastafarians physically demonstrated their rejection of and alienation from mainstream society.

Both head and facial hair were sacred to the many Rastafari who from 1934 wore beards. They neither trimmed nor shaved. Still, they were not locksmen. Their hair was not matted, because, although they did not trim, they combed. Any hair, regardless of texture, will grow into knots if left uncombed, more so if it had been exposed to water. To acquire matted locks one must refrain from combing or brushing it; soon the strands curl into tufts, which become heavier and heavier the longer they are left to grow uncultured. When such hair is the tough curly hair of Africans, the knots tend to begin almost from the very root.

It is not quite accurate to say that prior to the Youth Black Faith no one matted locks. Derelicts did. These were people who, because they had lost touch with reality, had no reason to conform to the acceptable human standards of behaviour. They lived in the open on sidewalks or under trees, foraged among the refuse, talked only to themselves or not at all, were unwashed and foul-smelling. They were outcasts. The prototype was Bag-a-wire. Bag-a-wire was well-known because it was said that that he had been a close follower of Marcus Garvey on whom Garvey had set a curse for his treachery. The name Bag-a-wire seems to be an elision of "Bag and wire," from the clothes he wore: burlap or crocus bags held together by wire threads. Society treated him as an outcast: people shunned and children used to stone him. The Dreadfuls and Sons of Thunder knew this was precisely the model society would have of them when they chose the matted hair. Wato explains:

> It appears to I many times that things that the man comb would go out and do, the man with the locks wouldn't think of doing. The appearance to the people when you step out of the form is a outcast. When you are dreadlocks you come like an outcast.

They elected to wear their hair matted, like the outcasts from society, because not only were they treated thus, but they did not consider themselves part of it. As Ethiopians, they wanted out. Some even went as far as adopt the burlap dress of derelicts, so much so that for many years Rastas were thought to be dirty people. *Dutty* (dirty) *Rasta!* became a curse word. It was even alleged that they matted their hair with grime and dung.

Debate inside the Youth Black Faith became heated. The issue was not whether hair was sacred or not, but whether combing was profane or not. To the Dreadfuls it was. If being clean shaven was one way of conforming to society, so that one's actions could be indistinguishable from those around, so too was combing. In other words, those who combed had the same in common with those who were beardless: they conformed. Thus the beard really did not separate the children of Israel from the children of Babylon, but the outcast did.

Had there been any developments to suggest that beards, though equated with the Rastafari, had become socially more acceptable? An interesting column in *The Star* of 30 April 1954 had the following to say:

> The popularity of "Beards" is increasing rapidly in the city. Even members of the higher social stratum have now gone in for hirsute rearing. This new fad has both ideological and economic backgrounds, namely: the suggested visit of the Emperor Haile Selassie, and a recent increase in the price of razor blades.

The mooted visit of His Imperial Majesty came against the background of a sustained heightening of the Back-to-Africa movement in Jamaica. From as early as 1945 a march was staged under the slogan "Give us work or send us back to Africa," thus linking external migration with the bad

Leonard Percivall Howell (1898–1981), founder of the Rastafari movement in the 1930s. Howell, a Garveyite, lived in Panama and the United States for two decades before returning to Jamaica and starting the movement. Photographer unknown, c. 1930s. Courtesy of the National Library of Jamaica.

internal economic situation, which would have been felt all the more bitterly given the high hopes the year before with the first elected government under universal adult suffrage. Many, having no intention of waiting on the government, actually left for Liberia in 1948, in what was seen as the start of a minor trek.

Indeed, the Back-to-Africa movement was quite respectable, receiving wide support from the elected politicians. Isaac Barrant, who rose from the lowly status of a labourer to become a popular representative in the Jamaica Labour Party (JLP) Government in the late 1940s and 1950s, was a consistent supporter. In 1948, B. B. Coke, another Black member in the JLP Government, moved the following motion in the House:

> Whereas there is great desire on the part of many Jamaicans today to migrate to Liberia for economic and other reasons;
>
> Whereas great difficulties are being experienced by these Jamaicans in obtaining the necessary funds so that they may travel and establish themselves in that Country;
>
> Be it resolved that the Government of Jamaica favourably consider the removal of all hindrances in the way, and the proffering of full aid of those would-be migrants.

The text of the resolution, unanimously passed, makes it quite clear that the movement was not confined to a fringe. The Rastafarians were not the only ones seeking to leave for Africa.

In such a climate, Back-to-Africa marches, such as the one led by the Garveyite Z. Munroe Scarlett in August 1950, which included one of the founders Rastafari, Archibald Dunkley and his King of Kings Ethiopian Mission, were a common enough event around Kingston. Thus, when the People's National Party tried to get the Governor to invite His Imperial Majesty to Jamaica in May 1954, the Party had widespread support behind it. The Governor took the request to his Executive Council [which] turned down the request to invite the Negus of Africa to visit Jamaica on grounds that there are "small numbers" of Jamaicans who would be a source of embarrassment to him and Jamaica. There can be no doubt that the Rastafari were meant. But at the same time, the Council was at pains to point out that the Emperor was held by its members "in highest esteem."

What seemed to have been taking place was a co-optation by the society of some of the main symbols of separatist identity. It had quite suddenly become respectable to have relations with the two independent African nations, Ethiopia and Liberia, and to talk of migration there. The word "Africa" no longer stood completely for savagery and darkness. This was the full import of the "ideological background" suggested by the *Star* columnist. No doubt, "decent" people could now be counted among those who hold African heads of state and their countries in esteem.

This co-optation created the need for new symbols of resistance and identity among the people, where interest in Africa was at no time confined solely to the question of migration. Jamaicans have always felt a genuine affinity with the people of the continent. In the mid-1950s, the feelings of solidarity were with Kenya. In January 1953 a large public meeting in Jones Town passed a resolution calling on Britain to withdraw her troops from Kenya and instead seek alternate ways of dealing with the Mau-Mau. The word "Mau-Mau" soon became a catchword used to express defiance. By

1954 there was a well-entrenched criminal gang calling itself the Mau-Mau, strong enough to battle with the police for "several hours," before their leaders were captured.

And so, while identification with certain leaders and peoples of Africa was no longer the source of shame it once was before Marcus Garvey, identification with the Mau-Mau now became, for an important segment of the urban masses, one way of expressing exactly how they felt about the society.

The members of the Youth Black Faith were adamant that they did not belong in Jamaica, and so they developed a more aggressive stance against the state and the society. From their Trench Town headquarters they staged a protest demonstration in support of Kenyatta in April 1953, when it was announced that he had been sentenced to seven years in prison for organizing and directing the Mau-Mau. To both state and society, the Mau-Mau were "terrorists," but to the Rastafari they were freedom fighters. A group of Rastafari defied the Central Housing Authority and began to rebuild the day after being evicted from government lands. Their slogan as they set about their work was "Mau-Mau!" And one "Bearded man" was actually fined £20 for preaching the "Mau-Mau doctrine," for saying, that is, that "the people of Kingston should organize themselves so we can 'chase the White man out of this country.'" In April 1954 when the Youth Black Faith members were arrested for marching through the city without a permit, they had no particular objective in mind other than that the Brother Arthur had received a vision that they should. It was exactly one year since Kenyatta was imprisoned. They not only refused to give their names, but created such a disturbance in court with biblical quotations and unknown tongues that the judge had them gagged, strait-jacketed and examined by Monsignor Gladstone Wilson, a psychologist. It was several weeks before they could reappear in court, whereupon Mr Justice Duffus simply admonished and dismissed them. Said Brother Arthur,

> Same time we here 'pon the work, same time Kenyatta there 'pon the work in Kenya. So this Youth Black Faith is the first throughout the whole world march for freedom!

To identify with the Mau-Mau was to identify with people regarded as criminals and antisocial elements. The Youth Black Faith conceived of themselves as a people struggling to leave a society to which they felt they did not belong. They took on a more aggressive, noncompromising stance. This they symbolized in adopting a new approach, a new way of presenting themselves: the dreadlocks. The Dreadfuls or Warriors were the first to start the trend, and as their hair grew they became even more "dreadful." According to Kurukang, who credited himself for introducing the nyabinghi dance into the Youth Black Faith, the debates were heated. The Dreadfuls were very vociferous and quarrelsome. They were so uncompromising that they brought about a split, as those who could not take the new order "shif up," that is, departed their various ways. By 1960 there were two Houses, the House of the Dreadlocks and the House of Combsomes. In 1961 when an official mission was being sent to Africa to examine the possibilities for migration there, the three Rastafari members of the delegation included one young Dread. By the middle of the 1960s the Combsomes had all but vanished.

Pleasure Island

Esther Chapman

Expanded air travel hastened tourism's growth after World War II. As cruises were no longer the main way to get to Jamaica, tourists from North America and Europe could arrive more quickly and stay longer. To meet this increasing demand, new hotels developed, particularly along the North Coast. Then as now, the winter season was the busiest. The island was marketed to foreigners as an ideal holiday destination with plenty of sunshine, sea, and scenery. In her 1951 guidebook Pleasure Island, *British expat Esther Chapman commented on this early period of Jamaican tourism. Chapman points out Jamaica's diversity of offerings and emphasizes its affordability.*

Whatever may be said by the people of Jamaica in regard to their political and economic difficulties, there has never been any question about the superb qualities which make the island so admirable a tourist resort. Not so many years ago, there were two hotels in the island, both owned by the United Fruit Company, the Myrtle Bank, and the Titchfield. This hotel was destroyed by fire, but the annexe survived, and this, with modern additions, is the present hotel. These two hotels were lordly establishments run less for profit than to provide suitable accommodation for the pampered passengers of the company.

Then Mrs. Ewen, a well-known resident of St. James, bought a charming little house on the cliffs at Montego Bay called Casa Blanca; she opened it for guests, and from this beginning the tourist trade of Jamaica has stemmed. Dr. Barker, the famous osteopath, spread far and wide the medicinal and invigorating qualities of the bathing at Doctor's Cave.

Casa Blanca spread its wings on either side of the original house. It added and improved year by year, without detracting from the original character. It built and acquired cottages on the land side of the road which, in the cause of progress, it has again torn down to replace them by its new and luxurious annexe; it has diverted the road for straightness and garden space. It began as the centre of the tourist industry and it has remained its hub. Around

Tourist map of Jamaica. Artist unknown. Previously published in Esther Chapman, ed., *Pleasure Island: The Book of Jamaica* (Kingston: Arawak Press, 1951). From the Rare Book Collection at the University of the West Indies, Mona, Jamaica, call number FI869.C5 1951.

it has sprung a true resort, with enormous charm, of which its terrace remains the focusing point. At this writing Sunset Lodge is the newest—as it is the most fashionable—hotel and has helped to add to the celebrity of a centre to which all its units have contributed. The life of the fashionable Montego Bay resort gravitates to the Casa Blanca terrace, Doctor's Cave Beach, the Beach View bar, and the Fairfield Country Club. A number of admirable establishments of varying character, which cater to visitors with variable purses, together combine with its lovely sunshine, its incomparable bathing, and its flavor of fashion and enjoyment to create a holiday centre unsurpassed in the world.

Montego Bay is the only resort of its kind in Jamaica and perhaps on the earth, for it is a smart Continental-type holiday spot in the loveliest of the tropical islands surrounded by the most beautiful of seas—the delightful Caribbean—astonishing those who see it by its changing and ever-deepening beauty. But all along the coasts of Jamaica, and up in its hills, there are hotels, or clusters of hotels, which offer equal though different delights. In the last few years, a colony of winter visitors or settlers from colder and more austere climes has dotted what is called the North Shore with delightful villas, has bought country properties perched on the hillsides overlooking the tree-fringed coast, and has been helping to support a chain of new hotels, small and large. Tower Isle, the finest and largest hotel in the British West Indies and one of the most luxurious in the hemisphere, was completed in January 1949, and immediately became the centre of the life of the area. In its shadow nestles the tiny Fern Brae hotel; and along to the west stretches a chain of new hotels. Here, as well as at Montego Bay, the roster of the winter residents includes names famous in the world of art, theatre, fashion, and affairs. These distinguished residents, or semi-residents, are part of the life of the country during its tourist months, which are becoming increasingly numerous and soon will stretch from end to end of the year.

The North Shore and Montego Bay attract most of the visitors, winter and summer; but there are people who never want to leave Port Antonio, where the Titchfield and the San San Beach Club are their gathering points. There are those who seek more secluded places, for there are beaches with good bathing all round the island, with the exception of the metropolis, around which the sea bathing is far from perfect. In the hotels of Kingston and its attractive suburbs, however, most hotels have their own fresh-water pools (Myrtle Bank has a salt-water one); and some people prefer to stay at Manor House, Courtleigh Manor, Mona or another of the comfortable hotels around the capital, from which they may tour the country and see its natural life.

The whole island is tourist material; for everywhere there is beauty, everywhere the sun shines, everywhere there is richness of scenery and softness of air. The breezes blow by day and night to temper the hot sun; but that sun is grateful indeed to skins roughened by the winds of the northlands.

Jamaica, most delectable of tourist lands, is accessible by sea and by air. Visitors from Britain used to consider that only a prolonged stay justified the long sea-voyage; now the distance can be spanned in a day or two. The cost is as variable as the accommodation; luxury hotels can command high rates, and, indeed, cannot afford not to charge them. But there are all kinds of places, from the finest hotels to modest guest-houses at reasonable rates. There is a place for the honeymoon or other couple who regards this as the holiday of a lifetime and will spare no money to make it perfect; and there is a welcome for the school teacher who wishes, by travel through island at moderate cost, to enlarge his travel experience. There are variations in climate, choice of food, degrees of luxury, means of recreation to suit everyone . . . and always, everywhere, the bounties of Nature in her most generous mood.

Hurricane Charlie

Spotlight

Like almost everywhere in the Caribbean region, Jamaica is vulnerable to natural disasters in the form of earthquakes and hurricanes. In the twentieth century, in addition to the 1907 earthquake, there were several major hurricanes. The impact of these disasters was often compounded by the poor infrastructure and poverty of the communities they affected. The worst was Hurricane Charlie, which lashed the eastern and southeastern part of the island in August 1951. Charlie caused over 150 deaths and left thousands homeless. In its aftermath the Jamaican government pursued a new housing policy that would eventually become the Ministry of Housing, an important office that oversaw major projects in Kingston's redevelopment. Referred to as "government yards," these projects would significantly alter Kingston's urban communities such as Trench Town, which was redeveloped in the mid-1950s. For this and other reasons Jamaicans would remember the reach of Hurricane Charlie's destruction well into the next century. This article appeared in the Jamaican magazine Spotlight *shortly after the hurricane.*

"Angrier Dan Ebber"

Roaring in from the southeast Caribbean at a rain-filled 125-mi. clip, tearing, clawing and ripping with murderous fury, the worst hurricane since 1903 struck Jamaica at 9:15 in the night, Friday, August 17.

By daylight the terrifying monster of the elements was gone. Behind, it left a harrowing calling card on which was engraved the most heart-sickening and anguishing picture of destruction in all the island's known history of disasters.

One hundred forty-two men, women and children lay dead amidst an estimated £16 million of wreckage; 30,000 were left with only the gray, frowning sky for a ceiling. It left the 145-by-50-mile island's 1.3 million inhabitants to fight a running battle with famine for the next 18 months at least.

Surveying the ocean of wreckage (giant trees uprooted or stripped clean of branches, whole villages laid flat, houses smashed to matchwood or hurtled chains away from their foundations, zinc sheeting draped high in the

The Spanish Town Court House became the home of hundreds of homeless people in the wake of Hurricane Charlie. A mother is seen with baby in arms and another leaning on her. Photographer unknown. From the *Gleaner*, August 1951. © The Gleaner Company (Media) Limited.

air over telephone poles that still stood up, debris-choked roads, devastated fields), oldtimers shook their heads sadly. Said a dazed survivor ironically at daybreak next morning: "De good Lawd musta been angrier dan ebber last nite wid Jamaica; Him sure rough up de place bad."

From Port Morant in the east, the monster travelled along the plainsland to far into the western hinterland, ricocheting off the foothills below the Blue Mountain hogback across the island, its madness aggravated by the rain that made every rivulet a raging Niagara.

Omen? All day Friday the sky had been heavy and brooding. Radio Jamaica had alerted the people on what to do before and during the hurricane that had been growling in the Caribbean for several days before. Some had taken the warnings seriously enough to batten down things, fill bathtubs with clean water (that looked like unstrained tea next morning), or be ready to head for prearranged shelters of refuge during the night if the worst came. Some of the shelters were churches. As it turned out, not a single church in the hurricane's path escaped. Some were ripped wide open and would be useless for a long time to come. (An omen, said the cynics, that churches serve no good purpose these days.)

In the days that followed, as relief and rehabilitation agencies went grimly about their tasks, as bodies began stinking in the debris or were fished out of the sea, the tales were told. They were tales of agonizing death, of heroic deeds, of utter loss of earthly possessions, of heartbreak and sorrow.

Jamaican East Indians

Laxmi and Ajai Mansingh

The indentured labor scheme that brought workers from India ended in 1917. The last group of repatriated Indians left Jamaica in 1929. By then, thousands of time-expired indentured workers and their descendants had come to call Jamaica home. The large influence of Indian culture in Jamaica is identifiable most readily in cuisine—curried meats have become a staple of the Jamaican diet—and the inclusion of Indian practices in national festivities. In this selection, two major historians of Indians in Jamaica consider the postindentureship experience of the Indian community and its influence in the twentieth century.

Almost two-thirds of the indentured immigrants remained in Jamaica, willingly or otherwise. Besides official hurdles, personal circumstances forced many to remain in Jamaica permanently.

The shortage of women in the Indian community forced many men to develop relationships with Afro-Jamaican girls and therefore found it practical to settle down in Jamaica, despite their love for the motherland. Others had developed an inescapable network of relationships within the indentured community through marriages. Many dreamed of a better economic future in Jamaica and took their chances.

Unlike Trinidad and Guyana, there was never any settlement in Jamaica which could be called an Indian village. The island did not have available land for the indians to purchase. They were thus forced to move into already established communities. The first Indian settlements started on the periphery of plantations in Clarendon and Westmoreland in the late 1850s, where 1,399 adults of the 1845–1848 group and their 92 children had settled. By 1861, their numbers had grown to 2,226, including those who had landed here during 1860–1861. More Indian settlements started to spring up in the 1870s, as the immigrants of the 1860s became eligible for cash bounties and land allocations.

Urban migration started in the mid-1850s when a few Indians were employed at Liguanea Plains in St. Andrew. Their numbers rose to 200 in 1881, 900 in 1891 and 967 in 1910. Approximately 94 per cent of the Indians still lived in rural communities, 9,830 in settlements and 7,500 on plantations. To-day [1995], 40 per cent of an estimated 50,000 Indians live in the metropolitan area and another 15 per cent in Spanish Town, Portmore and other urban centers in the island.

Kingston Pen (now Tivoli Gardens) was bought in the 1920s by Dhanukd-dhari Tiwari, an 1885 immigrant. The sixty-five-acre property, which had five sections—Newland, Ackee Walk, Back O' Wall, Grassyard and Maranga Lane—soon became the centre of Hinduism and Indian culture in Jamaica. About five hundred Indian families cultivated vegetables and flowers on the leased lands. Most jewellers from the country also moved here to establish the centre of Indian jewellery-making in Jamaica. In fact, Kingston Pen, Denham Town and the Four Mile were known as Hindu Town, until the 1960s.

The termination of the indentureship scheme in 1917 severed the umbilical cord between India and its indentured children in Jamaica. As the s.s. *Satlaj* sailed to India in 1929 with the last of the returnees, the thirty-thousand-strong Indian community in the island had to abandon any plan for returning to India. They now faced the challenge of integrating with the rest of Jamaica actively or passively. It required a philosophy and a strategy which the Indian leadership of the time never realized. The problem was exacerbated by the choices which the colonial Jamaica offered—become a Christian and thrive, or remain a Hindu or an Indian and continue to struggle. Many succumbed to the economic pressures and changed their religion; some cut off all cultural ties with the Hindus, but they could not do anything about their Indian features. Others succumbed partially and retained strong cultural links with the Hindus. Just as the colonial pressure was waning in the 1950s and 1960s, Afrocentricism raised its head in Jamaica in the 1970s. All Jamaicans were expected to find their roots in Africa. This home away from home began to look like a blind tunnel to enterprising Indo-Jamaicans and many chose to emigrate to the emotionally less stress-ful greener pastures elsewhere.

Indian culture has always been under severe pressure in Jamaica. It thrived in settlements where their numbers were viable. The new arrivals from India infused fresh blood, enthusiasm and determination in the community. The postindentureship era deprived the Indo-Jamaicans of cultural "blood-transfusion" and depleted their density below the threshold of cultural viability in many areas. If the social and economic disadvantages of being a Hindu or Muslim forced many Indians to embrace the religion of the rulers as far back as the 1860s, isolation from Indian settlements and concentrations forced most Indians to gradually succumb to demands and norms of the greater society.

However, some aspects of Indian culture survived in the homes of the isolated Indo-Jamaicans. The joint family system continued, but in most instances, it became a joint yard family system in which brothers with nuclear families share almost all the benefits of a joint family system except economic resources and their distribution according to the needs. Even when sons and daughters moved out to find work or to establish businesses, strong family ties have been maintained. The sacrifice of Indian parents in sharing their meager resources with children, relatives and close friends, providing better educational opportunities for their children, and showering them with love and concern continue to be the strong features of Indo-Jamaican family life. The sense of oneness thus instilled in the next generation ensures good old-age care for even the socially downtrodden parents.

The speaking of Hindi in Indian homes has been on the decline since the 1940s. In the 1970s, less than 10 per cent of individuals over fifty years of age and a few younger individuals could still converse in Hindi. Today, only some of the older folk understand Hindi, few speak it fluently, and even fewer can read or write it. The Western way of addressing relatives and offering greetings has been adopted by all. There are a few who sing Hindi songs. Most of the estimated fifty-thousand-strong Indo-Jamaicans enjoy Indian music, but do not understand the lyrics.

Indian traditional attire has been abandoned almost completely, except by the priests who wear the *dhoti* and *kurta* when performing religious duties, and some ladies who may wear a *saree* or *shalwar kurta* during festivals.

Indian food is the only aspect of culture retained by Indo-Jamaicans. Roti, daal, ethnic vegetables and such as flat beans and mango, and curried goat and fish are cooked by many Indo-Jamaicans. Until the 1960s, they grew all types of daal and vegetables for their own community needs.

Marriage and common-law unions with other racial groups have been on the increase since the 1960s. Today, there are no more than a score of families who do not have a non-Indian relative through marriage. Some Indian families still do not allow their daughters to date, but arrange social contacts with eligible Indian bachelors. Indo-Jamaican girls have a serious problem finding suitable, educated, ambitious and considerate Indian boys. The fact that five times as many girls go for higher education as Indo-Jamaican boys has widened the gap between the two sexes with regard to knowledge, values and economic potentials of the two sexes. A survey conducted by the authors in 1985 of one hundred single Indian girls across the island revealed that seventy-three of them preferred to marry suitable Indo-Jamaican boys. In practice, however, most end up marrying suitable Jamaicans of any ethnicity.

Blackness and Beauty

Rochelle Rowe

*Race has always influenced judgment about women's beauty in Jamaica. As nation-
alism became increasingly significant, efforts to redefine ideals of feminine beauty
to include black women became important too. Historian Rochelle Rowe explores
a contradictory effort to assert the beauty of black women—the "Ten Types—One
People" beauty contest, which began in 1955—as part of the celebrations that marked
the three hundredth anniversary of the British conquest of Jamaica. Although the
competition included black women as part of the "Miss Ebony" category, they were
presented as merely one of ten of Jamaica's "types," although they constituted the
vast majority of Jamaica's female population. In this, the competition foreshadowed
independent Jamaica's national slogan, "Out of Many, One People," which emphasized the country's mixture of heritages rather than its population's predominantly
African origins.*

In 1955, Jamaica celebrated a national festival, "Jamaica 300," that commem-
orated three hundred years of Jamaica's history as a British colony. A highly
visible part of the year-long celebration was the "Ten Types—One People"
female beauty contest, which attracted three thousand participants and ran
in the national tabloid, the *Star*, from May to December. The contest comprised ten separate competitions, each of which represented a category for a
specific skin tone. "Ten Types" produced ten winners, one from each competition, who would all reign as beauty queens with no overall winner pre-
siding. The titles euphemistically pertained to races, ethnicities, and colors,
including "Miss Apple Blossom," "Miss Allspice," and "Miss Ebony." The
ten categories, expressed through the female entrants' bodies, were paraded
alongside each other to suggest a racially harmonious Jamaica.

As part of "Jamaica 300," the "Ten Types" contest was designed to express
the idealized model of a plural Jamaica. The contest would indicate to both
domestic and foreign audiences that Jamaica had resolved the so-called race
problem, thereby establishing Jamaican modernity. Much like Brazil's official myth of racial democracy and the melting-pot rhetoric of the United

Ten Types, 1955, an image promoting the Ten Types—One People beauty contest, show-ing the winners of each section of the contest. The caption labels the women, left to right, as Miss Ebony, Miss Mahogany, Miss Satinwood, Miss Allspice, Miss Sandal-wood, Miss Golden Apple, Miss Jasmine, Miss Pomegranate, Miss Lotus, and Miss Appleblossom. Photograph taken for the Stationary Office, London, by an unknown photographer. Previously published in Rochelle Rowe, "'Glorifying the Jamaican Girl': The 'Ten Types—One People' Beauty Contest, Radicalized Femininities, and Jamai-can Nationalism," *Radical History Review* 103 (2009): 36–44.

States, "Ten Types" would serve as a metaphor for Jamaica's successful as-similation of once disparate peoples in democratic harmony.

The *Star* launched "Ten Types" in May 1955 as a uniquely inclusive beauty contest, the first of its kind, with a plural political message and a cleverly implied critique of the all-white "Miss Jamaica" contest summarized in the "Ten Types" slogan, "Every lassie has an equal chance." While it is impor-tant to distinguish "Ten Types" from the racially exclusive "Miss Jamaica," both pageants represented the interests and tactics of the establishment, relying as they did on commercial sponsorship, press exposure and the in-volvement of the Jamaica Tourist Board. Publicity for "Ten Types" appeared regularly in the *Star* and the *Gleaner* and revealed the grand scale of the con-test and the organizers' commitment to demonstrating its national scope. The "Ten Types" competition would tour the island, "uncovering a wealth of feminine charm," almost scouring the countryside for Jamaica's hidden beauties. There would be seven months of preliminaries between the launch of the contest in May and the final unveiling of the winners at Christmas.

The process resulted in ten separate beauty queens, each one crowned alongside her fellow queens as a national representative:

Miss Ebony—A Jamaican Girl of Black Complexion.

Miss Mahogany—A Jamaican Girl of Cocoa-Brown Complexion.

Miss Satinwood—A Jamaican Girl of Coffee-and-Milk Complexion.

Miss Golden Apple—A Jamaican Girl of Peaches-and-Cream Complexion.

Miss Apple Blossom—A Jamaican Girl of European Parentage.

Miss Pomegranate—A Jamaican Girl of White-Mediterranean Parentage.

Miss Sandalwood—A Jamaican Girl of Pure Indian Parentage.

Miss Lotus—A Jamaican Girl of Pure Chinese Parentage.

Miss Jasmine—A Jamaican Girl of Part Chinese Parentage.

Miss Allspice—A Jamaican Girl of Part Indian Parentage.

"Ten Types" attempted to universalize a feminine standard by showing that women of differently raced bodies could conform to a recognizable Western ideal. The selected beauty queens were all, unsurprisingly, slim and petite in frame. In the photograph they are posed in a row, tiptoed, hands on hips, heads turned to face the camera. The array of slim-figured women in identical poses reframed discourses of racialized othering. It suggested instead a universal beauty standard to which all Jamaican women could conform, and furthermore that the differently raced ethnic groups of Jamaica could assimilate to modernity.

The imagined color categories of the "Ten Types" parade appeared to decimalize the Jamaican demographic profile. That is, they appeared to give some measured proportionality to the division of Jamaican society into tenths, as though each category represented a tenth of the diverse whole of the population. In the process, they confined the most frequently occurring skin shade—the dark brown skin of obvious African descent—to only one of these categories. Moreover, the visual array gave primacy to the categories that referenced obvious racial mixes, those that reflected the ethnic composition of the colored middle class. In the parade of feminine beauty, brownness was imagined expansively and occupied a number of the given categories. The "Ten Types" panorama of feminine beauty, which attempted to deliver a multiracial model of plural Jamaica, was therefore weakened by what it revealed about the persistent unease with the place of blackness in the new political order at this heightened moment of cultural nationalism.

Chinese Jamaica

Easton Lee

Despite its small size, the Chinese community has played a prominent role in Ja-
maican society and history. Chinese people began arriving in the island in the mid-
nineteenth century. Along with East Indian migrants, they were recruited princi-
pally for plantation labor. Migration to Jamaica was part of a much larger pattern of
emigration from southeastern China in this period. It continued into the twentieth
century in spite of intermittent state regulations to restrict it. Although many Chi-
nese families left Jamaica for North America in the 1970s, a new wave has arrived
since the 1980s, many finding work in hospitality and as laborers on major construc-
tion projects. The 2011 census recorded 5,099 Jamaicans as people of Chinese ethnic
origin.[1] *Chinese Jamaicans have played a prominent role in the retail trade in dry*
goods and supermarkets. They have also made notable contributions to Jamaican
culture, industry, religion and politics. Several leading politicians, entrepreneurs,
clergymen, and record producers have been of Chinese origin. Easton Lee's personal
account of his life growing up as the son of Chinese grocery store owners in rural Ja-
maica highlights the sometimes-challenging experiences of the Chinese during their
early years of settlement in the island.

I remember my father building his own shop. It was about 20' × 12', and
there were three rooms at the back. One was about 10' × 10', another was
about 12' × 14', the third, which was about 10' × 8', was the dining room; and
that was your life. This was fenced round and had a gate and a lock, one
gate to the front and one to the back; and it was always a source of humour
in our family that the only time you walked through the front gate was
when you were going to church with my mother, who was Jamaican, on
a Sunday morning. Your life was entering in the shop and going out of the
shop so you didn't leave the place when the shop was closed, which in any
event wasn't for any long (I am amused to hear that it is eleven hours that
we worked; it was more like eighteen hours a day). The experience was like
this: you would be awakened by your parents at 4:30, you had to meet the
bread van that was passing to deliver the bread for the shop and at the same

time begin to prepare for the pit men and for people who were going to the fields who needed their half-a-penny sugar, their two-pence bread or penny bread and half-penny salt-butter, two ounces of saltfish or whatever they needed to take to the field with them. Now by the time this was finished, the parents had gotten awake and breakfast was made, and you were fed and sent off to school, and because we lived near to the school we were kept back until five minutes to nine when the first bell rang. And then at lunch time you would hurry back. When everybody else was playing cricket you had to hurry back to the shop so that the old people could get their chance to eat lunch and then you would stay with them until the bell rang again and you ran back to school, so there was not much of extra-curricular activities for us because we always had to be in the shop. In our family today, everybody showers the last thing before going to bed; it's a habit no matter what you did, no matter where you went, no matter if you had showered at 10 o'clock to go to a party and came home at 1 o'clock—you showered again before bed, because this had become a habit that started with nobody wanting to go to bed smelling of mackerel and saltfish.

Earlier settlers sent to China for their families, for their wives and their sons. In their shops they employed only Chinese because they didn't trust anybody else and they employed only relatives because they didn't trust some other Chinese as well. Their money was circulated among themselves, and such exclusivity bred, as it was bound to, resentment among the native population, and even, at times, ambivalent treatment from representatives of the British Crown. The Chinese community reacted as if they were in fact a society within a society. They developed and financed their own institutions: the benevolent society, a public school where they taught Hakka as well as English and bookkeeping, a newspaper, a sanitarium, a wholesalers and retailers association, athletic and dramatic clubs, a Chinese cemetery. And when they looked outward for support it was to the Chinese Ambassador in London. The experience with and the impression of the first groups of Chinese were to last a long time among the non-Chinese population. They were thought to be weak and unable to do hard work. Certainly the background of these Chinese people would suggest something else. Many other myths would spring up about the Chinese like with every other minority, I suppose, and the black population, anxious to assert their superiority, spread these myths and stories and ridiculed the Chinese in the practices of their culture. I can remember it being said that you were weak because you were Chinese; because you ate rice, you were very weak; and you were afraid of dead people, which was certainly not true because in the organization of the Chinese society specific people had specific functions, and if somebody died it was the older woman in the house who took care of that. There was no need for anybody else to deal with it. Another of these myths was that all Chinese were very short, but my own father was 5'11" (and my mother 5'2", so you can see where my shortness came from). The Jamaican women who later had children with Chinese men were told that this was a wrong thing to do because your blood was now poisoned and you would be unable to have children for any other man. My Jamaican grandfather was very upset when my mother and father got together because Chinese were cannibals and they would eat the people they came into contact with. And because of these myths that sprung up, the Chinese clung very closely together and formed their own society. My own father would journey from Appleton near Appleton Estates where we used to live all the way up to Mandeville on a Sunday just to meet with his friends at great expense; and the more the pressures from the outside came, the more they clung together.

The capital which they accumulated was passed on to their sons, note sons, not daughters, because in the Chinese way of reckoning your daughter is not your child because she will marry and the name will change, and the child born to my daughter is not considered among Chinese to be grandchild because the name has changed.

So it is either cash or kind that was passed on to the sons and it is very difficult for people outside of the Chinese way of life to understand the slow passion with which the Chinese worked and accumulated what they accumulated. It is very difficult for them to understand how it is that my father would look at me and say "I am sorry—no shoes, no clothes, you do with what you have. You want the book, here is the book; you want the food, here is the food." Now I realize that we were eating a much better balanced diet than most of these children with whom we were associating at the time, because my father insisted on meat, and on fish, and eggs, and milk, and rice, and cornmeal porridge and those kinds of things. I mean, anything you wanted to eat you could get. Any book you wanted, you could get, but you didn't ask for clothing other than what could be afforded. You were told, "I am sorry, you are going to school barefooted for the rest of the month because the shoe you have mashed up is the only one you are going to get. You won't get any more until Christmas or some other time." So it was a case of ordering our priorities. Things like curtains and fancy things in the house—no way. The basics were what were provided.

Note

1. *Population and Housing Census, 2011, Jamaica: General Report*, vol. 1 (Kingston: Statistical Institute of Jamaica, 2012), xiv.

Bauxite

Sherry Keith and Robert Girling

Postwar Jamaica saw a dramatic expansion in bauxite mining in the central hills of the island. Bauxite, the raw material for the production of aluminum, was increasingly important as a crucial component of aircraft and automobile manufacture. Successive Jamaican governments hoped that bauxite production would provide a route to development, but as Sherry Keith and Robert Girling explain in this article written in the 1970s, control of the international bauxite industry by a small number of vertically integrated North American companies made it difficult for Jamaica and other countries with substantial bauxite reserves to benefit from their extraction. The blast-mining method of bauxite extraction also damaged the environment, resulting in loss of agricultural and residential land, water contamination, and deforestation. Keith and Girling, both American, worked for the Jamaican government in the early years of independence.

Bauxite may not be as well-known to North America's pop culture as reggae or ganja, but it is more widely consumed. For aluminum has become one of the most common metals in the U.S. In heavy industry, aluminum goes into every U.S.-produced automobile; it is used extensively in the space program, and, perhaps most important in measuring aluminum's strategic importance, is the fact that 80 percent of an airplane's weight is accounted for by the metal. Understandably, the government has designated aluminum as one of the thirteen strategic metals. Not only does the U.S. depend on imported bauxite for about 85 percent of its needs, it also depends on Jamaican bauxite, which supplies about one-half of U.S. annual imports.

The story of the U.S. aluminum industry began in Pittsburgh in 1888, with the founding of the Pittsburgh Reduction Company, known today as Alcoa (the Aluminum Company of America). Alcoa began mining bauxite in the Caribbean as early as 1916, when it moved into Guyana (then British Guiana), and later into Surinam. The [Second World] war marked the beginning of a period of intense worldwide expansion of the aluminum industry, as the companies searched for cheap sources of high-quality bauxite ore.

With the [postwar US government] decision to depend on imported bauxite, the U.S. aluminum companies turned their attention to Jamaica. The island soon became a key link in the companies' strategy to internationalize their operations, and the major supplier of bauxite to North America. Jamaica was in several respects a model arena for expansion. Because of the island's proximity to the U.S., Jamaican ores were much cheaper to transport than the bauxite being mined in Guyana and Surinam, which were located more than twice the distance from U.S. Gulf Coast ports. In addition, the exceptionally high quality of Jamaica's ores made them relatively cheap to refine. Moreover, the ease of mining bauxite in Jamaica—where ore deposits are located six to twelve inches below the surface, as compared to as much as fifty feet in Guyana—gave the siting of mines on the island a further economic advantage for the companies. Another drawing card was the cheap and abundant labor available in Jamaica. In 1953 the unskilled bauxite worker earned an average wage of about $13 a week, just slightly more than the sugarcane cutter working full time during the harvest. Finally, the political climate of Jamaica during the late colonial period was relatively controlled, with the two major political parties strongly wedded to the parliamentary traditions established by the British. Confidence in the political stability of the late colonial regime was undoubtedly matched by the companies' confidence in their ability to come out on top in any dealing with the Jamaican government. The companies' control over every aspect of the worldwide aluminum industry, and Jamaica's lack of experience in the bauxite industry, gave the aluminum giants an overwhelming advantage vis-à-vis the government.

Presented with such favorable conditions, the aluminum companies moved rapidly into Jamaica, beginning with the purchase of vast tracts of bauxite lands in the forties. In 1943, Alcoa's former Canadian affiliate, Alcan Aluminium, established Jamaican Bauxites Ltd. as a fully owned subsidiary. Shortly thereafter, other major North American aluminum companies began to explore and make extensive property acquisitions. In 1944 Reynolds Metals entered the island and simultaneously began experimentation in the U.S. to develop a process to handle Jamaican bauxite ores. Permanente Metals (forerunner of Kaiser) began to buy up bauxite reserves abroad after taking over excess government smelting capacity in the U.S. following the war. The company purchased over forty thousand acres of bauxite-rich lands in Jamaica, which were to supply Kaiser's smelting and refining plants for the next two decades. In the early fifties, the companies began to develop their newly acquired reserves. Kaiser built a huge mining complex on the southwest coast of Jamaica. The company also developed its own railway line, road network, and its own port facilities where the ore could be stored, loaded and shipped to Louisiana for processing. Both Reynolds and Alcan also made large investments in mining and port facilities at this time. Alcoa continued to rely on its reserves in the U.S., Guyana and Surinam until 1960, when it too opened operations in Jamaica. It was not long before the companies began to build refineries alongside their mines in Jamaica and other countries. As early as 1953 Alcan built the first alumina refinery on the island—the Kirkvine works—but the major expansion of refining capacity took place in the early sixties.

The Jamaican investments became one piece in the companies' global strategy. For Jamaica, this meant that the development of its bauxite resources was decided by the companies' plans and operations elsewhere. The other side of the coin was the companies' growing reliance on Jamaica, as they restructured their refining, reduction and marketing capacity in North America to accommodate Jamaican bauxite. This dependence was later to give the Jamaican government some leverage over the companies. The U.S. government was in many respects a silent partner in the Jamaican venture. In addition to the guaranteed markets of the government stockpile and state subsidization of electric power to run the U.S. refineries, the companies received government financing for a large portion of their original investments in Jamaica. Reynolds, for example, received over $8.5 million from the U.S. government to finance its mining and processing facilities, which covered 85 percent of its total investment outlay. This partnership between transnational capital and the U.S. government is the origin, as well as the strength, of the North American chains that bind Jamaica until the present.

The arrival of the bauxite companies in Jamaica was met with great expectations by all Jamaicans, but especially the ruling circles. The government believed that the development of bauxite would have the effect of spreading industrialization rapidly to other sectors of the economy. In fact, this was only partially the case, principally because the companies were not interested in reinvesting their profits in other industrial activities within Jamaica. Furthermore, the ripple effects in the economy were limited because the bauxite industry required relatively few inputs which could be purchased locally. Most of the necessary components—heavy earth-moving machinery, forty-ton trucks, petroleum, caustic soda used in refining alumina—were not produced within Jamaica, but rather imported from the industrialized countries.

Because the bauxite industry was 100 percent foreign-owned, and generated relatively few jobs locally, the main contribution of the industry to the Jamaican economy was in the form of royalties and taxes paid to the government by the companies. By 1968, the government derived 14 percent of its tax revenues from the bauxite/alumina industry. This revenue, however, was relatively small by comparison with the value which the industry was generating for the companies themselves. But vertical integration of the bauxite/aluminum industry made it difficult for Jamaica to increase its share of the profits for several reasons. First, it was not easy to establish a market price for bauxite ore upon which to base taxation. Because each company owned all three stages of production—mining, refining and smelting—bauxite was never offered on the market; rather, it was "sold" by subsidiary to parent company for a "transfer price" established by the company itself. The companies consistently undervalued the price of Jamaican ore, which kept down their tax payments to the government. In 1950, with the first agreements between the bauxite companies and the government the payment was about $0.40 per ton. When the Jamaicans discovered how the companies were undervaluing the price, a new agreement was negotiated setting the tax at about $1.85 per ton. This agreement remained in effect until 1971, when the rate was raised to $2.40 per ton—still extremely low considering that smelted aluminum ingot was selling for approximately $500 per ton in the U.S. Moreover, the companies' position of dominance in the aluminum industry throughout the world kept the Jamaican government conciliatory toward them for over two decades. Even if Jamaica objected to their pricing policies, there were few prospects for alternative bauxite buyers. It was not until the government was confronted with severe social and economic crises that it chose to take an aggressive stance vis-à-vis the industry.

As the grip of the bauxite industry on Jamaica's economy tightened, the industry's presence caused important changes in the labor force. With the entry of the bauxite companies into the island, the situation of the peasantry deteriorated. The acute land shortage was further aggravated by the more than 100,000 acres of land purchased by the companies in their race to secure bauxite reserves for the future. Much of this land was purchased from small farmers, who in turn used the cash to leave the countryside and migrate to the cities or move abroad. Between 1945 and 1968 the total acreage under cultivation in Jamaica dropped by 18 percent. The bauxite industry created relatively few jobs because of its capital intensive nature. With all of the mining done in open pits, the industry relies more on heavy machinery than on labor power. And most bauxite workers are machine operators rather than pick and shovel miners, responsible for running the trucks, cranes and giant earth-moving equipment. The $300 million the companies invested in Jamaica between 1950 and 1970 created only about six thousand new permanent jobs, and in 1976 employment in the industry stood at less than seven thousand people (only 0.6 percent of the labor force).

As with all mining operations, aluminum production requires a large capital investment for plant and equipment, an investment easily running into the hundreds of millions of dollars. This is mainly because of the massive electric power requirements of the "pot lines" where oxygen is electro-chemically separated from alumina to produce aluminum. In fact, the key raw material for aluminum is not bauxite but electric power, with energy costs accounting for a quarter of the cost of finished aluminum products. The enormous capital requirements of the industry have helped determine the international division of labor within it. While the U.S., Japan and Western Europe produced only 11 percent of the entire world's bauxite in 1976, they smelted 57 percent of the aluminum. The major companies control all stages of production—from mining bauxite to refining alumina to smelting aluminum as well as marketing. They even have their own shipping lines. Were Jamaica to seize control of its bauxite mines and alumina refineries, it would have great difficulty in marketing its products, for the companies would act in concert to boycott its ore.

The West Indies Federation

Michele A. Johnson

The West Indies Federation was established in 1958 as a self-governing unit within the British Empire, with the intention that it would eventually become an independent nation. Made up of ten provinces, of which Jamaica was one, it won the allegiance of many nationalists, in particular those in the People's National Party. The Jamaica Labour Party opposed Jamaica's participation, however, fearing that membership would mean that Jamaica ended up financially supporting the federation's smaller members. In 1961 PNP premier Norman Manley called a referendum on Jamaica's membership in the federation, hoping for an endorsement that would settle the debate in his favor. Instead, the antifederalists won with 54 percent of the vote, and Jamaica withdrew. Eric Williams, prime minister of Trinidad and Tobago, famously commented that "one from ten leaves nought," and indeed the federation did collapse the following year. Here Jamaican historian Michele Johnson explains the run-up to the referendum, and the arguments made by campaigners on both sides.

By the constitution of 1944, which gave Jamaica more autonomy and universal adult suffrage, there appeared to be a distinct imperial commitment to decolonisation, perhaps even independence, and if that, preferably under the umbrella of the West Indian Federation. The idea of federation was not new in the Colonial Office, although few attempts survived the rough seas of mercantilism and soon sank under the weight of peculiar island concerns and jealousies.

A conference was scheduled for September 1947 in Montego Bay, to begin the discussions which might lead to a federal whole.

Delegates at the Montego Bay conference were not of one accord. Alexander Bustamante, leader of the majority in the Jamaican government and also leader of the Jamaica Labour Party (JLP), raised concern about the cost of the proposed federal government, about the power it would wield, the benefits of a federation of islands, at different levels of development, but altogether poor, suffering in "filth, mud, squalor." By the end of the conference, Bustamante's position had changed to the point where he said that the "wilderness of doubts" that surrounded the conference had been "cleared up and wiped away." Norman Manley pointed to existing and planned collaborative efforts and questioned the opposition to federation, explaining its bases in uncertainty, fear or vested interests. Manley then pronounced that if the islands failed to unite then "we are damned and purblind and history will condemn us."[1]

Following a series of conferences including those in London in 1953 and 1956, and another in Trinidad in 1955, with thorny issues such as the site of the federal capital supposedly resolved, the West Indian Federation was finally launched in 1958. It had been a trying period, but the basic structure of federation was in place and functioning. By 1960 it seemed the time had come for the federated islands to take the final step in a process begun more than thirteen years previously: that of independence.

In the meantime, some Jamaicans had come to question the benefits of federation membership. The growth of the economy, especially in newly emerging industries, made many increasingly wary of possible federal control, particularly after Grantley Adams, the federal prime minister, asserted that the federal government could "levy its own income tax . . . and make it retroactive to the date of the Federation."[2] Bustamante, then leader of the opposition, swung into action, demanding Jamaica's withdrawal from the federation unless its interests could be secured. Manley agreed. Increasingly, however, Bustamante portrayed the differences as Jamaica against "the rest" and claimed to be the island's champion.

Unexpectedly, on 31 May 1960 the nation was informed that the JLP had withdrawn from the federal by-elections which were scheduled to be held in St Thomas. In addition, the party declared its absolute, irreversible opposition to the concept of federation. In a quick response, Manley announced that a referendum would be held in 1961, so that the people could decide whether or not Jamaica was to remain in the federation. The stage was set for the referendum campaigns.

As the campaigns unfolded, it soon became clear that a cornerstone of the federal ideal, interisland unity, was to be put to the test. The major focus here was on Jamaica's political association with the small islands, with whom they would "dwell together in unity." While some presented the nine other islands (Trinidad and Barbados were sometimes excluded) as underdeveloped backwaters that would "drag down" Jamaica, others focused on the economic successes or potentials of the islands and on the promotion of a West Indian identity.

Those who campaigned for federation spoke directly to the antifederalist (or JLP) assertion that the small islands would be a drag on Jamaica.

H. G. White agreed with the antifederalists (or antifeds) that the islands were poor, but argued that the UK would give grants for their development and that Jamaica should not begrudge help to the islands because "the richer the people of the small islands become, the more they will buy from us." Further, there was a reciprocal relationship between giving and getting: "If you don't give you won't get"—what harm could there be in helping?[3]

From a completely different angle, some profederation advocates (or profeds) like "Small Islander" played down the islands' poverty and instead examined their resources, refuting the claim that there were none. S/he spoke of Barbados' industrialisation, Trinidad's rich natural resources, sea island cotton and arrowroot production in St Vincent, and spices in Grenada as indicators of progress and potential. Supporting this view, Henry Moe claimed that teachers' lifestyles in the "so-called poor islands" were better than those of their Jamaican counterparts. Wilton Neblett took this argument a step further, comparing the revenues of the "nine so-called pauperised units" with Jamaica's: the former did better both in absolute terms and on a per head basis. The other units, advised Neblett, should start "reviewing their stand on Federation with Jamaica," what with her poor revenues, colour prejudice, the scourge of Rastafarianism and high illiteracy rate.[4]

Many among the profederalist campaigners pointed to the poverty of the small islands, but argued that an alliance was nonetheless beneficial since Jamaica might one day gain from unity. They spoke of Bustamante's hidden motives for moving against the federation. They tried to focus on the collective conscience, talking about agreements made, about the unworthy action of leaving struggling comrades behind. And they argued that inasmuch as Jamaica shared a common history with those islands, perhaps it should share a common destiny with them. Although a large number of Jamaicans might have embraced the cliche bandied about by the profederalists about "unity being strength," they neither knew that common history nor cared to share a common destiny with small islands poorer than their own.

The antifed position was helped by big island arrogance and ignorance. Few were the Jamaicans who knew anything about the islands that they shared colonial status with. For many Jamaicans, the others were dismissed with disdain as small islands which could have little if anything to offer to a former pearl of the Caribbean. The very idea of West Indian unity was under siege as the antifeds delivered the message not that only was there no discernible benefit to living together in unity with the small islanders, but that there could be extreme disadvantages in any such move. The small islands were underdeveloped, they were Jamaica's competitors on the world market, and because they did not like Jamaicans or were jealous of them, they were simply waiting to have the island within the clutches of federation so that they could collude in her destruction and overturn gains which had been made.

When the campaign ended and voting was complete, Jamaicans awoke to the results on the morning of 20 September 1961. Red letters trumped the *Gleaner's* headline: "It's Jamaica—Alone . . . The People Vote against Federation." Of the electorate 60.44 percent had voted, and the *Gleaner* told of the "decisive 'No' with a clear majority of 35,535."[5]

Notes

1. Great Britain Colonial Office, Conference on the Closer Association of the British West Indian Colonies, Montego Bay Jamaica, 11–19 September 1947, Cmnd. 7291 (London: HMSO, 1948), 20–23, 57, 62, 110, 116.
2. *Gleaner*, 31 October 1958.
3. H. G. White, *Gleaner*, 24 August 1961.
4. Henry Moe, *Gleaner*, 6 September; Wilton Neblet, *Gleaner*, 7 September 1961.
5. *Gleaner*, 20 September 1961.

Rastafari and the New Nation

Michael G. Smith, Roy Augier, and Rex Nettleford

As Jamaica moved toward independence, the discontent of the growing Rastafarian movement seriously challenged the political class. Government fears were stoked in 1960 when some Rastafarians joined an unsuccessful armed rebellion led by Ronald (aka Reynold) Henry. Henry's attempted rebellion provoked widespread alarm among middle-class Jamaicans. Recent research by Robert A. Hill suggests that this was the context in which the University College of the West Indies (UCWI; now UWI) commissioned anthropologist Michael G. Smith and two colleagues to write a report on the Rastafari movement. Completed quickly, the report presented a different view of Rastafari to what at the time was the commonplace demonization of the movement. It called on the government to facilitate repatriation to Africa and to end persecution of members of the movement, along with wider social measures such as the provision of housing, sanitation, and other services to low-income communities in Kingston.

The UCWI was invited by Ras Tafari Brethren to tell the public what the movement stands for, how it is organised, and what the brethren want. As we have shown, the movement is not homogenous, and most of its members recognise no single leader or group of leaders. Nevertheless, certain common desires can be formulated.

All the brethren want to be repatriated to Ethiopia. There is no agreement, however, on what should happen in the meantime. The majority recognise that they have to live, and would welcome efforts to provide employment, housing, water and other amenities. There is, however, a very vocal minority which regards any effort to help Ras Tafari brethren in these ways as a plot to keep them in Jamaica. They profess themselves to be violently opposed to any measures which might have the effect of rehabilitation.

At a meeting held on July 15th between the UCWI team, the Principal and a large number of the brethren, it was agreed that the following is a fair statement of what Ras Tafari brethren want. In commenting seriatim, we also include our own recommendations.

1. The Ras Tafari brethren all want repatriation.
2. All the brethren want local recognition and freedom of movement and speech, which are essential human rights.
3. All want an end of "persecution" by Government and police.
4. Some brethren want improved material, social and economic conditions until repatriation.
5. Some brethren want educational provisions, including adult education and technical training. Many brethren are skilled men seeking employment.
6. Some brethren have suggested that a special fund be set up, to be known as the *Ras Tafari Rehabilitation Fund.*
7. Others have asked for a radio programme to tell Jamaica about their doctrine; some for Press facilities.

The goals and needs are specific and operational. There is nothing inherently impossible about them. The most important are also the most difficult and the most generally wanted. Of these, repatriation, that is, return to Africa, is undoubtedly the most passionately held and widespread demand of the Ras Tafari brethren.

Repatriation

We are strongly of the opinion that the Government of Jamaica should take the initiative in arranging for the emigration to Africa and settlement therein of Jamaicans who wish to go there. Several reasons lead to this conclusion.

1. Every citizen has a right to emigrate if he so desires, and to change his nationality if he so desires.
2. While many Ras Tafari brethren would stay in Jamaica if they found work and good social conditions, a large number have strong religious and emotional ties with Africa, which cannot be destroyed.
3. Jamaica is overpopulated, and cannot provide work for all its citizens. Every effort should be made to facilitate emigration.
4. Jamaica now facilitates the settlement of emigrants in England; from a racial point of view emigration to Africa seems more appropriate.
5. Substantial emigration to Africa will not be possible unless the Jamaica Government takes certain initiatives.

The first step is to find out which African countries are prepared to receive Jamaicans. There is evidence that the Emperor of Ethiopia has granted a few hundred acres of land on a trial basis for settlement of "Black People of the West." His willingness to admit Jamaicans to Ethiopia should be formally explored. Others mean by "Ethiopia" the continent of Africa, and would be glad to emigrate to any African country.

The first step is therefore to send an official mission to visit several countries of Africa, and seek permission for Jamaican immigration. Such a mission should be led by a prominent Jamaican, preferably not identified with one of the political parties. It should include civil servants, and prominent Ras Tafari brethren. Since the movement has no universally accepted leaders, this presents rather a difficulty. The various groups will be able to nominate people to discuss with the government the necessary preparations, and also to go on the mission. However, if the mission fails, the brethren will probably repudiate their representatives. Failure of the mission would not prove to the brethren that repatriation is a mirage. This should not be used as an excuse for failing to take the initiative. Emigration is necessary, and the government has a duty to discover whether it is possible, and to exploit every possibility.

Recognition

The Ras Tafari cult is unique, but it is not seditious. Its adherents have, and should continue to have, freedom to preach it. Their demand for freedom of speech and freedom of movement is wholly justifiable.

The Public should cease to believe that all Ras Tafari brethren conform to a stereotype.

Those Ras Tafarians who advertise themselves by wearing beards or the dreadlocks are shunned by the public. They have difficulty obtaining work. In every part of the world, including Africa, people who insist on looking different from their fellow man tend to be persecuted by their fellow men. This is not a justification for persecution. The public should learn to recognise that religious people have a right to wear their hair long if they wish to do so.

Some teachers cut the hair of Ras Tafari children, so the parents react by keeping the children away from school. Some of these parents are asking for special schools for their children. There is a much simpler remedy: the Minister of Education should prohibit teachers from cutting the hair of children without their parents' consent.

286 Smith, Augier, and Nettleford

The Police

The police and the Ras Tafaris are in a state of exasperation with each other, which can lead to no good.

The police have had to cope with a violent section of the movement, and have had to conduct security operations designed to discover the limits of violent intention. Such operations are seldom gentle. Add to this the complications of ganja hunting, plus the fact that policemen share the public's prejudice against men who wear their hair long, and it is not surprising that there have been many cases of arbitrary action by policemen against innocent people.

This has had the unfortunate result of wasting a valuable opportunity of enlisting Ras Tafari support against violence. Many Ras Tafari brethren were shocked by stories of stocks of arms, of foreign mercenaries, and or murder of Ras Tafaris, and so the moderates, who are the great majority, might have been enlisted in stamping out violence. Instead, by telling all Ras Tafari brethren alike as outcasts, the public and police have stimulated their sense of common grievance, and may have strengthened rather than weakened the ideological respect for violence.

The police have to keep in touch with potentially violent sections of the movement. Apart from this, they should leave innocent Ras Tafari brethren alone, stop cutting off their hair, stop moving them on, stop arresting them on minor pretexts, and stop beating them up. Violence breeds violence.

Social Conditions

Any self-respecting Jamaican who passes through such slum areas as the Foreshore Road, Back o' Wall, Davis Lane or the like cannot but be ashamed.

Several of these slums result from squatting on private land. No water is available. Pit latrines are illegal in Kingston; human waste is deposited between the shacks. KSAC [Kingston and St. Andrew Corporation] carts will not enter upon private land to collect rubbish, so that too is deposited between the shacks. If these people were not squatting, the landlord would be obliged to provide water and sewage disposal.

The trouble is that squatting is tolerated, but not recognised. It is tolerated because the Government is not building sufficient low-rent houses to eliminate squatting. It is not recognised because to recognise it might involve buying the land from landlords in areas where the market value of land is counted in thousands of pounds per acre. And because it is not recognised, the squatters get no amenities.

This nettle must be grasped. The building of low-rent houses should be accelerated. At the same time, there is little prospect that houses will be built fast enough to absorb the squatters—having regard to the rate at which Kingston's population is growing. The owners should face up to the fact that they have lost their land. Government, in turn, should pay them compensation, based on the price paid by an unwilling buyer to an unwilling seller, and should forthwith arrange for water, light, toilet facilities and sewage collection on these settlements.

Training

West Kingston as a whole is sadly in need of civic centres, which could serve several functions, such as technical classes, youth clubs, child clinics, or book distributions points. Playing fields are also sadly needed. If such centres are established under suitable Wardens skilled in this work, provision should be made for Ras Tafari brethren to use these facilities to the full, along with other citizens. Special efforts should be made to give young people of whatever persuasion technical skills, and to raise standards of literacy and general education. If Government provided sufficient funds, the ucwi might open a University Settlement in West Kingston.

The Methodist Church has been active, but all the churches could usefully do more social work in West Kingston. The Government should invite the Ethiopian Orthodox Coptic Church to establish a branch in West Kingston.

Economic Assistance

The basic need of Ras Tafari brethren, as most of the people of Kingston, is regular employment. Given regular employment, the brethren could afford better housing and other social amenities, and their feeling of alienation would greatly diminish.

Unfortunately, the rate of capital investment in Jamaica is not adequate to provide employment for all at the current level of wages. One must therefore consider how the people could help themselves by self-employment.

Some Ras Tafari brethren believe that, given financial aid, they could establish cooperative workshops, where they could produce commodities for sale to each other, with a surplus for sale to the general public. There are many skilled brethren who could work within this framework. The idea should be discussed, and an initial experiment made.

Similarly, some Ras Tafari brethren are prepared to build themselves houses, on the cooperative self-help plan, which has proved successful in Puerto Rico, Trinidad, Surinam and elsewhere. They should be given the chance to do so.

SUMMARY OF RECOMMENDATIONS

In the preceding chapters we have made the following recommendations.

1. The Government of Jamaica should send a mission to African countries to arrange for immigration of Jamaicans. Representatives of Ras Tafari brethren should be included in the mission.
2. Preparations for the mission should be discussed immediately with representatives of the Ras Tafari brethren.
3. The general public should recognise that the great majority of Ras Tafari brethren are peaceful citizens, willing to do an honest day's work.
4. The police should complete their security enquiries rapidly, and cease to persecute peaceful Ras Tafari brethren.
5. The building of low-rent houses should be accelerated, and provision made for self-help cooperative building.
6. Government should acquire the principal areas where squatting is now taking place, and arrange for water, light, sewerage disposal and collection of rubbish.
7. Civic centres should be built with facilities for technical classes, youth clubs, child clinics, etc. The churches and the UCWI should collaborate.
8. The Ethiopian Orthodox Coptic Church should be invited to establish a branch in West Kingston.
9. Ras Tafari brethren should be assisted to establish cooperative workshops.
10. Press and radio facilities should be accorded to leading members of the movement.

VI

Independence and After

Jamaica, the first of Britain's Caribbean colonies to become a nation-state, achieved independence on the night of 6 August 1962. The country's leadership promoted unity in nation building exemplified in the new motto, "Out of Many, One People." However, as Norman Manley, the principal creator of the motto, recognized, the concept was a lofty ideal yet to be achieved. In reality, Jamaica's class tensions and unequal distribution of wealth became more visible after British rule. The needs of the urban majority were often neglected in elite constructions of national goals. Visions from the top collided with the demands of marginalized Jamaicans, particularly urban youth, whose political and racial consciousness was influenced by global currents. Members of this group were angered because change of sovereignty did not transform enduring state practices of violence, hierarchy, and exclusion.

Jamaicans demanded more substantial transformation than independence could deliver from its national leaders. Inspired by the cultural changes of the 1960s, and particularly by the international Black Power struggle, young Jamaicans were drawn to an Afrocentric and, in some cases, socialist politics. These tensions led to conflicts throughout the first decade of independence, most notably the Coral Gardens incident of 1963 in which state security forces attacked a Rastafarian community, and the demonstrations that followed the banning of university lecturer Walter Rodney in 1968.

More frequent were the clashes in West Kingston, a tightly connected series of impoverished communities vulnerable to explosive conflict. Politicians from both parties developed policies for improving the urban infrastructure, often promising far more than could be achieved. In doing this they may have intended to channel the restless energy of the young into industry and a shared sense of national improvement. But by promoting urban residential patterns that followed party lines, their actions set the country on an opposite course. As party politics evolved, the rivalry between the JLP and the PNP for state control intensified. Each party resorted to violence to gain advantage. The coalescence of these forces—urban discontent, diminished popular commitment to national goals, social division, and growth in radical black consciousness—would define the years of PNP leadership under Prime Minister Michael Manley.

Manley's 1972 election brought fresh optimism much needed after the misgivings of the late 1960s. Many Jamaicans regarded Manley's leadership style as a fusion of the measured intellect of his father, Norman, and the magnetic populist charm of Alexander Bustamante. His election campaign drew on popular ferment, using Rastafarian symbols and presenting himself as a manifestation of the Old Testament prophet Joshua, chosen by God to lead the Israelites to the promised land.

Charisma proved insufficient to repair the fissures that widened in his first term. When in 1974 Manley declared democratic socialism as the political model for Jamaica, the partisan battle turned ideological. The JLP under the leadership of Edward Seaga labored to discredit the government. Each side had its enforcers, party affiliates willing to wage war against rivals for the sake of state control. Jamaica was violently divided.

The state's approach to the economy reflected its new orthodoxy. The bauxite production levy of 1974 was intended to increase government revenues from the mineral at a time of serious economic hardship following the global oil crisis and recession of the previous year. The move was designed to assert sovereignty in the face of multinational control and reduce Jamaica's dependence on foreign capital. The more immediate effect was that bauxite companies reduced activities in the island, causing further economic dislocation. Manley's program also included social legislation such as a minimum wage, maternity leave provision, and a national housing policy that developed a project of house building for the urban poor. The Manley years also saw a flourishing women's movement in Jamaica, as well as transformations in the everyday politics of race; with black pride ascendant, discrimination against dark-skinned Jamaicans came to be much less socially acceptable.

Manley admired Fidel Castro's policies but wanted to avoid Cuba's road toward dependence on the Soviet Union. He hoped to transform Jamaica's exploited position in the world economy without the nation becoming part of the Soviet bloc. As part of this vision, the Manley government encouraged relationships with newly independent states in Africa and Jamaica's neighbors in Latin America and the Caribbean. Though often more symbolic than material in consequence, state visits from the heads of state of Tanzania, Mozambique, Venezuela, Guyana, and Vietnam, and a much-publicized visit by Castro in 1977, reflected the PNP's foreign policy position.

Manley's actions greatly improved Jamaica's profile as a significant player in majority world diplomacy. His leadership of the Non-Aligned Movement was part of this effort. In the Cold War context, Jamaica's involvement with the Non-Aligned Movement, along with Manley's support of Cuban efforts in the fight for Angolan liberation, his passionate denunciation of imperialism, and the influence of international companies alienated the powerful United States. Agents of the US Central Intelligence Agency fomented conflict on the island, hoping to destabilize Manley's government. The PNP won another landslide victory in 1976, but Jamaica was more fractured than ever. The combined crises led to increased crime, violence, political unrest, mass migration, and social division. A capitulation to the International Monetary Fund (IMF) in 1977 distanced some leftists who were once among Manley's supporters.

Although in many ways Manley's program was moderate, it was met by strong resistance from his opponents in the JLP, from the traditional Jamaican elite, and externally, from the United States. Manley's government responded with firm policies, including the creation of a jury-free Gun Court in 1974, and imposed a state of emergency from June 1976 to June 1977, during which citizens were detained without trial. As this suggests, the 1970s was a period of increasing political polarization and a decade that heralded the institutionalization of a political violence that had begun over the previous decade. Much of metropolitan Kingston was separated into communities that became known as "garrisons," controlled by gangs affiliated to either the JLP or the PNP. The election of 1980, won by the JLP, was characterized by intense political violence, with official records counting around eight hundred dead.

Beyond, although linked to, Jamaican politics, the independence period was a time of cultural flourishing, particularly in music. The transitions of these years were narrated in new commercial styles of music: ska, referred to as the "national sound"; rocksteady; and especially the enormously popular reggae, which emerged in 1968 and exploded with international recognition in the 1970s. Reggae's leading personality was Bob Marley, who became a global superstar, while countless other musicians contributed to a thriving locally oriented music industry. Reggae music and the principally Rastafarian musicians who represented it insisted on an alternative vision for the young nation, placing its blunt realities firmly in historical and global contexts. Global youth gravitated to the music not only for the creative force of its sound, but also for its rebelliousness. Reggae's popularity has been one of the most enduring outcomes of this period.

A Date with Destiny

Daily Gleaner

Jamaica became an independent nation on 6 August 1962. Trinidad and Tobago would follow a few weeks later, on 31 August; the next Caribbean country to attain that status, Barbados, did not gain sovereignty until 1966. Alexander Bustamante became the first prime minister of independent Jamaica, having defeated the People's National Party under Norman Manley in elections in April. Although the PNP had held power between 1955 and 1962, its defeat in the West Indies Federation referendum of 1961 led to Manley's resignation and the holding of new elections.

Independence for Jamaica was a moment of optimism, as this article from the national newspaper the Daily Gleaner *suggests. For some, though, it was also tinged with regret and caution: regret at the failure of the West Indies Federation and, for Norman Manley and his supporters, disappointment that the People's National Party would not lead the nation into independence. A cartoon that was published in the* Star *ten days after independence (not reproduced here) suggested the anxiety of the transition moment. It represented the new nation as a rocket launching into the unknown from the planet of colonialism, while its captain hoped that the "engines" of faith, confidence, and unity wouldn't fail.*

Jamaica becomes the world's newest nation at midnight tonight. At that hour with the bands playing, with bonfires burning, with thousands cheering, the Union Flag of the United Kingdom will be lowered for the last time as the official flag of this island and in its place will rise the Black, Green and Gold standard of the Independent Jamaica. When this has happened a major milestone in the island's history will have been reached, the dream of hundreds of Jamaican patriots will have been realised and the efforts of many men will have climaxed with achievement.

In the Western Hemisphere, traditionally the area of freedom, if only from European domination—the area of Marti of Cuba, Toussaint L'Ouverture of Haiti, and Simon Bolivar of South America—Jamaica is the first new nation in approximately 60 years. Not since Panama, backed up by United States warships, declared its independence from Colombia (shades of

Cousins and political rivals Alexander Bustamante (*left*) of the JLP and Norman Manley (*right*) discuss independence in 1962. *Jamaica Constitutional Conference London 1962*,
photographer unknown. From the National Library of Jamaica, identifier D0002080.
Courtesy of the National Library of Jamaica.

Bolivar) on November 3, 1903, has this Hemisphere witnessed the birth of a
new Nation. Jamaica's nationhood is therefore of significant importance for
this Hemisphere.

   Tonight Jamaica will begin a new era of Independence for the territories
of the Western Hemisphere, blazing a trail which will be followed in a few
days' time by Trinidad and Tobago and perhaps in the future by other territories still holding allegiance to European powers. The time-old aims of
Simon Bolivar that no man in the Western Hemisphere should be subject
to any external power may well be achieved. It is the present pattern of the
world. It is the present thinking of the world.

The Meaning of Independence

Government of Jamaica

During the lead-up to independence, the government launched an extensive media campaign to inform Jamaicans of the value and importance of the country's new status. As part of that campaign this pamphlet was widely distributed. It outlines the expected changes that were to follow the transition from colony to independent nation. It also indicates the sort of country the state had envisioned in 1962.

The Meaning of Independence

On the 6th of August this year, Jamaica will become an independent nation after more than 300 years of British rule.

What does Independence mean?

In the first place, it means that for the first time in our history we will be on our own. We will be responsible for all our affairs, both at home and abroad.

In the second place, it means that, also for the first time in our history, we will be citizens of *Jamaica* not citizens of the United Kingdom and colonies as is now the case. We will travel abroad on Jamaican passports under the protection of the Jamaica Government.

In the third place, it means that the future of each of us and the future of our country will lie in our own hands.

Our Government will be responsible to us and to us alone.

Our Government in Independence

When we become independent, our Government will have new responsibilities.

It will take over our foreign affairs which are now being handled by the British Government.

It will appoint Jamaicans to represent us in overseas countries. Our rep-

A government pamphlet titled *Independence: What It Means to Us*, issued in August 1962, informing Jamaicans of their status in the new nation. From the Rare Book Collection at the University of the West Indies, Mona, Jamaica, call no. F1888 .A3 1963. Courtesy of the Jamaica Information Service.

resentatives will look after the welfare of Jamaicans living abroad and will see that we get the very best prices for the goods we produce.

Our Government will apply for Jamaica to be a member of the United Nations. When we become a member, for the first time our country will have a voice among the leading nations of the world.

Our Government will provide us with a defence force to keep law and order in Jamaica.

Our Government will also make defence agreements with powerful countries which will ensure our protection.

Playing Our Part as Citizens of an Independent Jamaica

If we want our country to prosper and be respected by other nations of the world, each and every one of us should make it a point of duty:

- To love our country and be proud of its achievements.
- To accept the responsibilities of free citizens of a free democracy.
- To work hard and take pride in whatever work we do. Every job well done will add to the prosperity of ourselves and our country.

- To show respect and courtesy not only to our fellow citizens but to the stranger within our gates.
- To respect the constitution under which we are governed and at all times accept the decision of the majority in our democratic nation.

The Motto of our Country is . . .

OUT OF MANY, ONE PEOPLE

The Assets We Have

Norman Washington Manley

If independence meant a triumph for the struggle for self-government that began in the 1930s, for its architects it was also an occasion for reflection on that journey and the path ahead. Norman Manley offers such a rumination in his September 1962 address to the PNP's national conference. Manley led Jamaica through the federation years and shepherded the discussions with the British government on the terms and timing of constitutional decolonization. As premier of Jamaica—a post that ceased to exist after 1959—Manley introduced several far-reaching policies intended to improve Jamaica's institutions. His strong support for federation suffered a blow with the referendum he called in September 1961. In the wake of that loss, and with the discussions for independence well underway, Manley called a general election for April 1962. He was defeated by Alexander Bustamante, his cousin and opposition leader. Manley continued to lead the PNP, which was again defeated in 1967. The 1962 loss was most upsetting for him and his followers. As he implies in the speech, it denied Manley the "privilege" of being the first prime minister of independent Jamaica.

If Manley felt bitterness at his and his party's loss, it was not apparent in this sober assessment of what had been achieved and the challenges to come. In his address to the conference, Manley placed himself and his generation among the island's nation builders who struggled for freedom from colonial rule. His party, which stood for a form of democratic socialism strongly influenced by Fabianism and the British Labour Party, had been criticized by his JLP rivals as being ideologically distant from the everyday needs of Jamaicans, a point emphasized by the charismatic Bustamante. But Manley succinctly defends his ideas and actions to the party faithful, referred to as comrades, clear in his assertion that Jamaicans were the country's greatest assets. Amid the excitement over independence, Manley accepted that the legacies of three centuries of colonial rule would take time to dismantle. The way ahead would depend less on him and the party's founders. The generation of independence had to accept the charge of making Jamaica a truly free nation defined by greater levels of social equality and economic sustainability. Manley's inspiring words in the face of two major defeats reflect his insistence that nationalism be placed above party political victory.

Comrades, I thank God that I have lived to see twenty-four years of the work of the party crowned with the achievement of independence for our blessed and beloved country (*applause*).

I look back on the long years of our struggle. I look back to the days of our early beginning when we first began to rouse Jamaica to her destiny as a nation in the world. I remember the hard and bitter struggles of the past. I remember the small handful of comrades that joined us. I remember the sacrifices they made. I remember the mockery they endured. I remember the suffering they withstood. I remember how some of them, nameless today and unsung, gave their lives that Jamaica might throw off 300 years of colonial bondage, might lift up their hearts to aspire to all that independence means and freedom for a people.

It is true that we have been denied the privilege of achieving power at this moment, but no one can deny us the accomplishment of our work in this country (*applause*). And many marveled how it was that we who were not in the seats of power acknowledged as the authors of the greatest of our land at this time (*applause*).

And now I am going to speak to you about the challenge of this time as we close one book of our history, a book which from the beginning could foresee its own end, and open another book in our history, the end of which no man can foresee, but it will roll on from generation to generation as we seek to build a nation worthy of our sons and daughters in this land.

Comrades, it is one thing to become free; it is another thing to build a real nation of your country (*applause*).

But, comrades, we start our nationhood with some great assets. One of the good things is the long time that it has taken us to evolve our life into freedom as a people. We have learned much over the past half a century. We have learned most of all over the last twenty-four years in this country; and we have only got to remember the lessons we have learned to make sure that we can find the right way for the future.

We gave this country for seven and a half years a Government that knew how to use power with restraint and respect for human decencies in the land. We gave this country for seven and a half years a Government which believed in the realities of democracy, which allowed all men to walk the land free from fear and free from oppression.

We have one third great asset in this country, moving into nationhood, and this is the quality of the people of the land, a people tough and resilient, taught by adversity to endure hardship with patience, given some special spirit of loyalty to inspire them in their devotion to the causes they espoused, a people well understanding right from wrong, well understanding decency in government, well understanding justice and the rule of law. And those are great assets for a country to start with. And I say what I have so often said, if Jamaica fails it is Jamaica's leaders that have failed, not Jamaica's people.

Comrades, we must never forget that we start with all the legacies of 300 years of colonial rule. We would be foolish if we did not understand that you don't throw off all the patterns of behaviour and thought that colonialism brings upon a people merely by becoming free. We have tried hard in this country to overcome them, but they are not yet overcome. In the old days each man sought his own good in the country and each man that made his way up turned his back on where he came from, and each man who achieved a high place on the ladder went steadily striving to bow the knee to wherever power was to be found in the Colonial Empire. Those patterns prevail in this country today and there are still men who in true colonial style serve one party only, the party in power—the PIPs who bow the knee and scrape and cringe and deny and falsify principles so as to protect themselves and their positions. Maybe it is common all over the world, but it is particularly common in societies that have known colonial rule for generations.

And I say one last thing. When I look into the future of Jamaica, I ask you to remember the three great tasks that confront us at this time as people. First, foremost and above all, to make come true this great motto that I am proud of having played a part in formulating when I was Premier of Jamaica: "Out of many, one people." We are not one people today. We are many. That is history. That is colonialism. That is our particular history. That is the problem before all Jamaica today—how to make "out of many, one people." That is a problem that we have understood for many years and that is something that our party must dedicate itself to achieving in this country.

We have another basic, fundamental problem, and that is how to continue to build our economy so as to create a society which offers the reality of equal opportunity to all people and offers the opportunity of decent Christian lives to every man, woman and child in the land.

As a nation our third great problem, and it would mean so much to us, is to present ourselves to the world so that we can mean something in the world of free peoples and free nations. In other words we want a meaning-ful foreign policy in Jamaica as a nation.

History now gives us the role to create the new things which will make that nation live and endure in the world to come. So let no man quarrel with history or question the judgments of the Architect of the universe.

Rastafari and the Coral Gardens Incident

John Maxwell and Mortimo Togo Desta Planno

Not a year into independence, a tragic episode occurred in Coral Gardens in St. James parish that was a harbinger of the class and cultural tensions that would emerge in independent Jamaica. The victims of the violence were members of the Rastafarian community living in the area. Rastafarians were generally viewed negatively across the island, feared for their antiestablishment beliefs and reviled for their appearance. State forces disdained the Rastas, or "beards men," and considered the movement a threat to national security. This hostility was clearly in evidence following an event in Montego Bay on Holy Thursday, 11 April 1963. Rudolph Franklyn, a Rastafarian farmer in Coral Gardens embittered by an ongoing land dispute, imprisonment, and mistreatment by the police, attacked a gas station and other buildings with the aid of a handful of supporters. Security forces on the orders of the government descended on the area, and over one hundred Rastas were arrested, tortured, or beaten. The actions were unjust and bore heavily on the community. News of the Coral Gardens incident led to a wider debate about Rastafari in the island, and some prominent journalists wrote sympathetically about the Rastafarians. Several supporting articles appeared in the political paper Public Opinion. *Two such are included here. In the first selection, published not long after the event, one of Jamaica's best-known journalists and broadcasters, John Maxwell, recounts the experience of someone he knew, William Cole, who was brutally beaten and falsely imprisoned. The second is a letter by Mortimo Planno, an impressive young Rastafarian leader from West Kingston who became a major figure in the movement.*

Oh, It's Hard to Be Poor

JOHN MAXWELL

"Oh, it's a hard thing to be poor in this country, especially if you wear a beard, Mr. Mac," he said to me.

He was William Cole, carver in alabaster and Rastafarian. A gentle, quiet little man who minds his own business and troubles no one. The girls at JBC [Jamaica Broadcasting Corporation] buy his ashtrays and his lamps as do the girls in other offices and shops in Kingston and Montego Bay. He has lived in Montego Bay for the past five years or so, because he finds a good market in selling his alabaster carvings to tourists. Lately he has been living with his common-law wife and their two-year-old child at Deeside, a small town in Trelawny, near the border with Saint James and about ten miles from Falmouth.

On Good Friday he was at home, minding his own business doing a little carving when he heard about "an occurrence that happens between some fellows and the government the day before" in which some people were killed.

At about 3 o'clock on Good Friday "a body of people come down on me with gun and stick and started to break the house door with a force, and demands me out of the house. My wife get frighten and run with the baby. They come into the house and find me under the bed because I heard them crying for me to come out so they could beat me . . . a man lift up the sheet of the bed and point his gun at me and I came out. They start with their stick dem and they gun to murder me in the worst condition. Then they take me away to the Deeside lockup.

"They say 'we locking up all you people who carry beard.'"

From Deeside he was taken to Wakefield, where he was manacled to another Rastafarian, Vincent Ellis, who had been trying to buy a ticket to see a film at the Wakefield movie house when he was "captured." On the way to Falmouth, Mr. Cole said, "The same continually murderation was going in the police transport. They mashed out my toenail with their police boots, spit in my face and juk me with they batons. But the worst position was in Falmouth.

"At Falmouth they asked me my name and I told them and they began again to murder me and Ellis all the while telling us 'go back where you come from.' It was about 15 to 16 of them was in the station beating us. One of them was a police in uniform.

"Some of them had batons and some had all kind of big stick and it was in the station there that they try to kill us. They beat us until Ellis' foot swell big so, and they beat me until my hand burs' and they break my knee-cap besides which they hit me in my back so bad that my semen run out of my line for three days straight."

He lost consciousness in the police wagon on the way to Montego Bay but they continued to beat him according to his fellow prisoner Ellis who was still shackled to him.

About three days after he was jailed at Montego Bay he lost consciousness in the cell. "The prisoners shouted out that I was dead and the police got a doctor to see me. He said I should get three days' hospital treatment but the police only close the door and left me there.

"In the cell there were about 18 of us and three bunks. Some of us slept on the bunks, taking turns according to who was most badly hurt, most of us slept on the concrete, resting our heads on each other for pillow. Some had to stand up because we couldn't all sleep at the same time. We had to sleep in shifts. Those that were standing up sang and talked to keep themselves awake."

William Cole was brought before the court about a week after he was jailed. He was charged with an unspecified beach of the Road Traffic Law. He pleaded not guilty because his £150 car which he uses to transport alabaster for carving had been parked for some months as it was in need of parts. He was granted £25 bail and was bailed by a relative of his wife's.

He went to a doctor and he was treated for his injured hand which was so mangled that the bone was affected. The doctor treated him for his other injuries.

He then employed a lawyer and when he went to court the second time he found that the charge had been altered and was now "Contemplating of creating war," in his words. His lawyer, Hewart Henriques, successfully argued that no evidence had been presented, no accusers had appeared and Mr. Cole was freed.

He discovered meanwhile, that his carvings which had been stored in the house of another Ras in Montego Bay had been stolen or destroyed when the Ras, Alan Blackwood, had been arrested in the police round-up. Mr. Cole's nephew, Vincent Cole was also arrested and beaten. He was set free by the judge who told him that "he must hold his peace for a year."

Mr. Cole told me that in jail in Montego Bay the food was not good, mainly lemonade or sugar and water and bread served in old oil-cans. When he was transferred from Montego Bay to Falmouth, the day before he was given bail, he had more serious complaints to make about the food.

At Falmouth Mr. Cole and another prisoner, a man named Isaacs, found ground glass in their food. When they shouted to tell the policeman on duty he said: "Me no business wid dat—a unoo kill people."

It was not until he had been in jail for some days that William Cole was able to get any clear idea of what had caused him to be taken there along with all the other Rases. "We got to understand what happen at Rose Hall and we got to understand that Bustamante said to bring all Rastas dead or alive."

It has been an instructive experience for William Cole, whose every word I believe. He is a victim of his beliefs and of public hysteria. He has got several beatings, being badly injured, has had to spend nearly £30 of money he does not have on lawyer's and doctor's fees, has lost months of work and material smashed and stolen; has, most important of all, had his legal rights trampled on and he does not know where to turn for redress.

William Cole is only one of many more whose stories you will never hear. But if we are serious and honest when we talk about "constitutional rights" we must hear these stories and we must attempt to remedy the wrong and damage done. If the Prime Minister can be serious for a moment, he must realise he owes it to some bearded citizens, indeed to all of us, to order an inquiry into the aftermath of the incidents at Coral Gardens.

Whatever we might feel about the Rastas, we must remember that they are no less human because they were beards and worship God in a slightly less conventional manner than other Christians. If we agree to their persecution we are agreeing with Hitler, Eichmann & Co. And we are agreeing with them if we do not raise up our voices and pens to insist that their rights must be respected.

Out of pure self-interest you might also remember: it may be your turn next.

Rastafari

MORTIMO TOGO DESTA PLANNO

Many people have made statements against the Rastafarian movement which they know not of.

Who is the Rastafarian? One who accepts that His Majesty Haile Selassie is the Messiah. We Rastafarians draw our theory from the King James version of the Bible. In Revelations chapter 5, John was caught up in a vision where a Book was seen closed with seven seals. "And no one in the heaven on the earth or under the earth was able to open the book or look thereon." And John wept because there was no one worthy to open the book, but an angel said unto him, "Weep not: behold, the Lion that is of the tribe of Judah, the Root of David, hath overcome, to open the book and the seven seals thereof."

Haile Selassie is the Conquering Lion of the tribe of Judah and with this and other revelations in the Bible we base our theory of our Emperor worship.

Our claim of repatriation and restoration is well accepted in Ethiopia— I'm a witness to that.

The Rastafarians have recognized themselves as a society and often show their approval and disapproval of public affairs. One Rasta even contested the independence elections.

The UCWI report, that the Rastafarian movement is large and heterogenous should be given priority treatment. According to the UN Human Rights charter all are free to hold and express their opinions without interference. To many, the Rastafarians' opinions should not be heard.

We are of the opinion that we are Ethiopians by virtue of our Royal Ethiopian blood, transcended and descended down through the lineage of our forefathers. We were taken to these shores as slaves. The UN Declaration of Human Rights says everyone has a right to a nationality and no one shall be arbitrarily deprived of his nationality nor denied the right to change his name.

Someone is violating the International Laws, not the Rastas, not Ethiopia.

He who knows not, and knows not that he knows not, needs teaching. Let's teach him. Many misunderstand the Rastafarians in this community, some even think we ostracize ourselves from the Jamaican society. No, the time has come when new things are happening. Our desires to be sent to Ethiopia are still in the balance.

May I ask these questions: If Ethiopia is prepared to settle the Rastafarian movement, should they be sent to Ethiopia? What if the Rastafarians do not want to be integrated into a Jamaican nation?

Country Boy

The Heptones

Adjustment to urban life was often hard for the thousands of rural youth who migrated to Kingston in the 1950s and 1960s in search of opportunity. The separation of "town" and "country" was pronounced. The city, though full of activity, was unknown; navigating its social and geographical borders required fast learning from the newcomers. This 1974 song by popular vocal group the Heptones narrates the typical experience of a country boy who has relocated to Kingston. The narrator chastises the country boy for his unawareness of popular city landmarks, most of which are alien to him. The country boy, however, pretends to know the city well, and the song also mentions the involvement of some rural youth in criminal activity.

A-true, a-true
Everything I say
A-true, a-true
Everything I say

Country boy, you're running up and down
Country boy, you go on like you know town
You nuh know bag-a-wire, you nuh know Race Course
You nuh know Pearl Harbor, nuh even know light post

A-true, a-true
Everything I say
A-true, a-true
Everything I say

Country boy, and no one knows your name
Country boy, Kingstonian get your blame
You nuh know Denham Town, you nuh know Hunt's Bay
You nuh know Parish Church, boy, get out of me way

I said, a-true, a-true
Every word I say

A-true, a-true
Everything I say

Country boy, you shooting up the place
Country boy, you with your ratchet in your waist
You nuh know uptown, you nuh know downtown
You nuh know 'round town, not even know Camperdown

I said, a-true, a-true
Everything I say
A-true, a-true
Everything I say

Oh, country boy
Oh, country boy

How to Be a "Face-Man"
The Star

Jamaican men have always been keen followers of mainstream fashion, often creating sartorial trends of their own. In the mid-1960s the popular men's style included an appropriation of European fashion with a unique Jamaican stamp: tight clothing, darkened glasses, slim ties, shortened trousers, and a porkpie hat. Men who paid close attention to their appearance were called "cha-cha bwoys" or, more commonly, "face men." This 1965 sketch parodies the dress style of a face man. The so-called Rude Boys of the 1960s would popularize this style, which would be copied internationally by followers of Jamaican music and culture. The colorful description pokes fun at the careful preening men take to project a tough image.

SO YOU WANT TO BE A FACE-MAN!
Don't worry if you aren't "facially" perfect! . . . Here's the formula for being one of those "groovy" face-mans!

[*Clockwise from top left*]

- Your hat should be small enough to comfortably cover your low, "continental" haircut.
- "Darkers"! These will make you look a goggle-eyed goldfish.
- While a cigarette-holder will add sophistication, as will rings.
- Cufflinks are a must and gold is always preffered [*sic*].
- Red elastic belt to match equally red 'kerchief.
- "Hip-pockets"! Dont [*sic*] worry if you cant [*sic*] get into them, you can keep your change in another. . . . . . . Equally tight, of course!
- Pants should be as tight as possible and need not match jacket. Should stop 5 inches above ankle.
- Black, high-heeled, elastic side, pointed toe shoe (?)
- White socks to add a splash.
- Red 'kerchief which should hang loosely from back pocket. Carry two if possible.

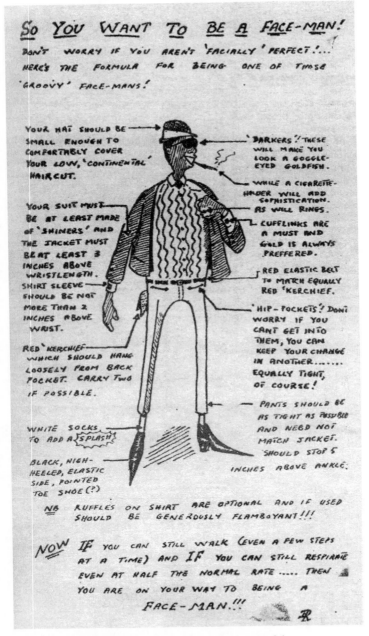

A humorous dissection of the style of Jamaican men of the 1960s. "So You Want to Be a Face-Man," artist unknown. From the *Star*, 21 May 1965, 3. © The Gleaner Company (Media) Limited. Image used by permission of the National Library of Jamaica.

- Your suit must be at least made of "shiners" and the jacket must be at least 3 inches above wristlength. Shirt sleeve should be not more than 2 inches above wrist.

<u>NB</u> Ruffles on shirt are optional and if used should be generously flamboyant!!!

<u>Now</u> IF you can still walk (even a few steps at a time) and IF you can still respirate even at half the normal rate. . . . . then you are on your way to being a FACE-MAN!!!

Cancer in West Kingston

Edward Seaga

This controversial 1966 radio broadcast by Edward Seaga, who at that time was JLP minister for development and welfare and later served as prime minister (1980–1989), speaks to the emergence of political violence between supporters of Jamaica's two main parties. Before he became a politician, Seaga had conducted research on African Jamaican culture and religion in poor communities both in Kingston and in the countryside. He also worked as a record producer and promoter. This background gave him an intimate knowledge of his West Kingston constituency and a rapport with its residents that many other light-skinned and well-off Jamaicans lacked.

The broadcast justifies the bulldozing in July 1966 of informal settlements along the Foreshore Road (now Marcus Garvey Drive) and in Back o' Wall (now Tivoli Gardens). The destruction of these communities was part of a broader program of redevelopment of the area, but was also an attack on their existing residents, particularly the Rastafarian community Back o' Wall. The thickly overcrowded squatter communities with no amenities were destroyed and replaced by the well-designed Tivoli Gardens. Previously the area had largely supported the PNP, but the new residents were fiercely loyal to Seaga. Tivoli Gardens became one of the most established "garrison communities." Using hostile language in which PNP supporters are described as a cancer that must be "cut out with a surgeon's knife," Seaga argued that coercion was an essential part of redevelopment because of earlier PNP activity. He accused his opponents directly of supplying guns.

In a certain way, West Kingston is perhaps the most difficult area in Jamaica; in another, it is perhaps the most colourful. When all other lights are dimmed it is the corner bars, and supper shops, the revival meetings and small churches, the bustling market places and street corners, the Coney Islands and gambling halls, the sound systems of West Kingston that are the last eyes to close in the face of the City. People who know the West love the fullness of its life; it is hard for a man to hide from activity here and all its people live each other's lives in daily incidents of discussion, tempered with raucous humour, earthy thought, easy acceptance, or bitter abuse. Many will agree perhaps for various reasons that there is no-where else in all Jamaica like West Kingston and those who know it intimately love it intimately as I do.

Packed in approximately one square mile much of which is occupied by May Pen's acres of dead, some 20,000 persons live under the most densely populated conditions in Jamaica—over 200 to the acre. The man who lives in St Andrew on a one-third acre lot of land with his wife and 2 children must realise that a lot of this same size would house over 70 persons in West Kingston. Who are those people? For the most part humble, decent folk; people who earn their living as tradesmen or craftsmen, unskilled labourers, and household helps, factory hands and Government staff, pedlars and higglers, shopkeepers and bartenders. They have the same ultimate aims that most Jamaicans share: to earn a living and own a home, to feed and care, to clothe and educate, and when Saturday night comes to have enough left over for a dance or a drink or a show.

But there is another West Kingston: home of the samfie man, the ginnal who preys on the poor, the gambler and the criminal, the men who smoke the weed and tear the flesh, men who don't eat with knives but make their living with them.[1] These are the Cancer of West Kingston. They cluster in cells, build by attacking the healthy until they establish an area of malignant growth.

The Foreshore Road and Back o' Wall grew up this way. First, a few harmless squatters, then a few more; then a small assortment of wrong-doers followed by the big criminals. In the midst of all this crept the subversives and political element. The outlines of a camp of terror were marked out. Beyond this line let no stranger go; within this line let no men talk of what he saw or what others did.

This is how the *Star* of July 30th described the Foreshore Road Shanty Town which Government recently bulldozed as stories of the life of hell created there were leaked out by fearful residents: I quote the *Star*.

> It began as an ordinary criminal gang of young "rudies" being trained to pick handbags and the like, or to "lasso" a victim to rob him; but certain other strong-arm members of the Rasta cult, with the connivance of politicians and their henchmen directed their attention to terrorism in the squatter area for political reasons for which they are paid large sums of money.
>
> It became organised sometime around the early part of June, last. They roamed the compound daily sorting out those who did not share

their views and anyone who showed resistance was beaten and otherwise tortured and "marked for death," according to the story of one who stoutly opposed the gang. People were forced to swear allegiance to the gang during regular rituals held at the gang base opposite the intersection of Foreshore Road and Industrial Terrace, where bombs and ammunition and firearms were distributed to the members by politicians or their henchmen. Old men and women were tied with rope to trees for long periods and flogged with wire covered with cloth until blood flowed from their bodies. The gangsters were also armed with spears and firearms. . . .

This is not my description; it is the description of people who lived in the Shanty Town as squatters, as given to the *Star*. They were in a position to see all that went on behind the scenes. They were able to see what I was not permitted to see for in my four years as Member of Parliament I was never able even once to trespass into this Camp because the dominating element was so violently opposed to the JLP that an armed team would have been needed to force entry. Members of the public will recall how the Police had to organise a massive assault of hundreds of men to get in there. Squatters in the area who sympathised with the JLP were beaten, thrown out, and their belongings destroyed.

Into this camp entered certain politicians and certain Trade Unionists, together with subversive persons all opposed to Government. In early June the criminal element were given guns in large numbers. Dynamite was introduced for the first time in our history as a weapon to destroy people, not fishes. Men were trained to use these weapons, but the big plan was for election time. The organisers of this plot did not foresee that the men would quarrel amongst themselves and begin to use these weapons on each other. This they did which eventually brought the police into the picture, only to be attacked by hundreds of rounds of shots and dozens of sticks of dynamite from the well-schooled hooligans.

The people know the rest of that story: the area was bulldozed. What has happened since then? Two things: Firstly, the criminals have shifted their headquarters to a tight area around the PNP Headquarters in Regent Street occupying premises in Bread Lane, Chestnut Lane and Charles Street within shouting distance of each other. They have set up the same strategy of driving out all residents who are of opposite political views so as to create an area of operation within which no one will divulge what is going on.

Even young boys of 12–15 years have now been conscripted into a group called the "Young Murderers." Their jobs are to scout and carry messages

An aerial photograph of the demolished shacks on Foreshore Road in 1966. The forced clearing and displacement of the inhabitants of this squalid area led to the construction of Tivoli Gardens, which Edward Seaga intended as a model community for western Kingston. *Bulldozing of Back-o-Wall, West Kingston*, photograph by Jack Tyndale-Biscoe, 1966. From the Jamaica Archives and Records Department, Kingston.

and hide weapons. In this small section men walk with guns stuck in their waist, new and strange guns. Innocent passers-by are stopped, questioned, beaten, shot and now even murder has been committed, for on Monday past a group of men dragged a JLP supporter from his bicycle and while he was held one put a revolver to his neck and fired. He died a few days after. Another camp of terror is born.

Some weeks ago during the disturbances two sticks of dynamite were thrown into my Ministry, but fortunately they did not explode. Soon after that an attempt was made to blow up the Esso Oil Refinery which adjoins the squatter area, with the use of dynamite. This also failed. If it had not, half of Kingston would have been blown off the map and thousands injured and killed.

The records show that during this time the only improvement provided by Central Government entirely for West Kingston followed on an outbreak of violence which led to the demolition of squatter shacks in Dungle. The

PNP did not use bulldozers, it is true. They simply turned fire hoses on the occupants as they do in Alabama and washed them away. As things grew worse their leader Manley is reported in the *Daily Express* as telling them one memorable night in 1961 at Coronation Market, speaking to the same people they now profess to love—and I quote from the *Gleaner*—"I will show them who is power in this country." Referring to a noisy element in the crowd who drew his wrath, the Premier said, "If they don't get out of here I will lead the crowd and give them one backside here tonight. I shall help the people to put them off the street. I can take the PNP and rub them out, rub them out till you can't find them. I declare war on them from tonight and we shall walk the streets of Kingston and clear them from the streets."

To understand West Kingston today one has to understand this past neglect. Covering the sore with the skin-coloured powder of police patrols is no more than a temporary measure. Until the gunmen are caught and guns seized there will be no real peace. Medical science, with all its skills and centuries of research has found no other way to deal with a cancer than with a surgeon's knife, and this cancer in West Kingston has to be cut out with a surgeon's knife.

Note

1. "Samfie man" and "ginnal": Jamaican terms for a confidence man or trickster. [Editors' note]

Birth of the Sound System

Norman C. Stolzoff

Anthropologist Norman Stolzoff traces the political and social evolution of Jamaica's distinctive musical landscape. This passage explains the material and cultural context in which sound systems playing recorded music became the heart of Jamaica's music scene, thus allowing for the rise of the DJ. Stolzoff draws on interviews with old-timers from Jamaica's postwar music scene, particularly Hedley Jones, a pioneering engineer and sound system builder, and Vaughn "Bunny" Goodison, a popular radio disc jockey and sound system operator.

Given the shortage of live dancehall music [after World War II], people started looking for musical alternatives.

By the start of 1950, [Hedley] Jones was specializing in building amps on demand for aspiring sound system men such as Roy Johnson, a sales agent for D&G bottlers. Johnson called his sound system, replete with the largest speakers anyone had seen, the House of Joy. Sound systems now began to proliferate in the Kingston area and to spread to the country parishes. Most of these sets were built by Jones and two technicians, Fred Stanford and Jacky Eastwood, whom he trained.

When Hurricane Charlie struck the island in 1951, all industry, including the sound system business, was temporarily stalled for a few months. After Jamaica had recovered from the hurricane, the sound system bounced back and "took everybody by storm," as Jones put it. Stanford and Eastwood had left Jones during the months after the hurricane when it was impossible to work. Venturing out on his own, Stanford went to work for Duke Reid, servicing his equipment and building new sets for his friends. Eastwood went on to work for Clement Seymour "Coxsone" Dodd. Coxsone, an ex–migrant farmworker who brought records back with him from the United States, called his set the Downbeat sound system. Once Duke Reid and Coxsone got into the sound system business, things were never the same on the Jamaican music scene. They became the two most important soundmen in the history of the business. Their innovations and entrepreneurial leadership carried the sound system to an unprecedented level, breaking barriers in many areas. As their popularity grew, each of them started putting together additional sound systems so that they could play different locations on any given night. It was reported that Coxsone had four separate sound systems operating at the same time, with two in Kingston and two in the countryside. Coxsone and [Arthur] Duke Reid also were the first to go into the studio to record music exclusively for the sound system.

The Dancehall as an Alternative Cultural Space

With their rising popularity, the three most popular sound systems (Tom's, Duke Reid's Trojan, and Coxsone's Downbeat) outgrew the house party circuit. They started holding their events in dancehalls throughout the country.

Bunny Goodison told me:

> Most of the dancehalls were what you call lodge halls. These were like fraternal organizations, you know. And they practice all kind of brotherly activity like helping people, and there was a degree of spiritualism to it too.

Some dances were not associated with lodges, however. They were held in abandoned yards, fixed-up old buildings, and at private homes. As the sound system caught on in the dancehalls, or lawns, the playing field became more competitive. Some of the larger dancehall sessions would have up to eight sound systems in "one big lawn," each vying to be the crowd's champion sound for the night. Larger dances were kept in the lodge halls, because the smaller venues could not accommodate the size of the sound equipment and audience. It is important to note the location of these dancehalls. They were all at or below Cross Roads, in the downtown areas of Kingston.

The Sound Clash

From this point in the mid-fifties on, the competition between Coxsone and Duke Reid—and those other sounds vying for the third spot—grew more intense. The sound systems had to compete to survive, to stay even with their rivals. Initially these competitions started when two sound systems were playing separate venues, sometimes in the same vicinity, and each sound would attempt to attract the crowd to their dance. On these occasions, many patrons would wait outside on the street to see which sound was playing better. To pull the crowd into their particular dance, the sound

Arthur "Duke" Reid (1915–1975) was a pioneering Jamaican producer and
sound system operator. He entered the music industry in the early 1950s
after a stint as a police officer in Kingston. Reid would find local fame
when he entered the nascent recording industry in the late 1950s. His
Treasure Isle label—named after a liquor store he also operated in downtown Kingston—became incredibly popular in the ska era of the early
1960s. Reid was at the forefront in Jamaican music's transitions from ska
to rocksteady and reggae. It was his early successes as a sound system
operator that cemented his legend. He often emerged the victor from
sound system clashes at Kingston's dancehalls throughout the 1950s. In
this photograph taken after one such contest, a proud Reid displays his
arsenal of speakers carefully posed close together for the photographer.
In the image Reid gently places a record on the turntable to underline his
preeminence as a sound system operator with one of the best record collections in the island. Photographer unknown, c. 1950s. From the cover
of the album *Hog in a Cocoa* by the Skatalites, Esoldun LG2-1016, 1991.

operations would string up steel horns in trees, point them out toward the
street, or if nearby, toward the other dance, trying to drown out the other
sound system's music.

    In the next phase of these sound system wars, two or more sounds would
play against each other in the same dancehall. These head-to-head duels
were known as clashes.

    Usually, the crowd's response determined who won a clash, although
occasionally judges were called on to select the winner. For the most part,
these sound battles were fought fairly. However, sometimes supporters,
who felt that their sound was about to lose, would practice unsportsmanlike
tactics on the other sound. According to Bunny Goodison: "They had sound
system, where if the guy feel he was threatened, he would do some sabotage

on a sound. The followers saw that their sound was being threatened and would either cut the wires or do something to it and damage it and shock the sound and do something, you understand?" The backers of particular sounds tended to reside in the same area that the sound originated from. This association of sounds and the inhabitants of certain areas would later become the basis of violent rivalries with the introduction of party politics and gangs of hired gunmen.

Rudie, Oh Rudie!

Garth White

The Rudie or Rude Boy was a misunderstood figure in mid- to late 1960s Jamaica. The term was popularized in song to denote a tough, unbowed male persona given to challenging authority. Rude Boys were often associated with criminal activity in West Kingston. A wave of ska and rocksteady songs addressed the Rude Boys either by praising their defiant "badness" or chastising them for social disturbance. The image and style of the Rude Boy would outlive the era. In later years it was adopted by youth in Britain. In this important assessment from 1966, Garth White emphasizes the complexity of the Rude Boy subculture in Kingston, asserting that the disaffected youth were a forceful product of a society that failed to recognize their marginalization.

A large percentage of "rude bwoys" are long past this stage of development. Hatred in their forebears, along with other factors, has assumed proportions large enough to result in its internalisation at an early age. It is becoming observable that this is an almost inevitable quality of the entire urban "lower class" youth. By youth is meant those persons ranging from fourteen to twenty-five years of age. With few exceptions that majority of youth coming from the lower 60% of the population that shows [sic] approximately 19% of the National Income is angry. Angry to the point of violence. The only restraining factor may be the lack of comprehensive organisation. And the hatred is pointed not only against the settler and his descendants, but also to all that class of persons who occupy the middle rung in the society. Rude bwoy is that person, native, who is totally disenchanted with the ruling system; who generally is descended from the "African" elements in the lower class and who is now armed with ratchets (German made knives), other cutting instruments and with increasing frequency nowadays, with guns and explosives. This last condition and to some extent a lesser ambivalence toward the culture of the metropolitan orientated "other" society is what really distinguishes between the rude bwoy and the other angry elements in similar station. In addition rude bwoys are largely centred in those urban areas that suffer from chronic depression and to which migration from rural areas was largely directed in the '50s and '60s. There is, however, evidence of an increasing militancy among the youth centred in and around the sugar belt. In rural areas it is seen that more ready availability of food tends to obscure other injustices.

In many cases the rudie intuitively knows the symbols of distorted Western culture. He knows that his music, ska, is given token appreciation by persons who call a reshuffling of the U.S.-based "Cashbox" hit parade—a Jamaican hit parade. He knows that his women's faces do not adorn lavish advertisement bill boards showing washing machines or someone gently tapping a 23-inch television set. His women are the women who are lucky if they fall into the group of householders who eke out an existence on £300 per annum. Approximately nine out of ten households in this country live on below £300 per annum.

Surely this is not far removed from slavery.

Aspects of Rudie Culture—Music and the Dance

Rude bwoy was heralded in a selection from Studio One (recording studio of Clement Dodd) by Roland Alphonso as early as late 1962. But another musical ode, this time by the "Wailers" in late 1965 signalled that rude bwoy was no passing indulgence but a very real element. Whatever the middle and upper classes may have to say about the quality of ska presentations, their usefulness as indicators of the thought of the other society—predominantly black—cannot be overemphasised. The number of rudie tunes on the airwaves reflects the increased status accorded Rudies by this other Afro-Jamaican society. Here it must be admitted that radio requests are often from middle class youths who to some extent are acquiring, or are in the process of acquiring, the symbols of rudie culture. Rudie culture items such as shoes, hats, music, stripped bicycles, etc. are sometimes possessed by these, but to what degree rudie culture is internalised is yet a matter of conjecture. The metropolitan-orientated society is simultaneously apprehensive of the Rudie, confused as to who he is and what he represents, and yet his influence is pervading even the bastions of the middle-class. Symbols of his culture are appearing everywhere. Sound-systems, for example, are being used by the traditionally conservative and Victorian school-boards. A good sound-system usually consists of an amplifier of about 300 watts, anything between 5 to 10 speakers enclosed in boxes of cedar or mahogany. Prior to middle-class acceptance, these systems supplied dance music in halls, lawns and the like. Price of admission could vary from two shillings for the Saturday night to five shillings on the holiday day and night session. The music played is ska, although American negro pop music enjoys some popularity. Notable among this "pop" music are records of people like The Impressions, Shirley and Lee. It must be noted that before the emergence of ska, music supplied by the sound-system medium was usually from this source and old names like Fats Domino, Bill Doggett and Louis Jordan are one-time stars. Ska is one of the means of expression of the "lower class." It is a propagandistic music and with increasing force it has acquired the role of commentator on the society. It is now reflecting the increased militancy of the class it generally represents. "Good Good Rudie" and "Let Him Go" are tunes related to West Kingston. A tune by the "Ethiopians" in its opening lines says:

> "I'm gonna take over now
> For I know that
> And I know
> Our time has come
> We must wear that crown."

The Rudie "dance," an extension of the principle that resulted in the slowing down of tempo in ska music, has not "cooled down" the lower class native. Rather it has caused numerous fights and recently even gang warfare at these dances. The muscular tension now finds outlet in gang wars. The fraternal blood-bath allows for procrastination of the choice, nonetheless inevitable, of armed resistance to the oppressors.

Violence, Politicians and Gangs

At first the only degree of organisation was that exerted by the existence of a common "corner." By "corner" is meant simply in most cases, junctions of two or more roads. But in the last months of 1965, organised gangs in a sense that overstepped the necessity of a common home area emerged. This is not to say, however, that many gangs were not now organised around the fact that the majority of members came from one area, say Felix City in Jones Town. With increasing urgency, these gangs are gaining some sense of purpose other than self-interest. They know that they are to be instrumental in the effort of the burdened lower class to throw off the national bourgeoisie.

The entry of the politicians clouds the issue somewhat. The tradition of political patronage manifested by both parties has canalised to some extent the potential mass violence in many urban areas along party lines. Nevertheless the greater end is still recognised by rudie, i.e. his ambitions to help liberate the "sufferer."

From recent events (West Kingston), it can be inferred that the stage is set. For example, early in 1966, the area around Pa[y]ne Avenue was bulldozed. Later on it was Industrial Terrace and adjoining areas. Where were these people, the large majority already at and below subsistence level, to go? The hundreds of hungry youths who of necessity had to move in amongst the dead in May Pen cemetery have in fact become certain of the imminence of a direct confrontation.

1968 Revisited

Rupert Lewis

Students of the UWI demonstrated in October 1968 in response to the government's ban on reentry to the country of Dr. Walter Rodney, a Guyanese lecturer in African history. As Rupert Lewis explains in this selection, Rodney's radical black nationalist and socialist political views significantly influenced black consciousness in Jamaica. Rodney offered a powerful critique of the social inequalities of 1960s Jamaica. In his short tenure as a university lecturer Rodney, a graduate of the UWI, had tapped into this pulse through his discussion sessions with poor Jamaicans in Kingston and rural communities. He drew on the Rastafarian model of grounding or reasoning in developing this practice. The JLP government under Prime Minister Hugh Shearer was concerned about his radicalism and socialism. The ban was put into immediate effect when Rodney returned to Kingston from a black writers' conference in Montreal. The protest exposed social divisions and the role of the state in protecting middle-class interests.

Rodney's expulsion by the Jamaican government was based on fears that his interaction with the leading figures at the grassroots could lead to the emergence of a radical political ideology taking hold among them and that instability would ensue if such a political movement became an oppositional force threatening the political system of independent Jamaica that was barely six years old. The possibility of a link between the intellectuals and the masses seemed to be a source of paranoia in the ruling Jamaica Labour Party, but so far no hard evidence of Rodney trying to overthrow the Jamaican government has emerged. What emerges is hostility by the political elite to black nationalism coupled with cold war anticommunism, and narrow-minded Jamaican nationalism which portrayed Rodney as a foreigner from Guyana who was interfering in national politics.

Walter Rodney had contacts with Rastafarians and left-wing individuals from the early 1960s when he was an undergraduate at the University of the West Indies, and he renewed these contacts in 1968. His groundings in the urban ghettoes of East and West Kingston and in the countryside acted as catalysts to the growth in social and political consciousness. The oppressive conditions of life for the poor and the determination of groups of activists to initiate social protest were ongoing in the early 1960s.

A brilliant lecturer, in the few months he taught at Mona [Rodney] made a deep impression on his students. His talks at the UWI Students Union on Black Power had both campus and off-campus support. He was not connected to any organization neither did he build any. He would accept invitations from youth and community groups, Rastafarian groups and high school students. Groundings took place anywhere people wanted to hear about African and Caribbean history and politics or discuss the black power and civil rights movement in the United States.

He was very critical of his colleagues at the university for their failure to initiate direct dialogue between people at the grassroots and academics. While he spoke, the special branch men in attendance took detailed notes. He did not enter the Jamaican situation with ready-made solutions, but his travels throughout the country and groundings with so many groups led to the government of the Jamaica Labour Party deciding to declare him persona non grata. Rodney was one of a number of intellectuals in the 1960s against whom the Jamaican government took action because their ideas, travel destinations, and political connections were deemed to be subversive of the national interest.

The State and the Intelligentsia

The Jamaican state had targeted progressive intellectuals and used measures such as the seizure of passports, banning orders on individuals and literature to restrict their influence.

On July 18, 1968, Roy McNeil, the minister of home affairs, banned "all the publications of which Stokely Carmichael is the author or coauthor; all publications of which Elijah Muhammad (otherwise called Elijah Poole) is the author."[1] On January 30, 1968, he had banned the *Crusader*, which was edited by the African American nationalist Robert Williams. A year before in May 1967 the Undesirable Publications Law had been revised to include all English-language publications coming from Moscow and the international organisations financed by the USSR, Peking and Cuba. The publications by Stokely Carmichael and Malcolm X were widely available in the United States, so they were easily accessed by Jamaicans who had travelled to the United States or who had family living there, but police raided the homes of activists associated with Black Power activities and Walter Rodney and seized this literature.

Rodney's visits to Cuba and the USSR as a student were part of the charges brought by Prime Minister Shearer to justify the banning order. Roy McNeil, the minister of home affairs, in the debate following the exclusion order on Rodney had said, "I have never come across a man who offers a greater threat to the security of this land than does Walter Rodney."[2]

Frank Davis, who worked with the Special Branch in Kingston and was directly involved with the Rodney case, admitted that the reason for banning Rodney was that he "was charismatic at the grassroots level and had a following among intellectuals."[3] It was this relationship with the working people that constituted the main fear of the Shearer regime, which was shaken by the demonstrations following the ban on Rodney. It was the circumstances surrounding the ban on Rodney which provoked widespread protests but the conditions for the protests had been in the making throughout the 1960s.

The aircraft which brought Rodney back from Montreal where he was attending a Congress of Black Writers landed at 2:20 p.m. on Tuesday, 15th October. However it was not until 9:00 p.m. that the students learnt that he was refused re-entry and confined to the aircraft. A meeting of students on the campus was advertised for 11:00 p.m. in Mary Seacole Hall. The meeting of some 900 students unanimously accepted a resolution to march the following day on the officers of the Minister of Home Affairs and the Prime Minister and the deliver two petitions.[4]

The students originally intended to hire buses to go to the office of the prime minister to lodge their protest. But when the buses did not turn up on the morning of October 16th, the students decided to walk into town. Neither the students when they set out nor Prime Minister Shearer appreciated the significance of their actions. The students set out quite innocently wearing their undergraduate red gowns to distinguish themselves and their protest. Their actions were largely a response to the victimization of a lecturer and his family.

Ralph Gonsalves, who was president of the UWI Student Guild, wrote a detailed account of the march and the political decisions he had to make. One of the most important decisions was not to follow the silly advice of those who wanted to march into West Kingston, as that would certainly have led to political violence and considerable loss of life. As it turned out, the student march and demonstrations were joined by urban youth who in response to police repression did considerable damage.

The mass response to the Rodney ban took the government by surprise and the violence and destruction of property played into their hands to the

UWI student protestors run after being confronted by police on the Mona Road in St. Andrew, October 17, 1968. Photographer unknown. © The Gleaner Company (Media) Limited.

extent that it fuelled views that the 26-year-old Walter Rodney was a bogey-man who had a plot to overthrow the Jamaican government. The *Gleaner* of October 18th reported the death of two people. Many buses were seized and used to block roads, 13 buses were destroyed, 72 damaged, in addition to over 90 buildings; 11 policemen were injured and about 23 people were arrested on various charges. In the parliamentary debate on the following day Rodney was depicted as the evil-mind behind the violent resistance and was made out to be the mastermind of both student unrest and mass protest. Edward Seaga, who represented the Jamaican government on the University Council, took a very hard line against non-Jamaican students and staff who were involved in the protests. The 1968 riots and the attention paid to Walter Rodney were a result not so much of economic disaffection but the failure of the brown middle-class-led nationalist movement and the propertied ethnic minorities to come to terms with reversing centuries of racial oppression and denigration. As Rodney pointed, in 1968 the racial question was out in the open "in spite of all the efforts to maintain the taboos surrounding it."[5]

The demonstrations were the clearest indication of growing mass opposition to the JLP that had been elected in 1967 for a second term. Large sections of the urban youth were to be drawn into the PNP by Michael Manley, who in 1969 succeeded his father as leader of the PNP. It was a period that was to lead to the renewal of the political parties with the entry of middle-class radicals such as D. K. Duncan, Arnold Bertram and others into the PNP, Bruce Golding and Pearnel Charles into the JLP, the formation of the Workers Party of Jamaica and the ideologisation of Jamaican politics in the 1970s.

Notes

1. See *Jamaica Gazette* (publication of the Government of Jamaica) Supplement July 18, 1968.
2. Jamaica Hansard 1968/1969, 395.
3. Frank Davis, interview by author, Kingston, 3 June 1991.
4. Ralph Gonsalves, "The Rodney Affair," *Caribbean Quarterly* 25, no. 3 (1979): 3–4.
5. Walter Rodney, *The Groundings with my Brothers* (London: Bogle-L'Ouverture), 1969, 14.

The Visual Arts

Anne Walmsley and Stanley Greaves

Jamaica's vibrant visual arts scene became internationally noted in the middle years of the twentieth century, as British cultural historian Anne Walmsley and Guyanese painter Stanley Greaves explain. Edna Manley, a major sculptor in mid-twentieth-century Jamaica and wife of PNP leader Norman Manley, was a principal shaper of the Jamaican visual arts movement. In addition to producing major artistic works of her own, she developed the infrastructure of the visual art scene, helping to found the Jamaica School of Arts and Crafts in 1950. As with other domains of Jamaican cultural life, the art movement reflected social divisions. Elite artists such as Manley initially determined the standards. Wider interest in the works of nonelite artists, a general shift toward cultural nationalism after independence, and the advent of the Edna Manley College of the Visual and Performing Arts led to the broadening of Jamaica's art scene. Since then Jamaican art has become more bold and varied. The work of self-taught artists, often producing art that engages with religious themes, has been an especially important feature. This overview identifies the major developments and influences in Jamaican art.

Jamaica's modern movement in art is dated from 1922, the year when Edna Manley (1900–1987) arrived from Britain. Art training in London, exposure to European modernist styles such as Cubism, and an interest in African art all influenced her early work: from *The Beadseller* (1922), based on a Mandeville market woman, to *Negro Aroused* (1935). Her half-Jamaican parentage and her marriage to Norman Manley, a lawyer turned politician, resulted in close identification with the Jamaican people, their aspirations and potential. Together the Manleys assumed leadership of the early nationalist movement in Jamaica and ensured a close alliance between politics and art.

Edna Manley first showed work in Kingston with the Armenian-born fellow sculptor Koren der Harootian (1909–1991) in 1931. Her solo show six years later included *Negro Aroused* (1935), which drew a wide public response, resulting in purchase by the Institute of Jamaica (IOJ). The Institute had, since its late nineteenth-century foundation, built up a substantial collection of pre- and post-Emancipation art. Manley's was its first modern work and regarded as the nucleus of a permanent gallery of Jamaican art.

Edna Manley's description of the island's artists and their work in 1934 as "a few anaemic imitators of European traditions, a few charming parlour tricks," referred to her own white and brown social elite. Artists of the black rural and urban working class of Manley's generation were as yet invisible. All art of the 1930s was made against a background of impoverished living and working conditions.

By 1940 young artists of promise had come to Edna Manley's notice. They were encouraged in their work through informal gatherings at Drumblair, the Manleys' home, and several soon attended art classes taken by Edna Manley and der Harootian at the IOJ's Junior Institute. The artists included David Pottinger (1911–2004) and Ralph Campbell (1921–1985), who took as their main subject Jamaican people and activities, [and] Albert Huie (1920–2010), [who painted] the Jamaican landscape. All their work was driven by a nationalist ideology and painted in styles based on European Post-Impressionism.

Other artists born early in the century developed independently, with other inspiration. Carl Abrahams (1913–2005), initially a cartoonist, turned to painting after seeing work made by the British artist Augustus John (1878–1961) on a visit to Jamaica in 1937. Alvin Marriott (1902–1992), who showed sculpture in a solo exhibition in 1934, won a British Council art scholarship. An ardent admirer of Marcus Garvey and his Universal Negro Improvement Association, Marriott made many portrait sculptures of Garvey and later National Heroes. Namba Roy (1910–1961), a Maroon of the Cockpit Country, practised inherited skills in carving first in Jamaica, then, to acclaim, in Britain. David Miller Jnr (1903–1977) began working in wood with his father and is best-known for a later series of fine Afro-Jamaican heads. John "Doc" Williamson (1911–2006) made stylized portrait sculptures from local alabaster. The wooden carvings of Mallica Reynolds (Kapo) (1911–1989) of the 1940s to the 1960s are unequalled in their expressive artistry, with themes from the Afro-Christian Revivalist religious practice in which he was a preacher.

Display opportunities for artists of Jamaica were provided by the IOJ through an annual national exhibition and, in 1945, for those of the region in *West Indian Paintings*. The IOJ's Arts and Crafts Committee had long urged an independent art teaching institution. Thanks to a donated building, some government funding and Edna Manley's impetus, the Jamaica School of Arts and Crafts (JSAC) opened at the da Costa Institute in 1950.

Artists formed a succession of groups during the 1950s and beyond. Most were short-lived; the exception is the Jamaica Guild of Artists (founded in 1977), which continues to exhibit and promote its members' work. The Jamaica Artists' Association, from the elite of colonial society, opened an art gallery and held exhibitions featuring leading local artists: Campbell, Dunkley, Huie, Pottinger.

Black consciousness continued to develop. Painting and sculpture expressing Afro-Jamaican Christian and Rastafarian beliefs became more widespread. Kapo had turned to painting in his Zion Revivalist yard in Kingston's Trench Town. Work made by Everald Brown (1917–2002) for his Assembly of the Living on the Spanish Town Road was first seen outside its religious setting at the Creative Arts Centre, UWI, in 1969. The *Annual National Exhibition* of 1970 showed paintings by twenty-six artists including several Rastafarians; Ras Daniel Heartman, who showed *Mystic Presence*, was especially popular with the viewing public though ignored by art pundits. Brown received an honourable mention, and Kapo first prize for *Sweet Oranges*.

Artists returning to or arriving in Jamaica in the 1960s brought new perspectives from training and travels elsewhere. Osmond Watson had been introduced to the ideals of Marcus Garvey as a child, and Garveyism was for him, as for many other artists, a potent force. It was strengthened during Watson's student years in London through opportunities to see traditional African sculpture; this, with the Modernist styles to which he was also exposed, became an important source for his future work: for example, paintings of John Canoe masqueraders in an individual Cubist style, woodcarvings which recall African masks and reflect Afro-Jamaican religious rituals. Australian-born Colin Garland (1935–2007) brought a fresh eye and approach to painting in Jamaica, especially through his distinctive use of Surrealism. It was, however the three artists who, in 1964, formed the Contemporary Jamaican Artists' Association (CJAA), whose work, individually and collectively, dominated the decade following independence. All had studied abroad and travelled widely: Eugene Hyde (1931–1980) in the USA; Karl Parboosingh (1923–1975) in the USA, France and Mexico; and Barrington Watson (b. 1931) in Britain, the Netherlands, Paris, Italy and Spain. Their paintings introduced then new styles such as neo-figuration and Abstract Expressionism.

Barrington Watson, as dean of studies at the JSAC (1963–1967), was influential in training the first generation of postindependence artists; full-time students first graduated in 1963. The next artist appointed to head the school, by now the JSA, was Karl "Jerry" Craig (b. 1936) in 1971, home from art training and work in art education in Britain, where he was an active participant in the Caribbean Artists Movement (1966–1971). Craig established a four-year programme at the JSA with new studies such as textiles, jewellery and art education, and oversaw the school's relocation to the Cultural Training Centre (1976). Following the death of Edna Manley in 1987, it was renamed the School of Art, then of Visual Arts, within the Edna Manley College of Visual and Performing Arts (EMC). As the premier art-teaching institution in the Anglophone Caribbean, it has long attracted students from elsewhere in the region.

Better Mus' Come

Delroy Wilson

A reggae classic, singer Delroy Wilson's most popular song (written by Everald Metcalf) expressed the sentiments of many Jamaicans ten years after independence. The singer's lament for improvement against a repressive system reflected a new consciousness that emerged in reggae music in 1968. This new militancy became its most recognizable feature in the next decade. The song was appropriated by Michael Manley's 1972 election campaign, which used "Better Mus' Come" as its slogan.

Yeah, yeah, yeah

I've been trying a long, long time still I didn't make it
Everything I try to do seems to go wrong
It seems I have done something wrong
But they're trying to keep me down

Who God bless, no one curse
Thank God I'm not the worst

Better mus' come one day
Better mus' come, they can't conquer me
Better mus' come, yeah

I've been trying a long, long time
But I can't make it
No one to give me a helping hand
They only tryin' to keep me down

Who God bless, no one curse
Thank God I'm not the worst

Oh, my people get a seat
They're trying to take advantage of me

Better mus' come, better must come, yeah
Better mus' come one day
Better mus' come, yeah, yeah, yeah, yeah, yeah

I've been trying a long, long time still I can't make it
Everything I try to do seems to go wrong
It seems I have done something wrong
But they're trying to keep me down

Who God bless, no one curse
Thank God I'm not the worst

Better mus' come one day
Better mus' come, they can't conquer me
Better mus' come one day, better must come
Oh, better mus' come one day, better must come

Better mus' come one day
Better mus' come
Better mus', ooh

Bob Marley's Fame

Ed McCormack

Robert Nesta (Bob) Marley is among the world's most famous faces. In his brief life Marley transcended Jamaican music and became extraordinarily influential. Marley was born on 6 February 1945 into a poor rural family in Nine Mile, in Rhoden Hall, a community deep in the hills of the northern parish of St. Ann. At a young age he moved to Kingston with his mother, Cedella, eventually pursuing a musical career. He enjoyed fleeting local success in the mid-1960s when he formed the vocal group the Wailers, which included Peter Tosh and Neville Livingstone (Bunny Wailer), two other youths who like Marley lived in the impoverished community of Trench Town. After several fits and starts, the group became local favorites at the beginning of the 1970s with hit songs such as "Small Axe" and "Trenchtown Rock." Greater success arrived in 1973 when the Wailers, by then devoted Rastafarians, were signed by Island Records mogul Chris Blackwell. A year later they stopped recording as a trio. This was, however, the beginning of Marley's phenomenal global rise. A series of solo albums released under the name Bob Marley and the Wailers and including an augmented band established his international reputation as a revolutionary musician. A failed assassination attempt in Kingston in December 1976 drew widespread attention. Marley continued to release outstanding albums and tour the world for the rest of the decade before succumbing to the melanoma that began in his right foot and claimed his life in May 1981 at only thirty-six. Since his death his fame has grown exponentially. Jamaica's current renown owes a great deal to his success. Indeed, Marley remains the most recognizable symbol of Jamaica, with a greater following than any of his successors.

This 1976 article from the premier US rock magazine, Rolling Stone, *captures Marley at the ascendance of his international stardom. The massive attention paid to his 1975 album,* Natty Dread, *and its follow-up,* Live!, *which was recorded that summer at the Lyceum Theatre in London, inspired dozens of rock music journalists to travel to Jamaica to interview him as he was completing recording of his* Rastaman Vibration *album, which would be followed by a breakthrough summer tour of North America, the UK, and Europe. The article was accompanied by Marley's appearance on the cover of* Rolling Stone, *a signal of the far reach of his fame.*

When I first encountered Bob Marley he was sitting in an upstairs window-sill in his house on Hope Road, smoking the inevitable spliff and study-ing the brilliant tropic treetops, deep in herbal meditation. In fact, Marley was so whacked out of his skull that it was possible to study him in perfect nubian-carving profile for several seconds before it even dawned on him that he had company.

Driving up, the first thing you noticed was the silver gray BMW parked in the driveway. Hope Road is a relatively affluent street of respectable middle-class dwellings within spitting distance of some of the worst slums in the Western Hemisphere. Hope House, surrounded by a spacious overgrown yard with several smaller structures out back (one of which is being con-verted into a recording studio), is still palatial by local standards. Surely Marley must have watched us drive up. As he sits there, looking surprisingly like Ché Guevara with his celebrated dreads stashed in an oversized beret, one can only speculate on what grave matters preoccupy him. Now that even *Time* magazine has acknowledged Marley as "a political force to rival the government," perhaps he is considering the not-so-remote possibility of a surprise raid from the governor general's white colonial headquarters, less than a mile down Hope Road. At least that would explain the tense hush that hangs over this house, making it seem like a guerrilla encampment. Given the uniqueness of his position, however, it seems just as possible he is calculating the effect that the upcoming parliamentary elections in Kings-ton might have on the sales of his latest single, a scathing political statement called "Rat Race."

Anyone naive enough to wonder aloud why such a righteously rebel-lious, nonmaterialistic culture hero would own the same kind of car Mi-chael Manley drives will be treated to a taste of fine Rasta logic: BMW stands for "Bob Marley and the Wailers." And why does he submit to so many photo sessions? "I tell you what," Marley says, "if the amount of records sell the amount of photo dem take—great! More than 2 million photo dem take already!"

Not to imply that Bob Marley has been bending over backward or any-thing. Stu Weintraub, Marley's American booking agent, told me it was touch and go and *soon come* for a hell of a long time before he finally got Bob Marley and the Wailers to play in the States.

"Every two weeks another emissary would arrive from Jamaica to tell me it was either on or off again. . . . It went on for so long that when I finally met Bob, when he finally showed up in my office in New York, I said, 'So, you're a real flesh and blood person! I was beginning to have my doubts!'"

From the beginning, Weintraub refused to let Marley and the Wailers open for any other act—not even the Rolling Stones, who offered the golden opportunity to expand a growing cult following when they asked to have the Rastaman as the opening act on their last tour.

"Naturally, I had to wonder if I was doing the right thing. How can you turn down a gig like that and not wonder?! But my feeling was that although not enough people knew about Bob Marley yet, he was already on his way to becoming a tremendous star . . . and stars don't open, they *headline*."

Weintraub says he was finally convinced he'd been right all along when the turnout for the most recent American tour surpassed even his expectations.

"We could have filled large stadiums like Madison Square Garden easily," Weintraub tells me. "But instead I chose to present Bob in medium-sized halls, in more intimate surroundings, where he could come across as what he is—a profoundly religious man expounding a profoundly religious message."

Marley himself will tell you that he submits to invasions of his privacy by foreign writers and photographers more to spread the gospel of Rastafarianism than for fame or gain.

"Mos' time me no see nobody but I brethren, I family," he says with a sweeping gesture of the arm, as though to embrace his extended family who are standing around, his five-year-old son Robbie playing with a miniature car in the yard and a pretty, brown-skinned woman smoking a spliff as though it were a Virginia Slim and gazing pensively down from the upstairs window where we first found him.

"Mos' time me no see nobody but dem, an' jus' stay heah an' wit I music an' I meditatin', mon. But sometime I like to talk to scribes for dem dat slow to catch onto I message, mon. Sometime it good for I and I to talk, 'cause sometime it cleah de air, mon . . . you understand?"

The public myth must be protected, especially now that some reggae purists are complaining that his latest American LP, *Rastaman Vibration*, seems noticeably diminished in roots and perhaps a shade too rock & rolly. But the album's sales, according to the people at Island Records, have already topped his previous three LPs combined and the album is still climbing the charts, goosed along by his recent tour. Most of these detractors may not be ready to relegate Bob Marley to the commercial limbo where Jimmy Cliff, the first reggae artist to become well-known in the U.S., now languishes. But these critics now point to Burning Spear, a group heavily into African chants, as the group to listen to if you want to hear some nitty-gritty roots, rude and raw.

Bob Marley brought bitter political rivals Prime Minister Michael Manley and opposition leader Edward Seaga onstage to join hands. It was a powerful gesture intended to bring an end to the political violence and bloodshed that had wracked Jamaica. In June 1978 Marley was awarded the United Nations Peace Medal of the Third World for his commitment to ending the strife in his homeland. Photograph by Adrian Boot, 1978. © Bob Marley Music Inc. Used courtesy of the photographer.

Like the folk purists who screamed "sellout" when Bob Dylan went electric, such critics are missing the point that Marley, like Dylan, has transcended genre—that he may even have transcended roots! You only have to see him onstage, a dancing dervish, dreadlocks windmilling, to realize that here is a rock & roll star.

Yet, Marley seems genuinely committed to his faith, and when he talks about the pilgrimage he soon plans to make to Ethiopia, it is clear that his heart remains in the highlands of that mythic mecca. "It I dream, mon, every Rastamon's dream, to fly home to Ethiopia and leave a-Babylon, where de politicians doan let I an' I brethren be free an' live we own righteous way. Dat's why I goan der buy land an' bring my family back wid me, mon, because a-Babylon mus' fall. It true so much wickedness mus' end, but when? Me an' I brethren no want to wait no more, 'cause our Jah, him tell us go home to we Ethiopia an' leave a-Babylon to perish in it own wickedness, mon. I doan know why . . . but it mus' be . . ."

Then Marley seems to brighten and he says, "It take many year, mon, an' maybe some bloodshed mus'be, but righteousness someday prevail. . . . Yeh, mon, me know, 'cause everywhere we go when we play outside Jamaica, all ovah the whorl, I see I dreadlock brethren everywhere . . . a-growin' up strong like herb stalks in de field. . . . Yeh, mon, it gladden I heart to see Natty Dreadlock him everywhere growin' strong . . . it *future*, mon."

Ganja Smoking

Daily News

The smoking of marijuana—"ganja" or "the herb"—became a great public con-cern in Jamaica during the early twentieth century, when the colonial government outlawed its use. Punishment for ganja smoking was strictly enforced in the early independence years through the Dangerous Drugs Act. Offenders were arrested and imprisoned for up to eighteen months for possession of marijuana, regardless of quantity. An active public media campaign aimed at youth discouraged use by em-phasizing harmful side effects, criminal sanctions, and mental health problems that could arise from abuse. Jamaica's political class and religious groups also attributed the country's high crime rate to ganja smoking. The efforts were controversial. Many Jamaicans believed the punishment for recreational use was excessive. A vigorous debate on ganja use extended into the 1970s. At the center of this debate were Ras-tafarians, who smoke ganja for religious reasons. Rastafarians have long believed in the medicinal properties of cannabis. The popularity of reggae music, which pro-moted Rastafari culture, including the smoking of "herb," further raised attention around its use in Jamaica. The image of the ganja-smoking reggae singer led to the false impression outside the island that ganja smoking was legal in Jamaica. In the summer of 1975 the rebellious reggae singer Peter Tosh released a promarijuana anthem, Legalize It, which was eventually banned from airplay. Nonetheless, the song's release reinvigorated local discussions about marijuana use and its effects on the island's youth. As this newspaper article from July 1975 indicates, younger Jamaicans were not convinced about widespread claims against ganja use. The per-spectives of members of a local youth club are representative of the wider arguments around ganja smoking in Jamaica.

Four decades later, in 2015, the Jamaican government amended the Dangerous Drugs Act by decriminalizing though not legalizing ganja use. Personal use of less than two ounces became a ticketable offence. The government further opened discus-sions around the cultivation of marijuana for its therapeutic properties. Notwith-standing these progressive measures, the issues raised in this article remain alive in local debates around marijuana.

The use of marijuana is widely regarded as a serious social problem. In the USA and in many other countries, ganja is legally classified with the true narcotics, cocaine and opium derivatives, and its sale and distribution are prohibited.

However, recently one American state, Alaska, legalised the smoking of ganja, leaving much speculation as to what will happen as a result.

Youth Forum today seeks to bring out some youth views on whether or not ganja smoking in Jamaica should be made legal.

To do this we join the Cross Roads Police Youth Club, while their meeting is in progress in the recreation room of the station. Of the club's 101 members, 11 persons including the club's president I. Seizas join the debate and all except one feels that ganja smoking should be legalized.

Seizas, who is 28 and a photographer, leads off the debate by saying that in his opinion ganja is free but it is man who is not free to smoke ganja. He says to prove this point we must observe that whenever someone is smoking ganja and the police appear, it is not the ganja which is carted off to jail but rather the smoker. Hence his stance that ganja is free.

He goes on to say that the smoking of "herb" should be made legal as it is a "sacrament" which has been in use from ancient times which was used by Moses, and later Jesus Christ.

Twenty-two-year-old Anthony Depass, a school teacher, expressed the view that ganja, unlike alcohol, does no harm to the human system and he sees no reason why its smoking in private should not be made legal.

Depass says that he had never seen any medical evidence that ganja causes madness as is suggested by many persons. On the other hand, alcohol has caused heart disease of one form or another and hundreds if not thousands die every year from cirrhosis of the liver caused by excessive use of alcohol.

Using this evidence, Depass feels that it is the smoking of ganja and not the drinking of liquor which should be given protection of the law. He however spelled out the circumstances under which the smoking of this "herb" should be made legal.

"There should be stringent rules laid down, which would permit herb smoking in private homes and other sanctuaries," said Depass. He feels that to indulge in a sacrament on the bus, or in a cinema is sacrilegious and is not done by true "brethren."

He was supported in this view by a 43-year-old welder, Roy Mitchell, who explained why people indulged in the smoking of ganja. He said that there were those who had evil intentions but before enforcing this they indulged in weed smoking and then carry out their deeds. This he said is not typical of the true brethren and is misleading to the public, who feel that it was the herb which caused such behaviour.

Gladston Cummings, a printer, agrees with him. He feels that like some rum drinkers, there were those herb smokers who only indulged in the custom to be called "Rastas." "These are not Rastas they are rascals," one member piped in.

But 15-year-old Lascells Pusey goes to the Bible for his contribution to the debate. "Grass is for the animals and herbs for the healing of the nation," he suggests. If God placed herbs on the earth why should not man be able to partake of it freely, he asks?

He went on to point out that being a one-time asthma sufferer it was ganja-tea which cured him of this ailment, thus instilling in him the relief of true medicinal qualities of ganja.

However, crafts man George Brown feels that if ganja smoking was legalized in Jamaica, Government earnings could be increased if the growing and sale of the herb was controlled and taxed like tobacco.

There would be added employment, foreign reserve build up, and instead of taking all smokers before the courts, legislation would only outlaw public smoking of ganja, Brown suggests.

Anthony Depass injects still another solution to the legalising of the herb, as he feels that the best rope, paper and medicines are produced from ganja. If this was legalized and grown with proper government supervision and proper medical research Jamaica would be on the way to producing a sick-free society and a nation second to none, Depass said.

Mitchell spoke of an eternal peace which would be possible with the legalising of ganja. He said that from time immemorial men sat down at the conference table and smoked the "peace pipe." The Indians and the white men did it, and leaders of great nations have done and are continuing to do it, he said.

The only dissenting member was 24-year-old police constable Alphonso Madden, who said that in his opinion ganja smoking should not be legalized as there were those who would still not stick to the letter of the law and would openly smoke the "weed" in defiance.

He said that Jamaicans usually were people who took everything to extremes and it was for this reason that he could not support any attempt to legalise this custom. However, he was of the opinion that there were persons who smoked ganja who were peaceful and otherwise law abiding citizens who were making meaningful contributions to the society.

We Are Not for Sale

Michael Manley

Prime Minister Michael Manley excelled at oratory. His address at the PNP's thirty-eighth annual conference on 19 September 1976 at the National Arena rates as one of his best. The opposition JLP and business interests regarded his policy of democratic socialism as the source of the country's terrible economic woes. A vicious party conflict had caused the deaths of hundreds. Manley also faced resistance from the United States, over his support of Castro's Cuba and the potential for socialism in Jamaica. Manley's opponents genuinely feared that Jamaica would become a one-party socialist state. In June 1976 Manley declared a state of public emergency that would remain in force for the next year. The violence continued nonetheless, and many Jamaicans chose to migrate, mostly to North America. Manley's administration fought hard to maintain its position as the country splintered. This situation added tension to Manley's address. The clever repetition of the refrains "We know where we are going," "Not for sale," and "We are going forward with socialism" emboldened party supporters—referred to as "comrades"—and would become popular clarions among those who stood in solidarity with the party's socialism. Partly on the strength of his passionate commitment, Manley was reelected prime minister in the violent general elections of 15 December 1976. Manley's supporters viewed his second mandate as popular reaffirmation of the government's socialist path.

We are struggling to build something new and we may suffer while we struggle, but the suffering that you endure when you struggle is worth enduring because you know what you are fighting to build and because you know where you are going.

And we know where we are going.

And Comrades, the reason why we were in that condition, because we the Jamaica people were trapped; we were trapped in a world system that we call imperialism and we were trapped in a local system that we call capitalism. And we set about, we set about in 1972 with your mandate for change, but we realized that there could be no change in this country unless we were prepared to change the system. Unless we were prepared to join the international struggle against imperialism, and unless we were prepared to reorganize Jamaica to replace the capitalist system with a socialist system.

Inside Jamaica, we are also determined to replace and change and remove the system of capitalism and replace it by building brick upon brick, step by step, the new system of democratic socialism.

And Comrades, when you look at the things we have done, you ask yourselves, why does the clique hate us so? Why do they fight us so? But first of all, let me remind you who the clique is. I am going to tell you who the clique is. The clique are the controllers of capital who resist change. The clique are the beneficiaries of imperialism who resist change. The clique are the developers who abscond with the people's money and take up residence abroad, skulking away like thieves in the night, leaving citizens to suffer behind them. Those are the clique and the ones that stole the money of the poor people with their houses. They lay about in Miami, loll about in Toronto, and they dream of the day when we will be defeated so that they can come back to scalp the people some more. But let the word go to them in Toronto—those who stole the people's money, and let it go to them in Miami, that they will never live to see that day.

And one day the laws of the world may be such, one day the laws of the world may be such that people who committed economic crimes in Jamaica, who stole poor people's money for houses, who went away with the money like thieves in the night, and who now take the sweat and the labour of the Jamaican people to enjoy themselves abroad, let them beware. One day the laws of the world may be such that the hand of justice will reach out from Jamaica and snatch them back to come to trial at home.

But the clique, the clique are there, and they are spending their money like wine, and how has the clique operated and why do they operate? The clique operates first of all because they realize that this government would not accept a Jamaica that was controlled in the interest of a minority and that we are going to build a Jamaica that was controlled by the majority of the people.

What did the clique do? First of all, it took final control of the Jamaica Labour Party and the Jamaica Labour Party is now the instrument and the yo-yo of the clique.

Who remembers the yo-yo? The yo-yo and the Labour Party are one and the same. Their first strategy was to take control of the Labour Party and the Labour Party of today is not the Labour Party of thirty years ago.

Look at what we have lived through. In 1973 we began to feel the lash of world inflation, the prices for the wheat that you take to make the flour and use the flour to make the bread and the dumplings, all of a sudden, the price went up five times; and the mother with her little pot, looking to cook the Sunday meal, had begun to ask, "Can I afford the dumpling, because the wheat from abroad cost five times?"—we took that blow. We couldn't do anything about it except prepare to change the world in time.

The oil prices one "lick" raises four times. This little country paying out $160 million a year now to buy the same oil, and the thing that saved Jamaica was the bauxite levy; the bauxite levy which was the use of the sovereign power of a Third World nation to put multinational corporations under "heavy manners."

And when I look outside there are those with a motive to put us in our place and teach us a lesson, and tell us who are we to believe that we can tell a bauxite company what taxation to pay? Who are we? Who are we to stand behind Cuba when she goes to the liberation of Angola by the defeat of the fascist and apartheid troops of South Africa?

And they say who are we, poor little Jamaica, who are we to mix up in all that? Well, I will tell you who we are. We are Jamaicans and we little but we "tallawah."

And having told you who we are, I will tell you why—because we know that for 300 years we have lived under that system and all we got was slavery and when we didn't get slavery, we got bad sugar prices and when we weren't getting bad sugar prices, we were getting hovels to raise our children. We know what that system has meant for us. We know what the masses got when the bauxite buildings were being built in Jamaica; they got nothing. And we are not for sale.

We are not for sale. And tell them anytime they are willing to deal with an honourable Jamaica built on principle, sovereignty, pride and dignity, then we will talk the investment of the money. But if we are to return to our knees, they can keep the money, we will find another way.

We know where we are going. We are creating a new man. We have begun the building of socialist man. We are working towards the day when there will be no more masters and no more servants but only one together in the Lord.

And we are learning now to go not upon our knees, but as true, sovereign, human, dignified human beings, because we know where we are going.

And we will remember then the Basic Schools that we built, because we know where we are going. We will remember the Day Care Centres that we are building because we know where we are going.

A political cartoon by Livingston McLaren from the *Daily News* that parodies three different views of Michael Manley's democratic socialism. From *Livingston McLaren's Selected Editorial Cartoons* (Kingston: Daily News, 1979). Courtesy of the National Library of Jamaica.

The National Youth Service that we have started, because we know where we are going.

The Pioneer Corps that is going forward, because we know where we are going.

And we are going to that place—they believe, they believe—bless their craven little hearts, they believe that we are going without the Middle Class, but they are wrong. Look about you. Look about you. Look about you.

And my Comrades, there is now equal pay for equal work because we know where we are going.

We have a Minimum Wage Law now because we know where we are going.

We have protection for workers now because we know where we are going.

We have a Family Court for mothers now because we know where we are going.

So my Comrades, go ye forth you warriors of socialism and gather us a harvest of victory. Be disciplined. Be worthy. In the name of every child in every hovel anywhere in Jamaica or in the world, in the name of every black man working out his days in the indignity of his servitude in Southern Africa, in the name of every mother whose heart is in agony as she gazes upon her baby and asks, "What is there for you, my little one?" In the name of every Jamaican who cares for justice, in the name of every youth who has died, in the name of Sam Sharpe, in the name of Paul Bogle, in the name of George William Gordon, in the name of Marcus Garvey,

In the name of Norman Manley,

In the name of every victim that ever lived, in the name of every martyr that ever died, we will not fail. We shall overcome.

Zig-Zag Politics and the IMF

George L. Beckford

The 1976 electoral victory gave Manley and the PNP a resounding mandate for democratic socialism. Yet it was not long before stronger tensions emerged over the path to be taken. The economic pressures of the mid-1970s were enormous. The cost of almost all imports, especially petroleum, increased in the aftermath of the 1973 "oil shock." In an effort to address these difficulties, the PNP recruited faculty at UWI's Mona campus to develop an alternative economic strategy for Jamaica. George Beckford, a respected political economist who spent much of his professional and personal life advocating for Jamaica's small farmers, was among the team that produced the Emergency Production Plan in 1977. With his progressive peers, Beckford was stirred by Manley's public stand to defend Jamaica against all forms of US imperialist encroachment. The plan they created, commonly referred to as the "people's plan," drew on Beckford's earlier analysis of Jamaica as a "plantation economy," oriented originally toward the needs of its colonizers, and now toward those of multinational capital. It aimed to create an alternative Jamaican economy that met its own needs, especially in food, rather than depending on imports. Its vision shared much with those of nationalist center-left governments across Latin America and the Caribbean in the 1960s and 1970s. Rather than full economic control by a socialist state, the "people's plan" envisaged a "mixed economy," in which agriculture and industrial workers would occupy a central role and the state would direct the most significant economic sectors. A vibrant publicity campaign underlined the energy that the team and their supporters put into the plan.

To its authors' distress, Manley's government backed away from the plan as it was about to be implemented. In the face of intense internal and external pressure, Manley signed a deal with the IMF in 1977. The deal gave Jamaica access to IMF loans in exchange for commitment to an "open" economy highly dependent on imports and exports, devaluation of the Jamaican dollar, and radical cuts to government spending on social programs. The decision disheartened Beckford and his allies. Beckford and Michael Witter, his colleague and a fellow member of the team, vividly documented the experience in Small Garden . . . Bitter Weed, *written at the end of the decade. The book detailed the plan and outlined the economic*

challenges the country contended with after the IMF deal. It was a powerful indict-
ment of Manley's about-face and its long-term consequences. Beckford and Witter
penned separate closing commentaries to the book. In his epilogue—the following
selection—Beckford framed the effort of the Production Plan team as part of Jamai-
ca's battle against imperialism in the 1970s. In the December election, according to
Beckford, "the electorate gave Manley and the PNP an overwhelming mandate to
pursue the Democratic Socialist alternative." In his analysis of Manley's decision
by April to move Jamaica away from a radical agenda toward an arrangement with
the IMF, Beckford expressed deep personal distress. He depicted Manley's actions,
especially those of his government representatives who were clandestinely meeting
with the IMF while the Production Plan was being designed, as a betrayal of the
country for which he would never be forgiven. It was Manley, he argues, who "took
the critical decision to keep Jamaica handcuffed to imperialism": "history will
never absolve him!" This anger reflected the profound disillusionment of many intel-
lectuals with Manley's economic policies during his second term. Manley always
maintained that he acted in the nation's best interest, and he was deeply upset by
Beckford's comments.

The massive defeat of Michael Manley's People's National Party (PNP) in
the October 30, 1980, electoral contest was a logical result of a process that
began on or before December 15, 1976. We describe and analyse the struggle
against imperialism, led by Manley's PNP government between 1974 and
1979, and the reaction of imperialism to that struggle.

The most crucial year of that period was September 1976 to September
1977. It was in September 1976 that Manley and the Jamaican people declared
unequivocally that WE ARE NOT FOR SALE. WE KNOW WHERE WE ARE
GOING, at a mass meeting in the National Stadium. Unknown to the Jamaican people, the then Minister of Finance (David Coore) and senior officials of the Bank of Jamaica (Governor Arthur Brown and Co.) were busy at
that very moment negotiating with the International Monetary Fund (IMF)
to "sell" Jamaica by ensnaring the economy deeper in the net of imperialism. The Finance Minister had made a firm commitment to the Fund at
a September meeting in Manila, Philippines. And between September and
December 1976, Bank of Jamaica officials held secret meetings with IMF officials deliberately "disguised as tourists" on the northern coast of Jamaica.

Meanwhile the PNP launched a militant anti-imperialist electoral campaign that presented "Democratic Socialism" to the Jamaican people as the
answer to centuries of exploitation under colonialism and imperialism. The
opposing Jamaica Labour Party (JLP) offered what they called "Nationalism": in reality, Jamaican capitalism in association with imperialism.

In the election held on December 15, 1976, the electorate gave Manley and the PNP an overwhelming mandate to pursue the Democratic Socialist alternative. Right after this electoral outcome a small group of political economists from the University of the West Indies alerted the General Secretary of the PNP (Dr. D. K. Duncan) and Prime Minister Manley of the consequences of an IMF agreement and the 40% devaluation of the currency which that entailed.

Prime Minister Manley commissioned us to prepare an alternative to the IMF, in the spirit of the electoral mandate. The first document was submitted to him late December 1976; and discussions arising from it led to a declaration made by him in a national broadcast of January 5, 1977, that his government would reject the IMF solution and chart the nation on a "self-reliant democratic socialist" path. This position was re-emphasised and elaborated in a second broadcast on January 19, 1977, by which time the UWI political economists had elaborated the Democratic Socialist alternative in two other documents.

The Prime Minister's speech of January 19 promised the nation that an Emergency Production Plan would be formulated by March to guide government policy and action for the rest of 1977 and that by year-end a Five-Year Development Plan would be ready for public scrutiny. To facilitate this, he invited members of the UWI team to take up key positions in the state planning, policy and mobilization bureaucracy. The most important of these appointments were Dr. N. P. Girvan to be Chief Technical Director of the National Planning Agency with Dr. M. Witter as his Economic Adviser; and Mr. L. G. Lindsay as Chief Technical Director in the newly created Ministry of National Mobilization and Human Resource Development.

The National Planning Agency (NPA) organized a Task Force of state and university technocrats, trade union representatives, and other interest groups, while the Ministry of Mobilization invited suggestions from the Jamaican public. Over 10,000 responses were received from the public in a two-week period. And these were integrated into a massive three-volume plan submitted by the NPA to cabinet on March 23, 1977. That plan was subsequently rejected by government. For a month later, on April 22, 1977, Prime Minister Manley presented to Parliament an Emergency Production Plan, 1977–78, that involved capitulation to the IMF and imperialism.

The mandate of December 15, 1976, was betrayed there and then. The IMF and imperialism finally succeeded in removing the Manley government on October 30, 1980.

Part of the price Mr. Manley would have to pay to receive IMF assistance would be to put the left wing of his party "under heavy manners." The first

IMF agreement was signed in July 1977; and at the annual party conference in September, Manley took to himself tasks, in both party and state, that had been the main responsibility of the leader of the left wing—Dr. D. K. Duncan; thereby forcing Duncan's resignation from his dual role as General Secretary of the PNP and Minister of National Mobilization and Human Resource Development.

Eventually, more information and documentation will become available to provide us with much more in-depth analyses of the critical conjuncture that existed in Jamaica in the four months between December 1976 and April 1977. Most of this is perhaps only now available to the one individual, Mr. Michael Manley, who took the critical decision to keep Jamaica handcuffed to imperialism. In the book itself we have offered a very brief and unsatisfactory analysis of "what factors triggered the turn-back of Prime Minister Manley . . ." One thing is certain, history will never absolve him![1]

Note

1. Beckford here pointedly references Fidel Castro's famous 1953 statement in court, "History will absolve me," emphasizing that in his eyes, Manley has failed to do for Jamaica what Castro had done for Cuba. [Editors' note]

Yesterday / Today / Tomorrow

Oku Onuora

Oku Onuora was one of the founders of a new fusion of verbal and musical arts, for which he popularized the term dub *poetry. Onuora defined a dub poem as one "that has a built-in reggae rhythm."*[1] *Born in 1952 and originally named Orlando Wong, Onuora became a Rastafarian and community activist in Kingston in the 1960s. He began to write and perform poetry while incarcerated in Fort Augusta prison. He was released on parole in 1977 and published his first written collection,* Echo, *from which this poem is taken, the same year.*

This poem, like much of Onuora's work, is overtly political. It is an implicit attack on Michael Manley's use of pan-Africanist and socialist rhetoric, suggesting that the PNP were co-opting the ideas of people they previously dismissed as ignorant.

yesterday
I said:
bongo man
congo man
dread
I
      Rastafari
roots
I talked about:
Garvey
pan Africanism
Socialism
Nkrumah
Ghana
Nyerere
Tanzania
Castro
Cuba
Liberation

Struggle

Yesterday
you said:
>   bongo man
>   congo man

primitiveness
       dread
outrageous
       I
ignorant
              roots
foolishness
                    Garvey
no big thing
                         pan Africanism
                    socialism
irrelevant
       Nkrumah
       Ghana
       Nyerere
       Tanzania
       Castro
       Cuba
Catastrophe
       liberation
from what?
       struggle
subversive

today
I say
what I said yesterday

today
you say:
>   bongo man
>   congo man
>   dread
>   I

A Helper's Story

Sistren, with Honor Ford Smith

The Sistren Theatre Collective was founded in 1977. It produced improvised plays that stemmed from its members' desire to make visible the experience and suffering of Jamaican working-class women. In 1986 the collective published Lionheart Gal, *a collection of autobiographical narratives, written in patwa. The life story extracted here provides one of the few detailed descriptions of what was always one of the most common occupations for women: household work. As well as describing the day-to-day experience of such work, the testimony also hints at the important changes in relationships between employers and domestic workers in the 1970s due to the introduction of minimum wage legislation.*

Di first ting ah going tell yuh is what really mek me conscious of how dis life do me. Ah been working from ah was seventeen years old until now and all di lickle money dat ah work only go fi food and rent. Ah don't have none save. Di lickle money is too small to save.

Di first job ah ever do was a domestic servant. Ah do it fi three years. Ah was living in Alexandria in di country wid me family. A Big Man in di district had a big property. His son grow up and come to town and was working at Hanna's shops as one of Hanna's big supervisor. After him get married, him wanted a helper, so him come down and ask me faada if him can let me come and me faada say "Yes." Dat was how ah come to Kingston.

Ah was di washer and do di cleaning and tidying of di house. Dem have anodder lady who cook. It was stop pon premises. Di gardener deh one side by himself inna one room wid only a lickle bed and one table in deh. Me and di cook share a room. Inna it we have two lickle single bed fi me and she and one lickle table inna di middle, to put anyting we had. We suitcase was put down at di odder side pon di floor or pon one box. Di table was di place weh we eat.

A bell connect from fi-dem room to fi-we room. Every morning at five o'clock dat lady ring dat bell. Breakfast have to ready, for Mr Iris have to be on di road by six thirty to reach work by seven. Him a di manager so him

360 Sistren, with Honor Ford Smith

carry home most of di key dem and him open di shop in di morning. Ah had
to get up and go in di kitchen and get di breakfast. Dem had a big breakfast.
Green banana and mackerel or egg and bacon and tea and toast and corn-
flakes different. As di breakfast finish and him go tru di gate, me start tidy
di house and mek up di bed. It was him and him wife and him madda in a
two bedroom house. Me mek up di bed and sweep out di house. Di cook
start look after whatsoever she cooking for lunch or she do lickle ironing.

By eight o'clock ah finish tidy out di house. Ah had to wash and iron every day for di man change a white shirt every morning and every evening.
Every week you have fourteen shirt fi wash fi him, fourteen underpant,
fourteen marina, fourteen pair a socks. When him come in from work in
di evening, him tidy and put on one. When him go a him bed, him tek off
dat and put on him pyjama. In di morning, him wake up and put on one
clean suit fi go a work, so ah have dat amount of clothes to look after fi di
man plus her clothes and de madda's. By twelve o'clock yuh have to put di
clothes on di line. When him come for lunch, it was a small lunch. We have
to find our own lunch. She never give we lunch. She only give us breakfast
and dinner. We buy banana and mackerel or saltfish and we cook dumpling.
Sometimes we used to buy bread or biscuit and dat least we fi di week.

At two, yuh start pick up di clothes to iron dem. She never allow di
clothes dem to dry on di line. She just make dem half quail up and den yuh
pick dem up, fold dem, damp dem and start press dem.

Yuh iron till four thirty. At dat time she say, "Yuh can stop iron now and
go tidy yuhself." Yuh put away di clothes and by five yuh go to bathe and
change yuh clothes.

Six o'clock is dem dinner time—table set and dey have a big dinner—
steak or chicken, vegetable. Dey don't eat much starchy food. Di cook finish
dinner and dish it out. My duty was to go round di table wid it in di waiter.
Yuh serve di meat first, den di rice, den di vegetable. Dem only tek out a
small amount each time. Yuh put di rest pon a side table and stand up beside
it. If somebody want anodder piece of someting dem say "Can you bring
whatever-it-is?" and yuh tek it up and yuh serve and yuh go back go stand
up side a di food again. If a next somebody want a piece a meat, dem say
"Can you bring the meat?" And yuh bring it. It go on like dat until everybody's stomach is filled. When yuh see everybody close dem knife and fork
yuh know dem finish eat and yuh can clear di table. If dey want coffee, dey
ask. Den when dey finish and everybody get up from di table yuh go in go
tidy di kitchen.

It end up dat is a whole lot of dishes since everyting dat cook have to go
into a separate dish. All dose dishes have to wash and pack up and all di pots.

Yuh sweep di kitchen. At eight thirty yuh finish work fi di night—dat is if dey don't have visitors. Sometimes dey have visitors dat come before dinner and mek dinner an hour late. So instead dey have dinner at six, it might not be until seven thirty. Den yuh finish work nine or nine thirty. Di pay was twenty five shillings per week. Yuh got one evening off a week and one Sunday a month.

After ah worked deh for a long time, Jill, same country gal like me, came to work next door. Both of us never know anywhere in town, but since me and she get di same evening off we used to go out togedder. Di evening off start twelve o'clock. After yuh finish yuh lickle washing, yuh go Cross Roads to a matinee. Yuh come home by eight because dem don't want people coming in dem yard late.

Me and dem get on all right. Di lickle wife did kind a miserable. She push yuh round and sometimes when she see di tings dem done and notten no deh fi we do, she find work give we. We must come down wipe down di wall or come dust out some ole big cupboard dem have all bout inna di housetop.

To tell di truth di job was very boring, but in dose days we just accept di fact. We, di young people, wasn't so crazy like di young ones now. Everyting was quieter. Yuh stay in dat job for months before yuh find a friend yuh could change thoughts wid. After serving dinner some a di helpers dem in our area don't stop pon premises, dem go home and have their domestic work to do. Dey have to come out by seven di next morning. It change a little now, because during di seventies di government pass di minimum wage law. It say yuh must only do eight hours a day and it fix di wage; but some a dem who stop pon premises still have it hard.

After ah was working deh three years, ah find out seh me pregnant. As ah reach five months pregnant, me lef di work. Dem never even know seh me pregnant. Ah stay in town wid Amy, di helper from next door who never stop pon premises. Di baby faada never di a help me. When me lef di work, me leave deh wid nine pound save out a di twenty-five shilling a week and das what me use and live till me go back a work. Me never tell me faada seh me pregnant for him would a quarrel. And him did quarrel when him hear, after di baby born.

VII

Jamaica in the Age of Neoliberalism

Edward Philip George Seaga became the fifth prime minister of independent Jamaica on 1 November 1980. Seaga led the JLP back into power with the largest electoral sweep in Jamaican history. Jamaicans looked to the new government to craft a way out of the misery, violence, and "tribal" party divisions that had left hundreds dead and the country bitterly divided. Seaga, a decidedly more conservative leader than Michael Manley, took the country far from the democratic socialism of the 1970s. The new prime minister committed his administration to advancing the neoliberal reforms that had started in the last three years of Manley's administration. These reforms led to a contraction of the local economy that most affected farmers, workers, the urban poor, and small-scale businesses.

When Manley returned to power in 1989, alternatives to neoliberalism were fewer than at the start of the decade. The end of the Cold War contributed to the dissolution of what remained of 1970s-era radicalism. Manley's second administration and that of his PNP successors deepened the country's indebtedness to external lending agencies. By the 1990s the country was suffering from economic instability.

The readings in this section illuminate the far-reaching effects of neoliberal policies in Jamaica since the 1980s. The most pronounced consequences have been economic. The high level of debt that accrues from international loans has contributed to low growth rates and high import-dependency. Jamaica has one of the highest debt-to-GDP ratios. To cope with these conditions, a robust informal economy has developed. There has been much creativity in the informal sector, especially among the ICIs (Informal Commercial Importers)—commonly referred to as "higglers"—who have successfully established alternative markets through trade in a range of foreign-made goods. Illegal activities have also become more persistent since the 1980s. Transnational criminal networks including drug trafficking, smuggling, and fraud have increased crime and corruption at all levels of society. The grave social result of this has been steady emigration from the island and alarming homicide rates. While the tourism sector continues to dominate, both legal and illegal informal activities remain significant. In 2001 the informal economy contributed 43 percent of GDP.[1]

The social divide across class and color lines has proved both resilient and flexible. Alternative economic activities since the 1980s have expanded access to wealth for some Jamaicans. This has led to a modest improvement in social relations. Where previously postsecondary education was available almost exclusively to the children of middle-class Jamaicans, a wider cross section of Jamaicans can now attend the island's universities. This has led to an expansion of a well-trained professional class, amplified by the return of skilled Jamaicans after years of living abroad. No longer is the middle class exclusively light skinned, although there remains a strong association between lightness of skin and access to resources. Meanwhile, the expansion of the middle class has also increased the dominance of middle-class codes of behavior in "uptown" culture and everyday life. The privileging of lighter skin, often regarded as the epitome of beauty, has led to an increase in the practice of skin bleaching for aesthetic reasons.

Jamaican culture has, as always, reflected on these changes. Reggae, while still globally significant, is now overshadowed by its variant dancehall, a musical form with an altogether different sound, style, purpose, and expression. The emphasis on material wealth, "slackness" (explicit lyrics describing sexual acts in explicit detail), exaggerated masculinity, and self-aggrandizement of post-1970s Jamaica have become distinctive though not exclusive features of dancehall music. Although harshly criticized by Jamaica's elite, dancehall remains an important vehicle for expressing the views of Jamaica's poor majority.

Dancehall lyrics are generally delivered in Jamaican patwa. The conscious embrace of patwa by popular music performers reflects a wider attitude of contemporary Jamaicans, who after suffering decades of denigration of the language now more confidently claim it as an integral part of their national identity. As some of the readings in this part make clear, Jamaican pride has strengthened in recent years. This is partly a result of the country's remarkable cultural influence beyond the Caribbean. The fascination with Jamaican reggae that began in the 1970s expanded tremendously in the following decades. There have been foreign-born reggae artists who perform in their native languages. Global communities have embraced the music's protest themes of "truth and rights." Reggae was incorporated into the global mainstream, where it now remains, despite evolutions in its performance and style. Annual reggae festivals from California to Cologne, the influence of reggae and dancehall on global youth music—reggaeton, dubstep, and hip-hop, for example—and the astounding successes of a new generation of Jamaican athletes such as Usain Bolt and writers such as Marlon James have inspired renewed international fascination with Jamaica. At the same time, young Jamaicans are more closely tied to foreign culture than their predecessors. The advent of digital media and global social networks facilitated by the internet have had no small effect on the cultural evolution and mores of the island.

Political relations have improved considerably since the 1980s. General elections since then have for the most part taken place without violence. The acceptance of neoliberal economic policies by both parties has further blurred the policy differences between the JLP and the PNP. Political control of the inner-city gangs has also changed. The powerful ghetto "don," a ruthless community chief who administers extrajudicial authority, has superseded the once dominant hold of the politicians over various constituencies. In May 2010, at the request of the state (under the leadership of a JLP prime minister, Bruce Golding), the security forces launched a military incursion in the JLP's West Kingston stronghold of Tivoli Gardens. The incursion aimed to serve a US extradition warrant on reigning don Christopher "Dudus" Coke. The government declared a state of emergency to enable this action, leading to the deaths of dozens of innocent people. For many, the Tivoli massacre demonstrated the Jamaican state's contempt for the poor.

Foreign visitors continue to flock to Jamaica, with limited awareness of the island's troubles. The enormous hotels of the North Coast and the large cruise ships that dock in Ocho Rios and Falmouth have kept tourist numbers high. In 2017 Jamaica surpassed previous records, with over 4 million total arrivals to the island.[2] Many tourists are insulated from the harsh realities of Jamaican life by all-inclusive packages, which perpetuate the skewed appearance of an island paradise. Tourists experience a life unknown to the overwhelming majority of Jamaica's 2.7 million people, of whom at least 8 percent are unemployed and 14.5 percent live below the official poverty line.[3]

Jamaica since 1980 has seen a weakening of some axes of power. The election in 1992 of Percival James (PJ) Patterson symbolized the island's changing racial politics. Patterson, who did not have the same color and class background as Manley and Seaga, became the longest-serving politician in that role, remaining in power until 2006. He was then followed by Portia Simpson Miller, also a black Jamaican, who became the first woman to occupy the prime ministerial role. These political figures symbolize broader changes in Jamaican society. Although class divisions remain sharp, it is no longer the case that white or light skin is a principal requirement for leadership or success. After more than fifty years as an independent nation, Jamaicans in the twenty-first century are divided by many things, but for the most part they share a pride in their nation and its people's achievements.

Notes

1. *The Informal Sector in Jamaica* (Inter-American Development Bank Region 3, Economic and Sector Studies, December 2006), 1.
2. Claudia Gardner, "Record 4.3. Million Tourist Arrivals in 2017," *JIS News*, Jamaica Information Service, https://jis.gov.jm/record-4-3-million-tourist-arrivals-2017/, accessed 10 January 2019.
3. Statistical Institute of Jamaica, http://statinja.gov.jm/, accessed 10 January 2019; Mcpherse Thompson, "UNDP: Poverty in Jamaica at 14.5%," *Jamaica Gleaner*, 21 July 2017, http://jamaica-gleaner.com/article/business/20170721/undp-poverty-jamaica-145.

Nine Months of Turmoil

Barbara Nelson

The violence that colored Jamaica's 1970s climaxed with the bloody general election of 30 October 1980. That year, according to official figures, at least eight hundred Jamaicans were murdered—the real number was likely much higher—in politically motivated violence. It was also one of the longest election campaigns in the country's history. As prime minister, Michael Manley was free to call an election at any point within his five-year term, and beginning in the summer of 1979 rumors circulated that in 1980 Jamaicans would go to the polls, though constitutionally Manley had until 1981 to call a general election. By then party rivalries had become so marked that the wearing of political colors (green for the JLP and orange for the PNP) could be met with harassment from die-hard party supporters. The anticipation of an upcoming election throughout the year encouraged an escalation in violence. Among the most tragic episodes in those months was the 21 May burning down of the Eventide Home, a home for the indigent and aged.

Manley and the PNP appeared confident of reelection in spite of the brutality. With more than a year left in office Manley announced a general election at a mass meeting attended by an estimated 150,000 supporters in Montego Bay. His declaration "150,000 strong can't be wrong" became a bolstering party slogan. Contrary to these hopes, the PNP retained only nine out of sixty seats in Parliament. In this article, which appeared four days before the polls opened, journalist Barbara Nelson describes the events leading up to the election, the efforts to stem the tide of violence, and the scars that the campaign had already inflicted.

On February 3, 1980, Prime Minister Michael Manley announced that we would be holding general elections this year. The country, he said, "needs to settle down" so in order to settle the question of the economic strategy to be pursued in the immediate future, a decision was taken to vote by October.

The nine-month period of gestation has been one of turmoil and escalating violence. The most serious incident to have occurred so far was the assassination of junior Minister and MP Roy McGann and the killing of his bodyguard Acting Corporal Errol White on the morning of Nomination Day, October 14.

The killing unprecedented in the political [history] is another statistic in the growing number of people—men, women, children, babies, 470 in all—who have died since January.

Of the 470 who died violently, 359 have been killed by gunmen. The security forces, on the other hand, have killed 144 suspected of being criminals.

In January the number who died violently was 11; February, 15; March, 7; April, 28; May, 28; June, 60; July, 125; and August, 31. In September 57 people died violently. Those who died included 21 members of the security forces.

The pattern of violence can be related directly to certain measures that have been introduced, by the greater involvement of the Jamaica Council of Churches in the political process and by the reaction of the man in the street to any kind of harassment or violation of human rights by the security forces.

One of the outstanding aspects of the election period has been the use of the media, in particular JBC [Jamaica Broadcasting Corporation] Television, by demonstrators particularly from the lower income groups who spoke of attacks on their communities by terrorists and intimidation by members of the security forces.

After the declaration of elections for 1980, violence started to erupt in one or two places, particularly in the Corporate Area.

On April 29 gunmen clad in military-type uniforms and toting automatic weapons shot dead four young men and wounded several others at a dance at Gold Street. A fifth man died later in hospital. This occurred in Central Kingston on Gold Street.

By the end of April and the beginning of May the violence was stepped up and each of the two political parties claimed victims from the spate of killings. Some people called for Interpol to help in the situation and various organizations expressed concern at the violence.

In May, too, Opposition Leader Edward Seaga wrote to JDF Chief of Staff Brigadier Neish asking if the security forces could contain the terrorism to allow free and fair elections.

Brigadier Neish replied that the Army's presence had significantly reduced violent crime. Mr. Seaga said then that violence was a part of the PNP's plot—a military solution strategy planned in their effort to win the upcoming elections.

Early in the election period the Jamaica Council of Churches issued guidelines on the conduct of candidates who planned to present themselves for selection. That was in May. Later on the JCC established a Monitoring Committee which heard complaints from people about the actions of candidates and their supporters.

Edward Seaga greets supporters on the campaign trail in 1980. Photographer unknown. © The Gleaner Company (Media) Limited.

Crime Stop

In September Operation Crime Stop went into its second phase, offering rewards of $60,000 for the arrest of the 12 most wanted men.

In September, too, Operation Crime Stop paid out the first $5,000 reward to the person who gave information leading to the recovery of an MI enforcer sub–machine gun loaded with 26 rounds of ammunition.

The island is now experiencing repeated eruptions of violence, not only in the Corporate Area but also in the rural areas. Political meetings have been stopped, students, children and older people have been injured as a result of repeated clashes between political supporters.

Do the security forces feel equipped to deal with the obvious escalation in violence now that the elections are just days away? We can only hope that this is so.

Seaga v. Manley

Carl Stone

Political scientist Carl Stone was Jamaica's most respected pollster. Here Stone compares the governing practices of the PNP and the JLP, and more specifically their leaders Michael Manley and Edward Seaga. He concludes that the difference between the two and the respective decades they led the island was marked in leadership style and popular expectations: Seaga was a managerialist and Manley a populist. Stone accurately predicted that the pendulum would swing away from Seaga-style managerialism and that Manley and the PNP would sweep the 1989 general elections.

The relationship between economic progress and how Jamaicans vote has been a puzzle for most of us. I have spent the last almost twenty years studying and researching it and have written many books about it but it continues to be a puzzle.

The puzzle is based on the fact that Jamaican voters often change government or turn against parties in power in periods when substantial economic progress is being achieved.

Tourism today is the highest area of growth in the Jamaican economy. The tourist areas have experienced an explosion of employment, construction, investment expansion, business, income and increased prosperity. Yet the tourist towns voted more for Mr. Manley in 1986 than the rest of the country.

In my January 1988 Stone Poll, 86 percent of the voters interviewed (in an enlarged tourism subsample) admitted that they are experiencing substantial improvements in income and economic opportunities since the tourism boom under Mr. Seaga's government. Yet a majority of them want a change and wish to vote for Mr. Manley.

There are usually concrete issues which motivates many voters to get rid of governing parties notwithstanding positive gains that are associated with their policies.

In 1972, social issues (not economic issues) swept the J.L.P. out of power. The people saw the growth and the prosperity and the material progress but felt that the economic cake was not being fairly distributed. The appeal of a Michael Manley promoting social justice and a fairer sharing up of the economic cake was decisive in inducing the swing voters to get rid of the J.L.P.

In 1976, these P.N.P. policies designed to try and share up the cake better caught the imagination of the youth and the poor classes and won Michael a landslide victory although the economy had begun to slide backwards. By 1980, the long and fast skid backwards economically had wiped out all the gains from the P.N.P.'s distributive policies, and poor management of the economy lost Manley the 1980 election.

Anticommunism simply helped to increase the P.N.P. vote deficit, but the real dominant issue influencing the swing voters islandwide against the P.N.P. was economics.

Today, the puzzle of the complex relationship between voting choice and economic trends has returned.

As I have stated time and again in this column, if you look at trends in production, savings and investment, employment, growth, export and import growth, financial management, and changes in real income, there is absolutely no doubt that since 1980 Mr. Seaga has managed the Jamaican economy better than Mr. Manley did in the 1970s. Michael is an outstanding leader but facts are facts.

Outside Help

To be sure, Eddie [Seaga] has had more outside help than Michael had, and the private sector has been more part of the solution than part of the problem in the 1980s compared to the 1970s. But let's not forget that bauxite was booming in the 1970s and it collapsed in the 1980s. But in the arena of results Eddie's economic management has been superior to Michael's.

Yet the polls show that people want Michael to return to power. The J.L.P. is not likely to win more than fifteen or sixteen seats in Parliament when the votes are counted, although the country is experiencing for the first time since the 1960s a trend towards economic buoyancy, recovery and upturn led by tourism, export manufacturing and construction.

The J.L.P. can only change its almost inevitable political fate if it can convince most of the swing voters between now and election day that they are likely to be worse off under Manley than under Seaga. That's easier said than done.

Politics and political choices turn as much on perceptions as they do on reality.

In the realm of perceptions, Manley's political assets are overwhelmingly powerful and Seaga's assets deficient. In the realm of the reality of policy results and more effective public management, Seaga's assets are much stronger than Manley's.

Fundamentally, the voters see the choice as a choice between a good manager (Seaga) and a good trade unionist (Manley). The good manager generates benefits by increasing production, income and cash flow. Some voters prefer to have a good manager running the system. The good trade unionist deals with social justice, fairness, equity and justice of the poor and downtrodden.

The majority of voters today feel that the good manager (Seaga) is failing to share up the cake equitably and insist that the country needs the dispensation of a good trade unionist (Manley) to ensure more equity. That perception explains why [in] the booming tourist towns where progress under Seaga is acknowledged, the majority of voters want a change. That perception is going to be the basis of Mr. Manley's election victory in 1988.

Manley's political image is that of the man in today's Jamaica most committed to sharing up the cake equitably and taking care of the needs of the poor. Some swing voters feel that the good manager (Seaga) is partial to the rich and the powerful and that a political change is necessary to adjust the balance of class power in the country.

The electoral choice between Seaga and Manley is a choice between managerialism and populism. Populism clearly has the majority support right now. But far more is at stake here in the choices we will be making than whether the P.N.P. or the J.L.P. rules.

Jamaica is now at a very important political crossroads.

Born Fi' Dead

Laurie Gunst

The American writer and historian Laurie Gunst lived in East Kingston during the 1980s. Her partly autobiographical account exposed the intimate relationship between Jamaican politicians and the gun culture of downtown Kingston. It also charted the transformation of island-based political gangs into transnational drug businesses, who drew profits from the transshipment of cocaine from South America to the United States. As she explains here, through a narrative about her personal experience with gang members "Brambles" and "Kenty" and their friend "Lyrics," the rise of the cocaine business had the serious side effect of promoting the use of the drug among Jamaicans.

"If you interested in this cocaine bizness," Brambles said, "the way it ties in to politics an' ting, you could do a lickle research in Negril. I 'ave a friend there who juggles coke, an' he could tell you some stories about the white wife."

That was the phrase of the moment, a perfect description of the drug's foreign origins and its power to lay waste. Cocaine was a novelty, a fairly recent addition to the island's pharmacopoeia, but it was quickly becoming the next bad dream, as it always does. Tourists had brought it to Negril in the late 1970s, where it was soon de rigueur for whites and their rent-a-dread consorts. But across the island in Kingston, cocaine made a different kind of entrance.

The drug started showing up in the pockets and noses of JLP gunmen just before the 1980 election. That was a coincidence no one cared to probe. But it was said by Carl Stone, the UWI professor and political scientist, that the drug was partly responsible for the sickening nature of the violence during that time—atrocities such as the killing of children and the mutilation of pregnant women. Stone called 1980 "the reign of the wall-eyed gunmen."

Whether or not Seaga was feeding cocaine to his paladins, the JLP definitely controlled the trade. Jamaica became a major Caribbean transshipment point for the drug when Seaga came to power, and several of his government ministers were said to be involved in protecting its movement into and out of Jamaica. The police—most of them badly paid and poorly trained country boys who were easily corrupted—were cut in on the trade. By the time I moved to Kingston in 1984, cocaine was everywhere. The Chinese controlled the uptown market and the JLP had it to themselves in the ghettoes, which was why it was easy to come by in Labourite enclaves like Southside. By 1984 crack was already replacing powder cocaine in the ghettos; since Jamaicans were given to smoking ganja, it was natural for them to take to the smokable (and cheaper) form of cocaine.

But islanders were slow to awaken to the drug's menace. Foreign political consultants and aid agencies had crammed it down their throats that ganja was their country's major peril, and the Americans didn't seem too worried about Jamaica's cocaine problem—it was ganja they were forever spraying with lethal herbicides and burning with flamethrowers. But the Americans would soon have reason to worry about Jamaica and cocaine. In 1984 the Drug Enforcement Administration sounded a quiet warning in its annual intelligence report: "Increasing evidence of cocaine traffic in Jamaica is of concern both because of the threat to the local population and because it involves foreign criminal elements. Some Jamaican traffickers are believed to have switched to cocaine because of the relative ease with which it can be shipped, in comparison to marijuana, and because of the large profits to be made."

What the report neglected to say was that Jamaica's entry into the Caribbean transshipment trade dovetailed neatly and brutally with the island's American-funded ganja-eradication program. As the ganja barons found it harder to get their product off the island, they began to piggyback their shipments on the cocaine trade. And it wasn't long before the local market became a lucrative sideline; the friend Brambles wanted me to meet in Negril was one of the local ganja dealers who had made the shift from the "Weed of Wisdom" to the "White Wife."

Cocaine hit the local population with a force that was not unlike the way alcohol devastated Native Americans in the nineteenth century. As one of Brambles's Foster Lane friends said, "The first time I tek it, it mek I feel dazzled-like." Soon he was hooked on the dazzle, selling every stick of the furniture his mother had left him and pimping his baby-mother for his high.

We left for Negril, with Kenty riding shotgun, on a cool early morning and took the Junction road, the steepest and most beautiful route over the Blue Mountains. The road was no wider than a cart track in many places, empty as a bush path except for country people on foot or riding donkeys.

Soothed by the bucolic loveliness of the landscape, Brambles lost his usual edginess and became serene. We stopped so many times along the way, buying roasted corn and paper cups of scalding soup straight from vendors' kettles, that it took us the better part of the day to reach Negril. Kenty wanted to check his grower in the outskirts of town, so we dropped him off at a red-dirt footpath into the hills and then went to find Brambles's friend.

His name was Lyrics; in patois, someone who "flies lyrics" is a genial con artist of the first rank. "I don't know how we goin' to find him," Brambles said. "I mean, what kind of mood he's goin' to be in. Sometimes he licks the pipe for days and days, an' then he's in no shape to reason."

Lyrics's yard was high up in the district called Red Ground, perched on a hilltop with sweeping views of the sea. We parked the car and walked, panting up a steep, rock-strewn path with hummingbirds darting through the bush and goats trailing their ropes as they browsed. Lyrics was sitting in a porch swing that hung from a huge mango tree, drowsing in the shade. He greeted Brambles as if he had known his old friend was coming.

"You gwan' live long!" Lyrics said, the Jamaican way of saying that you'll have good luck for showing up just as someone is thinking about you. Lyrics was smoking herb, and he was in a mellow mood, but as we began talking, he waxed eloquent about his ups and downs with cocaine. He liked talking about the drug, and he had the addict's classic fascination for his substance: dread of its consequences coupled with no will to quit just yet. He was bitter, but he was still in thrall to the White Wife.

Sunsplash 1984

Roger Steffens

The success of reggae on the 1970s world stage contributed to commercialization at home. While Bob Marley remained the unrivaled leader of the genre, he was ably assisted by dozens of other highly successful Jamaican musicians, such as Peter Tosh, Jimmy Cliff, Burning Spear, Black Uhuru, and Third World, who took Jamaica's music to markets far beyond the Caribbean. Then and now, the steady demand for Jamaican musicians to perform to overseas audiences meant fewer opportunities to hear them on home soil. Enterprising Jamaican promoters saw the value in developing a summer reggae music festival on the island. This was not only aimed at Jamaican audiences eager to see their local heroes—now international stars—onstage. It was also marketed to tourist visitors enamored with Jamaica's cultural offerings. Reggae Sunsplash began on 23 June 1978 and would become the biggest annual reggae festival on the island for the next decade, before pulling up its stakes in the 1990s. Most of Jamaica's legendary performers, and several foreign acts, at one time or another faced the famously critical Jamaican audiences on a Sunsplash stage. Sunsplash became a mecca for die-hard reggae fans across the globe who made the pilgrimage every year to the all-night four-day festival. The sight of scores of people sleeping on flattened cardboard boxes dubbed "reggae beds" epitomized Sunsplash fan dedication. The transitions in the island's popular music from "roots" reggae to dancehall in the 1980s would be captured in the evolution of the festival, which saw more and more dancehall performers claiming their own space in the limelight. Some of the inherent strains in this transition are clear in reggae historian Roger Steffens's colorful report of the first two nights of Reggae Sunsplash 1984.

Night 1

Sunsplash 7 returned home this year to Jarrett Park in Montego Bay. Tommy Cowan began the show about 9 o'clock with a tribute to His Majesty, Haile Selassie I, then introduced Ras Michael and the Sons of Negus. Michael was garbed in clerical minirobes and Billy Jack black hat, making him look like a Tibetan from the Andes. His large group chanted a dozen shots with "Stop,

Look and Listen" and "Drum Song" being particular standouts. Marley's "Redemption Song" received a Frank Sinatra twist, white phosphorous bursting skyward during the words "through the power of the Almighty." A powerfully authentic opening.

The Rasta theme continued with the all-female African Woman group, whose five fine songs recalled the I Threes at their best. After a short break, Lloyd Parks and his We the People Band took the stage, backing the next four acts. Wearing a three-piece burgundy suit and bow tie, and sporting thick glasses ("I can't see too good"), Derrick Morgan did an exciting eight-song ska set. "Rudy's in Court," "Hey You Fatman" and "Blackhead China-man" were highlighted by his trapezoidal ska dancing, but he proved to be up to the minute "with my latest, 'Independence Time,'" singing about the "butterfly, hula hoop, the cool and deadly." One of this year's genuine discoveries from the past. A big cheer greeted the Mighty Diamonds, and although their set was abbreviated, they seem to have been many people's favorite act this evening. Beginning with new material like "Heads of Government" and "Wise Son," they recalled classics from the *Right Time* LP, and the soulful "There's No Me without You," during which Bunny did a great Satchmo imitation.

Next was the man who stole opening night in '83, Delroy Wilson, back to try it again. He was less successful this year. His four songs included a medley, and during a blazing Dean Fraser sax solo he danced a '40s hipster shuffle that led into some James Brown flourishes. But somehow contact was not made, and the audience stared stoically, proving once again that at Sunsplash there are never *any* certainties.

Conservatively attired in a grey sharkskin suit and white felt hat, the master toaster U Roy tapped through a tight six-tune set, including "Soul Rebel," "Kung Fu Fighting," and "Wear You to the Ball." His encore was "Chalice in the Palace," and the crowd dug it all.

The evening's second break allowed what Cowan called "the largest opening night audience in Sunsplash history" the time to browse through more than one hundred stalls lining the back half of the stadium. There seemed a disproportionate number of food booths, and hardly anyone selling records. Still I turned up a copy of Bunny Wailer's first Solomonic single, "Searching for Love," for a dollar at the Abyssinians' stall, and was amused to see the *Reggae and African Beat* for sale off the back of some dread's motorcycle in the middle of the field. Access to the shops was fairly simple, a matter of climbing over prone bodies loosely gathered on the grass. No seats, and no reserved section, created the most democratic and hearty vibes I've yet felt at a Sunsplash.

Freddie McGregor got the twelve-song set he should have had last year, and made the most of it. He did a funny imitation of Dennis Brown singing "Have You Ever," and on "Africa Here I Come" he added a natty dancer who lurched onstage doing a belly wind. "Bandulu" concluded with a capaella quintet outro, and earned a pair of encore tunes.

Another brief break, and then the final act: Burning Spear and his Burning Band. Spear walked out, uncharacteristically, with a lady on his arm, who came center stage with him, then walked off the other side. Spear had a blue English shop clerk's coat and a floppy Seven Dwarves roots cap. A dozen of his best-known chants were delivered skillfully, though sometimes too quickly. On "Foggy Road" Herman Marquis blew haunting harbor-horn sax, and on the standout "Slavery Days" the four-strong brass section sounded almost like speech when they blared the accusation "Do you remember the days of slavery?" Spear drew on a growing repertoire of movements: bird-flap jumping jacks, moshing-in-place crucifixions, and pitter-patter slow crawls. All in all a terrifically satisfying opening night, with a broad range of good performances.

Night 2

"We live next door, Jamaica, you can't make a move that we don't know!" announced the leader of the Cayman Islands' group Memory of Justice. A good hard-driving reggae band, featuring a keyboardist in a British judge's wig, M.O.J. lifted the crowd with the big hit "Me and My Crew."

Barry G emceed the second night, before an enormous backdrop of a sound system dance. He first brought out some dancers; then an inappropriate Yank-turned-Israeli who sang solo acoustic numbers in a Tim Buckley style to a befuddled crowd; and, after what seemed hours, the Sagittarius Band.

Sagittarius backed the next five acts, powerfully and effectively. Michael Palmer was first to join them, performing a pleasant half dozen songs, with "Gunshot" and his current scorcher, "Lick Shot," garnering nice audience reactions.

Young Edi Fitzroy sang conscious music like "General Penitentiary" and "First Class Citizen," the latter being one of the most stunning moments of the festival for me, if not for the mass of the somnolent audience.

It took the unannounced appearance of Brigadier Jerry to touch off the first true excitement of the Splash, well into Friday morning. From the first notes of the "Fame" spinoff called "Pain," the crowd shot to its feet and surged toward the stage. "Ganja Pipe a Burn" and "Hold Them Briggy" brought a well-deserved encore mixture of "The Boom" and some c&w [country and western] standards.

Toaster Charlie Chaplin followed immediately and, as with the majority of performers this year, was dressed in all black. Accompanied by three male dancers in camouflage fatigues, Chaplin speed-rapped through an antifreebase song, then seg'd into "You're Too Fat/Fire Down Below," while the three did Jane Fonda windmills behind his song. During a long dub jam, the four men changed into new costumes, and Mr. C. announced, "I can do anything Michael Jackson can do" and proceeded to spring into some of the "Thriller" dance steps, driving the Jamaicans to irie ites of frenzy. His fifth and final song, "Jamaican Girl," ended with the dancers swimming off stage on their bellies.

Josie Wales kept the vibe growing, prancing onstage in blue Chinese PJs and a conical straw hat. He had two backup dancers, and they did little routines while he paced the stage, furiously, back and forth for six songs. On the seventh, he was suddenly joined by Charlie and Briggy for a super trio jam that lasted nearly a half-hour. "Wha' dem a go do if Josie shut his mouth?" featured the Brigadier's limp-wristed imitation of Michael Jackson, target of much scorn throughout the fest, applying makeup and lipstick to his medically perfected countenance. Through it, all laughter and motion, was Charlie Chaplin pirouetting and splitting like a prissy ballerina, his Chinese clothing identical to Josie's.

Another brief break for a band change, and one of the most eagerly awaited of this year's crop of discoveries, Ini Kamoze, came on with Aswad's rhythm section. A new song, "Live Ista Live," was marred by an unsuccessful singalong, but "World a Music" ended his four-song set brilliantly, and left the crowd wanting more, but not knowing how to get it from Barry G. In a festival where soft bands were routinely granted ten songs, why should genuine standouts like Kamoze be hindered with four?

We left as Yellowman's slackness began to whip the crowd into a fulsome froth.

Walking Jewellery Store

Yellowman

Jamaica's changes in the 1980s were indicated in the dramatic transformation in its popular music. The "roots and culture" of the previous decade receded and was eclipsed by an innovative new variant of reggae: dancehall. The emphasis was still on the rhythm, but the advent of digital technology produced new synthesized sounds that won wide appeal among a younger generation. Dancehall artists—termed "toasters" or "DJs"—deliver lyrical rhymes over these beats with numerous artists laying lyrics over the same rhythm track. The sonic contrast in the music was but one distinction between dancehall and reggae. Equally noticeable was the language and content of the lyrics. Whereas reggae stars like Bob Marley sang in a Jamaican-inflected English readily accessible to an international audience, dancehall lyrics fully embraced Jamaican patwa, aiming more squarely at Jamaican and Jamaican diaspora listeners who understood the words and the references. Non-Jamaicans largely had to settle for appreciating the music's rhythm, culture, and style, while understanding relatively few of the words.

The personas of dancehall DJs are certainly striking. They typically exude toughness, emphasize sexual braggadocio, and celebrate the materialism that their predecessors of the 1970s eschewed. A focus on visible wealth and success has become a hallmark of the genre, similarly to US hip-hop, which drew strong influences from Jamaica. Dancehall culture of the 1980s reflected its materialism in dress, fashion, and music. Conspicuous displays of wealth included cars, clothes, homes, and, most importantly, jewelry. Dancehall's first international success was King Yellowman (Winston Foster). In "Walking Jewellery Store" from 1985, Yellowman praises his affinity for gold chains and expensive jewelry. As he states without a hint of modesty,

Nuh tell me bout nuh brass or nuh silver
Nuh tell me bout nuh lead neither copper
A strictly gold chain a weh mi prefer
Yuh know Yellowman yuh gold entertainer:
"Strictly gold mi wear a dat mi sure
Nuh tell mi seh mi rich nuh tell mi seh mi poor"

While some critics saw the DJs' adoption of the ethic of conspicuous consumption as a backward move away from "conscious" lyrics that explicitly advocated for social justice, many fans took vicarious pleasure in the brash display of wealth by black men from "ghetto" backgrounds, who made few if any concessions to middle-class behavioral norms.

> Well dedicate this one to all who own a Jewellery store
> Like the man called Mr. Tewani and Mistress Tewani

Yellowman dedicates the song to Gordon and Diana Tewani, owners of Mall and Tropical Jewellers, well-known Kingston jewelry stores:

> Yellowman a walking Jewel Store
> Yellowman a walking Jewel Store
> You know why?
> Because mi tell you once and mi tell you before
> Mi will walk from Kingston go ova Portmore
> And fly from Jamaica go ova Singapore
> Caw anywhere di gold deh mi haffi get more
> Mi a walking Jewel Store

The song is a boast of the importance of gold to his persona and as an unmissable sign of his success. Yellowman shows his commitment to sourcing gold in Jamaica and overseas.

> Yellowman a walking Jewel Store
> You know why?
> You look inna mi ears mi have a ears ring
> If you look pon mi finga twenty gold ring
> If a girl waan one dem betta kiss mi pon mi chin
> You know dem crown mi as di DJ King
> Mi a walking Jewel Store
> Yellowman a walking Jewel Store
> Nuh tell mi seh mi rich, nuh tell mi seh mi poor
> Mi wear twenty chain mi don't wear four
> Caw anywhere di jewel deh mi haffi get more
> Walking Jewel Store
> Yellowman a walking Jewel Store
> Nuh tell mi seh mi rich, nuh tell mi seh mi poor

But it is also a reflection of the material aspirations of Jamaican entertainers, the vast majority of whom emerged from consuming poverty. Conspicuous wealth, as Yellowman makes clear, is an expectation of their fame.

Mi wear twenty chain I don't wear four
Caw anywhere di jewel deh mi haffi get more
Mi a walking Jewel Store
Yellowman a walking Jewel Store
Yellowman a walking Jewel Store
You know why?
Mi have a likkle wife and she name Rosie
She a di Queen, Yellowman a di King
And dat's why mi buy har wedding ring
Tell you Yellowman a de DJ King
Everywhere mi see her inna it me haffi sing
"She wears my ring"

Yellowman continues a narrative familiar to fans and introduced in his 1982 song "Getting Married." Although frequently associated with slackness, Yellowman often celebrated his marriage to his wife Rosie in his songs. In this lyric he identifies Rosie's gold wedding band as a source of pride for him. Later songs, such as "Letter to Rosie," continued this narrative.

Lawd
Yellowman a walking Jewel Store
Yellowman a walking Jewel Store
Guess wha?
Nuh tell me bout nuh brass or nuh silver
Nuh tell me bout nuh lead neither copper
A strictly gold chain a weh mi prefer
Yuh know Yellowman yuh gold entertainer
Mi a walking Jewel Store
Yellowman a walking Jewel Store
Because
Tell you once and mi tell you before
Mi will walk from Kingston go ova Portmore
And fly from Jamaica go ova Singapore
Caw anywhere di jewel deh mi haffi get more
Strictly gold mi wear a dat mi sure
Nuh tell mi seh mi rich nuh tell mi seh mi poor
Mi a walking Jewel Store
Caw mi lef Kingston go down di country
No one nah wear jewel like me
Caw mi lef Boston to New York City
Lef New York City go dung a Miami

Di ongle one mi see inna jewel like me
Di ongle one mi see inna jewel like me
A di one weh dem call Mr T
A di one weh dem call Mr T
But wha
Mi a walking Jewel Store
Yellowman a walking Jewel Store
Mi walk from Kingston go ova Portmore
Nuh tell mi seh mi rich, nuh tell mi seh mi poor
Mi where strictly gold and a dat mi sure
Tell you mi a walking Jewel Store
You tink a lie?
You look inna mi ears mi wear earsring
Pon mi finger twenty-five gold ring
You know Yellowman a him a carry di swing
If you nah wear gold yuh nah say nutten
You know Yellowman jus' a ride di riddim
You know Yellowman im a King inna di ring
Mi a walking Jewel Store
Yellowman a walking Jewel Store
Yellowman a walking Jewel Store
You waan more?

Hurricane Story, 1988

Olive Senior

*Hurricane Gilbert struck Jamaica on 12 September 1988, killing forty-nine people
and causing intense destruction across the island. Olive Senior's poem here, from
her collection* Gardening in the Tropics *(1995), is one of a series that memorializes
this as well as earlier hurricanes that hit Jamaica in 1903, 1944, and 1951. The poem
draws attention to the economic effects of the hurricane in disrupting the small-scale
but essential international trade of women who "banked between [their] breasts."
It includes references to current and recent events: the name Imelda refers to Imelda
Marcos, wife of the Filipino dictator Ferdinand Marcos, who became famous for her
enormous collection of shoes, while "five flights a day to Miami / grounded" alludes
to Prime Minister Michael Manley's 1975 taunt to his opponents: "Jamaica has no
room for millionaires. For anyone who wants to become a millionaire, we have five
flights a day to Miami."*

My mother wasn't christened
Imelda but she stashed a cache
of shoes beneath the bed.

She used to travel to Haiti,
Panama, Curaçao, Miami,
wherever there was bargain

to catch—even shoes that
didn't have match. Back home
she could always find customer

come bend-down to look and talk
where she plant herself on
sidewalk. When the hurricane

hit, she ban her belly and bawl,
for five flights a day to Miami
grounded. No sale and her shoes

getting junjo from the damp (since
the roof decamp) and the rest
sitting in Customs, impounded.

My mother banked between her
breasts, lived out her dreams
in a spliff or two each night.

Since the storm, things so tight
her breasts shrivel, the notes
shrinking. Every night she there

thinking. Every morning she get up
and she wail: Lawd! Life so soak-up
and no bail out. To raatid!

Wild Gilbert

Lloyd Lovindeer

The dancehall song "Wild Gilbert" was a runaway success after the 1988 hurricane. Its clever lyrics appealed to the whole Jamaican population, at once evoking post-storm hardship and satirizing posthurricane profiteering and looting. Lines like "mi roof migrate without a visa" spoke to a broader context of Jamaicans' relationships to the wealthy world so close to the island. The song was played everywhere for months and remains popular.

Wa wa wild Gilbert! well Gilbert yuh gone ha ha
Now wi can chat behind yuh back
Wa wa wild Gilbert

[Chorus:]
Water come inna mi room
Huh huh
Mi sweep out some with mi broom
Di likkle dog laugh to see such fun
And di dish run away with the spoon
Come now come now come now

Unno si mi dish unno si mi dish,
Anybody unno si mi satellite d-dish
Unno si mi dish unno si mi . . .
Fire!
Rough!
We would like to express our sympathies
To those affected by Gilbert
Wa wa wild Gilbert

[Chorus]

Unnu si mi dish, unnu si mi dish
Anybody unnu si mi satellite d-dish

Unnu si mi dish, unnu si mi dish
Anybody unnu si mi satellite dish
Come!
Dish tek off like flying saucer
Mi roof migrate without a visa
Bedroom full up a water
Mi in a di dark nuh light nuh [water]
And true mi nuh have no generator
Mi seh
One cold beer cost ten dollar
Mi fish and mi meat spoil in di freezer
A pure bully beef full up mi structure
Come!
Full a bully beef, full a bully beef,
Mi caan get fi cook so mi full a bully b-beef
Full a bully beef, full a bully beef
Mi caan get fi cook so mi full a bully beef
Come!

[Chorus]

Water wet up mi shoes and ah wet up mi hat
Wet up mi daag and wet up mi cat
Wet up di bed wet up mi parrot
Water wet up mi what's it not
[Yuh mean yuh what not?]
No mi what's it not
Water wet up mi what's it not
Mi a look somewhere safe dry and warm
Di youth dem a loot in the raging storm
We tank di lord we never get hurt
Dem seh tank yuh lord for Mr Gilbert
Cause! Yuh si mi fridge! Gilbert gimme
Yuh si mi colour TV! A Gilbert gimme
Yuh si mi new stereo! A Gilbert gimme
Yuh si mi new video! A Gilbert gimme
Come now!

[Chorus]

Natty dreadlocks sidung inside
A look how Gilbert a gwaan outside

When breeze lick dong Mr Chin restaurant
Natty dread jump up and chant:
Lick dem jah! Gwaan go [dweet]!
A dem did gi di dread pork fi eat
Jook dem jah with storm and thunder!
Tear off dem roof and bruk dem windah!
Two sheet a zinc blow off a Joe house
Dread flash him locks and start to shout:
Selassie jah! King of Kings!
Show dem seh a we run tings
Blow weh dem house but mek dem survive
So when dem si I dem will realize
Is through I merciful why dem alive
Likkle after that Gilbert turn back
Lift off di roof off a natty dread shack
Him seh blouse and skirt Jah must a never know
Seh I an' I live right yah so!

[Chorus]

Showing Skin Teeth

A. Lynn Bolles

Since the mid-twentieth century, tourism has been Jamaica's single largest industry. Most of the jobs available in the tourist sector offer relatively low wages and depend on the worker's performance of friendly deference. Much debate takes place among tourists and middle-class Jamaicans alike about Jamaicans' alleged poor service ethic; governments of both parties have run campaigns aimed at getting Jamaicans employed in tourism or selling to tourists to be less "aggressive" or "harassing"; such campaigns have sometimes included intensive policing of tourist zones. Much less attention is usually given to the perceptions of those who, as workers in the tourist industry, are the targets of such campaigns. Anthropologist A. Lynn Bolles's work is an exception; here she presents extracts from interviews with three women who work in the resort town of Negril, in far western Jamaica. The interviewees share the experience of rudeness from tourists which must be confronted by "showing skin teeth," a patwa phrase that implies a false smile that hides frustration, hostility, or anger.

The Front Desk

"Margaret Bristol" has just come on duty as the clerk at the front desk of "Big Pink," a large family-oriented hotel. Margaret is working nights because she went out of rotation with the other clerks when she went on maternity leave. Actually, Margaret notes that she likes night duty because it's very quiet, and luckily nothing catastrophic has happened on her watch. As her day begins at nine o'clock in the evening, Margaret joins other workers whose hours on the job reverse night into day—the night shift. No matter the hour, the clerk at the front desk is critical to a well-run tourist establishment.

Being on the front desk is a low middle-management job. Margaret Bristol is well prepared for almost anything to happen. She left high school with good grades and high scores on the Cambridge Exams, but not enough for entry into the university. Margaret did not take commercial courses, but was able to easily pick up the routine of posting entries in lodge books, and being an overall "gopher" in the accounts office at Big Pink. What she enjoys about working in a resort is meeting and having conversations with guests. As she proved her merit in the hotel business, Margaret was given more responsibilities, changes in job status and increases in wages. It took four years before Margaret became the night clerk. In that job, she posts late entries, usually from bar tabs or late dinners on guests' bills, answers questions, and checks in late arrivals.

At about midnight one uneventful evening, Margaret became comfortable enough to talk about the pluses and minuses of her job. On the positive side, Margaret was pleased with her job situation, and saw a bright future for herself and Big Pink in Negril's tourist industry. Big Pink had a great reputation with many repeat visitors. During the height of the tourist season, January through March, things get really hectic because there are "so many guests on property," she says.

"The sheer numbers of people sometimes wears a person down when you are trying to help one person, one couple or one family at a time, and everybody is demanding something from you at the same time," Margaret states.

How do you handle the pressure? Tell me about handling people.

"Well," she said, "I hate late arrivals, especially large groups, lateness which usually has nothing to do with Jamaica. But something already set off the group, like a delayed takeoff because of weather, or worse, something wrong with the plane. So, by the time they arrive in Montego Bay, everyone is annoyed. People working ground crew is fit to be tied. They have to wait until the last plane come in. The time they (group of travellers) reach here, some have calmed down, at least they arrive safe and are on holiday. Others are just waiting for something else to go wrong. You know what I mean? They arguing with their husband or wife, or friend, everyone around them. It's usually a man, makes himself like a spokesperson for the group and starts with the demands, even when everything is in order. One time, one guy was sheer rudeness, calling bad words, carrying on and cursing. There was just one bellman, and even though I asked a security guard to help handle the baggage, nothing was to please this man. He pushed in front of the line and demanded to see the manager 'cause of 'inefficient staff' and 'don't you people move under a crisis?' I told him that I was the night clerk and that he had to calm himself, and just relax he would spoil his vacation. Real nice like. Well, that started off a whole heap of bad words and carrying on. I just kept on, took deep breaths, put on my best smile and got everyone registered and assigned keys."

What kind of smile?

"You know, show skin teeth and kept doing my work cause the man started to really annoy me to no end. You can't let these people trouble you."

The Tour Desk

Diana Smythe Jones is in charge of the tour desk in one of Negril's couples-only all-inclusives. Her job includes promoting trips for guests to visit sites off the property, linking up with excursion operations, making guests understand the cost and benefits of the trip (not included in the all-inclusive arrangement), and making sure guests are prepared for the trip, including reminding them to wear appropriate clothing, shoes, and other necessary equipment. Posted around Diana's desk are posters announcing the off-property trips, times, and costs just to make things clear.

Diana was just getting off the phone with the excursion agent for Wet 'n' Wild cruise party. She had another set of guests in front of her who wanted a less wild event for their day trip. Diana got out the brochure for these two couples to consider. They huddled and agreed for Diana to arrange a lunch-time party cruise to Booby Cay (a small island off the coast of Negril), that was good for a short trip, and great snorkeling. Diana carefully explained when the couples need to be at the resort's dock to be picked up by the cruise boat, what to wear, and when they would return—back at the resort's dock. The couples went off on their way for the business at hand—fun in the sun and sand.

Two hours later, one woman from the group came up to Diana at her desk and asked for an itinerary again. Diana smiled, went over the agenda once more. Just as Diana was preparing to leave for the day, the same woman came up to her and asked the same set of questions. Diana thought perhaps there was something medically wrong with the guest. Everything she had now said twice was in the brochure, except for the times. Maybe that was the problem.

The next morning, Diana told me, the same woman asked exactly where they were to be picked up for the cruise, "like I did not remember her and her pesky questions."

"I just show skin teeth, 'cause now this woman is annoying me. I remind her once again. Do you know that same woman never said thank you all those times she bothered me, and then the last time she had nerve to be rude! Like I should collect from their room and escort them down to the dock because that is what I am being paid to do. Can you imagine? The rudeness of some people," an exacerbated Diana recounted.

The Hotel Room

Miss Ida works in one of the older hotels in Negril. As times change, the clientele of this once in-high-demand hotel has shifted accordingly. Now, Miss Ida reports, "respectable guests from Canada, Germany and even the nice Americans" go elsewhere. "Now," she says "we get people from Italy who don't know how to behave."

"The Italy people who mostly young men come to Negril 'cause they hear about the nice beach, how things comfortable and so forth, and so on. Italy people dem also hear about ganja, drugs, and rum. That's why they here. Let me tell you something. One day, I go to make up a room. You know we make up the bed, change the linen, clean the bathroom tidy up. I knock, even though the Do Not Disturb is not on the door. No answer, so I let myself in. Well, there on the floor is this white Italy man, all dark and hairy and naked as the day he born. Empty rum bottles all over the place. (Later on I learn that on the table were leftovers of cocaine, but Miss Ida did not know what it was.) The room is a wreck and it smells bad, bad. There's holes in the walls. The bathroom is filthy with vomit. My dear I tell you. I turn on my heel to right out for the room to go tell the head of housekeeping the situation there. The man sits up, starts swearing in his language. He is showing himself to me and tells me that I better clean up this 'shit' (now he is talking in English). Now, I don't have to take that out-of-order business from anyone. You understand? I look at the man, give him skin teeth and leave the room. Can you stand it? A drunk white man demanding of me? Massa, dem days is done, you hear?"

Slackness

Lady Saw

Jamaican popular music includes a strong tradition of "slackness"—lyrics that describe sexual acts in explicit detail—that goes back to the early days of mento in the 1950s. Since then the state has frequently banned certain songs from airplay for their lewd lyrical content. Male dancehall artists' "slack" lyrics have often been criticized for presenting women as objects of rather than participants in sexual encounters, and Jamaican music generally has been heavily male-dominated. In the early 1990s this male domination was challenged by the lyrically talented and hugely popular live performer Lady Saw (born Marion Hall in 1969), who in songs such as "Stab up de Meat" and "Welding Torch" presented explicit lyrics that described heterosexual sex from the woman's point of view. In 2015 Hall went through a Christian conversion and became a gospel singer, performing as Minister Marion Hall.

In the heyday of her Lady Saw persona in the 1990s, Hall's music was condemned by many who disliked dancehall tout court for its slackness. She received far more negative attention than many male artists who sang slack lyrics. Members of the St. James Parish Council even tried to ban her from performing in the parish, which includes Montego Bay, Jamaica's second city and host to many important reggae events. Lady Saw and her supporters condemned these moves as representing a double standard, and she responded to her critics with a song that begins with the pointed question "Want to know what slackness is?" The song also emphasizes the gender bias in favor of male DJs, who were not subject to the same social attacks that Lady Saw had to endure: "It's a double standard ting / Slackness mek nuff man gone a farin International / a green dollars dem a bring."

"Slackness" was celebrated as a smart riposte to her critics and sparked discussion on the treatment of female performers in Jamaican culture.

Want to know what slackness is?
I'll be the witness to dat.
Unu come off a mi back.
A whole heap a tings out there waan deal with
An unu naa see dat.

Watch yah nah,
Mi seh:

Society a blame Lady Saw
fi di system dem create
When culture did a clap
Dem never let mi through the gate, now
As me say "sex" dem waan fi jump pon mi case
But take the beam outa yu eye
Before yu chat inna mi face

Slackness is
When the road waan fi fix
Slackness when government break dem promise
Slackness when politician issue out guns
So the two party a shot dem one anedda down

Charging her critics with hypocrisy ("society a blame Lady Saw fi de system dem create"), the song pointed to poverty ("Government say education it is always the key / But tell me now how de hell could it be / When the poorer class of people can't find de school fee"), political corruption ("slackness when government break dem promise"), and gun violence ("slackness when politician issue out guns"), rather than sexually explicit music, as the real problems in Jamaican society.

A syndicate of man waan fi flop me career
Saying, Lady Saw a lead the people dem astray
What happen to the nude beach dem have inna Mo Bay
And we own Sunday show dat is promoting gay?

The song also protests the class-bound double standards that meant that nude beaches aimed at tourists did not receive the same critique as dancehall music, and critiqued Royal Palm Estate, a popular Jamaican-produced soap opera that briefly featured a middle-class gay character ("we own Sunday show dat is promoting gay"). Lady Saw's lyric draws attention to and participates in a Jamaican religious conservatism that views homosexuality as immoral. Royal Palm Estate, the longest-running program of its kind on Jamaican television, frequently challenged conventions in its representation of sexuality. Whereas heterosexual relationships routinely featured on television, the introduction of a gay character produced public outrage so strong that the character had to be written out of the script. Lady Saw reveals her own position in this public debate by condemning the producers of the program for corrupting Jamaican morals. In doing so she aligns herself with popular homophobia to position the sexuality of her performance persona as "normally"

Marion Hall (formerly dancehall artist Lady Saw) delivers a testimony in song about her conversion to Christianity at an event held at the White House on 22 June 2016. Her appearance was part of a conference on the influence of Caribbean Culture and Heritage in the United States. Other artists who performed were Trinidadian Machel Montano and Etienne Charles and Haitian performers Emeline Michel and Dener Ceide. In her testimony Hall recounted the challenges she faced growing up in poverty in Jamaica and her past as a risqué dancehall performer. Since her baptism in 2015, Hall has started her own ministry and released several gospel albums. This image captures Hall at the end of her emotional performance, which featured Montano and Ceide as accompanists on guitars, in front of a crowd of enthralled spectators. L'union Suite, "Marion Hall Formerly Lady Saw Perform at White House Caribbean Heritage Month Celebration," YouTube video, 4:10, 23 June 2016, https://www.youtube.com /watch?v=98DB4BVUWiU.

heterosexual, against what many Jamaicans perceived as the perverse but protected homosexuality of tourism and middle-class Jamaicans.

> Well you say slack
> Don't point yuh finger at me
> Government say education it is always the key
> But tell me now how de hell could it be
> When the poorer class of people can't find de school fee
> Ban people, trust me dem wrong
> De only ban mi cyaan get must be my wedding ban
> Remember dis I'm a born Jamaican
> And no matter how dem try mi nah lef mi island
>
> Dem a blame Lady Saw . . .

Dem say me slack, but it's a double standard ting
Slackness mek nuff man gone a farin International
a green dollars dem a bring
But true mi nah bring enough dem tek set inna mi skin

Dem a blame Lady Saw . . .

Downtown Ladies

Gina A. Ulysse

Market women, known as "higglers," have been a mainstay of the Jamaican econ-
omy since slavery. With cheap air travel higglering became an international busi-
ness. Higglers, now renamed (at least in official parlance) as Informal Commercial
Importers (ICIs), travel regularly elsewhere in the Caribbean and to the United
States, usually Miami, to purchase clothing, shoes, and other goods they bring back
to Jamaica to sell. Gina Ulysse's ethnography of ICIs vividly describes the behind-
the-scenes life of downtown Kingston market arcades, as well as following her sub-
jects to Miami and back. Here she tells the life story of one of the main subjects of
her research, Miss T., and also describes life in the market as Miss T. prepares for a
trip to Miami.

Miss T. is dark skinned and comes from a traditionally lower-class family.
She describes herself as black. Currently in her early sixties, she started
out in the business during the early 1980s. Her foreign higglering activities were preceded by a long history of informal economic activities that
have made her one of the arcade's most experienced and fascinating traders.
She has been almost every kind of vendor existing within the continuum
of the trade. Her knowledge in this area, she quickly admits, she received
from her mother, who was a higgler. At a very young age, like most children of higglers, she accompanied her mother to the market on weekends,
thus learning about the trade. In her midteens, she left her mother's home
for Kingston to pursue her own economic activities. In the last forty-seven
years, she has been a tray girl, a food shop owner, a fish vendor, and finally
an ICI.

She began her career as an Informal Commercial Importer as a result
of the misfortunes of being a street vendor. The van that she used to both
transport and refrigerate her fish was stolen. Like most of the old-timers,
she began by exporting produce to Panama and importing goods in high
demand in Jamaica. On several occasions, she also travelled to Haiti, where
she bought plastic goods. On those trips, she would meet a friend, an inter-

preter, who accompanied her, since she didn't speak Kreyol. He negotiated her purchases. She buys in gross for both wholesale and retail purposes. She is an expert buyer who also purchases for other traders. She buys various goods including cereal, paper products, bric-a-brac, clothes and shoes. The wide variety of goods ensures that there will always be something to trade.

An Anglican since childhood, Miss T. believes that many trials and success are the result of having chosen God. "From the moment you open your business, you have to put God in front. . . . You either open your business with God or the devil." Her continued dedication, after twice losing everything in fires in her arcade stall (occupied since 1985), stems from an unfailing belief that God, who gave her the knowledge to do her work, will always take care of her. As she notes, "God comes first in everything. If not for God, me cannot sell."

Over the years, she has primarily sold shoes and some clothing. I have repeatedly visited her in the arcade during days when she could not sell a single pair of shoes or even a roll of toilet paper as there were no buyers. A person who does not accept defeat, she often reminds me that "in life, like in the business, some days are good and some days are bad. But with God all things are possible." She used to attend the Wednesday Falmouth market until it closed in 1997. The Falmouth market was primarily a wholesale market that promised some income, especially during the low buying season. She accumulated enough capital to purchase a pickup truck to minimize the exhaustion, discomfort and lack of safety of these trips. Before that, she, like other ICIs, rode on semitrailers that carry higglers and ICIs to market. Though she travels as her funds permit, she often expresses a desire to quit the business, since it is no longer profitable. With past profits from the trade, she purchased her home and pays for the education of her grandchildren. Despite the hard work, she notes that the business allows her to enjoy herself. An oldies music fanatic, she frequently attends shows. The trade also allows her to buy things that she wants and needs for herself and to travel to visit her children, who reside abroad.

I arrive at the arcade at 11 a.m. today. Miss T. has just arrived. She unlocks the gate and tells me to sit on the stool inside the stall. I sit down. Some of the shelves are empty because her stall was broken into last week. Her goosekiller comes in, and they unpack several boxes of clothing that are piled on top of each other in the corner where she stores her goods.[1] They are men's T-shirts and sport shirts, which are still on their hangers. She takes them out and hangs them vertically outside of her stall, all in a row like most other traders do. She also hangs several from the grid in the ceiling so the shirts are hung from above. We chat. No one comes by. She tells me she is buying her ticket [to Miami] on Monday. I ask her for the travel agent. She gives me the name and number, and then asks me if I want to call her on her cellular phone. I did not know to operate it. She says that I must be an idiot, "How you come from foreign and you don't know how you use a cellular?" I tell her that in the States only people with money have a cellular phone. She laughs, which I find annoying, and she proceeds to instruct me on how to use the phone. The whole time she is laughing at me; I feel distant from her and I keep thinking about our class differences and status symbols.

From the way she is talking, I realize that she is planning on travelling with somebody—Miss Z., an ICI whose stall is on the other side. Over the time I have spent visiting her, I observe that she has had no interaction with the other traders on her row. None whatsoever. They don't even say good morning. Across from her, the other ICI sits on her chair, her back facing the entrance to the arcade. The she moves her chair inside the stall.

While I was with Miss T. today, she has had three customers. She has sold two pairs of shoes, one of them to a young man who doesn't even haggle over the price. The other two customers haggle the price down. She starts saying she doesn't have time. "Don't touch my shoes if you're not buying," she warns him. He looks at the shoes then asks how much. She gives him a price. He quickly asks if she would take any less. She says, "No! If you don't want it, just go on." He makes another offer. She laughs and says she will only take off fifty dollars from her original price. He takes out money from his pocket and pays her. She gives the goosekiller his cut and hands over a couple bills to another man behind him who is outside but whom I had not noticed before. A man in a nearby stall starts to curse at the customer and calls him a "fuckery" because he bought the shoes from Miss T. and not from him. Apparently, the buyer had approached him first. She doesn't even flinch. While this man's aggression disturbed me, she does not seem concerned.

Around two o'clock, I take my little plastic container of vegetables out and begin to eat my lunch. She calls me Rasta and tells me that's why I like to go to the UVA, because I'm a Rasta.[2] While I'm eating. Miss Z., with whom she will be travelling, comes by. I introduce myself to her. The goosekiller comes back inside saying that nothing is going on out there. He leans over on the drum container and begins to stare at me. He picks another style of shoe and leaves.

Notes

1. A goosekiller is a street-based sales agent who works on behalf of a stallholder. [Editors' note]

2. As Ulysse explains elsewhere in her book, the United Vendors Association (UVA) was founded to represent the interest of vendors. Among its important founders were Garvey-ite Rastafari. [Editors' note]

Jamaica's Shame

Thomas Glave

Visible political advocacy by LGBT Jamaicans began in the 1970s, with the establishment of the Gay Freedom Movement by some gay men, largely middle-class and based in Kingston. The group published a newsletter (the Jamaican Gaily News*), wrote regular letters to the editors of the island's newspapers, and organized a Pride picnic and panel discussion in 1979. The AIDS crisis of the 1980s hit Jamaica hard and overwhelmed the ability of these early activists to continue public advocacy work. Nevertheless, a network remained in touch throughout the 1980s.*

Public debates about homosexuality reemerged in the 1990s. Thomas Glave was among the founders in 1998 of the Jamaican Federation of Lesbians, All-Sexuals, and Gays (JFLAG), which remains active today. Like other gay Caribbean writers and activists, Glave is at pains to emphasize the authenticity of same-sex love and desire, opposing a common rhetorical move that suggests that it is merely an import from the alleged liberal decadence of North America and Europe. Since Glave's essay, which highlighted the threat of violence faced by sexual minorities in Jamaica, debate has become increasingly intense. Portia Simpson-Miller broke with previous politicians by stating during the 2011 general election campaign that she opposed discrimination on the grounds of sexual orientation, although her government did little to improve the legal position of LGBT Jamaicans. Jamaica has had a regular gay pride festival since 2015, although notably without a public march. Institutions such as the University of the West Indies have taken public action to oppose homophobia, and opposition to discrimination on grounds of sexuality has become the norm among middle-class Jamaicans, who regularly travel internationally. Even so, a majority of the Jamaican population continues to believe that homosexuality is wrong, and sex between men remains illegal.

Because, in fact, we are not noble. We are cowards, hypocrites. Hysterical in our hatred and ignorance, seeking to cast aspersions and impose ostracism via state and social persecution—death sentences—upon those whom we consider already damned. Upon lesbians and gay men: those whom we would briskly vilify as "sodomites" or "abominations"—denunciations heard in recent public discussions about homosexuality in Jamaica. But how swift and smug our judgements. How devoid of simple human compassion. How shallow our reasoning.

In truth, we, as a society, barely know what the word "humanity" means. For in failing to love and support our fellow humans who are gay and lesbian, we are hardly human. This is only one part of our shame.

Have we fallen so far into the abyss of historical amnesia that we have (wilfully, purposefully) forgotten? Forgotten that only as recently as the last century our ancestors, who burned and rioted against their masters so that we might bask and shine in freedom's ennobling light, perished beneath the plantation's whip, withered in cane fields beneath vicious suns, opened ravaged thighs to rape, to torture, to unimaginable degradation? To utter inhumanity?

Slavery, it was called. Slavery. Black bodies packed thousandfold into ships, black hands manacled at the wrist. Flesh ripped, feet broken, brands steamed white-hot into skin. They are not humans, they are animals, the masters said. So echoed the innumerable colonizers who followed them— who, late into this century, believe that we, as black people, "out of many, one," were unfit to govern ourselves: to make laws as human beings for ourselves, and live, peacefully, lovingly, nobly, amongst ourselves.

In our present willingness to persecute and destroy our gay and lesbian brothers and sisters—our children, parents and aunts, grandparents, uncles, cousins, and friends—have we proved our masters correct?

With such a brutal history—need we say it?—we should be the noblest people in the world. Self-governing at last, survivors of the most heinous atrocities against humanity the world has ever known, we should long ago have acquired a braver, more generous, more noble imagination: the ability to envision goodness, even greatness, in all things and, most of all, in ourselves; the ability to love ourselves—all of ourselves, irrespective of colour, class, gender or sexual orientation. But we have not. Our flag flies proudly, yet we are not proud—or we are so falsely, mired in the arrogance that, writ large, adores dishonesty. In our present mean-spiritedness and self-enslaving ignorance, we are quickly on our way to becoming worse off than what many have consistently attempted to make us.

I am gay. Jamaican. And proud to be both. That flag of green, black and gold is my flag; that national anthem, my anthem; those people in Cross Roads and St Mary and Clarendon—every parish—mine. All mine. I am them. Of them. The blood of my ancestors yet tells me so. Many of my fellow Jamaicans, however, would not have it be so. "You shoulda dead, bwoy," they would say; "Gwan with that nasty foreign business," they would say.

(Indeed, some of them have said.) "We shoulda kill you the first chance we did get," they would say. Shot, stabbed, stoned. Boom bye-bye. It has been said.

Dead? Me, and my lesbian sister and gay brothers, who are sisters and brothers of us all? Cutlassed down in Half-Way-Tree? Shot on Molynes Road? Burned out of house and home (or to ashes) in St Catherine?

No, no. Absolutely no. It cannot be so. For we are here: we are you, we are part of you. We are Jamaican, human, alive. Your neighbours and your friends. Your helpers, coworkers, bosses. We serve your food in restaurants, clean your streets, fix your cars and bury your dead. We nurse you and your loved ones back to health in hospitals and bring forth your children (and our own, for many of us also are parents) into the world. We tidy your homes and live in them. We process your loans and bank accounts, and teach your children. We drive the taxis you hail, arrest the criminals you fear, catch the fish that you fry and steam, repair the roads upon which you walk, and even fly the planes and steer the boats that carry you to places beyond your most hopeful dreams. And in this there is a kind of nobility, for—like many other members of this society—we do a great deal without asking much in return, except that we be allowed to live our lives without fear of being harassed or gunned down.

We are, indeed, everywhere: like you. But you have not often asked us who we were because you did not want to know, and even when you knew, you denied it. Thus you were able to say, "Me never know a gay smaddi yet," or "Battyman, man royal, the whole heap a them nasty so"—without acknowledging that the woman who sold you yams and breadfruit this morning or last night might be a lesbian, that the man who drove the bus you rode to work might have gone home later to the kisses and love of another man, that the women who work as security guards, or pharmacy clerks, or as sidewalk vendors on Orange Street and King Street might be dreaming of loving each other—what is normal and true. That we have always been here has always been true in Jamaica. We are not a new "fashion," not something brought back by an ICI from Curaçao or North America. We are not a disease, nor are we damned.

We are none of the terrible things many would have us be. But we were not asked compassionately where we were or how we lived, and so—as far as many were concerned—we did not exist. But how ignoble is such imagining; how it reeks of narrow-mindedness and spiritual selfishness. If we honestly intend to occupy this earth, and the country, in each other's human service and in peace, these hateful prejudices are far from the best imagining of our lesbian and gay sisters and brothers we as Jamaicans can do. Such mean imagining in actuality pays dim tribute to the formidable legacies handed down to our brilliant national heroes, and to figures such as the late, great Bob Marley and Michael Manley—visionaries who believed, not coincidentally, in the transcendent and enlarging possibilities of freedom.

Regarding deliberations on homosexuality (and so many other critical matters facing us in this country), I charge my fellow Jamaicans with the necessary human task of becoming more noble. I exhort us to be great, spiritually and in the acts which that spiritual magnitude will motivate. I press us toward compassion. We are not there yet. None of us can love as our greatest, grandest selves while we continue to despise and denigrate so many who are, ultimately, ourselves—our fellow citizens, lesbians and gay men included. The masters' lesson of oppression, like their brands on our ancestors' flesh, still burn into our brains. Our greatest prophet-singer admonished us: we must free ourselves from mental slavery—from bigotry, hatred and self-oppression. He knew that none of us would ever be truly free until we all were. As members of the modern world, we must know that freedom cannot be granted selectively: we cannot grant freedom to some as we continue to oppress—"downpress"—others. We must work toward a nobility of the imagination and spirit that rejects the shame of our ignorance, as we recognize that all of us, heterosexual and homosexual, deserve equal, loving places in society. Until we do so, we will continue to bear the marks of the master and the weight of our shame—our *dis*-spiriting prejudice and ignorance. Anti–Third Worldists and cultural imperialists need not dominate and manipulate us with spurious promises and seductions of foreign aid if we are willing to alienate and destroy our own.

And so, in this season of God, nearing the close of one of the most violent centuries humankind has ever known, I pray—words offered up to all who will hear: that I and my lesbian sisters and gay brothers will not, as we come forth in love and honesty, be harassed, or killed, or maimed, in this green, troubled land of our own people and ancestors—this island of so many joys and sorrows. I pray that we all will, in this nation that might be great, walk peacefully away from shame, toward our potential human nobility. The slaves are dead, the masters decayed in their graves; the future, while never assured, can yet be ours, together. We are poised in the present moment, in which all things may change, all ignorance be transposed to knowledge; from knowledge shall come compassion, and from compassion, nobility.

Our ancestors and national heroes knew this. Dying for us, they spoke it. They speak to us still.

So we are at the beginning. A new beginning in this season of God.

Thus is my faith in my own people that—standing tall—we may all hear.

Hear each other. Attend each other. For once, in unity. Heterosexuals. Homosexuals. All configurations abiding, reconfigurings emergent. Wealthy and poor, female and male. Together. Alive. Here. Now.

Kingston, Jamaica
December 1998–January 1999

Woman Time Now

HG Helps

In 2011 Portia Simpson-Miller became the first female prime minister of Jamaica. Her ascension owed much to social changes of the 1970s and her own considerable strengths as a charismatic political leader in a male-centered political culture. As this short political biography reveals, Simpson-Miller drew her support from a large base of Jamaicans from the majority population. She reflected their own aspirations far more than her mostly middle-class male predecessors. Their faithful devotion to her often overwhelmed her rivals. She took over as prime minister when P. J. Patterson stepped down in 2006, and although she lost the general election the following year, she retained her party's loyalty, leading it to victory at the next general election in 2011. After serving as prime minister from 2011 to 2016, Simpson-Miller retired from representational politics in 2017.

Running around as a skinny, shy young girl at Marie Hill Primary School in what is now the constituency of North Central St. Catherine, Portia Simpson presented no warning signs that she had political ambitions, let alone that she would one day become prime minister of her native land.

After all, the school that she attended at the start of the 1950s had itself, done nothing spectacular to raise anyone's antenna that even within another fifty years one of its own would hold its name aloft in glory.

Even in Wood Hall, where she was born on December 12, 1945, thoughts of that district turning out someone of political significance were tantamount to political blasphemy.

Fast-forward a half-century later and the name Portia Simpson, now lengthened by the matrimonial acquisition of Miller, would resonate with thunderous effect across the length and breadth of this North Caribbean island of 2.8 million inhabitants.

Simpson Miller upset the status quo and the Boys' Club by becoming the first woman prime minister in 2006. She again rewrote the pages of history in December 2011 by repeating the feat and joining her mentor, Michael Manley, as the only politicians since Jamaica gained independence in 1962 to have served as prime minister, lost and returned to political office as leader of the country.

Her entry onto the political playground as a councillor of the Kingston & St Andrew Corporation in 1974, paved the way for a more meaningful call-up to the altar of service, for by 1976 she was elected member of parliament for South West St Andrew, a move that was to prove telling.

She had won a seat that was previously foreign territory to the PNP and in the process reversed a deficit of several thousand voters, an achievement that baffled political commentators.

Simpson Miller's first call to higher national service came in 1976 when Manley appointed her parliamentary secretary for local government in the Office of the Prime Minister.

Since then, she has held full ministerial responsibility for labour, welfare and sport, first in 1989; followed by tourism and sport; local government, community development and sport; before becoming prime minister in 2006, retaining the sport portfolio and acquiring the traditional defence responsibility.

Getting to that position though was not all smooth sailing for Simpson Miller, a former president of the PNP's Woman's Movement, who struggled along the way in her quest to beat PJ Patterson to the tape in the race for leadership of the PNP in 1992.

But after following in Patterson's shadow for fourteen years while he oversaw significant infrastructural and telecommunication developments to the society, it was time for Simpson Miller to make her move again to the prime minister's office, Jamaica House, as the chosen one, in February 2006.

Jamaica embraced her with optimism and hope. Some even toyed with the slogan "Woman Time Now." The changes had gone down well and the population except for the hardline JLP supporters, was prepared to be patient with her.

Later, Simpson Miller, who up to the time of her elevation was one of the PNP's longest-serving vice-presidents, defied the odds to achieve the lowest inflation rate in Jamaica's mordant era. 5–8 per cent by official data for the fiscal year 2006–2007.

Regarded as the most popular politician since Alexander Bustamante and Michael Manley, Simpson Miller's often verbal protestations for better living conditions for Jamaica's poor and disadvantaged, continue to win her favours in the eyes of the proletariat, the unemployed and the downtrodden.

A Wild Ride

Robert Lalah

Taxicabs, noticeable by their red license plates, crowd the main thoroughfares of Jamaican cities. They are usually tightly packed with passengers, play loud music, and bear distinguishing names or advertisements for upcoming entertainment events. Equally common is the sight of cabs zipping in and out of traffic through narrow spaces or even creating an alternative lane on the sidewalk. The experience of a taxi ride in Kingston can be harrowing and revealing, as journalist Robert Lalah discovered in this account of a ride with a typically strongly opinionated taxi driver.

I should've known that this was going to be weird. The car was missing a headlight and I could hear the engine rattling long before it came around the corner. Still, when the taxi pulled up, I was happy, especially since it was more than fifteen minutes late. The driver, however, was quite pleased with himself and boasted about how fast he had driven to get there "on time."

I had poked my head inside when the car stopped, and glanced at the driver. He was huge, with a big head. Because he was so tall, he had to hang his head just so he could fit inside. He reminded me of those clowns who squeeze themselves into tiny cars at the circus. For a moment, I thought about telling him this but, when I sat in the car and realised that he could perhaps crush me with his thumb, I decided against it. Anyway, off we went. Our location: Spanish Town. Our destination: Kingston. Inside the car smelled like pine leaves and there was a furry cloth covering the seats. The windows were tinted and there was an air freshener in the shape of a tree, hanging from the rearview mirror. There was a yellow cloth tucked under the emergency brake and the driver, who goes by the moniker "Number 7," kept taking it up to wipe something or the other in the car.

We sat in silence until "Number 7" pulled on to the Spanish Town bypass.

"You know a from when di govament claim 'bout dem a go build up dah road yah? A fool dem tek poor people fah, you know? All dem do a promise and den dem nuh do nothing," he said, looking at me for a reaction. I made a gesture with my eyes and I guess this encouraged him to go on and on. "All dem do a thief poor people money and go pan vacation wid dem wife and dem ting deh. Dem only care 'bout themselves," he said.

Now, I'm sure that "Number 7" went on further on the matter, but I was busy staring in front of me. "Number 7" may be a good conversationalist, but his driving skills leave much to be desired. And that's putting it mildly. Every time the car in front of his slowed down, even a bit, "Number 7" would go into a tirade about how "these people take the driving ting as a play play ting." I didn't interrupt his ranting.

We were at a stoplight near to the hospital and before the light even went on green "Number 7" started tooting his horn and shouting for the driver in front of him to move his something or the other.

At more than ninety kilometres an hour, "Number 7" shot across the bridge on his way to the Mandela Highway. What bothered me most was that while he pressed his foot on the accelerator, he remained calm, almost nonchalant about the whole affair. Meanwhile, I was sweating profusely and holding on tight to the fabric on my seat. My eyes were wide when I looked at him and said, as calmly as I could, "You can take your time, you know, I'm not really in a rush." Much to my consternation, this had little effect on "Number 7," who now decided to strike up a conversation about the police.

"Every time dem waan seize man cyar. Is like dem nuh waan do nothing else. As dem hold you and realise dat you nuh have no insurance, dem waan tek weh yuh cyar. Is what happen to dem people yah?" he said. I wasn't able to give a response. My eyes were glued to a woman ahead of us crossing the road with a baby in her arms. She was, by now, directly in front of us, and "Number 7" showed no signs of slowing the car down anytime soon. I was silent, but in my head I was screaming, "Lawd have mercy!"

Luckily, "Number 7" swung the car around the woman in the nick of time and then made some comment about "dem people yah who love run crass di road when dem see people a come."

I was really in no mood to argue with a burly man, but couldn't help telling him that he could have slowed down a bit sooner when he noticed that the woman was crossing the road. I should have anticipated his response.

"No man! You haffi shake dem up. Dem galang like is fi dem road. Dem fi know dat is cyar and truck man run road."

I didn't respond. There was little point, really.

By now, we were on Spanish Town Road. I remembered a newspaper article I had read about a week earlier which said that this road was a major crash spot last year.

I glanced at my watch and tried to convince myself that I would be at my destination and away from this maniac in only a few minutes.

"You see how di young bwoy win di competition? Yes man! Di woman dem gwaan like dem want tek over everyting. Mi glad how di yout put har inna har place," he said.

I saw myself hurtling toward the back of a truck and whispered a prayer for the preservation of my soul after my impending death. With only one eye open, I breathed a sigh of relief as the car swung around the truck, missing it by mere inches.

"Dem company yah dat a redundancy di people dem now. Wah you really think a gwaan?" He didn't give me a chance to respond. "Is pure politics! All dem waan do is keep di people dem inna poverty. Marcus Garvey done tell dem," he said, while barely missing the tail of a dog that ran across the road.

"Di two phone company dem inna tings wid dem one another. People nuh realise dat di two a dem a work wid dem one another fi mek more money off di poor people dem," said "Number 7."

Ironically, his phone rang soon after and I wondered how much worse he could possibly drive, while distracted by a phone call. Luckily, he didn't accept the call and mumbled something about his babymother and money. I didn't care. I could see my destination now and, as the car came to a screeching halt, I thanked him and the heavens above for my survival.

I hopped out of the car and watched as "Number 7," in his mobile death machine, shot down the road and out of sight.

Skin Bleaching

Carolyn Cooper

Jamaican cultural critic Carolyn Cooper discusses the widespread use of chemical products—often with dangerous side effects—to lighten the skin. Cooper understands skin bleaching as a product of Jamaica's discriminatory color hierarchies, in which lighter-skinned people are systematically valued above the darker-skinned. Still, she also investigates the knowingness of many practitioners of bleaching, seeing the practice as often a form of role-play rather than an attempt to fully take on an identity as light-skinned or "brown."

There is a disturbing trend in the Caribbean today for Black women to bleach their skin in an attempt to approximate the standards of Euro-American ideal beauty, especially its mulatto variant. This bleaching of the skin—usually only the face and neck—is an obvious attempt to partially disguise the racial identity of the subject. The mask of "lightness," however dangerous in medical terms, becomes a therapeutic signifier of status in a racist society that still privileges melanin deficiency as a sign of beauty. And there is decided ambivalence about the use of these bleaching agents. Some obvious bleachers, when confronted with the question, "Why yu a bleach?," cunningly attempt to conceal the evidence. A recurring explanation for the "coolness" of the skin is the claim "is because mi work in air condition office." This adds yet another layer of disguise to the subject, for many such respondents may, in fact, be unemployed.

For me, the most alluring account of this refusal to admit that one is bleaching the skin comes from a young woman who sells in Kingston's Papine Market, whose face, all of a sudden, began to assume an unusual ghostly whiteness, a vivid contrast with the rest of her body. When I nosily commented on what had happened to her face and asked why she was bothering to bleach, she rather airily informed me that I was mistaking her for her sister. Now, it is true that this young woman does have a sister who is a little darker than she, and who sometimes sells in the market too. But I know them both well enough not to confuse them. An equally nosy man who works in the market observed in a stage whisper, "Is because she know seh she spoil up herself mek she a tell yu bout a her 'sister'" [It's because she knows that she's spoilt herself why she's telling you that she's her "sister"]. In this young woman's case, role-play manifested a clear desire to deny her basic identity. She has since stopped bleaching, her natural skin colour has returned and every now and then I jokingly ask how her sister is doing. She laughs—with me, I hope.

It is not only women who feel obliged to wear the mask, as the following anecdote illustrates. A panel discussion was held in December 1999 at the Mona Common Basic School, where students in the Caribbean Institute of Media and Communication at the University of the West Indies were screening a video on bleaching that they had made as part of a research project on the theme "Love the Skin You're In." At the event, a young man who had participated in the study acknowledged the fact that bleaching was harmful to the skin and said he was planning to stop. But he is a DJ who knows the value of looking good on his own terms. Let me recount his explanation, not quite verbatim, but as best as I can recall it, for why he would continue to bleach for a little while longer: "Christmas a come an mi ha fi look good. Mi a go gwaan bleach. An when yu see mi ready fi go out, mi a go put on one long sleeve ganzie and wear mi cap. An dem wi tink a one browning a come through" [Christmas is coming and I have to look good. I'm going to continue bleaching. And when I'm ready to go out, I'm going to put on a long-sleeved jersey and wear my cap. And they will think that it's a browning coming through].

First of all, I feel perversely obliged to disabuse the young man of that fantasy. No one, I told him, would ever mistake him for a browning. And, in any case, he needed to look in the mirror and see that he was perfectly handsome as a Black person.

In retrospect, I do seriously wonder about the appropriateness of my intended reprimand to my skin-bleaching DJ. Not just the issue of my bad manners in pointing out the obvious, but more so the haunting question of whether the young man's understanding of what he was doing was much more sophisticated than I was willing to allow at that time. What remains so fascinating in his narrative is his rather practical sense of seasonal brownness. He knew that being brown, however achieved, was not really an essential part of his identity. Light skin color was a fashion accessory that would stand him in good stead during the festive season. Somewhat like the bright lights that decorate the Christmas landscape, light skin color, however fleeting, would give the DJ added visibility. The metaphor thus underscores both the elements of fantasy as well as the conscious awareness of role-play that are so subtly intertwined in these dancehall discourses of desire.

Furthermore, the DJ's metaphor of "coming through" signals his conception of the color line as a barrier that must literally be breached, so that he can become socially visible. And it takes a lot of cunning, Anansi style, to make the breakthrough possible.

Tragedy in Tivoli

W. Earl Witter and Livern Barrett

This pair of readings provides two perspectives on the May 2010 military incursion in Tivoli Gardens, an inner-city community in West Kingston which was both a JLP stronghold and a "garrison community" dominated by the "Shower Posse" gang. The Tivoli incursion, which occurred under a state of public emergency, came after a prolonged period of diplomatic tension between Prime Minister Bruce Golding's administration and the United States. As the first reading explains, the dispute concerned a US request for the extradition of Christopher "Dudus" Coke, a prominent "don" in Tivoli, for drug trafficking and related crimes in the United States. In violation of Jamaican law Golding enlisted the support of a US law firm to act on the government's behalf in its dispute over the extradition treaty. When this was revealed, Golding was compelled to authorize the request and commanded the security forces to serve the warrant for Coke's arrest. The action triggered events that led to the deaths of over seventy Tivoli residents. In September 2011 Golding resigned as prime minister—the only Jamaican prime minister to do so for political reasons—partly as a result of the damage the extradition affair had done to his leadership. The Tivoli incursion is the most serious of a pattern of events in which the Jamaican state has used deadly military force against poor Jamaicans.

The first reading is from the report submitted to Parliament by Director of Public Prosecutions Earl Witter in April 2013. Based on recommendations in this report, a Commission of Enquiry into the events was held between 2014 and 2016. At the enquiry several residents of Tivoli Gardens gave emotional testimony of the horror of the events. The second is a newspaper report that describes the statement of seventy-two-year-old market-woman Adina "Rosie" Derby, who lost her son and was herself shot by security forces. The Tivoli Enquiry's final report included hard-hitting criticisms of the government. It recommended that Tivoli residents receive compensation for harm done to them and their families as a result of the incursion and that the government make a formal apology. Prime Minister Andrew Holness issued the apology in December 2017, and the government approved compensation of J$200 million (more than US$1.5 million). Even so, critics note that many harmed *have not received appropriate compensation and point out that no one was charged with any crime as a result of the violence of the incursion.*

The Siege: Earl Witter's Report to Parliament

BACKDROP OF THE "INCURSION" OR "SIEGE"

7.0.0. Unfolding of material events could be said to have begun on the night of May 17, 2010. The then Prime Minister, Mr. Golding, announced in a nationwide television and radio broadcast that the Minister of Justice would, after all, issue an authority to proceed under the Extradition Act, 1991, S.13 (1), in relation to a request by the United States of America (the USA) for the extradition of Christopher Coke. The requisition had been received on August 25, 2009. Coke was wanted for trial in the USA on drug trafficking and gun-running charges but was now a fugitive, ignoring entreaties to surrender himself and evading capture. His whereabouts were known to a few only.

7.1.1. The fateful disclosure ended a period of some nine months, during which the Jamaican Government vacillated over its response to the extradition request. It had come under ever mounting pressure from the government of the USA, the local Church, private business sector and "civil society" groupings, to forgo any or any further court proceedings in the matter. The issuing of the authority to proceed had been kept on hold, pending the outcome of those proceedings. But following upon that announcement, events took on a momentum of their own.

7.1.2. MARCH ON DOWNTOWN KINGSTON. A large throng of West Kingston women, nearly all of them dressed in white, marched into downtown Kingston. They were protesting the signing of the authority to proceed and Coke's imminent arrest. The women displayed fierce loyalty to him. At least one of them considered him "next to Jesus." Others would "dead fi Dudus."

ANNOUNCEMENT OF A STATE OF EMERGENCY; MR. GOLDING'S SECOND NATIONWIDE BROADCAST. On the afternoon of Sunday, May 23, 2010, the Government announced that the Governor General had declared a State of Public Emergency. In another nationwide television and radio broadcast that night, Mr. Golding appealed to all law-abiding citizens to remain calm. He said that threats against the safety of the Jamaican people would be driven back. The State of Emergency had been declared based on "information" from the Security Forces that actions were being carried out which posed significant threats to law and order in the Corporate Area.

7.1.5. By the evening of May 23, hundreds of well-armed and camouflaged soldiers in full battle gear and drawn from various battalions of the JDF [Jamaica Defence Force] and JNR [Jamaica National Reserve] had descended upon West Kingston. They accompanied hundreds more armed policemen (a great many of them masked) drawn from various divisions of the JCF [Jamaica Constabulary Force] and ISCF [Island Special Constabulary Force]. Armoured vehicles and bulldozers (to be used in breaching barricades) were deployed.

7.1.6. A command structure provided for splitting up of the territory into "sectors." Cordons were established. One, in particular, was tightly placed around Tivoli Gardens, the supposed encampment of Christopher Coke. Illegal gunmen loyal to Coke and recruited from West Kingston and beyond were said to have taken up position there, prepared to take on the State Security Forces. The battle lines were drawn. Night fell. Electric power supply to Tivoli Gardens was cut off, intentionally or not. The community was thereby plunged into darkness.

JCF ANNOUNCEMENT OF OPERATIONS

8. On Labour Day, Monday, May 24, 2010 (a public holiday), the JCF announced that earlier in the day it had launched an operation in Tivoli Gardens and surrounding areas of West Kingston. The joint military/police operation, a news release stated, was

> aimed at executing a warrant issued by the courts of Jamaica for the arrest of Christopher Michael Coke otherwise called "Dudus" as well as to restore the area to stability after three consecutive days of barricading by criminal elements and wanton attacks on the police force. During the operation, seven members of the Security Forces were injured. Six of the seven were shot, one succumbed to his injuries. The other was injured in an accident. The operation is still ongoing and the Security Forces are resolute in bringing the area to stability so that law abiding citizens of West Kingston and its environs can get on with their lives in peace. The Security Forces are reminding the residents of Kingston and St. Andrew that there is a limited State of Emergency in effect and residents are asked to remain indoors.

MR. GOLDING ADDRESSES PARLIAMENT

8.1. The following day, Tuesday, May 25, Mr. Golding told a sombre House of Representatives that since Sunday, May 23, several roads in West

Kingston had been barricaded, impeding the movement of pedestrian and vehicular traffic as well as normal police law enforcement operations. He continued:

> Intelligence gathered by the security forces indicated that in anticipation of the execution of a warrant for the arrest of Christopher Coke, heavily armed men were preparing to attack members of the security forces. Intelligence further suggested that criminal elements in other communities intended to launch attacks on the security forces in order to divert attention and resources from the focused operation of what the situation in West Kingston required.

8.2. On Saturday night, May 22, a police patrol car had been attacked by gunmen on Mountain View Avenue, East Kingston. Two policemen had been killed and eight others injured, Mr. Golding said. During that night and next morning, "several police stations in and outside of the Corporate Area" were attacked by armed men using guns and molotov cocktails. These included police stations in West Kingston and Rockfort in East Kingston and Spanish Town, St. Catherine. The Hannah Town and Darling Street police stations in West Kingston were set on fire and extensively damaged.

8.3. The joint police/military operation launched in Tivoli Gardens, he indicated, was meant to bring an end "to this spate of lawlessness and to restore order and calm to the affected areas." The security forces encountered "sustained and sporadic [sic] gunfire" and in the exchange that ensued, he said, "several" persons were confirmed dead, including a member of the JDF. "Several" others, including twelve (12) JDF soldiers, had been injured. The police had reported that "twenty-six" (26) persons were confirmed dead, but it was likely that the number was higher.

Rosie Tells Her Story

LIVERN BARRETT
An elderly Tivoli Gardens woman yesterday recounted how she took a bullet to the back as she, along with other family members, rushed her wounded son to hospital on a handcart during the 2010 police-military operations in her west Kingston community.

Seventy-two-year-old Adina Derby insisted during her testimony to the west Kingston commission of enquiry, being held at the Jamaica Conference Centre, downtown Kingston, that she was shot by a policeman moments after she ran past him in chase of the handcart transporting her son

A heavily armed Jamaica Defense Force soldier alongside civilian residents of Tivoli Gardens, Kingston, in the aftermath of the May 2010 incursion during which at least seventy-three civilians were killed. State authorities treated all Tivoli residents as supporters and possible harborers of Christopher "Dudus" Coke, the "don" of Tivoli Gardens, who was being extradited to the United States on drug trafficking charges. Security forces entered Tivoli to arrest Coke, who evaded capture until a month later, when he was found in a roadblock outside Kingston. This image comes from footage produced by an Al Jazeera journalist, part of a group of foreign journalists escorted into the area by police a couple of days after the military invasion, while the area remained under military occupation under a state of emergency. Showing the armed and armored solider on the left and the unarmed, smaller, fearful civilians on the right, the image suggests the heavy force used against the entire population of the area during the raid and its aftermath. The schoolgirl appears to be leaving for school—like other Tivoli residents, forced to go about her daily life surrounded by intense military force. Mexico Shoots, "AJE Jamaica Tivoli Gardens Aftermath," YouTube Video, 0:16, 27 May 2010, https://www.youtube.com/watch?v=6M0QC80V2ZM.

to Kingston Public Hospital (KPH) with what she described as a gunshot wound to the chest.

"When me run past him, me hear sup'n go so 'blow' and me drop," Derby recounted of the May 24, 2010, shooting.

"Me feel like is a balloon blow up inna me. Me get up and me run off and me drop. . . . A three times me get up and drop," said the woman affectionately called "Rosie" about the injury that would change her life for good.

The lifelong Tivoli Gardens resident also blasted the security forces for the way the operation was conducted, charging that "dem come wid blood inna dem eye fi kill off everybody."

"We are human beings . . . [If] you come fi somebody [Christopher Coke], you come the right and proper way," she underscored.

Derby testified that amid the fierce gun battle still raging in the west Kingston community, she had to abandon her son and seek refuge in a nearby yard.

"Me did haffi run fi my rescue. Me couldn't mek him dead and me dead. . . . Probably if me neva lef him, me woulda dead too and the other rest a people [pushing her son on the cart] would a dead to," she surmised.

"'Rosie" testified that her son—who was shot when he went to the second floor of the family's two-storey home to get phone signal—later succumbed to his injury.

She admitted, during cross-examination by Deborah Martin, one of the attorneys for the Jamaica Constabulary Force (JCF), that she did not know if soldiers, police or gunmen shot her son.

She also disputed claims that, in her statement to the public defender's office in 2010, she did not indicate that a member of the JCF shot her.

"From me get shot, me tell dem say a police shoot me," she insisted.

Derby said hours after she was shot, a group of soldiers transported her to the University Hospital of the West Indies (UHWI), and praised them for the treatment she received.

Derby revealed that she spent nearly a month at the UHWI and pointed to the physical and emotional scars that still linger more than four years later.

"I don't even like talking about this, because I don't like to remember it," she muttered in-between her testimony, noting that she still walks with a limp.

The Cell Phone and the Economy of Communication

Heather A. Horst and Daniel Miller

Heather Horst and Daniel Miller assess the impact of the defining technology of the late twentieth and early twenty-first centuries: the cell phone. Their work is based on ethnography in a rural central Jamaican community and in a low-income housing development in Portmore, a busy city on the southern coast of St. Catherine parish. They refer to these places by the pseudonyms Orange Valley and Marshfield. Horst and Miller argue that for low-income Jamaicans, the cell phone provides a means of extending established communication patterns. In particular, it facilitates the circulation of small amounts of cash and credit and thus enhances both connections and dependencies. They suggest that Jamaicans tend to be at once highly economically individualistic (avoiding shared budgets within families, for instance) and strongly connected to large numbers of people, often across substantial distances.

Whereas many individuals do not possess the basic capital to create small-scale businesses, it is clear they do use the cell phone within their day-to-day survival strategies. As one goes deeper and deeper into the daily budgets of low-income individuals and households and considers the way they simply get by from day to day, one starts to see why the phone, far from being peripheral or an additional expense, is actually the new heart of economic survival. For low-income individuals, what finally matters are not earnings that come from employment or the incomes resulting from entrepreneurial activity and sales, but rather support that comes from other people—people who "have it." Of the households in Marshfield, 70 per cent received money from others, including other family members, boyfriends and partners, baby-fathers and friends in Jamaica and abroad; 48 per cent received one-third of their income from others and 38 per cent of the households surveyed in Marshfield survived exclusively through social networks and the patronage of others. In contrast to Marshfield, small-scale farming plays a significant role in the economy of Orange Valley, where 64 per cent of the households we surveyed supplement their income through small-scale farming. In many cases, small-scale farming produces surplus food and fruit, which can be sold, traded or exchanged for acts of goodwill. Nonetheless, 34 per cent also meet their day-to-day needs exclusively through their social networks, which include immediate family, boyfriends, girlfriends, neighbours, acquaintances and a host of friends. The bottom line in both sites is that over a third of households have no "income" in the sense of anything they earn through capitalized labour. They exist only through their ability to obtain money from others.

Keisha perhaps best illustrates the ways in which social connections and social capital operate in Jamaica. A thirty-three-year-old woman who lives in a shared rental flat in Marshfield after growing up in Orange Valley, Keisha has always been considered "bright." Over the past decade, she has worked as a secretary at a factory in Kingston as well as in telesales at a Portmore company. When she became pregnant with her daughter, she decided to quit her job to care for her new baby. With the support of her married baby-father (\$JA10,000 per month) and the small profits from the sale of an average of twenty-five Digicel phonecards each week, Keisha was able to meet her basic monthly rent payment and food expenses, which totalled \$JA8,400 per month, as well as her hefty phonecard habit of \$JA2,400 monthly. However, she often had to source money and cards from one of her boyfriends or skim a little off the top of the money that Keisha's sister Carmen sends monthly to support her three children whom Keisha looked after during the day.

After over a year at home with her daughter, niece and nephews, Keisha decided that she wanted to go back to school and further her studies. When Keisha announced her plan to attend teacher's college, she called and met with her baby-father, boyfriend and sister, who offered their support. While Keisha had some savings from her previous job, they said they would try to help her with her school fees of \$JA60,000. Because she had to board at the school as a student (no children allowed), her sister, who was not working at the time, also agreed to take on the full responsibility for their sister Carmen's three children as well as Keisha's daughter Aaliyah. Aaliyah's father's sister also said that she would look after Aaliyah from time to time. A local grocer offered Keisha a short-term position crunching numbers in their books and, to help with school fees, he gave her an advance on her salary to help her pay the remaining part of her school fees. However, books, uniforms, shoes and other incidental expenses had not been purchased. Two weeks before the start of term, Keisha turned to her cell phone and scrolled through the numbers. After passing by Adrian, Alston, Andrea, Bups and

Cuzzi, Keisha saw the name of a local businessman who always encouraged her to continue with her education. She called him and explained that she had been accepted for school and paid her fees but needed money for books and supplies. However, he told her to come by later in the year since he had recently extended himself helping others. After she hung up, Keisha scrolled through her phone again, calling Doreen, an old coworker from her telesales days, "Miss D," her office procedures teacher, Shernette, a friend whom she used to go out with, and another friend from school days, Tomoya. Over the weekend she also tried her niece, who had a good job in Spanish Town; another former coworker; a former teacher; a friend; and her daughter's godmother.

In all, Keisha phoned fourteen people. She asked some individuals for money for her school books and other individual for uniforms. She asked Tomoya for help with school shoes and requested money for towels from her daughter's godmother since her tattered "yard" towels were too embarrassing to bring to school. In the end, she received $JA1,000 for the towels from her daughter's godmother and another $JA2,500 from a combination of her teacher, a former coworker and her friend working in Spanish Town. These three people managed to "have it" at the time and were willing to share their money with Keisha. In addition, Keisha's sister living and working in Florida sent her $JA6,000 ($US100) to help her out. Although Keisha had helped a number of people that she called when she was still working at the bank, it was not necessarily these same people who helped her set herself up in her new course. Some of the people Keisha helped out had their own situations to deal with. Others simply said they could not help her. It all just depended upon who had the money to help her then and if they felt prepared to give at that moment. Moreover, when she originally took down the numbers of the people she called in her phone book, Keisha had no idea at that time that she would be attending school or that she might be one day asking for their help. Rather, she just knew that it was "good to have friends."

Low-income Jamaicans may not articulate the importance of connections in terms of social capital, but they are quite aware of the way that Jamaicans use friendship, kinship and other ties as a coping strategy. Andrea describes the way Jamaicans "operate":

Sometimes mi watch the TV and see some likl piple a foreign now like Africa an so forth like that, Delhi, this an. Jamaica is like, you can see a fren and seh "beg yuh a hundred dolla" and dem gi yu. But dem places

I doan think they can, maybe dem neighbour they can beg an sumting like that.

[Sometimes I watch the TV and see little people "in foreign" like in Africa and Delhi. In Jamaica you can see a friend and say "beg you $JA100" and they will give it to you. But in those places I don't think they can, maybe they can ask a neighbour.]

What Andrea makes clear is that, in Jamaica (and perhaps elsewhere), the difference between being poor and not being poor is having friends and family that you can call upon in a time of need, even if it is $JA100 for transport to visit a friend who may have no visible financial prospects. What the poorest individuals really lack is not so much good food, but these critical social networks. The cell phone, and its ability to record and recall up to four hundred numbers, is therefore the ideal tool for a Jamaican trying to create the ever-changing social networks that Jamaicans feel are ultimately more reliable than a company, employer or even a parent or spouse alone. This feature, perhaps more than any other, represents the critical economic impact of the cell phone in Jamaica.

Middle-class Jamaicans often remarked disparagingly about the amount of money low-income Jamaicans appeared to spend on their phone. They told us that, even when people came to plead poverty or ask for state relief or other forms of assistance, they made no attempt to hide their constant usage of the phone, let alone its possession. What came across again and again in such conversations is the degree to which middle-class Jamaicans had become completely isolated from the experience of those they were discussing. They simply had no idea why the phone, so far from being seen as a luxury that added to one's expense, had come to be seen as the necessity that was vital to mere survival. To other low-income Jamaicans, the possession of the phone was mute testimony to the need for keeping open communication with others, the very opposite to being a symptom of extravagance. Overall, the cell phone is about as effective an instrument as can be imagined for assisting in low-level redistribution of money from those who have little to those who have least.

Unsustainable Development

Esther Figueroa

Bauxite and tourism have transformed key areas of Jamaica's landscape. Even more noticeable are the myriad large all-inclusive beachfront resorts that spread across the North Coast. The state has promoted these sectors in order to bring in foreign investment and jobs. But their development has had dire ecological consequences. Existing environmental laws are not strictly enforced in vulnerable areas such as the marine environment of the northern and southwestern coasts, and this has led to much damage to the island's natural heritage. Local communities have also frequently suffered displacement and loss of business. Filmmaker and novelist Esther Figueroa is a member of a committed group of Jamaican environmentalists. In this section of her novel Limbo, *the main character, an environmentalist named Flora, travels with her partner Jerome from the cruise ship destination of Falmouth to bauxite mining communities in St. Ann and is struck by the social and ecological damage of "sustainable development" projects on the countryside.*

In the late afternoon, Flora and Jerome walk through Falmouth holding hands like tourists. They would take a tour if one could be taken, but those are only available when the cruise ships are docked, and despite all development efforts being focused on the new pier—the minister has said only the roads that are needed for the development will get attention—who knows how often ships actually will arrive, once, twice, thrice a week? There jutting out far into the sea, where once had been nothing but seawater, is the brand new Historic Falmouth, a concrete complex of shops, restaurants, and entertainment for cruise ship visitors—even a replica pirate ship with staged battles. The fishing beach is now a paved parking lot with imported palm trees and trolleys standing ready to transport passengers.

The courthouse is no longer cream-colored, but canary yellow, and has the colors of the Jamaican flag embossed onto its crown. The color choices confuse Flora, but since the original courthouse that was built in 1815 was damaged in a fire in 1926, and this one an inexact replica, why get hung up on verisimilitude? Why not paint it red to keep the duppies away?

They drive over to the mouth of the Martha Brae, where the river enters the eastern edge of Falmouth harbor at Glistening Waters, and walk alongside the river, startling herons into flight. The growth is too thick to get very far. They promise each other to come back and kayak to Jerome's, and he can pull her up the river.

They drive into the community of Rock to the little dock that holds three fishing canoes. They can't find their friend Monty who will be transporting them. His daughter says he "soon come."

At Benny's Bar, Flora is recognized as the Environment Lady, and as word spreads, people start congregating. Monty comes in looking for them and joins in the conversation, which is now raging about the cruise ship pier, the dumping up of the old fishing beach (they are not pleased with the new location of the fishermen's co-op and are now being charged a fee to park their boats), the dredging of the harbor (why would you be stupid enough to choose a shallow harbor prone to silting to park the largest cruise ships in the world?), the damaging wave action now that the reef is gone (has no one noticed that the old seawalls are collapsing?), the loss of the fish nurseries (they need bigger boats with stronger engines so they can go fish in Cuban waters), and they all concur that the luminescent lagoon will be next to go. Since many combine fishing with taking visitors out on tours, they will be financially ruined: no fish, no glow, no money. Their women have to be out in the hot sun under tarpaulin selling, because the Parish Council has mashed down the market and not built the new one that had been promised. They bulldozed the people's homes and dumped them in the hills where they have no water or on a nice pretty place to park. It is with resounding agreement they articulate that development in Jamaica is only for the Big Man, and them, the Little Man, can expect nothing.

Almost all of St. Ann has bauxite deposits, and the Dry Harbour mountains are a major source of bauxite mining. Flora has studied the area to death. A third of her dissertation and two chapters of her book focus on mining in these districts, places with strange names: Tobolski, Philadelphia, Alexandria, Inverness. But they are going to just outside of Gibraltar, to a place with the most lovely of names: Lime Tree Garden.

They pass crater after crater, pit after dug-out pit, and mound after piled-up mound; the red earth stains everything so that even something brand-new looks decrepit. The degraded soil can't grow anything, so the "reclaimed" lands are just endless grasslands and shrubbery, with the occasional sports and community centers. The bauxite companies are fond of football fields in the land they have hollowed out, so you will be standing looking down into what had once been a hill and find a field with goalposts and sometimes even a small clubhouse.

They drive into what unmistakably had once been a thriving community, homes with yards and fertile soil to grow food. Houses with delicate details of fretting, or carefully placed porches and verandas, that reveal the work of skilled carpenters and builders, but they have been abandoned for decades, windows shattered, paint peeling, walls fractured, roofs leaking. They stroll over to a large yard with a cluster of lime trees; only the foundation of the house remains and steps that lead to what had been the entrances. Flora leads Jerome to three graves that lie side by side. Moss has grown over the stones, and the names are difficult to read, but Flora knows who they are—her mother's family, the Turners, come from Lime Tree Garden—this home belonged to Mrs. Scott, her mother's primary school principal, and the graves are of Mrs. Scott's parents, Douglas and Agatha, and her sister Agnes. What had been the property next door, but is now a crater at the edge of the graves, belonged to Milton's maternal family, the Maises. Flora's mother's family home is up the road a bit, right where they are still extracting bauxite, a gaping chasm where the huge machines dig into the earth and pull out her insides. When the bauxite company bought all the land and they had to relocate, May was sent to Kingston to finish her schooling. She lived there with her maiden aunt Flora; all the rest of May's family migrated to England. Some of the people in the region took plots of land far away in Cockpit Country or moved to towns, but most got on a boat and left, and land that had supplied generations of Jamaicans with food was lost.

She doesn't want to go over to the pit; she doesn't want to look in. She doesn't want to see the machines, hear the jeers of the men at work. But she wants to show Jerome where she comes from, where her mother didn't get to complete her growing up, and why she never talks about her mother's family; they were gone, they were a hole in the ground, she never knew them. Half of herself had been dug up and sent away so that others could land on the moon, could explode rockets in the air, could live in the space age, could eat their TV dinners and their fast-food wrapped in aluminum foil, could have modern, clean, convenient lives, so that we all could long for buildings that touch the sky and for fast cars. "Donkey seh world no level," some of us are the sacrificed.

The Case for Reparations

P. J. Patterson

British prime minister David Cameron's 2015 visit to Jamaica was dominated by the call that Britain pay reparations for the damage done by slavery and colonialism. Such claims have a long history but had recently been given official weight by the establishment in 2009 of a Jamaican National Commission on Reparations and in 2013 of a similar body by CARICOM. Cameron's speech to the Jamaican Parliament did not address the issue of Britain's responsibility for slavery; instead he stated that "as friends who have gone through so much together since those darkest of times, we [the Caribbean and Britain] can move on from this painful legacy and continue to build for the future."

The reaction from Jamaicans was overwhelmingly negative. One of the most widely circulated responses came from former prime minister Percival James Patterson. Patterson, a member of the PNP, was the longest-serving prime minister, holding office from 1992 to 2006. In his open letter to Cameron, Patterson rebuked the British PM and called for "reparatory justice."

Dear Prime Minister Cameron,

We who belong to the Commonwealth Parliamentary Association and cherish the value of the Westminster tradition should seek continually to foster rather than diminish it.

Given the honour which you were afforded to address the Joint Sitting of Jamaica's Parliament on Tuesday, September 30, 2015, the traditional Parliamentary right of debate and reply could not be exercised by any of our Members who were in attendance. As I watched your presentation, knowing them on both sides of the aisle as I do, their good behaviour which you commended ought not to be interpreted as acquiescence in everything you said.

Prime Minister, the most noble intentions were jarred by those portions of your address which asserted that slavery was a long time ago, in the historical past and "as friends we can move on together to build for the future."

428 P. J. Patterson

Your host, The Most Hon. Portia Simpson-Miller, in her gracious
welcome referred to the difficult issue of reparation which should be
discussed in "a spirit of mutual respect, openness and understanding as
we seek to actively engage the U.K. on the matter."

You chose instead to throw down the gauntlet.

Mere acknowledgement of its horror will not suffice.

It was and still is a most heinous crime against humanity—a stain
which cannot be removed merely by the passage of time.

The attempt to trivialise and diminish the significance of 300 years of
British enslavement of Africans and the trade in their bodies reflects the
continued ethnic targeting of our ancestors and their progeny for discriminatory treatment both in the annals of history and in the present.

The 180 years of slavery in Jamaica remain fresh in living memory.
There are people alive in Jamaica today whose great-grandparents were
a part of the slavery system and the memory of slavery still lingers in
these households and communities.

Those 180 years were followed by another 100 years of imposed racial
apartheid in which these families were racially oppressed by British
armies and colonial machinery. The scars of this oppression are still
alive in the minds and hearts of a million Jamaicans.

To speak of slavery as something from the Middle Ages is insufficient. For our communities its legacies are still present in their memory
and emotions. To reject this living experience is to repudiate the very
meaning and existence of these people's lives.

How can we simply forget it and move on to the future? If there is no
explicit admission of guilt now, when will be the proper time?

You argue that Britain abolished the slave system and the credit for
this resonates in the British Parliament today and shows British compassion and diplomacy.

Where is the prior confession that Britain fashioned, legalised, perpetuated and prospered from the slave trade?

Indeed, the facts speak to a different explanation. In Jamaica the
enslaved led by Sam Sharpe tried to abolish slavery themselves three
years before your Parliament acted. The British army destroyed these
freedom fighters and executed their leaders.

This attempt to destroy the seed of freedom and justice in Jamaica
continued for another hundred years. In 1865 the peasants sought to
occupy Crown lands in order to survive widespread hunger. The British
government sent in the army and massacred those people, executing
Paul Bogle, George William Gordon and other Leaders.

Furthermore, the British Act of Emancipation reflected that the enslaved people of Jamaica were not human but property. The 800,000 Africans in the Caribbean and elsewhere were valued at £47 million. The government agreed to compensate the slave owners £20 million, and passed an Emancipation Act in which the enslaved had to work free for another four to six years in order to work off the £27 million promised slave owners.

It was they who paid for their eventual freedom.

The enslaved paid more than 50 per cent of the cost of their market value in compensation to slave owners. This is what your Emancipation Act did. The enslaved got nothing by way of compensation. The Act of Emancipation was self serving and was designed to support British national commercial interests alone.

You have refused to apologise. Yet your government has apologised to everyone else for horrid crimes. Are we not worthy of an apology or less deserving?

Mere acknowledgement of the crime is insufficient. The international community and international law call for formal apologies when crimes against humanity are committed. The UN has deemed slave trading and slavery as crimes against humanity. The refusal to apologise is a refusal to take responsibility for the crime. In a law-abiding world this is not acceptable.

Contrary to your view, the Caribbean people will never emerge completely from the "long, dark shadow" of slavery until there is a full confession of guilt by those who committed this evil atrocity.

"The resilience and spirit of its people" is no ground to impair the solemnity of a privileged Parliamentary occasion and allow the memory of our ancestors to be offended once again.

The Caribbean people have long been looking to the future. This is what we do in our development visions, but these legacies are like millstones around our necks. We look to reparatory justice as the beginning of shaping a new future. We invite Britain to engage in removing this blot on human civilisation so that together we can create a new and secure future.

ONE LOVE.

Yours sincerely,
P. J. Patterson
Former Prime Minister,
Jamaica (1992–2006)

These Islands of Love and Hate

Kei Miller

Kei Miller, a celebrated poet, novelist, and essayist, offers sharp insights into Jamaican realities. Miller has been at the forefront of a postindependence generation of Jamaican writers who look critically at the contradictions of the island's past and its relationships with Britain and the United States. In his writing Miller considers the weaving of these contradictions into the fabric of Jamaican life. He has a perceptive twenty-first-century vision that contemplates the gains, missed opportunities, and marks left by the island's bitter struggle for self-assertion. In this 2008 essay, Miller casts his attention on the powerful coexistence of love and hate in the Caribbean and Jamaica in particular, exploring how much of this reality is consciously hidden from those who see only the glossy sheen of the tourist hotels.

If you go on vacation to Jamaica, it is not likely you will get to see or experience it. Around the beachfront property in which you are staying, there will be a high fence. Like all fences, it keeps things out. Mainly, it keeps the Caribbean out. The problem is, you will not see the fence. The landscape artist did his job well—he managed to give the whole resort an illusion of openness—the beach on one side bordered only by the horizon, the perfectly manicured lawns on the other, opening out onto island life behind it, verdant mountains rising in the distance. The fence is invisible. Of course there have been tourists—you may have been one of them—who naturally perceived it, who felt for its weaknesses and, with a deep breath, escaped into the beautifully ugly, the violently magical, the tragically wonderful thing that is the Caribbean, the place where I grew up. But that story, of tourists who escape finally into their true destinations, discovering then that paradise is at once uglier and more amazing than any brochure could have had them imagine, is not often told. It is not often told because it is neither a good nor a bad story. It simply is.

Its opposite, however, is almost always a bad story, and one that is increasingly told. For there are moments when it is the Caribbean on the other side that places its large, dark hands against the fence, and feels for weaknesses. Sometimes it isn't tourists that break out, but the Caribbean that breaks in. How many times have we bowed our heads upon hearing this story—Catherine and Benjamin Mullany who visited Antigua for their honeymoon last year, Claudia Von Weis who went to Cuba, Melanie Rose Clarke who came to Jamaica for a wedding,[1] people who found themselves suddenly in the actual place they had flown to—saw it, experienced it, and died for it. In a way, their story isn't new, for hundreds of years people have been discovering the islands of the Caribbean and falling in and out of love with them.

I grew up in Jamaica. But if you ask me what it was like growing up on an island, I would tell you—it never felt like an island. It felt like a country, which is what it was. It felt like the world, which is what it was. None of us live in the whole world at any one time. We live in small portions of it, and we get to know that small portion. I would say, however, that a hotel in the Caribbean *is* like an island—because it is a small place cut off from the world around it. Who can blame the hotels for doing what they do and for being what they are—fenced off, cut off, sterile enclaves that offer Caribbean culture to their guests in the same way that they offer Caribbean rum—diluted, safe, with pineapples and a cute umbrella? Full-proof Caribbean culture can be dangerous, so for the evening's entertainment the tourist is only given a band of toothless men playing banjos and, throughout the day, smiling women in floral skirts serving mangoes and plantain chips. The tourist watching this parade of pleasant, smiling minstrels will inevitably comment on how slow and easy the pace of life is in the Caribbean. They will have little inkling of the struggle that is always underneath those songs plucked out on the banjos. Who can blame the hotels from shielding tourists from reality? This is the thing they wanted to escape from anyway. But hotels are inevitably controlled by big money interests intent on making even more money, and here is the sad truth of things—if tourists feel at least a little terrified of outside, of the real Caribbean, they will keep themselves (and their money) put. It is a careful balancing act, this—making tourists feel safe enough to come to the Caribbean, but not so safe as to venture into it.

There is such a large thing to say right now, about tragedies like the ones in Antigua and Jamaica and Cuba, and how the assurances given by Antigua's Canadian-born Commissioner of Police or Jamaica's British-born Assistant Commissioner of Police (as if to assure the world that the savage natives do not police themselves) and all the promises of beefed-up security around the hotels, how an unfortunate kind of tourism is being perpetuated in the Caribbean. The tourist is encouraged not to ever really know or to be suspicious of his host. But that thing is truly large and I do not know how to say it exactly. It would have to be a nuanced thing; it would have to make several allowances. After all, big hotels did not create the outside world they seek to protect tourists from: they only exploit it.

Besides, there is an even larger thing to say about the outside world that comes in occasionally—about the Caribbean. It is this world that, for brief moments, whenever there is a tragedy, many will try to understand. It is this world that will be explained through history and sociology, that will be summarized by statistics, GDP, indices of poverty, unemployment rates, homicide rates. But the scientific language of statistics and the language of sociology does not offer a template or vocabulary to talk about this larger thing that I want to talk about—about love and hate, and how these things have been brewing in Jamaica, if not the whole Caribbean.

I was born in Kingston. I was born in the time when the word was "love." It was the time of White Flight. It was the '70s. In those days, Jamaica's most charismatic Prime Minister, Michael Manley, mounted a stage and said four words which would become a mantra for the poor. "The word is love," he said. The word is love.

To repeat it now makes it sound like a strange, nebulous thing, a thing without any real substance or meaning. And that was its exact danger. It was a powerful thing that had no meaning. It was like an Old Testament prophecy—it took root in the hearts of the disenfranchised, and they believed that this word would change them and their situations. But it was only rhetoric. In essence, they were empowered into nothing. The strange irony is that the time when the word was love was actually a quite hateful time.

Many, of course, do not and cannot see it this way. After all, so many good things happened. Poor black people who had been previously denied so many good things, who had believed wholeheartedly in their wretchedness and in their physical ugliness, finally began to believe something bigger. To this day there are those who count the decade of the '70s as a success, and maybe in a certain way it was. Many Jamaicans found out suddenly that they could love themselves and who they were—the image they saw in the mirror. They could also look forward to their own possibilities, the things they could suddenly achieve. The big problem was that the government had given them all this hope, all this love, this wide sense of possibility, but little way of achieving it.

Jamaicans have always been inventive. Many decided they would achieve their possibilities for themselves. What helped was that at this very moment, the large-scale importation of illegal guns had begun. Take note of the following recipe: arm people with a message and then with a machine gun, and they will believe that the second thing can achieve the first; they will believe that guns can achieve love.

You cannot fault people for trying. They tried and they are still trying now. Of course, it doesn't work. And neither sociology nor homicide statistics can pinpoint the moment when the prophesied love turned into hate. As much as people began to love themselves was as much as they began to hate everything that had oppressed them before, every system that had kept them down—the police, the upper class, the middle class, the government, businesses, the school system, the English language. You see, in that hateful time when I was born, the time when the word was love, all over the island a resentful people began to commandeer vehicles and houses and parcels of land. They drew frightened owners from out of their homes and cars and farms, dumped them onto the streets, and the captors would say triumphantly, "The word is love."

In the time when the word was love, many left. Largely, they were white and Chinese Jamaicans who no longer felt safe. They took their capital with them, leaving Jamaica in an even sorrier state than it was before. Some of these class-war refugees settled in the lands of their summer vacations: Canada, America, England, even Wales like Jeanetta did. Jeanetta became a kind of mother to me when I first moved to Britain. Staying at her home one Christmas, I asked her why she had left Jamaica. I was too young to remember the '70s as I had only lived in that decade for its last year. So she told me, "I was just tired of saying I was sorry. I didn't know how to say it anymore. The island I loved turned around and hated me. They hated me for being white." That same evening in Wales, a neighbour came over and looked at my dark skin and smiled. She declared, "Oh Jeanetta, finally! A proper Jamaican!" I know this statement made her sad, and I realized that this thing which happened in the '70s—when the majority of Jamaicans began to love themselves and began to hate others—is a complex thing with many truths to it, and many repercussions, and a tragic history projecting itself into the future. I used to imagine Jeanetta back in Jamaica, and I would imagine her in the safe island of a hotel—fenced off from the Caribbean she grew up in and still loves, hoping that it would not break in on her. I only stopped imagining such a thing recently, because Jeanetta really has gone back. She lived in Wales for twenty years, but it is the Caribbean she has always loved.

I have switched places with Jeanetta, and sometimes from this new country, I look back to Jamaica and it is hard for me to understand my own deep love for the place, a country that is occasionally full of such indefensible hatred. And yet, there is something special that grows out of it all—this mix of paradisiacal beauty and poverty, of passion and politics. I understand what it means to be an artist in the midst of all of that—to be a prophet in the midst of Babylon. I understand the power of Peter Tosh, who wrote "Get Up, Stand Up," or Buju Banton, who came from Salt Lane, or Bounty Killer, who grew up "as sufferer but naah mek him children grow up tun sufferer." Or of Bob Marley flashing his locks and singing over and over, "One love, One heart!" And maybe it is this song, playing in the background of so many "Come to the Caribbean" commercials, that convinces potential tourists that the Caribbean Sea really is full of love. And it is. These islands are full of so much love. But sometimes that love goes so deep, it arrives on the other side as its opposite.

Note

1. Miller is referring to well-publicized cases of tourists who were murdered or went missing while on vacation. [Editors' note]

VIII

Jamaicans in the World

For more than five centuries Jamaica has been a country of migrants. Until full freedom from slavery in 1838, migration was largely *to* the island; the vast majority of those arriving came against their will, forced into slavery. Since abolition, Jamaicans have joined their neighbors in the global South in an enduring exodus in search of jobs and a better life. Many moved to North America. But large numbers of Jamaicans have migrated elsewhere. For instance, during the 1880s, around thirty thousand Jamaicans migrated to work on infrastructure projects in Panama and Costa Rica.

The United States–led construction of the Panama Canal beginning in 1904 recruited a foreign labor force that included more than forty thousand Jamaicans, 60 percent of the total. The vast majority of these workers were men. Others moved to work on Central American banana plantations and in Venezuelan oil and gold production. After World War I, seventy-five thousand Jamaicans migrated to work on the Cuban and Dominican sugar plantations.[1] By the 1940s, the United States' agricultural sector increasingly attracted the bulk of emigrants. The post–World War II period also saw the arrival of the "Windrush generation" to the UK.[2] Thousands of Jamaicans moved to the United Kingdom, which deliberately sought migrants from colonies to fill shortages in important sectors of the economy. For many Jamaicans, migration has been a repeated experience, as people set up home in new lands when opportunities become available. Those who moved overseas had frequently migrated earlier from rural Jamaica to the capital. And migration has had a profound effect on Jamaicans in Jamaica as well as those in "farin" ("foreign," the patwa term for other countries), producing a society that has long had deep and strong connections to many other parts of the world.

Migration patterns have also been determined by the policies of receiving countries, which have often changed at a dizzying pace. Until the 1920s, Jamaican migration to the US was relatively unregulated, but the 1924 Immigration Act instituted a system of quotas for specific countries. For Jamaicans the situation was worsened by the discriminatory 1952 McCarren-Walter Act, which imposed tight restrictions on Caribbean migration. Jamaican migration to other places was also affected by policy changes. During the Great Depression of the 1930s Jamaicans, along with many other West Indians, were deported from across the Caribbean as host countries sought to limit the impact of the economic downturn. Britain's postwar solicitation of migration from the empire (including the Caribbean) came to a sudden end in 1962 with the passage of the first of a series of Commonwealth Immigrants Acts, which restricted what had previously been rights of Jamaicans and other citizens of the Commonwealth (established in its current form in 1949) to settle in Britain. At around the same time the possibility of migration to the United States reopened: the quota system that had been instituted in 1924 was abolished in 1965. These shifts in state policies were usually driven by domestic debates that took place without reference to the needs of sending societies. Yet they have had important consequences for would-be Jamaican migrants.

Jamaicans have been "pulled" by the possibilities for work in other places, but also "pushed" by the lack of opportunities at home. Indeed, for much of its recent history Jamaica's primary export has been its people. Their migration provided a means of escape as population expanded without significant economic development. After World War II, increasing mechanization of agriculture and a turn to capital-intensive industries such as bauxite mining meant that the limited economic growth that took place rarely provided secure employment opportunities. The migration of Jamaicans has had a substantial effect on economy and society back home, as remittances in money (facilitated by the growth of international money transfer companies like Western Union) and in material goods (sent via ubiquitous barrels) helped many households survive. On the other hand, the enduring desire of large numbers of skilled workers and professionals to leave has had negative consequences for national development.

As the flow of material goods from the diaspora back to Jamaica suggests, overseas Jamaicans do not detach themselves from home. On the contrary, many return. Involuntary return migrants—commonly referred to as deportees—sent back by North American and British governments attract the greatest attention. But there has long been a community of voluntary return migrants of professionals and retirees who have reestablished themselves in Jamaica. Returnees sometimes find reintegration challenging, but as their numbers have grown in recent years, networks of people with similar experiences have eased such difficulties.

Jamaican emigrants have also made significant contributions to the

In the Canal Zone

Alfred Mitchell S.

Between 1904 and 1914 thousands of workers, most West Indian and many Jamaican, labored to build the Panama Canal that would link the Atlantic and Pacific Oceans, cutting the costs of moving goods and people dramatically. These workers followed in the footsteps of previous migrants to Panama who had worked to build the Panama Railroad in the mid-nineteenth century and an earlier canal project organized by France in the last two decades of the nineteenth century.

Work in the Canal Zone was dangerous, unhealthy, and exhausting, and black workers were subject to racial discrimination in wages and employment conditions. Known as the "silver men" because they were paid in Panamanian silver, they earned much less than the American workers who were paid in US currency. Even so, work on the canal was a source of significant income for West Indian migrants; back in Jamaica and elsewhere the image of the "Colón Man" came to symbolize the migrant who had made money overseas.

This description comes from an entry submitted to a competition run in the 1960s by the Isthmian Historical Society. The society advertised in fifteen newspapers throughout the Caribbean, offering prizes for the best accounts of life in the Canal Zone; it collected and published more than a hundred responses. Alfred Mitchell S.'s life story is characteristic of that of many Jamaicans who worked in the Canal Zone. He moved from Jamaica to Panama, and after the canal was completed he migrated to Honduras.

Mitchell S., Alfred; c/o Ronald Chessman, Electrical Dept., Tela Rail Road Company; El Progreso, Yoro, Honduras

I was brought from Jamaica at the age of 14 years old in the year of 1904, with my mother. I left school in 3 grade or 3 standard. Well, Mother was working and fortunately I got a job as water-boy on the Panama Rail Road docks, and same year Mother took me on the lines, to a place called Bas-Obispo Canal Zone. I worked there carrying water for a drilling gang; then I heard the transportation was employing youngsters for steam shovel checkers. There

West Indians working in the Canal Zone. To begin excavation, tripod pneumatic drills were lined up near each other and operated in unison. As of 1913, two men were required to operate each drill. The resulting holes were then loaded with dynamite. Even without the threat of explosion, the noise and vibration of the unison batteries of drills boring through rock and packed earth must have adversely affected unprotected ears and bones. *Pneumatic Drills, Culebra Cut*, photographer unknown, 1913. From the Panama Canal Museum Collection, Special and Area Studies Collections, George A. Smathers Libraries, University of Florida, Gainesville.

when I asked the yard-master at Lascascadas, then he asked me if I could read and write, I told him "a little"; that yard-master was Boreguard, and then J. C. Barnett. Then he gave me a book and Mother bought me a $1.00 watch. I worked there keeping around and my witts, also. Then the yard-master, J. C. Barnett called me one morning told me "you are going to do some braking on train, you are along with Conductor C. A. Shaw and Engineer W. G. Ford, they will take care of you." So I did as he told me. Well, I kept on being a brakeman for a long time, then he pulled me off the train and put me back in the office. Well, Sirs, I can tell you what I really saw and knew Bas Obispo and Lascascadas. Must really say those two places were the hardest spots, with a steam shovel; digging and meeting up against dynamite caps that were not exploded when the dynamite miners left, causes a lot of lives. Steam shovel pit men, they were called, also steam shovel engineers and crane men American Negroes and Spain Spaniards. I don't know how myself and my conductor did not get killed. It was an awful time.

Then I left there and went on working for the Panama R. R. Company. I knew General George W. Goethals and Mr. D. D. Galliard (thats why the name of Culebra Cut was changed to Galliard Cut). Mr G. W. Goothals would walk on the right hand side of Canal bank from Culebra Cut, stop looking at the works going on below, until he reached a placed they called Matachin, there board his motor-car by rail to Culebra, his residence and office. His motorman was an American by the name of Smallwood. Now, Mr. D. D. Galliard, he would walked down the Canal among drills steam shovel dynamite hole looking right down in 30 feet hole where they were loading dynamite. He would go to a steam shovel when it was not working and would ask the steam shovel operator "what's the matter?" The operator would made a reply "We are going to blow these big rocks with dynamite." He would say "good-by, take care of yourself." You should see Mr. Galliard getting out of sight over rocks, old ties and rails. That's what I see and what happen.

Life was alright, salary was small, but things were cheap. We did not feel it so hard. Lots of fevers: black water fever, typhoid fever and yellow fever. But Doctor Gorgas try his best by killing out a lot of mosquitoes, fumigating the houses using a lot of oil in the swamps or water that stand still, so as to do away with the malaria. So when the Canal was finish, boats passing through, people going home to their native land, I decided to leave, so I join the United Fruit Company and come on to Honduras, that's where I am making life right now.

A Diaspora Story

Lok C. D. Siu and Fernando Jackson

Anthropologist Lok C. D. Siu interviewed Fernando Jackson for her research on the Chinese diaspora in the Americas. Jackson's life encompassed multiple diasporas. His paternal grandfather migrated from China to Jamaica. There he married a black Jamaican woman. Jackson's father was born in Panama but spent his childhood in Jamaica. Jackson's maternal grandparents were of Portuguese, Chinese, and European descent, and moved to Panama from Guyana. Fernando himself was born in Panama, spent his own childhood in Jamaica, attended college in the United States, and finally settled in Panama.

I met Fernando through his son, a good friend of mine, who graciously helped set up the initial interview. We met for the first time at his home in a quiet, middle-class neighbourhood of Panama City. Being "part Chinese, part white, part black, and part indigenous," Fernando claims that he does not emphasize any one racial identity over the others. When asked, "How do you see yourself fitting into these different communities?" he responds, "Is there a category for mongrels? If so, that's the category I fit into." With brown skin and wavy black hair, he does not possess obvious Chinese features. Even his name, Fernando Jackson, gives no hint of his Chinese background.

> My paternal grandfather was Chinese and first immigrated to Jamaica before coming to Colón, Panama, in the late 1800s. He had owned a store in Jamaica, and it was there that he married my grandmother, who was a black Jamaican. After he married, he changed his surname from Cheng to Jackson in order to obtain a Jamaican passport. That's why my last name is Jackson, not Cheng. I am not sure why [my grandparents] decided to move to Colón. That was common back then, because my other grandparents also moved to Colón from Guyana. My [maternal] grandfather was Portuguese, and he married my grandmother who was a mixture of different backgrounds, including Chinese and

Caucasian. I don't have many memories of them. I only remember that my Chinese grandfather used to own a shop, and, from time to time, I could get a nickel from him. And my black grandmother, she was a nice fat lady who took care of us kids. My other grandmother was a good, caring person too, and my Portuguese grandfather . . . he left when I was very young. My father was born in Colón, and at a young age, he was sent to Jamaica for school. He didn't return until after high school, and when he did he worked in the shipping division of the United Fruit Company.

At first I was attending a public school in Colón, but because I was getting into so many fights with other kids, my father decided to put me into a private school. From there, I went to Jamaica. My father wanted me to learn English well, so he sent me to Jamaica. I guess he knew that knowing English is important. Afterwards, I applied for college in the United States, and I was accepted. So I left and spent the next four years in Chicago. So, in a sense, I spent much of my childhood and young adult life outside of Panama.

I was offered a job [in the United States] upon graduation; but, after spending six years in boarding school and four years in college, I just did not feel like being away from home anymore. In reality my ties to home were not strong, because [in] four years of college I had been home just once. Nevertheless, I did not want to stay in the United States any longer. Perhaps there was an unconscious desire to re-establish roots in Panama.

I have no trouble identifying with the Chinese community. However, it's not so much because of my Chinese heritage but that most of [the people in] my social circle are Chinese in varying degrees. Almost all the active members of Agrupa [Agrupación, a Panamanian Chinese organization] are my friends from many years ago. Setting up the organization was merely a way of providing an occasion for all of us to get together. People bring their friends, and they bring their friends, and that's how we deal with our membership. Many of the people in Agrupa went to school with me in Colón. We basically grew up together. In fact, we all got married at around the same time, and our kids were born within years of each other.

Going to Cuba

"Man-Boy"

In 1975 noted Jamaican sociologist and writer Erna Brodber conducted islandwide interviews of Jamaicans as part of a pioneering project titled Life in Jamaica in the Early Twentieth Century. *Brodber gave special attention to rural Jamaicans. Their revealing testimonies emphasized the diversity of life experiences among black Jamaicans and individual responses to more global issues of migration, race, political and social change, Garveyism, the 1907 earthquake, World Wars I and II, imperialism, and social activism. In addition, the testimonies provide unique insight into the texture of life in the island in the first half of the twentieth century. Brodber's interviewee is seventy-nine-year-old "Man-Boy," a rural farmer from Kellits in the parish of Clarendon. He was born in 1896 and survived the Kingston earthquake of 1907. Like many other young men of his background, he was enticed by the possibility of better opportunities for work in Cuba. Thousands of Jamaicans traveled to Cuba in the early twentieth century to become laborers in the sugarcane sector. In the following extract "Man-Boy" discusses his reasons for leaving Jamaica.*

So you went to Cuba. About how old were you when you went to Cuba?

19.

How you got to hear about this whole Cuba business?

Oh. My uncle was living in Panama, so he came home and I knew a few. In those days now Cuba open up with the cane business you know. You could get a lot of money. So I had decided to go to this Cuba, me dear. And in those days now we had sailing boats. It wasn't now like steamships and all like that. So the only way you could go is on a logwood boat and a sugar boat.

By a logwood boat you mean a boat that was going to sell logwood? So we were taking logwood from here and it was being sold in Cuba?

Yes. Sometime it go further than Cuba it go to all the islands, go to Cayman Is., and all that.

We were the people who were selling it?

Yes. In those days logwood was about £8 a ton. So I went on a sailing boat name the *Varona*.

About how many people were in the boat? How many people were making the trip over? I don't mean crew. I mean were making the trip over as migrants?

It was about 30.

So what happened when you reached Cuba now?

Oh, we came off at Santiago. Santiago de Cuba is the capital of the Oriente; so we came off at Santiago and we stop off there for the night. But that is not to say that we weren't kept outside there for, I think 2 days, 3 days, on the quarantine ground. Because in those days a medical service wasn't as good as now.

But you were fed by the host country, by the Cubans? They looked after you, or you had to buy food?

No, no. You have to look after yourself until you land; but they stop you off before you reach in at a place they call the quarantine ground so as to find out if you have, if the boat in general bring any disease or any malaria fever or anything. So the doctor have to come. I think that's how it went. And they bring the doctor come to that spot, and test everybody and you get vaccination and all like that before you go into the country. Because that was the system you know; because whether you bring disease or not, you have to stop a day or two outside the quarantine ground. And now when they prove that everything is fit now, they let you pass out and go on land. So after we land now we, in those days now everybody, you hear somebody asking about if you want to go to such a place and if you want to go to cut cane or . . .

Speaking Spanish?

Yes. And you have Jamaican men who interpret also so that you weren't in any trouble; for amongst the people who want you to go and work you have people who speak English and Spanish, so they will tell you what them say, you know. Anyway when we went off, after we landed there now we went to, the first place I went to, was place nearby to Guantanamo Bay in Oriente, I think the place was Bermita was the name of the place. A mill you know, and it was an American set-up too; so we had English-speaking people on it, that farm.

So how long did you stay in Cuba?

Well I stayed 3 years, the first time and I went back with me girl friend and—

From Jamaica? You took her from Jamaica?

Yes, and me finish up me 10 years—7 plus the 3 years, I spent and it was over there. I married over there.

What you mean you finish up the 10 years? Did you have a contract or something?

No. No. I spent 10 years there but I had a break in the first 3 years. I came out, came out for a 2 months, bring me girl friend over and we married over there and had me family there now, for the other 7 years.

What kind of work you did in Cuba?

Oh, I cut cane there for a few days and I do, the first thing I did was, used to do day work with the Americans when I entered the first time— brush yard or do some things around the stable and after that now I learnt that, cut a few, those are cane too, but I learnt that the best thing that I could get me money from was to drive a bull cart.

A bull cart? What's a bull cart?

The cart that draws the cane to the mill, or to the crane. Call it grua, in those days, in the language you know. Anyway the cart that draws the cane from the field, that the man cut the cane and the field, the cart that draws the cane to the scale house, that man make more money more than actually anybody in the whole set. Because the scale open at 2 o'clock and that man has to fix up the load of cane in the evening. And 2 o'clock the scale open so him is going to fight to get to the scale first and everybody fighting to get the first place in the scale. And after you weight out and you gone back to road, and the men know that load up here and you are coming back so they also wait out in camp and they are prepared to go with you, help you yoke up the bulls and to assist you in the first instance that you go, and them stay there and put up their lantern and cut cane until you come back and they load you again.

So they were doing quite a lot of the labour business for you?

Yes. But you work like an animal too because you have to hand every piece of cane. Then, twelve of them stay down on the ground giving you the cane up to heap. Buy you only have to pack it and fix it and tie it and step down and come and fix another lay, and cap it and step down and come and fix. And anytime the cart load up now, you drive off. And some of them could learn to yoke the animals to! So if you have a set of people who are working, that cutting the cane, and can yoke the animals, they can assist you in the night when you go the first trip because while you are yoking up one they are yoking the other.

So you never actually did any planting in Cuba?

No. No.

No actual farming. No cultivation. So when you came back here—

I either work around the centrifugals—they cure sugar. When the time is cold, we get into the factory. We work around the centrifugals because you warm inside, for you see you have electricity, electricity cures the sugar and steam bring it to you so the whole place is just hot you know. So in the winter we work in the factories, except when we were drawing canes.

Tropics in New York

Claude McKay

*Claude McKay (1889–1948), a well-known Harlem Renaissance writer, never ne-
glected his Jamaican roots. Born in Clarendon parish, he left for the United States
in 1912 to study at Booker T. Washington's Tuskegee Institute, then settled in New
York. As a poet and novelist, McKay gained extraordinary acclaim, including for his
novel* Home to Harlem *(1928) and classic poem "If We Must Die" (1919).*

*Throughout his illustrious career McKay remained connected to the West Indian
experience abroad. In this poem written in 1922, McKay's subject is the nostalgia
many immigrants in New York City felt for their Caribbean homeland. In a precise
and economical style McKay captures the contrasting landscapes of New York and
Jamaica and the sadness that reminiscences of home conjure for the immigrant.*

Bananas ripe and green, and ginger-root,
Cocoa in pods and alligator pears,
And tangerines and mangoes and grape fruit,
Fit for the highest prize at parish fairs,

Set in the window, bringing memories
Of fruit-trees laden by low-singing rills,
And dewy dawns, and mystical blue skies
In benediction over nun-like hills.

My eyes grew dim, and I could no more gaze;
A wave of longing through my body swept,
And, hungry for the old, familiar ways,
I turned aside and bowed my head and wept.

Little Brown Girl

Una Marson

The Jamaican feminist, nationalist, and writer Una Marson depicts the difficulties of displacement in this famous poem. Born in 1905 to a middle-class family in St. Elizabeth, Marson moved to London in 1932, where she worked for the BBC, eventually developing the radio programs Calling the West Indies *and, from 1943,* Caribbean Voices. *The latter became a legendary forum for Caribbean writers in Britain. Marson spent two years in Jamaica from 1936 to 1938, where she published the collection* The Moth and the Star, *which included "Little Brown Girl."*

Marson's work often centered the experiences of women, both in the Caribbean and in Britain. In "Little Brown Girl," which draws generously on her personal experience, she examines the racism and sexism black Jamaican women experienced while struggling to adjust to a foreign society. The poem narrates the encounter between the black foreigner and the white native from the unstable perspective of the latter. The white narrator views the unnamed object of her gaze as exotic, presenting her with question after question while reducing the empire to an undifferentiated mass of "brown girls," who might come from India, Africa, or "some island / In the West Indies." Yet the poem's narrative viewpoint shifts in the third, fourth, and fifth stanzas, where the "little brown girl" is briefly able to enunciate her own perspective, contrasting the Caribbean's diverse "friendly countryfolk" with the repetitive whiteness of London. Even the narrator is forced to concede that, despite the "lovely things" available to buy in London, it is ultimately a "dismal City."

Marson's use of color contrasts is one of the poem's most striking elements. Color terms here go beyond racial marking, to comment on physical space as much as on human skin tones. "Brown," "bronze," "copper-colored," "chocolate," and "black" are presented as ideals and "white" as unappealing. London is a "white white city," whereas the brown girl's homeland makes white people "get brown." The only whiteness to be found in the Caribbean is the "pearly teeth" of the cheerful rural ladies. Marson also uses the climate to stress the metaphorical separation between the two places. London is cold, in contrast to the physical beauty of the sunlit Caribbean; London's coldness leads to an enclosed, almost always "coated" and implicitly inward-looking population. The poem's sad closing line points to the harsh reality for the Jamaican migrant to 1930s Britain: the better life they hoped for was not to be found there.

Little brown girl
Why do you wander alone
About the streets
Of the great city
Of London?

Why do you start and wince
When white folk stare at you?
Don't you think they wonder
Why a little brown girl
Should roam about their city,
Their white, white city?

Little brown girl,
Why did you leave
Your sunlit land
Where we sometimes go
To rest and get brown
So we may look healthy?

What are you seeking,
What would you have?
In London town
There are no laughing faces,
People frown if one really laughs,
Everyone is quiet,
That is respectable;
There's nothing picturesque
To be seen in the streets,
Nothing but people clad
In Coats, Coats, Coats,
Coats in autumn, winter and spring,
And often in the Summer—
A city of coated people
But little to charm the eye.

And the folks are all white—
White, white, white,

And they all seem the same
As they say that Negroes seem.
No pretty copper-coloured skins,
No black and bronze and brown,
No chocolate and high-brown girls
Clad in smart colours
To blend with the complexion

And wearing delicate
Dainty shoes on dainty feet
That one can admire.
No friendly countryfolk
Parading the city
With bare feet,
Bright attractive bandanas,
Black faces, pearly teeth
And flashing eyes.
No heavy-laden donkeys
And weary, laden women
Balancing huge baskets
So cleverly on their heads
While they greet each other
And tell of little things
That mean so much to them.

Little brown girl,
Do you like the shops
And all the lovely things
In the show windows?
Wouldn't you like a coat
With a fifty-pound tag on it,
Or one of those little hats
In Bond Street?

Little brown girl,
Why do you look so hard
At the Bobbies
And the bookstalls
And the city lights?
Why do you stop and look
At all the pictures

A girl looks forlorn as she awaits a train at Waterloo Station in London. Photograph by Howard Grey. Bridgeman Images no. HGR3084879. Used by permission of Bridgeman Images.

Outside the theatres?
Do you like shows?
Have you theatres
In your country,
And from whence are you,
Little brown girl?
I guess Africa, or India,
Ah no, from some island
In the West Indies,
But isn't that India all the same?

I heard you speak
To the Bobby,

You speak good English
Little brown girl
How is that you speak
English as though it belonged
To you?

Would you like to be white,
Little brown girl?
I don't think you would,
For you toss your head
As though you are proud
To be brown.

Little brown girl,
Don't you feel very strange
To be so often alone
In a crowd of whites?
Do you remember you are brown
Or do you forget?
Or do people staring at you
Remind you of your colour?

Little brown girl,
You are exotic,
And you make me wonder
All sorts of things
When you stroll about London
Seeking, seeking, seeking.
What are you seeking
To discover in this dismal
City of ours?
From the look in your eyes,
Little brown girl,
I know it is something
That does not really exist.

Colonization in Reverse

Louise Bennett

Louise Bennett (1919–2006), popularly known as Miss Lou, was a pioneering folk-lorist, writer, actress, and poet. Bennett was born in Kingston, and after her educa-tion there she studied at the Royal Academy of Dramatic Art in London, the first Jamaican admitted to the prestigious school. A highly trained actress, Bennett was most comfortable performing Jamaican folklore songs and original work. From her days as a student in Kingston she was writing poems in patwa. Her reputation as a folklorist grew when she returned home and became a major cultural figure, ap-pearing frequently on stage, in print, and on the airwaves. She carefully researched the island's folk traditions and defended them passionately. She insisted that the country's cultural heritage should be preserved. Her efforts in this area inspired a generation of Jamaican poets and novelists.

A hallmark of her poetry was its reflections on Jamaican themes with humor and a keen sense of historical significance. This 1966 poem is one of Bennett's most recog-nizable pieces. Its subject is the mass migration of Jamaicans to England. The nar-rative of the poem, while specific to Jamaicans, could be applied to other immigrant communities from former imperial possessions that arrived in large numbers in the United Kingdom. The clever comic reference to Jamaican migration as "colonization in reverse" is punctuated by Bennett's insistence that this new pattern of migration is turning history upside down.

Wat a joyful news, Miss Mattie,
I feel like me heart gwine burs'
Jamaica people colonizin
Englan in reverse.

By de hundred, by de t'ousan
From country and from town,
By de ship load, by de plane-load
Jamaica is Englan boun.

Women arriving at Waterloo Station, London, 1962. The UK Parliament passed the Commonwealth Immigration Act in 1962, which limited the rights of Commonwealth citizens to migrate to the UK. All Commonwealth citizens not born in the UK or holding a UK passport were subject to immigration restrictions. The new act started on July 1. The "beat the ban" rush prompted thousands of Jamaicans to emigrate to the UK. They were among the last of the so-called Windrush generation to arrive. Photograph by Howard Grey. Bridgeman Images no. HGR3084883. Used by permission of Bridgeman Images.

Dem a-pour out o' Jamaica,
Everybody future plan
Is fe get a big-time job
An settle in de mother lan.

What a islan! What a people!
Man an woman, old and young
Jusa pack dem bag an baggage
An tun history upside dung!

Some people don't like travel,
But fe show dem loyalty
Dem all a-open up cheap-fare-
To-England agency.

An week by week dem shipping off
Dem countryman like fire,

Fe immigrate an populate
De seat o' de Empire.

Oonoo see how life is funny
Oonoo see de tunabout,
Jamaica live fi box bread
Outa English people mout'.

For wen dem catch a Englan,
An start play dem different role,
Some will settle down to work
An some will settle fe de dole.

Jane say de dole is not too bad
Bacause dey payin, she
Two pounds a week fe seek a job
Dat suit her dignity.

Me say Jane will never find work
At the rate how she dah look,
For all day she stay pon Aunt Fan couch
An read love-story book.

Wat a devilment a Englan!
Dem face war an brave de worse,
But I'm wonderin how dem gwine stan
Colonizin' in reverse.

A Farmworker in Florida

Delroy Livingston

Since World War II, Jamaican men—along with Mexicans, other Caribbean peo-ple, and workers from as far away as Thailand—have been traveling to the United States to do agricultural work as part of what became known as the Farmworker Program, or H☒ Program, after the visa that authorized their passage. Jamaican H☒ workers mainly traveled to Florida to work on citrus farms or sugar planta-tions. This was a system of temporary labor migration: H☒ workers' visa status did not allow them to settle in the US, to change jobs, or to bring family members with them. Nevertheless, the program was attractive to Jamaicans who had few options at home, and it was oversubscribed.

This interview with Delroy Livingston, who worked for four seasons cutting sug-arcane in Florida, discusses both the desirability of the work and the hardships that accompanied it. Livingston's account, featured in a book on migrant farmworkers in the US by anthropologist Daniel Rothenberg, suggests the pride in hard physical labor taken by many Jamaican men. Livingston emphasizes the roughness of his hands as a sign of his ability to work hard. Even while he stresses pride in being se-lected for the migrant labor program, Livingston's account of the physical, corporeal inspections undergone by men hoping to become migrant workers has disturbing resonances with earlier accounts of the inspection of enslaved people prior to pur-chase, suggesting some continuities in labor regimes over the centuries. Livingston's description of his Florida life suggests some sociability with the other workers in cooking, eating, and playing dominoes, but also a strong sense of loneliness and of living for the future, when he could return to Jamaica having earned enough to purchase material comforts: "furniture, a television, a VCR, a stove, a fridge, and a stereo."

Livingston's description of the "hardest work in the world" reveals his awareness of the racial hierarchies at play in the organization of this labor system, in which the only white man around was "the big man in the office." His account also speaks to an acute sense of exploitation by the agricultural companies who used many men's labor over decades, but then left them without any pension or other form of security.

From when I was eighteen I always tried to get a farmwork card to go and cut sugarcane in Florida. I go to the MP office and ask if they give me a farmwork card. Them always promise me. They take my name and say they call me.

I knew a lot of people who cut cane. They told me that it was hard work. I always like hard work. I like rough work. I like my clothes dirty. I'm not a person who dress in a necktie and those things. So, I always want to try cane cutting, to experience it. I respect a hardworking person more than a easy-working person. When you come in with a necktie, you're sitting all day, but when you're out there in the field, you work hard and appreciate your money better.

When I was twenty-four, they finally gave me the card. Then they give me a date to go to where the men who came from the U.S. test you to see if your body fit enough to cut cane. When you get there, you form a line with two or three hundred others.

Then the man question you. They want to see if you're tough. Them ask you if you feel that you can manage the work, and you answer, "Yes." Them tell you that over there it is very hot, and you say, "Well out here it very hot, too." Them say that over there it cold and you say, "Well, I try it." So, them say, "OK."

Then they look at your hand and your build. They take your hand, hold it, and squeeze the palm to see how soft it is. If your hand is soft, they say you cannot manage it because you have to hold that bill—the cane knife— and it mash up your hand. They say if your hand is too soft, the bill mess it up and then you can't work. If you tell them you're a farmer and you have a soft hand, they know you tell them a lie. When they look at my hand they say, "OK, that look all right." My hand look very tough, man, lot of corn in it, lots of roughness.

Then, they look at you. If you're too skinny or too fat, they don't want you. If you're fat, you cannot work fast, and if you're skinny, then you easy to die because the work is very hard. And if you were skinny when you go to work, you're gonna get more skinny because over there that work is hard. The first man stamp your paper and he send you on to another man who ask you the same questions or other questions. If you fail the questions, he send you out. They only select a certain number of men. I was a lucky one to go through.

Then they tell you that you have to go to a medical test in Kingston. There they test your blood, urine, pressure, and those things. They check you for sickness with a chest X ray and everything, to see if your body fit. If you pass the medical, then they sign all the papers, saying which camp you going to. Then they send you back home and say wait for a telegram. When the telegram arrive, you go back to Kingston, and they take you on a bus to the airport. Then they put you on a plane.

The first time I came on contract was my first plane ride. I was very excited. I tried to be calm, but the plane lift up off the ground, and then shoot up in the air. When I come off of the plane it was at night so I couldn't see a thing. We went straight to the bus and then off to the labor camp. I expected the camp to look good, but when I got there, it was just cane fields. As far as I could see, just sugarcane. I wonder what type of a place is this? All we can see is cane, the camp, and the sugar factory. It was like being in a desert of cane.

The camp is a long building with an upstairs and a downstairs. You sleep in bunk beds, one bed on top of the other. There are hundreds of workers on each floor. All you see are the same guys that you leave Jamaica with. Once in a while you see a white guy driving a truck, or a police officer. You're on a plantation, just praying for the five months to be up, praying to go home.

They wake you up at four o'clock in the morning to go to the mess hall. They give you two slice of bread, some porridge, and a cup of tea. Then you go to the field. Your rice trucks supposed to come there at eleven o'clock, but sometimes they don't reach you until one or two o'clock. In the fields, you don't have no time to even eat, not even five minutes, man. You don't come back until maybe three-thirty. You rest, make some rice, eat, play domino. It lonely, but you try to make friends. You sit around and talk. Sometimes you play cricket on a big playing field. When it Christmastime, you get up in the morning and they give you a ripe banana, an orange, and a piece of cake. That's your Christmas.

Cutting cane is rough work, man. I think it's the hardest work in the world. You have to keep your bill, your cane knife, real sharp. You have to have a hat because the sun too hot. You have to wear a iron hand and foot guard. Without the foot guard, you'd cut your foot off. You have to bend down and grab hold of the cane. You hold as much as you can in your hand and then you chop the root and lay it down. Then you cut off the leaf and put it on one side, and lay the cane on the other side. You have to do it all fast, very fast. If you don't cut fast, you don't make money.

When I was out there cutting the cane, the only thing I'd think about all the while I was working it, "I'll get some money, go back home, and buy a piece of land." That's the only thing I thought about. I always wanted a three-bedroom house. I never built it. I did achieve a lot of things by cutting cane though. I buy furniture, a television, a VCR, a stove, a fridge, and a stereo.

While we were there, all the people we saw were black. The only white is the big man in the office. And we don't see them. The big bosses is white and the white is not going to have other white men cut cane. The work is too hard for the white. The white can't manage it, so he have to get a black man. White people are weaker than the black. They use the black because the black can go all day long. White man will be boss, but he won't be cutting that cane.

In Kingston, they tell you they going to pay five dollars thirty an hour. This is what it says on the contract. When you get to Florida, they don't pay you by the hour, they pay you by how much cane you cut. They might pay fifty dollars for a row of cane, so a half row is twenty-five dollars and quarter row is twelve dollars fifty. When you come out of the fields, you get a ticket from the ticket writer that says how much cane you cut and how much money you earned. If you can cut fast and the row is fifty dollars, the ticket writer will write that you worked eight hours. But if you work all day and only cut a quarter row, the ticket will show you earned twelve fifty and only worked for two hours—even though you were out there for the full eight. The company rob you. You see, if they put you out for eight hours and you only make ten dollars, they supposed to build up your pay to about forty dollars, to make the eight hours' money. That's called "build-up pay." But the company don't want to do that, so they tell the ticket writer to put down the same hours as the money you earn. I always ask the ticket writer about it and he say that's what the boss tell them to do and they got to do what the boss say. You can't complain, because if you do, they send you home the next day. They'll claim you called Legal Aid on them. So you have to just go up there and learn to work fast.

When I just start to cut the cane, I used to earn a hundred and fifty dollars for two weeks. When I start to improve on cutting the cane, I would earn two hundred, maybe two hundred and fifty, that's after they take out the rice bill, the saving, and everything.

The workers are mistreated. You don't get a good bed or a proper meal. They don't respect you and they don't pay you right. They're very greedy, man. They make millions off the sugar, but you're the one in the field, doing the hard work. The companies don't care who you are. All they're interested in is that you get their work done. If you can't cut the cane good, they send you home. They told us that if they sent back a thousand today, they can get two thousand tomorrow, so it's no matter to them.

Now they've stopped bringing workers in to cut cane. I think that they should give us farmworkers some benefit like a pension or something. I'm not talking about people that spend a year of their life cutting cane. I'm talking about all those people who spent fifteen or twenty years getting nothing money and then going back home. They should get something from all that work. Just give them something, and they'll feel all right. But they'll get nothing, man.

Reggae and Possible Africas

Louis Chude-Sokei

Jamaica's culture traveled with the island's migrants. In metropolitan centers like London, where large numbers of Jamaicans settled, their music quickly gained an audience outside the Jamaican community. With the iconic success of Bob Marley and the international touring of his contemporaries, new audiences became more aware of reggae. Reggae's melodies, variety, and lyrics appealed to people from many nationalities who identified with its message of universal struggle against all forms of oppression. Reggae and its offspring, dancehall, now commands a large and devoted following even in faraway places with only tiny Jamaican communities. The music has had special resonance in Africa. During the apartheid era in South Africa, reggae or "roots" music became extremely popular among black youth who responded positively to its revolutionary image and veneration of Africa. Louis Chude-Sokei's analysis explains the deeper significance of reggae's appeal on the continent, arguing that reggae has contributed to multiple imaginings of Africa by Africans.

> Reggae is mine, reggae is mine
> Yeah yeah . . .
> Reggae is mine
> Yeah, yeah, yeah, yeah, yeah . . .
> —Lucky Dube, "Back to My Roots"

To return to a choice expressed in black or black masquerade, in his own words, Lucky Dube's switch to reggae was due to the acknowledgement that reggae was not simply a Caribbean or specifically Jamaican music. It had attained the status of a global or world cultural form and had carved out a transcultural and international space of popular dialogue, something that seemed to *invite* pan-African participation and continental echoing precisely due to its relentless references to and imaginings of Africa. For Lucky Dube and the myriad musicians and fans on the continent, despite its deep essentialism, reggae offered not an authentic or a true Africa but a series of possible Africas that could stand above and beyond the ethnic particularities of the continent and could enable the intrusion of merely literal Africans in the black diaspora's conversations and into its creation of foundational assumptions. At its most generously utopian, roots offered a vision of possibility that, because it framed itself in the language of African ancestry, functioned in contemporary Africa as a possible future and an enlarged, cross-cultural sense of tradition that masquerades and therefore authorizes itself via the mask of the past.

This new, possible Africa created a climate that welcomed and fed roots reggae and its globalizing of all currents of pan-Africanism and black radicalism in a music of popular protest. This was something that the continent would forever have to contend with because however alien it might have seemed as a concept or value, it ultimately authorized and authenticated itself in sound via the shared image, symbol and sign of Africa. It is this authentication of the various cultures, politics and identities of postcolonial Africa with the myth of a possible Africa that roots reggae sound must be credited for. No, it did not initiate this process, nor is it solely responsible for it (indeed, that process is the diaspora itself, structured as it is by sound and the black engagement with technologies of sound modulation). Considering reggae's often blithe indifference to contemporary continental realities, it should not necessarily be praised for it either. For example, due to a blind commitment to an unchanging *anciency* and a suspicion of modernity so complete as to erase the indebtedness to it, Rastafarianism has yet to be taken to task for its support for some of the continent's most reactionary regimes—most notably Ethiopia.

Yet despite, or perhaps due to, its contradictory and sometimes fanciful notions of black diasporic *anciency, roots* did take root on the continent in such a way as to help signal a transformation in how that continent both sees and hears itself across a global landscape. It is not an overstatement to say that this landscape continues to prove itself to be more attuned to speaking about Africa than actually listening to Africa speak. So it is not just sound and music here to be memorialized, nor is it simply the life of a remarkable musician like Lucky Dube, in whose wake new singers, producers, deejays and rappers emerge to continue redefining Africa in the language of the black diaspora. Herein lie not just centuries of the West's complex and varied representations and imaginings of Africa, but also the black diaspora's implication in this history of projection and construction, particularly since what we call the black diaspora is in fact an intimate component of Western modernity—not so much a "counterculture" as a constituent element, as collusive as it is resistant. However, despite its language of primal authenticity, those Africans seeking entry into the echo chamber of black modernity found in roots a language that, unlike most other languages, privileged them. In reggae these performers found not their roots or even their past. Instead they found a future, which ultimately means the ability to transform roots via the authorizing symbol of an Africa that they have grown to accept as inevitable.

Canadian-Jamaican

Carl E. James and Andrea Davis

Carl James and Andrea Davis address the crucial role that generations of Jamaican migrants to Canada have played in the development of Canadian multicultural-ism. They challenge the view that Jamaican migration to Canada began with the Canadian government's immigration policy changes of the late 1960s, pointing out that these changes actually intensified a centuries-old history of relocation from the island to its northern neighbor. Since the 1960s the overwhelming presence of Jamaicans among black foreign-born residents of Toronto, Montreal, and western provinces has had far-reaching implications for Canada's black population. This is visible in the popularity of the annual festival Caribana in Toronto, which is heavily Jamaican in orientation, and in the wide availability of Jamaican imported food in Canadian supermarkets.

Since Confederation of Canada in 1867, immigration has been seen as essential to boosting Canada's population growth, expanding the economy, and developing the society as a whole. The impact of Jamaicans in Canada, however, begins long before Confederation. The first group of Jamaican immigrants to settle in Canada—almost six hundred Maroons—arrived in Nova Scotia in 1796. They were followed in the mid-nineteenth century by an influx of "British subjects" from the British Empire. These pre-Confederation immigrants included influential Jamaicans, deeply loyal to the British Crown, who settled in British Columbia.

Until the 1960s, the "selective admission" of Canadian immigration laws, however, meant that few Jamaicans were able to migrate. Those who came were service (e.g., railway workers and coalminers) and domestic workers, and students. In the years following World War II, Canada—like the USA, Britain, and most other European countries—grew increasingly dependent on immigrants, not only to restore the population, but also to fill labour needs, particularly in the areas of domestic help (replacing women who went into the workforce during and after the war), nurses (to care for war veterans), and workers in the service industry. Jamaicans—particularly

Black Jamaicans—migrated to Canada during this period to work in these areas, and in so doing contributed to the racial, ethnic, linguistic, and cultural diversity that characterizes Canadian society today.

By the 1970s the numbers of Jamaican residents in Canada had grown exponentially. These Jamaicans were primarily professionals who met the new educational and occupational entry requirements—many of them nurses, teachers, physicians, and university students.

New immigration policies and practices that favoured highly skilled immigrants also meant that those Jamaican immigrants—entering Canada since the late 1960s with postsecondary education, professional skills, and occupational qualifications—better understood their rights within a democratic society such as Canada. These diasporan Jamaicans sought to benefit from former Prime Minister Pierre Trudeau's 1971 "policy of multiculturalism in a bilingual framework." This promise of a multicultural Canada likely motivated many middle-class immigrants to give preference to Canada as a place to resettle—instead of England and the USA, where hitherto Jamaicans had been going in larger numbers—with the expectation that their customs, values, and norms would be respected, if not accepted.

Today, Canadian society is made up of a population of people who are vibrant, educated, and technologically skilled—the majority of whom are first-, second-, and third-generation Canadians. Jamaicans are a vital part of the population, contributing to Canada's needs in education, healthcare, industry, domestic support, and service work. According to the 2011 Canadian census, approximately 260,000 Canadians identified as being of Jamaican descent, representing the largest group of Caribbean descendants residing in Canada—mainly in Toronto, Montreal, and Ottawa. Nevertheless, there is a prevailing notion that Jamaicans' presence in Canada—especially that of Black Jamaicans—is recent, or only historically accidental. This myth operated to deny the contributions of non-White peoples to the social, economic, and political development of the country. While Canada is perceived globally to be a welcoming liberal democracy, problems of racism and xenophobia continue to operate as barriers to education and employment opportunities and achievements, thereby exacerbating the struggle to realize the Canadian dream.

A Maid in New York City

Shellee Colen

Many Jamaican women in the United States work as domestics. Often initially un-documented, these women need the sponsorship of employers to regularize their sta-tus. They often live in the family homes of their employers, doing domestic labor and taking care of children, while their own children are looked after by relatives back home. Shellee Colen conducted intensive interviews with ten such women in New York City in the 1980s, including two Jamaicans. She uses these interviews to shed light on the emotional experience of domestic labor.

Most [of the women interviewed for this study] entered with visitors' vi-sas which they overstayed, becoming undocumented. To achieve their goals, including reunion with their children, they needed green cards. To get them, they turned to employer sponsorship in child care and domestic work, the main route for West Indian women (other than marriage to a permanent resident or a citizen, or sponsorship by certain closely related permanent residents or citizens). None knew of any West Indian woman (besides registered nurses, of whom there is a shortage in New York) who had been sponsored by an employer outside of domestic work.

Joyce Miller worked at her live-in sponsor job from 1977 to 1981. The couple for whom she worked, on the edges of suburban New Jersey, owned a chain of clothing stores. The wife worked part-time in the business and devoted the rest of her time to shopping for antiques, decorating, attending cooking classes, entertaining, traveling, and participating in her children's school. Joyce worked sixteen hours or more a day, was on call twenty-four hours a day, seven days a week, caring for the large house and three chil-dren for $90 a week ($110 at the time she quit). When she took a day off to see her lawyer, that day was deducted from her salary.

> The working situation there [was] a lot of work. No breaks. I work sometimes till 11 o'clock at night. . . . I get up early in the morning and I get up at night to tend the baby. I wash, I cook, I clean.

Isolation from kin, friends and community is a painful consequence of many live-in jobs. Immersion into a foreign world aggravates the loneliness and demoralization of many new migrants.

Joyce Miller found that the isolation of a black woman living in a white world had other consequences when people mistook her for a convict from the nearby prison when she did the shopping in town. When faced with a snowstorm on her day off, Monica Cooper paid several times her normal bus fare to "get out" of her suburban live-in job and come to New York. As she said, "There's no way on earth I'm going to have a day off and stay in there."

Despite the exploitation, several women feel gratitude toward their employers for sponsoring them. As Joyce Miller said: "That's why I give and take a lot of things. . . . A lot of things I let her get away with because I feel endebted to her." Like several others, she has maintained relations with her former employers, especially to visit the children.

In discussing the role of immigrant workers in New York, Joyce Miller said "they just want cheap labor . . . West Indians, or foreigners or what they want to call it." She indicated many ways in which undocumented workers support the U.S. economy, which include providing exploited labor, retaining immigration attorneys, and purchasing food, clothing, and household items to send home regularly to kin.

Monica Cooper pinpointed racism as a major influence on immigration policy and procedure, noting the differential treatment of different immigrant groups:

> I do feel the system is set up to make it harder for black people coming here. It's . . . to a larger extent . . . people coming in from the black countries or [some of the] Third World countries . . . that sense that they have special quotas.

In discussing the asymmetrical relations, every woman spoke most about the lack of respect shown to her by employers. What the worker experiences as lack of respect often appears to be efforts to depersonalize the very personal relations involved in the work and to dehumanize the worker in a variety of ways. On one hand are the personalized relations of the work, the worker's intimate knowledge of her employers, her responsibility for maintaining and managing the household to free its members for other activities, her possible residence in the household, and her nurturance, guidance, and care, both physical and affective, for the children. On the other hand are the wage relations of the work, and the depersonalizing, dehumanizing treatment of the worker.

The treatment here is terrible. . . . I think the employers should treat people much better because they're cleaning up after them to make the environment clean. They're helping them out. If they can do the work themselves, they [should] stay at the house or do the work themselves. Don't treat people like that.

Joyce Miller pointed out the unacknowledged need for the employee. She spoke of how her twenty-four-hour responsibility for the children and household freed her employers but at the same time was taken for granted by them.

She thought she had me there inevitably. She wanted me to be there forever. No one ever came there and stayed. Not because she's bad, but because of the work. The responsibility. It was a lot. She doesn't like to stay home. She had her baby [third child] and like in the space of two weeks she's gone. She's not there at day. She's not there at night.

At times, Joyce Miller felt taken for granted by the employers for whom she worked after getting her green card. They were a wealthy couple with an elegant co-op on the Upper East Side of Manhattan. The husband was a lawyer from a manufacturing family, while the wife, from a New York real estate family, was an aspiring magazine writer who was somewhat "spoiled" and very "untidy."

The thing I hate, everytime I clean the house, you know that woman make a mess. She throw everything on the floor. She leave all the cabinets open, you bump your head every time of the day. She leave all the drawers out. . . . I don't like things to be messed up. If I fix it, don't throw it down. If you use a thing, don't throw it on the floor. Put it in the hamper.

Food and eating are other arenas of dehumanization and depersonalization. Some employers left food for the worker to prepare for the children but none for the worker herself, though she might work an eight- to twelve-hour shift. Joyce Miller spoke of the classic situation in which, as a live-in worker for a young, wealthy family, she ate separately from the other members of the household.

I couldn't eat with them at the table. . . . I have to eat after they finished eating. . . . And then I eat in the kitchen. There are a lot of people who do that because they want us to know that we are not equal. That's my point of view. You are the housekeeper. I think the only reason why I was in their house is to clean. . . . Like olden days. . . . That's the part I hate. I hate that part because it's showing me a lot of things. You need things from me, but when it comes down to sitting at the table with you, you are going to show me separation there. I just don't like it.

The highly personalized relations of domestic work, especially that which is live-in, produce such phrases as "like one of the family." Joyce Miller said,

> Whenever they want you to give your all in their favor, or anyway to feel comfortable to do what they want you to do, they use the words "we are family." That's the one I hate. "You are one of the family." That's not true. That's a password as sorry . . . if you're one of the family, don't let me eat after you. . . . They say it to make you feel OK, but at the same time, they're not doing the right thing.
>
> Some of them don't even talk to you. They just want to know how their kid is or how the housework is going. They never one day ask you how you're feeling or anything else. . . . They're into their own little world and their own little life and leave you out, block you out like you're just nothing. And I think that really hurts a lot. Especially when people leave five, six kids in the West Indies and come here to do housework.

My Great Shun

Mutabaruka

Mutabaruka (born Alan Hope) contributed to dub poetry in the 1970s. This hybrid cultural form of verse drew on folk traditions, reggae aesthetics, and near exclusive use of patwa. Mutabaruka's trenchant poems on global black consciousness and the Jamaican experience made him a leading dub poet. Over the next two decades his fame grew thanks to his albums, frequent overseas tours, and hosting of a popular radio program in Jamaica, The Cutting Edge. *In this piece, Mutabaruka addresses the negative side of Jamaican migration (playfully rendered here as "My Great Shun"). It is also a comment on the fate of undocumented Jamaican migrants. The protagonist's "illusion" of an idyllic life outside Jamaica is shattered by the harsh reality of the situation abroad. In its place emerges a new dream to return to Jamaica.*

> Suh yuh jus fine out 'bout, de reality ova deh
> Lef yard seh . . . yuh wah run whey
> Now yuh a bawl . . . yuh wah cum back
> Betta cum quick before de door dem lack
>
> But yuh passport nuh up to date, suh yuh afi wait
> Si yuh grab de bait, si yuh grab de bait
> Dis a de dream yuh wanted to wear
> Now it tun inna nitemare
> There in de slums yuh sit ana wanda
> If de news is true or is jus propaganda
> Wid yuh Jamaican body an yuh foreign mind
> Standin' in de welfare line
> Tryin' to get everything yuh can get
> Neva knoo yuh coulda cold an sweat
>
> But yuh lef' tinkin' yuh woulda betta deh
> But tings nuh betta . . . betta weh
> Yuh visa expire, yuh afi tun lier

Yuh suh bold, sweatin' in de cold
You are so bold sweatin' in the cold

Bet yuh neva knoo tings was like dis
In de lan of opportunity an bliss
Bet yuh neva knoo seh
Suffaration deh every whey
But yuh lef' tinkin' yuh woulda betta deh
But tings nuh betta . . . betta whey

Now yuh tink of de lan yuh lef' behind
Quick san pullin yuh caught in de grime
In de lan of opportunity an bliss
Doin' funny tings jus to exist
Tryin' to get a piece of de pie
Livin' in their illusion an lie

Yuh so bold, sweatin' in de cold
You are so bold, sweatin' in the cold

Homecomers

C. S. Reid

Jamaicans living abroad are rarely disconnected from their home. Transnational networks have always existed between "yard" and "foreign" and are today maintained through remittances, seasonal work, and the sending of goods to family members at home in circular cardboard-reinforced containers. These "barrels" have become an omnipresent image of the contact that exists between families across the diaspora. Indeed, livelihoods can depend on the goods received in these barrels. The barrels sent back to Jamaica by absent parents represent psychological as well as material contact for all parties.

During special occasions it is not only the barrels that arrive but also Jamaican migrants themselves. Travel back home is especially busy at Christmas. The Christmas return by those who can afford it is a highly anticipated event in family life.

In this selection from 1980, columnist C. S. Reid highlights the importance of these "homecomers" to the Jamaican economy, pointing out along the way the contradictory treatment they receive at home. Importantly, Reid's comments were made at the end of a decade that witnessed a remarkable rise in Jamaican outmigration as a result of the troubling political situation.

This column would like to take the opportunity to greet those Jamaicans who came home for Christmas. They do not get as much attention as the genuine "tourists." They do not stay in hotels and so are not an important part of our "arrivals" statistics.

But in all the obscure little villages up and down Jamaica these past few days, much excitement and cheer have been brought to thousands of humble homes by Jamaicans who went away to Europe or North America to seek their fortune, and who have come home to pay a visit with the old folks at home.

Many of these folks are living in nicer looking houses than formerly, because those who went away did not forget. And this season they were able to go and do a bit of a splurge in the shops, because the "homecomers" also brought them spending money. Many usually ragged little boys and girls in the country sported fancy suits in the most gorgeous colours this Christmas because the "homecomers" cared.

Some have not been so lucky. The carefully packed barrels with their weird assortments of precious commodities are still sitting down at some northern airport, waiting on the airlines' promise to deliver by a date long passed. Meanwhile these same homecomers spend precious hours out of their meager vacation time in queues at Palisados and Montego Bay, hoping to receive and distribute their carefully selected presents before they themselves must go again, perhaps not to see home for another five or ten years!

It has been the misfortune of Jamaica for many generations, never to be able to provide a living for all her sons and daughters. They have had to get out or starve. By getting out they have rescued themselves and thereby also helped to rescue those who did not manage to "get out"—either by leaving them a little more space within which they survive; or by actively sponsoring brothers and sisters, and taking better care of old parents.

We have also hitherto been able to find someone willing to give hospitality to many of those who sought to get out. In the fifties and early sixties it was Britain. That country's immigration policies have become increasingly more conservative and racist since 1965. Canada and the United States, which used to be considered more racist by the "Liberal" Britons, have ironically been the ones to come to our rescue in recent years. Figures released by the United States Embassy here are very instructive.

I think it is very important that we do not alienate our fellow countrymen who are living abroad. We have succeeded in doing that to many already, and they have shown it by closing or running down their accounts with the Building Societies in Jamaica. This is sad. For we need our overseas relatives. We need them in individual families which are supported by them; and we need them nationally as a source of private investment and as a reservoir of acquired skills and expertise on which we can draw for nation building. Obviously the political parties are aware that they need the nationals overseas for their financial support to party funds!

Anyway, just now—To all our Jamaican "homecomers," who are making their living abroad, Welcome home. I hope you had a happy Christmas; and, wherever you go—a prosperous New Year!

Return to Jamaica

Emma Brooker

By the 1990s many of the "Windrush generation" of migrants who moved to Britain in the 1940s and 1950s reached retirement age. Some chose to retire in Jamaica, where they lived on pensions earned over decades of employment in British public services. They were comparatively well-off and could afford to build or buy houses, often on the North Coast or in the parish of Manchester. Return is often the fulfillment of a lifelong dream, but it is not always straightforward, as Emma Brooker's 1995 article emphasizes.

Since Brooker wrote, the situation of the Windrush generation in Britain has worsened. After 2010, British government policy toward movement of people became more severe and punitive. Because members of the Windrush generation had moved to Britain with full citizenship rights as imperial subjects, many did not acquire documentation to prove their status on entry to the UK or subsequently. In 2018 what became known as the Windrush scandal revealed that many British citizens born in the Caribbean were being denied healthcare or the right to work and that some had been illegally detained or deported. The scandal damaged British-Caribbean relations and led to the resignation of the home secretary, but the government's policy of hostility to migrants and migration continued.

In 1954, Eric Robinson boarded a banana boat in Kingston harbour with five hundred other hopeful young Jamaicans, and weathered a stormy three-week passage to Liverpool in search of "opportunity." Aged twenty-five, with an engineering qualification stuffed in his suit pocket and his chest puffed up with hope, Robinson had left behind his girlfriend and their baby daughter in order to take part, as a British subject, in the rebuilding of the motherland. "People said: 'Britain needs labour,'" remembers Robinson, who had seen the job advertisements placed in the Jamaican press by London Transport and the National Health Service. "These were great opportunities, and I was just following the others, part of a mass migration."

Like many Jamaicans who arrived in Britain in the fifties and early sixties, he had planned to stay for five years, save enough money to buy a plot of land in Jamaica and return to build a home for his family. In fact, it took him forty years, but last year he finally realised his dream and, leaving his daughter and grandchildren in Britain, returned with his wife to live in his birthplace, Yallahs, in southeast Jamaica.

He was not alone. Immigration from Jamaica accounts for the great majority of Britain's 900,000-strong Caribbean community, but it has not been the continuing stream that some people still imagine. An average of twenty thousand Jamaicans migrated each year to the UK in the mid-fifties and early sixties, but that flood has long since become a trickle. In 1994, a mere three hundred Jamaicans emigrated to the UK. The trickle of immigrants in the opposite direction, by contrast, is beginning to become a flood. Last year, around three thousand British nationals of Jamaican origin or ancestry emigrated to Jamaica.

This is the most dramatic realisation to date of a trend that has been gathering pace for most of the nineties (with an average rate of emigration of around one thousand a year). As more and more former immigrants— like Eric Robinson—reach retirement or receive redundancy payments, so the rate of return has accelerated. There are currently some twenty thousand Jamaican residents drawing British pensions—bringing in an annual revenue of £45m. And there are growing numbers of young people—some born in Jamaica, but most born and raised in Britain—joining the westward migration.

The British government seems unconcerned at losing these citizens; Jamaica is only too delighted to profit from our complacency. Returnees (a misleading but persistent term that embraces British-born descendants of Jamaican immigrants as well as returning first-generation immigrants), enriched by highly favourable exchange rates, have revived the island's building industry, often constructing lavish ideal homes for themselves. Indeed, they are now Jamaica's third biggest source of desperately needed foreign currency.

The Jamaicans who migrated to the UK in the fifties were mainly working class. Not so the returnees. The older generation now have their savings and pensions, while the younger generation are emphatically middle class: professionals, managers, small entrepreneurs. "People who were born in the UK or left here as small children are beginning to see the future in Jamaica," says Don Bryce, head of the Returning Residents Facilitation Unit.

The RRFU was created by the Jamaican government in 1993, the same year that import duties on cars and household appliances were waived. Bryce denies that the government is actively recruiting returnees, but it clearly sees the benefits of attracting skilled and professional people to the country. Derrick Heaven, Jamaica's High Commissioner in London, has toured British cities lecturing on relocating to Jamaica, and the RRFU keeps the CVs of would-be returnees on a database for Jamaican companies. As a result, thousands of educated, productive young people are now happily contributing to society in Jamaica rather than Britain.

The town of Yallahs is half an hour east of Kingston. On this harsh stretch of coast, Eric Robinson's newly renovated house and well-tended garden signal an affluence that marks him out immediately as someone who has spent time working in "foreign." Robinson now owns a farm in the hills which employs up to twelve local people. He looks back on his four decades in England with pride—"I served my sentence," he says—but he is delighted to be back in Jamaica. One of his great joys is to marshal locals into fund-raising activities—for a new county fire station, for example. "At the time of leaving England, I'd had enough," he says. "I wanted to get on to the next stage. I feel happier now. I can help other people less fortunate than myself." Yet there have been disappointments. After years of dreaming achingly of home, on returning to Jamaica he has found himself treated in some ways once again as an outsider. "In England initially when I wanted to buy something, I used to send a white person to the shop to get it for me. He'd get it at a reasonable price. Here I send a Jamaican who has always lived here. Otherwise they take one look at me and think, 'You've travelled, you've had plenty, we want what you've got,' and they'll charge me excess."

This experience is widely shared. No matter how "returnees" described themselves when they were in Britain—as British, as Jamaican or as Afro-Caribbean—once they set foot in Jamaica, they are, like it or not, English.

Brinette Rose, an Englishwoman in her early thirties who settled on the island with her husband David in 1993, was born in Coventry and had never left Britain at all until she visited Jamaica at the age of twenty-five. Nonetheless, "it was only in Jamaica that people started calling me English," she says. "At first I felt insulted, but now I feel there's a lot of things I learnt in Britain to be proud of."

The Roses have joined the growing community of black British expats who have settled among the wealthy Jamaicans of Mandeville, an affluent town perched high in the island's cool interior. Wet and temperate, smart and snobby, this town has been a favourite haunt of British colonials since they first seized the island from the Spanish in 1655. Today, seven-bedroom mansions with swimming pools and garages peep out from the tropical foliage cloaking Mandeville's circle of residential hills, along with more modest but still desirable dwellings such as the Roses'. It is easy to see why it is known as the Cheltenham of Jamaica. The Roses met ten years ago, in the

7–11 store on west London's Harrow Road. Their own parents had migrated to Britain with a view to improving their standard of living, but Brinette and David decided—five years ago, to be precise—that moving to Jamaica would give them a quality of life incomparably better than anything that they and their three daughters had or could realistically hope for in the UK.

For several years they barely saw each other as they worked for up to fifteen hours a day to earn money to make the move. Brinette worked as a care assistant for the local authority; David combined up to three jobs, working as an engineer for Leyland Daf, a minicab driver and a nighttime delivery driver. Finally the day came when they could leave their council flat—on a notorious, drug-afflicted west London estate—for the last time, and for the past two years they have been in Mandeville. David is running a small farm. They are, by any standards, well off.

"I felt that we were working very hard in Britain and not getting very much in return," says Brinette. "Put it this way: as black people in Britain, we couldn't go and live in the countryside. It doesn't seem to work. But out here we fit in." Except that, in some ways, they don't. One reason for the Roses' prosperity—and for that of many other returnees—is the devaluation of the Jamaican dollar which took place in 1991. This left many Jamaicans struggling to afford basic supplies. It also meant that the cost of the Roses' Jamaican mortgage fell—from £20,000 to about £4,000—and they have now paid most of it off in sterling. One pound currently buys around 52 Jamaican dollars (compared with 12 before devaluation); many Jamaicans earn as little as JA$800 per week.

The fact that they have reaped the benefits of what to other Jamaicans spelt financial ruin has meant that families like the Roses are viewed by some as pariahs. The result is an unfortunate siege mentality: like rich white British families ill-at-ease with their poorer, black neighbours (who, they suspect, resent them), they view many ordinary Jamaicans with fear and suspicion.

"I don't trust any Jamaicans," says Brinette.

"Coming to Jamaica has made you a racist," her husband teases.

Brinette protests: "I'm wary because the dollar is devalued against the pound: they look at you and think, fifty to one. The rumour goes round that the English have a lot of money. Some people despise you for that."

Two years ago, a number of returning residents were the targets of a spate of burglaries and attacks. Today, the doors and windows of Brinette's house are covered by metal security grilles, and a dog named Rambo guards the yard. "We don't have a gun yet," says Brinette, "but I want to get one."

"Many residents who have returned have expressed to us a feeling of alienation, a feeling of some hostility directed towards them," concedes John Small, a former assistant director of social services with Hackney Council who now runs the International Returning Residents Association in Kingston. "There's a certain amount of feeling, you've left and have done well and have returned to show off your wealth, and there's an aversion to that among Jamaicans. Perhaps there's some petty jealousy in there as well."

Whatever the reason, there are some returnees for whom the Jamaican dream becomes a nightmare. Most years, about fifteen families decide that they are unable to adjust to Jamaica, and make the return journey to Britain. "These are people who go there and expect a little England," says Mark Lobban, thirty-four-year-old chairman of the new British-based Organisation of Returnees and Associates of Jamaica (ORAJ). "They put themselves under a lot of stress."

Things Change

Buju Banton

Buju Banton (born Mark Myrie in 1973) recounts the difficult experiences of involuntary returned Jamaicans in this song. Since the 1980s, the US, UK, and Canadian governments have detained or deported thousands of first- and second-generation Jamaicans for criminal offenses and infractions of immigration status, placing the blame on the rise in Jamaican-related gang violence in metropolitan cities. The unfair association of largely working-class Jamaicans with gang- and drug-related crimes led to indiscriminate treatment of undocumented Jamaican migrants. Forced returned migrants were also stigmatized in Jamaica, where they were often assumed to be gangsters and criminals. In reality, studies of involuntary returned persons conclude that most of those returned to Jamaica have committed very minor crimes or immigration offenses.[1] For many forced to return, their drop in status from migrant to returnee is a source of ridicule by Jamaicans. Banton's song "Deportees (Things Change)" chastises the spendthrift Jamaican migrant who, in selfish pursuit of material gain in the United States, neglects care of his family in Jamaica. Forced to "start from scratch again," the deportee in the song is shamed for returning without anything to show for his time abroad.

Buju Banton is a controversial figure. He quickly became a legend in dancehall reggae when he first appeared in the early 1990s and broke Bob Marley's record for the most number one songs on the local charts. He remains a hugely popular artist in Jamaica and overseas. However, he attracted strong criticism abroad and from some Jamaicans for the violently homophobic lyrics of his early song "Boom Bye Bye," recorded when he was a teenager. In 2011 he was imprisoned in the United States for seven years for conspiracy to smuggle narcotics, and on his release in December 2018 he was forced to return to Jamaica in a case of life partially imitating art. He received a hero's welcome on his return.

Yes, well, tek dis from Gargamel,
uddawise known as Buju
Anytime yuh go a foreign
neva yuh dare t'row stone behind you

'Ca wicked t'ings will tek yuh
Watch mi nuh! Yuh hear!

[Chorus:]
T'ings change, now unno see seh life hard
Yuh neva use to sen' no money come a yard
Yuh wretch you, yuh spen' di whole a it abroad
Squander yuh money now yuh livin' like dog

Bwoy get deport come dung inna one pants
Bruk an' have no money
But mi nuh response
No abiding city, wan pressure fi mi ranch
An' when 'im dey a foreign 'im did important
But 'im neva did a look back, neva did a glance
Neva know 'im would a tumble ova like an avalanche
Mama dung inna di hole, an' 'im don't buy her a lamp
Not a line, not a letter, nor a fifty cent stamp
Him father want a shoes an' cannot go to remittance
When mi hear di bwoy get dep, yuh know mi vibes cramp
Send 'im back
Uncle Sam, cause 'im deh dey an' a ramp
An nuff yout' out 'ya wan drop inna di camp

[Chorus]

Wan' drop inna di snow from about seventy-nine
Neva get di chance cause it wasn't my time
An' mi hear yuh dey a foreign an' commit di most crime
An' mek a bag a money when mi couldn't mek a dime
(re)memba one time gon how yuh used to brag
Benz an' Lexus a wey yuh did have
Clarks and Bally whey yuh got in a bag
Clothes wey yuh no wear still have on nametag
Now yuh crash up, now yuh mash up, yuh neva did a plan
Yuh neva pay de check fi lay di foundation, mi holla

[Chorus]

Back together again, mi baby fren'
Dust off yuh clothes, an' start from scratch again
Back together again, mi baby fren'
Dust off yuh clothes, an' start, nuh true

Caught up in di world of di rich and di famous
Golden livity it haffi luxurious
Have all di girls in di world in a surplus
Massage yuh shoulder, bump some a bust
Request yuh coffee an' she pour it from di thermos
Cool an' kick back an' just a watch *Delirious*
Now yuh sorry, yuh neva (re)memba
Di almighty one in yuh days of splendor

[Chorus]

Note

1. Bernard Headley, "Giving Critical Context to the Deportee Phenomenon," *Social Justice* 22, no. 1 (2006): 40–56.

Jamaica to the World

Ingrid Brown

Jamaica's fiftieth independence anniversary coincided with one of the nation's greatest international moments: Jamaica's tally of a record twelve medals won by eighteen athletes in the 2012 Summer Olympics. Significantly the games were held in London, capital of the former empire. The Jamaican team, led by the charismatic Usain Bolt, fulfilled the extraordinary expectations of their native land and an ador- ing world.

    In Jamaica, the official Jamaica 50 festivities were grand. At the National Arena and in the nearby car park of the National Stadium, huge screens were set up for at- tendees to watch the track-and-field events live. For a full week this "independence village" was a beehive attracting thousands of Jamaicans from across the island and the diaspora. The village featured musical performances, Jamaican food stalls, games, souvenirs, and heritage boards that surveyed the entire history and heritage of the island since the Taíno.

    The highlight of the independence week was the 100-meter men's sprint finals, which almost by destiny, took place in London on the night of 5 August, the eve of In- dependence Day. The victory of Bolt and Yohan Blake, who placed first and second in the final, heightened the emotion of an event that was already full of meaning. For many Jamaicans at home and abroad Jamaica 50 will be memorable for the 6 August medal ceremony, when two Jamaican flags were hoisted in the Olympic stadium in London and the national anthem boomed from loud speakers. In many ways it was a reminder that the small island's triumphs stood high above everything else in its history.

    Jamaicans overseas made the most of the anniversary. Unsurprisingly, the mas- sive Jamaican community in the United Kingdom was ecstatic. This report from a Jamaican correspondent in London captures the infectious mood that accompanied that moment of immense patriotism.

Jamaicans, adorned from head to toe in black, green and gold, took to Lon- don streets last night with pride to celebrate Usain Bolt and Yohan Blake's gold and silver medal victories, respectively, in the long-awaited Olympic men's 100-metre finals here.

Pockets of Jamaicans gathered at city squares, parks, bars, and anywhere big-screen TVs were set up to blow whistles, wave flags and cheer on the athletes to victory in true Jamaican style.

At the entrance to the Olympic Park in Stratford, a group of Jamaicans formed a cheerleading team as they danced and coined their own lyrics to popular Jamaican songs, much to the delight of hundreds of passengers passing through the nearby train station.

Shouts of "Usain Bolt!" echoed throughout the bustling town square as the cheering group grew larger by the minute with more Jamaicans stopping by to join the celebrations.

Passersby, some draped in other countries' flags, stopped to celebrate with the Jamaicans, taking pictures with the Jamaican flag and doing Bolt's famous signature "To the world" pose.

Strangers who would never exchange a word struck up lively conversations on the streets and inside the train station as the whole world seemed to be celebrating Jamaica's victory.

International media stopped to get sound bites from the cheering crowd and even the usually stern policemen surrounding the park seemed to relax for the moment as the bustling train station was transformed into a festive venue.

"Jamaica ah 50 years tomorrow and this ah present," shouted Meshack McLean as he led the group in the singing of Tony Rebel's "Sweet Jamdown."

"Me love the unity and the togetherness with people of all race who are here to celebrate with us," he told the *Jamaica Observer*.

Sharlene Dunns was in her element as she was asked to pose for several pictures by non-Jamaicans who were fascinated with her outfit, which consisted of everything from black, green and gold hair to similarly coloured shoes.

"I am so proud to be a Jamaican, extremely proud," she beamed as she wrapped a flag close around her.

At the Maryland School, a few miles away, many Jamaicans left their flat-screen TVs at home and crammed into the school hall to watch the race, which was streamed via computer on a projector screen.

"I just wanted to be somewhere watching it with a lot of other Jamaicans because I knew we would have something to celebrate," said Marlene Shaw.

Michael Coore and Garvis Brady, who also came out in their Jamaican colours, said they were extremely proud to be Jamaicans in London at this time.

Evangelist Denise Chambers said she has not owned a television for years now, after she made the personal choice not to. However, it took a race like last night's to get her out to watch the event on big screen.

"It was fantastic, and I am glad Bolt came through because I was rooting for him," she said.

Collin Robinson said watching the race made him wish he was in Jamaica now to celebrate with the country.

"I am feeling very proud," he said.

Suggestions for Further Reading

General Works

Alleyne, Mervyn. *Roots of Jamaican Culture*. London: Pluto, 1988.

Arbell, Mordehay. *The Portuguese Jews of Jamaica*. Kingston: Canoe Press, 2000.

Besson, Jean. *Martha Brae's Two Histories: European Expansion and Caribbean Culture-Building in Jamaica*. Chapel Hill: University of North Carolina Press, 2002.

Black, Clinton V. *The History of Jamaica*. London: Collins Educational, 1983.

Cooper, Carolyn. *Noises in the Blood: Orality, Gender and the "Vulgar" Body of Jamaican Popular Culture*. London: Macmillan Caribbean, 1993.

Craton, Michael, and James Walvin. *A Jamaican Plantation: The History of Worthy Park, 1670–1970*. London: W. H. Allen, 1970.

Delle, James A., Mark W. Hauser, and Douglas V. Armstrong. *Out of Many, One People: The Historical Archaeology of Colonial Jamaica*. Tuscaloosa: University of Alabama Press, 2011.

Higman, B. W. *Jamaican Food: History, Biology, Culture*. Kingston: University of the West Indies Press, 2008.

Lalla, Barbara, and Jean D'Costa, eds. *Language in Exile: Three Hundred Years of Jamaican Creole*. Tuscaloosa: University of Alabama Press, 1990.

Le Page, R. B. (Robert Brock), and D. De Camp. *Jamaican Creole: An Historical Introduction to Jamaican Creole*. London: Macmillan; New York: St. Martin's, 1960.

Lewin, Olive. *Rock It Come Over: The Folk Music of Jamaica*. Kingston: University of the West Indies Press, 2000.

Marshall, Emily Zobel. *Anansi's Journey: A Story of Jamaican Cultural Resistance*. Kingston: University of the West Indies Press, 2012.

Stewart, Dianne M. *Three Eyes for the Journey: African Dimensions of the Jamaican Religious Experience*. Oxford: Oxford University Press, 2005.

Part I: Becoming Jamaica

Allsworth-Jones, P. *Pre-Columbian Jamaica: Caribbean Archaeology and Ethnohistory*. Tuscaloosa: University of Alabama Press, 2008.

Atkinson, Lesley-Gail. *The Earliest Inhabitants: The Dynamics of the Jamaican Taíno*. Kingston: University of the West Indies Press, 2006.

Hughes, Ben, and T. D. Dungan. *Apocalypse 1692: Empire, Slavery, and the Great Port Royal Earthquake*. Yardley, PA: Westholme, 2017.

Morales Padrón, Francisco. *Spanish Jamaica*. Translated by Patrick Bryan. Kingston: Ian Randle, 2003.

Pawson, Michael, and David Buisseret. *Port Royal, Jamaica*. Rev. ed. Kingston: University of the West Indies Press, 2000.

Pestana, Carla Gardina. *The English Conquest of Jamaica: Oliver Cromwell's Bid for Empire*. Cambridge, MA: Belknap Press of Harvard University Press, 2017.

Wheat, David. *Atlantic Africa and the Spanish Caribbean, 1570–1640*. Chapel Hill: University of North Carolina Press, 2016.

Wilson, Samuel M. *The Archaeology of the Caribbean*. Cambridge: Cambridge University Press, 2007.

Part II: From English Conquest to Slave Society

Amussen, Susan Dwyer. *Caribbean Exchanges: Slavery and the Transformation of English Society, 1640–1700*. Chapel Hill: University of North Carolina Press, 2007.

Bilby, Kenneth M. *True-Born Maroons*. Gainesville: University Press of Florida, 2005.

Brown, Vincent. *Tacky's Revolt: The Story of an Atlantic Slave War*. Cambridge, MA: Harvard University Press, 2020.

Burnard, Trevor G., and John Garrigus. *The Plantation Machine: Atlantic Capitalism in French Saint-Domingue and British Jamaica*. Philadelphia: University of Pennsylvania Press, 2016.

Dunn, Richard S. *Sugar and Slaves: The Rise of the Planter Class in the English West Indies, 1624–1713*. New York: Norton, 1973.

Dunn, Richard S. *A Tale of Two Plantations: Slave Life and Labor in Jamaica and Virginia*. Cambridge, MA: Harvard University Press, 2014.

Greene, Jack P. *Settler Jamaica in the 1750s: A Social Portrait*. Early American Histories. Charlottesville: University of Virginia Press, 2016.

Mulcahy, Matthew. *Hubs of Empire: The Southeastern Lowcountry and British Caribbean*. Baltimore: Johns Hopkins University Press, 2014.

Musical Passage: A Voyage to 1688 Jamaica. http://www.musicalpassage.org/.

Part III: Enlightenment Slavery

Brathwaite, Edward. *The Development of Creole Society in Jamaica, 1770–1820*. Oxford: Clarendon, 1971.

Brown, Vincent. *The Reaper's Garden: Death and Power in the World of Atlantic Slavery*. Cambridge, MA: Harvard University Press, 2008.

Gikandi, Simon. *Slavery and the Culture of Taste*. Princeton, NJ: Princeton University Press, 2014.

Heuman, Gad. *Between Black and White: Race, Politics, and the Free Coloreds in Jamaica, 1792–1865*. Westport, CT: Greenwood, 1981.

Higman, B. W. *Plantation Jamaica, 1750–1850: Capital and Control in a Colonial Economy*. Kingston: University of the West Indies Press, 2008.

Livesay, Daniel. *Children of Uncertain Fortune: Mixed-Race Jamaicans in Britain and the Atlantic Family, 1733–1833*. Chapel Hill: University of North Carolina Press, 2018.

Nelson, Louis P. *Architecture and Empire in Jamaica*. New Haven, CT: Yale University Press, 2016.

Newman, Brooke N. *A Dark Inheritance: Blood, Race, and Sex in Colonial Jamaica*. New Haven, CT: Yale University Press, 2018.

Patterson, Orlando. *The Sociology of Slavery: An Analysis of the Origins, Development and Structure of Negro Slave Society in Jamaica*. London: Macgibbon and Kee, 1967.

Petley, Christer. *White Fury: A Jamaican Slaveholder and the Age of Revolution*. Oxford: Oxford University Press, 2018.

Scott, Julius Sherrard. *The Common Wind: Afro-American Currents in the Age of the Haitian Revolution*. London: Verso, 2018.

Turner, Mary. *Slaves and Missionaries: The Disintegration of Jamaican Slave Society, 1787–1834*. Urbana: University of Illinois Press, 1982.

Turner, Sasha. *Contested Bodies: Pregnancy, Childrearing, and Slavery in Jamaica, 1770–1834*. Philadelphia: University of Pennsylvania Press, 2017.

Vasconcellos, Colleen A. *Slavery, Childhood, and Abolition in Jamaica, 1788–1838*. Athens: University of Georgia Press, 2015.

Part IV: Colonial Freedom

Barringer, T. J., Gillian Forrester, Barbaro Martinez-Ruiz, and Yale Center for British Art. *Art and Emancipation in Jamaica: Isaac Mendes Belisario and His Worlds*. New Haven, CT: Yale Center for British Art in association with Yale University Press, 2007.

Brodber, Erna. *The Second Generation of Freemen in Jamaica, 1907–1944*. Gainesville: University Press of Florida, 2004.

Eisner, Gisela. *Jamaica, 1830–1930: A Study in Economic Growth*. Westport, CT: Greenwood, 1961.

Hall, Catherine. *Civilising Subjects: Metropole and Colony in the English Imagination, 1830–1867*. Cambridge: Polity, 2002.

Hall, Douglas. *Free Jamaica, 1838–1865: An Economic History*. New Haven, CT: Yale University Press, 1959.

Heuman, Gad. *"The Killing Time": The Morant Bay Rebellion in Jamaica*. London: Macmillan Caribbean, 1994.

Holt, Thomas C. *The Problem of Freedom: Race, Labor, and Politics in Jamaica and Britain, 1832–1938*. Baltimore: Johns Hopkins University Press, 1992.

Paton, Diana. *No Bond but the Law: Punishment, Race, and Gender in Jamaican State Formation, 1780–1870*. Durham, NC: Duke University Press, 2004.

Satchell, Veront M. *From Plots to Plantations: Land Transactions in Jamaica, 1866–1900*. Mona, Jamaica: Institute for Social and Economic Research, University of the West Indies, 1990.

Sheller, Mimi. *Democracy after Slavery: Black Publics and Peasant Radicalism in Haiti and Jamaica*. London: Macmillan, 2000.

Shepherd, Verene A. *Transients to Settlers: The Experience of Indians in Jamaica, 1845–1950*. Leeds: Peepal Tree, 1994.

Smith, Matthew J. *Liberty, Fraternity, Exile: Haiti and Jamaica after Emancipation*. Chapel Hill: University of North Carolina Press, 2014.

Part V: Jamaica Arise

Bean, Dalea. *Jamaican Women and the World Wars*. New York: Springer Berlin Heidelberg, 2018.

Bennett, Wycliffe, and Hazel Bennett. *Jamaican Theatre: Highlights of the Performing Arts in the Twentieth Century*. Kingston: University of the West Indies Press, 2011.

Bryan, Patrick. *The Jamaican People, 1880–1902: Race, Class and Social Control*. London: Macmillan Caribbean, 1991.

Chevannes, Barry. *Rastafari: Roots and Ideology*. Syracuse, NY: Syracuse University Press, 1995.

Ewing, Adam. *Age of Garvey: How a Jamaican Activist Created a Mass Movement and Changed Global Black Politics*. Princeton, NJ: Princeton University Press, 2016.

Hill, Robert A. *Dread History: Leonard P. Howell and Millenarian Visions in the Early Rastafarian Religion*. Chicago: Research Associates School Times Publications / Frontline Distribution Int'l, 2001.

Moore, Brian L., and Michele A. Johnson. *Neither Led nor Driven: Contesting British Cultural Imperialism in Jamaica, 1865–1920*. Kingston: University of the West Indies Press, 2004.

Moore, Brian L., and Michele A. Johnson. *"They Do as They Please": The Jamaican Struggle for Cultural Freedom after Morant Bay*. Kingston: University of the West Indies Press, 2011.

Palmer, Colin A. *Freedom's Children: The 1938 Labor Rebellion and the Birth of Modern Jamaica*. Kingston: Ian Randle, 2014.

Palmer, Colin A. *Inward Yearnings: Jamaica's Journey to Nationhood*. Kingston: University of the West Indies Press, 2016.

Post, Ken. *Arise Ye Starvelings: The Jamaican Labour Rebellion of 1938 and Its Aftermath*. The Hague: Martinus Nijhoff, 1978.

Post, Ken. *Strike the Iron: A Colony at War. Jamaica, 1939–1945*. 2 vols. The Hague: Humanities Press, 1981.

Taylor, Frank Fonda. *To Hell with Paradise: A History of the Jamaican Tourist Industry*. Pittsburgh: University of Pittsburgh Press, 1993.

Timm, Birte. *Nationalists Abroad: The Jamaica Progressive League and the Foundations of Jamaican Independence*. Kingston: Ian Randle, 2016.

Part VI: Independence and After

Beckford, George. *Persistent Poverty: Underdevelopment in Plantation Economies of the Third World*. New York: Oxford University Press, 1972.

Bradley, Lloyd. *This Is Reggae Music: The Story of Jamaica's Music*. London: Grove, 2001.

Bryan, Patrick. *Edward Seaga and the Challenges of Modern Jamaica*. Kingston: University of the West Indies Press, 2011.

Clarke, Colin G. *Kingston, Jamaica: Urban Growth and Social Change, 1692–1962*. Berkeley: University of California Press, 1975.

Clarke, Colin G. *Race, Class, and the Politics of Decolonization: Jamaica Journals, 1961 and 1968*. New York: Palgrave Macmillan, 2015.

Gray, Obika. *Demeaned but Empowered: The Social Power of the Urban Poor in Jamaica*. Mona, Jamaica: University of the West Indies Press, 2004.

James, Marlon. *A Brief History of Seven Killings*. London: Oneworld, 2015.

Manley, Michael. *Jamaica: Struggle in the Periphery*. London: Third World Media Limited in association with Writers and Readers Publishing Cooperative Society, 1982.

Manley, Rachel. *Drumblair: Memories of a Jamaican Childhood*. Toronto: Vintage Canada, 1997.

Mars, Perry, and Alma H. Young. *Caribbean Labor and Politics: Legacies of Cheddi Jagan and Michael Manley*. Detroit: Wayne State University Press, 2004.

Morris, Mervyn. *Miss Lou: Louise Bennett and Jamaican Culture*. Kingston: Ian Randle, 2014.

Nettleford, Rex, and Rex M. Nettleford. *Jamaica in Independence: Essays on the Early Years*. Kingston: Heinemann Caribbean, 1989.

Sorgel, Sabine. *Dancing Postcolonialism: The National Dance Theatre Company of Jamaica*. Bielefeld, Germany: Transcript, 2007.

Steffens, Roger. *So Much Things to Say: An Oral History of Bob Marley*. New York: W. W. Norton, 2017.

Part VII: Jamaica in the Age of Neoliberalism

Chin, Staceyann. *The Other Side of Paradise: A Memoir*. New York: Scribner, 2010.

Cooper, Carolyn. *Noises in the Blood: Orality, Gender, and the "Vulgar" Body of Jamaican Popular Culture*. Durham, NC: Duke University Press, 1995.

Glave, Thomas. *Among the Bloodpeople: Politics and Flesh*. New York: Akashic Books, 2013.

Gunst, Laurie. *Born Fi' Dead: A Journey through the Jamaican Posse Underworld*. New York: Henry Holt, 1995.

Harriott, Anthony. *Understanding Crime in Jamaica: New Challenges for Public Policy*. Kingston: University of the West Indies Press, 2003.

Hope, Donna Patricia. *Inna Di Dancehall: Popular Culture and the Politics of Identity in Jamaica*. Mona, Jamaica: University of the West Indies Press, 2006.

Moore, Richard. *The Bolt Supremacy: Inside Jamaica's Sprint Factory*. London: Yellow Jersey Press, 2015.

Morris-Francis, Sherill, Camille Gibson, and Lorna Elaine Grant, eds. *Crime and Violence in the Caribbean: Lessons from Jamaica*. Lanham, MD: Lexington Books, 2018.

Nettleford, Rex. *Caribbean Cultural Identity: The Case of Jamaica. An Essay in Cultural Dynamics*. Kingston: Institute of Jamaica, 1978.

Stolzoff, Norman C. *Wake the Town and Tell the People: Dancehall Culture in Jamaica*. Durham, NC: Duke University Press, 2000.

Thomas, Deborah A. *Modern Blackness: Nationalism, Globalization, and the Politics of Culture in Jamaica*. Durham, NC: Duke University Press, 2004.

Part VIII: Jamaicans in the World

Brinkhurst-Cuff, Charlie, ed. *Mother Country: Real Stories of the Windrush Children*. London: Headline Books, 2018.

Cliff, Michelle. *No Telephone to Heaven*. New York: Plume, 1996.

Davis, Andrea, and Carl E. Davis, eds. *Jamaica in the Canadian Experience: A Multiculturalizing Presence*. Halifax, Nova Scotia: Fernwood, 2012.

Foner, Nancy. *Jamaica Farewell: Jamaican Migrants in London*. London: Routledge and Kegan Paul, 1979.

Golash-Boza, Tanya Maria. *Deported: Immigrant Policing, Disposable Labor, and Global Capitalism*. Latina/o Sociology Series. New York: New York University Press, 2015.

Hahamovitch, Cindy. *No Man's Land: Jamaican Guestworkers in America and the Global History of Deportable Labor*. Princeton, NJ: Princeton University Press, 2011.

Jarrett-Macauley, Delia. *The Life of Una Marson, 1905–1965*. Manchester: Manchester University Press, 1998.

Petras, Elizabeth McLean. *Jamaican Labor Migration: White Capital and Black Labor, 1850–1930*. Boulder, CO: Westview, 1988.

Putnam, Lara. *Radical Moves: Caribbean Migrants and the Politics of Race in the Jazz Age*. Chapel Hill: University of North Carolina Press, 2013.

Senior, Olive. *Dying to Better Themselves: West Indians and the Building of the Panama Canal*. Kingston: University of the West Indies Press, 2014.

Thomas-Hope, Elizabeth M., and Rose Mary Allen, eds. *Freedom and Constraint in Caribbean Migration and Diaspora*. Kingston: Ian Randle, 2009.

Acknowledgment of Copyrights and Sources

Part I: Becoming Jamaica

"Taíno Society," by Kit W. Wesler, previously published as "Jamaica" in *The Oxford Handbook of Caribbean Archaeology*, ed. William F. Keegan, Corinne L. Hofman, and Reniel Rodríguez Ramos (Oxford: Oxford University Press, 2013), 252–253, 259–260.

"Taíno Worship," by Ramón Pané, from *An Account of the Antiquities of the Indians*, ed. José Juan Arrom, trans. Susan C. Griswold (Durham, NC: Duke University Press, 1999), 25–27.

"The First European Account of Jamaica," by Andrés Bernáldez, previously published as "History of the Catholic Sovereigns, Don Ferdinand and Doña Isabella" in *Select Documents Illustrating the Four Voyages of Columbus*, vol. 1, ed. and trans. Cecil Jane (London: Hakluyt Society, 1930), 124–128.

"A Spanish Settler in Jamaica," by Pedro de Maçuelo, correspondence from 21 April 1515, reprinted in Spanish in "The Early History of Jamaica (1511–1536)" by Irene Wright, from *English Historical Review* 36 (1921): 85–88. Original letter in the General Archives of the Indies, Seville, Spain. Translated by Kathryn Burns for this volume.

"The Spanish Capital," by James Robertson, from *Gone Is the Ancient Glory: Spanish Town, Jamaica, 1534–2000* (Kingston: Ian Randle, 2005), 15–17, 21–22, 30–32.

"Slavery in Spanish Jamaica," by Francisco Morales Padrón, from *Spanish Jamaica*, trans. Patrick E. Bryan (Kingston: Ian Randle, 2003), 153–156.

"A Description of Spanish Jamaica," by Francisco Marques de Villalobos: correspondence from 8 November 1582, reprinted in *Jamaica under the Spaniards, Abstracted from the Archives of Seville*, ed. Frank Cundall and Joseph L. Pietersz, trans. Joseph L. Pietersz (Kingston: Institute of Jamaica, 1919), 15–16.

"The Economy of Spanish Jamaica," by Alonzo de Miranda: correspondence from 14 July 1611, reprinted in *Jamaica under the Spaniards, Abstracted from the Archives of Seville*, ed. Frank Cundall and Joseph L. Pietersz, trans. Joseph L. Pietersz (Kingston: Institute of Jamaica, 1919), 34–38.

"The Western Design," by Juan Ramirez: correspondence to King Philip IV of Spain, 24 May 1655, reprinted in *Jamaica under the Spaniards, Abstracted from the Archives of Seville*, ed. Frank Cundall and Joseph L. Pietersz, trans. Joseph L. Pietersz (Kingston: Institute of Jamaica, 1919), 51–52.

"Mountains of Gold Turned into Dross": (1) anonymous correspondence from 1 June 1655, reprinted in The *Narrative of General Venables: With an Appendix of Papers*

Relating to the Expedition to the West Indies and the Conquest of Jamaica, 1654–1655, ed. C. H. Firth (London: Longmans, Green, and Co., 1900), 136–139. Original letter in the Bodleian Library, University of Oxford (Rawlinson MS D.1208, f.62). (2) anonymous correspondence from 5 November 1655, reprinted in *The Narrative of General Venables: With an Appendix of Papers Relating to the Expedition to the West Indies and the Conquest of Jamaica, 1654–1655,* ed. C. H. Firth (London: Longmans, Green, and Co., 1900), 141–142. Original letter in the Bodleian Library, University of Oxford (Rawlinson MS D.1208, f.62).

"The Establishment of Maroon Society," by Robert Sedgwicke and William Goodson: correspondence to Oliver Cromwell, 24 January 1655, reprinted in *A Collection of the State Papers of John Thurloe, Esq; Secretary, First, to the Council of State, and Afterwards to the Two Protectors, Oliver and Richard Cromwell,* vol. 4, ed. Thomas Birch (London: Fletcher Gyles, 1742), 455–458.

Part II: From English Conquest to Slave Society

"Pirate Stronghold," by Nuala Zahedieh, previously published as "Trade, Plunder, and Economic Development in Early English Jamaica, 1655–89" in *Economic History Review* 39, no. 2 (1986): 215–216, 218–220, 222. © 1986 John Wiley and Sons, Inc. Reproduced with permission of Blackwell Publishing Ltd.

"Port Royal Destroyed," by an anonymous author, from *The Truest and Largest Account of the Late Earthquake in Jamaica, June the 7th, 1692: Written by a Reverend Divine There to His Friend in London, With Some Improvement Thereof by Another Hand* (London: Printed for J. Butler, 1693), 1–6, 8–9.

"White Servants," by the Government of Jamaica, from "An Act for Regulating Servants," 1681, in *Acts of Assembly, Passed in the Island of Jamaica; From 1681, to 1754, Inclusive* (London: Curtiss, Brett and Company, 1756), 1–6.

"The Rise of Slave Society," by Richard S. Dunn, from *Sugar and Slaves: The Rise of the Planter Class in the English West Indies, 1624–1713,* published for the Omohundro Institute of Early American History and Culture, Williamsburg, Virginia (Chapel Hill: University of North Carolina Press, 1972), 165–172, 175–177. Copyright © 1972 by the University of North Carolina Press. Used by permission of the publisher. www.unc press.org.

"African Music in Jamaica," by Hans Sloane, from *A Voyage to the Islands Madera, Barbados, Nieves, St Christopher, and Jamaica,* vol. 1 (1707), xlviii.

"A Maroon Tradition," collected by Kenneth M. Bilby, previously published as "'Two Sister Pikni': A Historical Tradition of Dual Ethnogenesis in Eastern Jamaica" in *Caribbean Quarterly* 30, nos. 3–4 (1984): 12–13, 20. © University of the West Indies, reprinted by permission of Taylor and Francis, Ltd on behalf of the University of the West Indies.

"Treaty between the British and the Maroons," by an anonymous author, from *The History of the Maroons, from Their Origin to the Establishment of Their Chief Tribe at Sierra Leone,* vol. 1, ed. Robert Charles Dallas (London: Longman, 1803), 58–65.

"African Arrivals," by Audra A. Diptee, from *From Africa to Jamaica: The Making of an*

Atlantic Slave Society, 1775–1807 (Gainesville: University Press of Florida, 2010), 60–66.
Reprinted with permission of the University Press of Florida.

"Spiritual Terror," by Vincent Brown, previously published as "Spiritual Terror and
Sacred Authority: The Power of the Supernatural in Jamaican Slave Society" in
New Studies in the History of American Slavery, ed. Edward E. Baptist and Stephanie
M. H. Camp (Athens: University of Georgia Press, 2006), 181–183.

"Two Enslaved Lives," by Trevor Burnard, from *Mastery, Tyranny, and Desire: Thomas
Thistlewood and His Slaves in the Anglo-Jamaican World* (Chapel Hill: University of
North Carolina Press, 2004), 217–218, 221–225. Copyright © 2004 by the University of North Carolina Press. Used by permission of the publisher. www.uncpress
.org.

"Increase and Decrease," by the Managers of Haughton Tower Estate, from *An Account of the Increase and Decrease of Negroes & Stock on Haughton Tower Estate for the
Year 1768.* Courtesy of the private collection of Nicholas James.

"A Free Black Poet," by Francis Williams, originally published as "A Poem in Honour
of Sir George Haldane, ᴋɴᴛ," in W. J. Gardner, *A History of Jamaica from Its Discovery by Christopher Columbus to the Year 1872*, trans. E. J. Chinnock (Kingston, Jamaica,
1909), 509–510.

"Jamaica Talk," by Frederic G. Cassidy, from *Jamaica Talk: Three Hundred Years of the
English Language in Jamaica* (1961; repr., Mona, Jamaica: University of the West
Indies Press, 2007), 1–9.

"The War of 1760–1761," by Edward Long, from *The History of Jamaica, or General
Survey of the Ancient Modern State of that Island: with Reflections on its Situations,
Settlements, Inhabitants, Climates, Products, Commerce, Laws, and Government*, vol. 2
(London: T. Lowndes, 1784), 447–458, 461–462.

Part III: Enlightenment Slavery

"Creole Society," by Edward (Kamau) Brathwaite, from *The Development of Creole Society in Jamaica, 1770–1820* (Kingston: Ian Randle, 2005), 306–311.

"Cane and Coffee," by Robert Charles Dallas, from *The History of the Maroons, from
Their Origin to the Establishment of Their Chief Tribe at Sierra Leone*, vol. 1, ed. Robert
Charles Dallas (London: Longman and Rees, 1803), lxxxviii–lxxxix, xci–xcvii,
xcix–cv.

"Women's and Men's Work under Slavery," by Lucille Mathurin Mair, from *A Historical Study of Women in Jamaica, 1655–1834* (Kingston: University of the West Indies
Press, 2006), 201–206.

"Although a Slave Me Is Born and Bred," by an anonymous author, recorded by
J. B. Moreton, from Moreton's *West India Customs and Manners: Containing Strictures
on the Soil, Cultivation, Produce, Trade, Officers, and Inhabitants: With the Method of Establishing and Conducting a Sugar Plantation. To Which is Added, the Practice of Training
New Slaves* (London: J. Parsons, 1793), 154–155.

"Capture and Enslavement," by Archibald John Monteath, previously published as
"Archibald John Monteith: Native Helper and Assistant in the Jamaican Mission

at New Carmel," ed. Vernon H. Nelson, in *Transactions of the Moravian Historical Society* 21, no. 1 (1966): 30–32.

"The Black Church," by George Liele, previously published as "An Account of Several Baptist Churches, Consisting Chiefly of Negro Slaves: Particularly of One at Kingston, in Jamaica: And Another at Savannah in Georgia" in *The Baptist Annual Register, for 1790, 1791, 1792, and Part of 1793. Including Sketches of the State of the Religion among Different Denominations of Good Men at Home and Abroad*, ed. John Rippon (London: 1794), 334–337. Reprinted as "Letters Showing the Rise and Progress of the Early Negro Churches in Georgia and the West Indies" in *Journal of Negro History* 1, no. 1 (1916): 71–74.

"British Missionaries," by Mary Turner, from *Slaves and Missionaries: The Disintegration of Jamaican Slave Society, 1787–1834* (Kingston, Jamaica: University of the West Indies Press, 1998), 7–9, 11–12.

"The Second Maroon War," by Representatives of the Trelawny Town Maroons, previously published as "State of grievances complained of by the Maroons of Trelawney Town, made this 19th of July, 1795, before the honourable John Tharp, James Stewart, General Reid, John Mowat, Jarvis Gallimore, Edward Knowles, and James Galloway, esquires; who went to the said town, in consequence of a letter sent to convey the wish of the Maroons to have a conference with them" in *The History of the Maroons, from their Origin to the Establishment of their Chief Tribe at Sierra Leone, including the Expedition to Cuba for the purpose of procuring Spanish Chasseurs; and the State of the Island of Jamaica for the last Ten Years, with a Succinct History of the Island previous to that period*, vol. 1, ed. Robert Charles Dallas (London: Longman and Rees, 1803), 325–326.

"Jonkanoo," by Michael Scott, from *Tom Cringle's Log* (Edinburgh: William Blackwood, 1833), 345–353.

"Provision Grounds," by Sidney Mintz, from "The Origins of the Jamaican Marketing System" in *Caribbean Transformations* (New York: Columbia University Press, 1989), 182–183, 189, 196–197, 202. Copyright © 1989 Jacqueline Mintz. Reprinted with permission of the publisher and of Jacqueline Mintz.

"The Liberation War of 1831," by Henry Bleby, from *Death Struggles of Slavery: Being a Narrative of Facts and Incidents, which Occurred in a British Colony, during the Two Years Immediately Preceding Negro Emancipation* (London: Hamilton, Adams & Co., 1853), 113–117.

"Apprenticeship and Its Conflicts," by Diana Paton, from *No Bond but the Law: Punishment, Race, and Gender in Jamaican State Formation, 1780–1870* (Durham, NC: Duke University Press, 2004), 78–80.

"An Apprentice's Story," by James Williams, from *A Narrative of Events, since the First of August 1834, by James Williams, an Apprenticed Labourer in Jamaica*, ed. Diana Paton (1837; repr., Durham, NC: Duke University Press, 2001), 6–8.

"Because of 1833," by Andrew Salkey, from *Jamaica: An Epic Poem Exploring the Historical Foundations of Jamaican Society* (1973; repr., London: Bogle L'Ouverture, 1983), 37–42.

Part IV: Colonial Freedom

"Free Villages," by Jean Besson, from *Martha Brae's Two Histories: European Expansion and Caribbean Culture-Building in Jamaica* (Chapel Hill: University of North Carolina Press, 2002), 161–164, 167, 171–174. Copyright © 2002 by the University of North Carolina Press. Used by permission of the publisher. www.uncpress.org.

"Cholera," by Samuel Jones: correspondence to Frederick Trestrail, 8 April 1851, from *Letters of Samuel Jones (1803–1877), a Baptist Missionary in Jamaica* in the National Library of Wales, Aberystwyth, UK, call number NLW MS 14424C.

"Black Voters," by Swithin Wilmot, previously published as "'A Stake in the Soil': Land and Creole Politics in Free Jamaica—the 1849 Elections" in *In the Shadow of the Plantation: Caribbean History and Legacy*, ed. Alvin O. Thompson (Kingston: Ian Randle, 2002), 22–325.

"Religion after Slavery," by Hope Waddell, from *Twenty-Nine Years in the West Indies and Central Africa: A Review of Missionary Work and Adventure, 1829–1858* (London: Thomas Nelson and Son, 1853), 187–190.

"Indentured Workers," by Verene Shepherd, from *Transients to Settlers: The Experience of Indians in Jamaica, 1845–1950* (Leeds, UK: Peepal Tree, 1994), 53–59.

"The Morant Bay Rebellion," by Gad Heuman, from *"The Killing Time": The Morant Bay Rebellion in Jamaica* (London: Macmillan, 1994), xiii–xiv, xvii, 3–5, 13–14.

"Dear Lucy," by George William Gordon, previously published as "Letter to Lucy" in *Illustrated London News*, 9 December 1865.

"Vindicating the Race," by the Rev. R. (Robert) Gordon, from *Jamaica's Jubilee; or, What We Are and What We Hope to Be* (London: S. W. Partridge and Co., 1888), 11–13, 15–16.

"August Town Craze," by Frederick S. Sanguinetti, 28 May 1895, from *Despatches from Henry Arthur Blake, Governor of Jamaica* in the National Archives, Kew, UK, call number CO 137/566, no. 165.

"Anansi and the Tiger," by Walter Jekyll (traditional folktale) previously published as "Annancy and Brother Tiger" in *Jamaican Song and Story: Annancy Stories, Digging Sings, Ring Tunes, and Dancing Tunes*, ed. Walter Jekyll (London: David Nutt, 1907), 7–9.

"The 1907 Earthquake," by Dick Chislett: letter to Jack Chislett, 16 January 1907, from the National Library of Jamaica, Kingston, Jamaica, MS 2051: Photographs and letters of the 1907 earthquake.

"Traveling from Kingston to Montego Bay," by Herbert de Lisser, from *Twentieth Century Jamaica* (Kingston: Jamaica Times Limited, 1913), 71–92.

Part V: Jamaica Arise

"Life in Rural Jamaica," by Lorna Goodison, from *From Harvey River, a Memoir of My Mother and Her Island* (New York: Amistad, 2007), 64–72.

"An Amazing Island," by W. E. B. Du Bois, from *Crisis* 10, no. 2 (June 1915): 80–81.

"Marcus Garvey Comes to the United States," by Marcus Garvey, originally published as "A Monthly Survey of Negro Achievement" in *Champion Magazine*, January 1917,

167–168. Reprinted as "West Indians in the Mirror of Truth" in *The Marcus Garvey and Universal Negro Improvement Association Papers: The Caribbean Diaspora, 1910–1920*, vol. 11, ed. Robert A. Hill (Durham, NC: Duke University Press, 2011), 87–90.

"Jamaica and the Great War": (1) "Jamaica's War," by the editorial board of the *Daily Gleaner*, 13 October 1915, 8. (2) "To the Women of Jamaica," by the editorial board of the *Daily Gleaner*, 6 October 1915, 8.

"Returning from War," by Glenford Howe, from *Race, War and Nationalism: A Social History of West Indians in the First World War* (Kingston: Ian Randle, 2002), 191–195.

"Self-Government for Jamaica," by W. Adolphe Roberts, from a 1936 Jamaica Progressive League pamphlet, *Based upon Addresses Delivered before the British-Jamaican Benevolent Association Inc. (New York) on July 15th and September 27th, 1936.*

"The 1938 Rebellion," by Richard Hart, from *Labour Rebellions of the 1930s in the British Caribbean Region Colonies* (London: Caribbean Labour Solidarity, 2002).

"Remembering the Rebellion," by Lucius Watson, from *Not for Wages Alone: Eyewitness Summaries of the 1938 Labour Rebellion in Jamaica*, ed. Patrick E. Bryan and Karl Watson (Mona, Jamaica: Social History Project, Department of History and Archaeology, University of the West Indies, 2003), 63–64, 68–75.

"Now We Know," by Roger Mais, from the Roger Mais Collection, UWI-Mona, Special Collections. Originally published in *Public Opinion*, 11 July 1944, 2. Courtesy of the University of the West Indies Library, Mona.

"Cookshop Culture," by an anonymous author, previously published as "Eating Goes Modern: Glance at the Cookshop of a Past Generation—and Then at the Popular Eating Houses of To-Day" in *Planters' Punch* 4, no. 3 (1940–1941): 11–12.

"My Mother Who Fathered Me," by Edith Clarke, from *My Mother Who Fathered Me: A Study of the Families in Three Selected Communities of Jamaica* (1957; repr., Kingston: University of the West Indies Press, 1999), 105–111.

"The Origins of Dreadlocks," by Barry Chevannes, previously published as "The Origin of the Dreadlocks" in *Rastafari and Other African-Caribbean World-views*, ed. Barry Chevannes (London: Macmillan, 1998), 77–86, 88–93.

"Pleasure Island," by Esther Chapman, from *Pleasure Island: The Book of Jamaica*, ed. Esther Chapman (Kingston: Arawak Press, 1951), 127–129.

"Hurricane Charlie," by anonymous, previously published as "The Hurricane: Angrier dan Ebber" in *Spotlight*, August 1951, 18–19.

"Jamaican East Indians," by Laxmi and Ajai Mansingh, from *Home Away from Home: 150 Years of Indian Presence in Jamaica, 1845–1995* (Kingston: Ian Randle, 1999), 88–116.

"Blackness and Beauty," by Rochelle Rowe, previously published as "'Glorifying the Jamaican Girl': The 'Ten Types—One People' Beauty Contest, Radicalized Femininities, and Jamaican Nationalism" in *Radical History Review* 103 (2009): 36–44.

"Chinese Jamaica," by Easton Lee, from "The Chinese in Jamaica: A Personal Account," in UWI-Mona Special Collections, F1896.C5 L423, 1977.

"Bauxite," by Sherry Keith and Robert Girling, previously published as "Bauxite Dependency: Roots of Crisis" in *NACLA: Reports on the Americas*, 25 September 2007), https://nacla.org/article/bauxite-dependency-roots-crisis.

"The West Indies Federation," by Michele A. Johnson, previously published as "'To Dwell Together in Unity': Referendum on West Indian Federation, 1961" in *Before and after 1865: Education, Politics and Regionalism in the Caribbean*, ed. Brian Moore and Swithin Wilmot (Kingston: Ian Randle, 1998), 262–270.

"Rastafari and the New Nation," by Michael G. Smith, Roy Augier, and Rex Nettleford, from *Report on the Ras Tafari Movement in Kingston, Jamaica* (Mona, Jamaica: Institute of Social and Economic Studies, 1960), 33–38.

Part VI: Independence and After

"A Date with Destiny," by the *Daily Gleaner*, previously published as "Midnight Tonight—A Date with Destiny," in the *Daily Gleaner*, 5 August 1962. © The Gleaner Company (Media) Limited.

"The Meaning of Independence," by the Government of Jamaica, from a pamphlet in UWI-Mona Special Collections, call number F1888.A3 1963. Courtesy of the Jamaica Information Service.

"The Assets We Have," by Norman Washington Manley, previously published as "Independence: The Assets We Have" in *Norman Washington Manley, Manley and the New Jamaica: Selected Speeches and Writings, 1938–1968*, ed. Rex Nettleford (Kingston: Longman Caribbean, 1971), 313–317.

"Rastafari and the Coral Gardens Incident": (1) "Oh, It's Hard to Be Poor," by John Maxwell, from *Public Opinion*, 7 June 1963, 4–5. (2) "Rastafari," by Mortimo Togo Desta Planno, from *Public Opinion*, 4 May 1963, 2.

"Country Boy," by Leroy Sibbles, from the album *Country Boy*, by the Heptones, Island Records Ltd WIP 6266, 1976. Words and music by Leroy Sibbles. Copyright © 1985 Universal—Songs of Polygram International, Inc. All rights reserved, used by permission. Reprinted by permission of Hal Leonard LLC. © Universal PolyGram Int. Publishing Inc./Universal Music Publishing Pty. Ltd. for Australia & New Zealand. All rights reserved. International copyright secured. Reprinted with permission.

"How to Be a 'Face-Man,'" from "So You Want to Be a Face-Man!," *Star*, 21 May 1965, 3. © The Gleaner Company (Media) Limited.

"Cancer in West Kingston," by Edward Seaga: transcript of broadcast from 28 August 1966, West Indies Collection HN223.84, University of the West Indies Library, Mona, 2–6.

"Birth of the Sound System," by Norman C. Stolzoff, from *Wake the Town and Tell the People: Dancehall Culture in Jamaica* (Durham, NC: Duke University Press, 2000), 41–45, 47–54.

"Rudie, Oh Rudie!," by Garth White, from *Caribbean Quarterly* 13, no. 3 (1967): 39–44. Copyright © University of the West Indies, reprinted by permission of Taylor and Francis Ltd, http://www.tandfonline.com on behalf of University of the West Indies.

"1968 Revisited," by Rupert Lewis, previously published as "Walter Rodney: 1968 Revisited" in *Social and Economic Studies* 43, no. 3 (1994): 7–56.

"The Visual Arts," by Anne Walmsley and Stanley Greaves, from "Jamaican Art," in *Art in the Caribbean: An Introduction* (London: New Beacon Press, 2010), 141–146.

"Better Mus' Come," by Delroy Wilson, from his album *Better Must Come*, Dynamic Sounds, DY-3324, 1971.

Part VII: Jamaica in the Age of Neoliberalism

the Imagination: Jamaica's Shame" in "Genders and Sexuality," special issue, *Small Axe: A Journal of Criticism* 7 (March 2000): 123–126.

"Woman Time Now," by HG Helps, from *Jamaica Observer*, 7 March 2013, 16–18. Used courtesy of Jamaica Observer Limited.

"A Wild Ride," by Robert Lalah, from *Roving with Lalah: Slices of Everyday Jamaican Life* (Kingston: Ian Randle, 2008), 81–83.

"Skin Bleaching," by Carolyn Cooper, from *Sound Clash: Jamaican Dancehall Culture at Large* (London: Palgrave Macmillan, 2004), 135–138.

"Tragedy in Tivoli": (1) "The Siege," by W. Earl Witter QC, from *Interim Report to Parliament concerning Investigations into the Conduction of the Security Forces during the State of Emergency Declared May, 2010—West Kingston/Tivoli Gardens "Incursion"—the Killing of Mr. Keith Oxford Clarke and Related Matters*. Office of the Public Defender, 29 April 2013, 19–26. (2) "Rosie Tells Her Story," interview with Adina Derby, conducted by Livern Barrett, previously published as "'I Don't Like to Remember It': Rosie Tells Tale of Being Shot by Police" in the *Gleaner*, 9 December 2014, A3. © The Gleaner Company (Media) Limited.

"The Cell Phone and the Economy of Communication," by Heather A. Horst and Daniel Miller, from *The Cell Phone: An Anthropology of Communication* (Oxford: Berg, 2006), 108–111, 113–114. © Heather A. Horst and Daniel Miller, 2006, "The Cell Phone and the Economy of Communication," Berg Publishers, an imprint of Bloomsbury Publishing PLC.

"Unsustainable Development," by Esther Figueroa, from *Limbo, a Novel about Jamaica* (New York: Arcade, 2014), 213–216, 224–226.

"The Case for Reparations," by P. J. Patterson, open letter to David Cameron, from the *Gleaner*, 8 October 2015, http://jamaica-gleaner.com/article/news/20151008/full-text-pj-slams-david-cameron-are-we-not-worthy-he-asks.

"These Islands of Love and Hate," by Kei Miller, from *Writing Down the Vision: Essays and Prophecies* (Leeds: Peepal Tree Press, 2013), 27–31.

Part VIII: Jamaicans in the World

"In the Canal Zone," by Alfred Mitchell S., originally published as "Letters from Isthmian Canal Construction Workers" by the Isthmian Historical Society as an entry for their "Competition for the Best True Story of Life and Work on the Isthmus of Panama during the Construction of the Panama Canal," 1963. Digital Library of the Caribbean, https://ufdc.ufl.edu/AA00016037/00080.

"A Diaspora Story," by Lok C. D. Siu and Fernando Jackson, from Lok C. D. Siu, *Memories of a Future Home: Diasporic Citizenship of Chinese in Panama* (Palo Alto, CA: Stanford University Press, 2005), 91–94.

"Going to Cuba," interview with "Man-Boy," conducted in 1975 by Erna Brodber, from *Life of Jamaica in the Early Twentieth Century: A Presentation of 90 Oral Accounts—Clarendon*, manuscript held at the Sir Arthur Lewis Institute of Social and Economic Studies, 10–35.

"Tropics in New York," by Claude McKay, from *Spring in New Hampshire and Other*

Index